HUMBERSIDE LIBRARIES

MUNBY & WATSON

Road Passenge   1.VII

REVIEWS OF UNITED KINGDOM

STATISTICAL SOURCES

Volume VII

Road Passenger Transport
and
Road Goods Transport

Reviews of United Kingdom Statistical Sources

Editor W. F. Maunder

Vol I	1.	*Personal Social Services*, B. P. Davies
	2.	*Voluntary Organizations in the Personal Social Service Field*, G. J. Murray
Vol II	3.	*Central Government Routine Health Statistics*, Michael Alderson
	4.	*Social Security Statistics*, Frank Whitehead
Vol III	5.	*Housing in Great Britain*, Stuart Farthing
	6.	*Housing in Northern Ireland*, Michael Fleming
Vol IV	7.	*Leisure*, F. M. M. Lewes and S. R. Parker
	8.	*Tourism*, L. J. Lickorish
Vol V	9.	*General Sources of Statistics*, G. F. Lock
Vol VI	10.	*Wealth*, A. B. Atkinson and A. J. Harrison
	11.	*Personal Incomes*, T. Stark
Vol VII	12.	*Road Passenger Tranport*, D. L. Munby
	13.	*Road Goods Transport*, A. H. Watson
Vol VIII	14.	*Land Use*, J. T. Coppock
	15.	*Town and Country Planning*, L. F. Gebbett

REVIEWS OF UNITED KINGDOM STATISTICAL SOURCES
Edited by W. F. MAUNDER
Professor of Economic and Social Statistics
University of Exeter

VOLUME VII

ROAD PASSENGER TRANSPORT

by

D. L. MUNBY
Nuffield College, Oxford

and

ROAD GOODS TRANSPORT

by

A. H. WATSON

Published for The Royal Statistical Society
and the Social Science Research Council
by

PERGAMON PRESS

OXFORD · NEW YORK · TORONTO · SYDNEY · PARIS · FRANKFURT

U.K.	Pergamon Press Ltd., Headington Hill Hall, Oxford OX3 0BW, England
U.S.A.	Pergamon Press Inc., Maxwell House, Fairview Park, Elmsford, New York 10523, U.S.A.
CANADA	Pergamon of Canada Ltd., 75 The East Mall, Toronto, Ontario, Canada
AUSTRALIA	Pergamon Press (Aust.) Pty. Ltd., 19a Boundary Street, Rushcutters Bay, N.S.W. 2011, Australia
FRANCE	Pergamon Press SARL, 24 rue des Ecoles, 75240 Paris, Cedex 05, France
FEDERAL REPUBLIC OF GERMANY	Pergamon Press GmbH, 6242 Kronberg-Taunus, Pferdstrasse 1, Republic of Germany

Copyright © 1978 Royal Statistical Society and Social Science Research Council

All Rights Reserved. No part of this publication may be reproduced, stored in a retrieval system or transmitted in any form or by any means: electronic, electrostatic, magnetic tape, mechanical, photocopying, recording or otherwise, without permission in writing from the copyright holders

First Published 1978

For bibliographic purposes this volume should be cited as:
Munby, D. L. and Watson, A. H., *Road Passenger Transport and Road Goods Transport*, Pergamon Press Ltd on behalf of The Royal Statistical Society and the Social Science Research Council, 1978

British Library Cataloguing in Publication Data

Reviews of United Kingdom statistical sources.
Vol. 7: Road passenger transport; and, Road goods transport.
1. Great Britain – Statistical services
I. Maunder, Wynne Frederick II. Munby, Denys Lawrence III. Watson, A. H. IV. Royal Statistical Society V. Social Science Research Council
(Great Britain)
314. 1   HA37. G7   77-30558

ISBN 0-08-022449-0

Printed in Great Britain by Cox & Wyman Ltd, London, Fakenham and Reading

Contents

Foreword vi

Introduction ix

Review No. 12 Road Passenger Transport 1

Subject Index to Road Passenger Transport 135

Review No. 13 Road Goods Transport 1

Subject Index to Road Goods Transport 121

Foreword

The Sources and Nature of the Statistics of the United Kingdom produced under the auspices of the Royal Statistical Society and edited by Maurice Kendall, filled a notable gap on the library shelves when it made its appearance in the early post-war years. Through a series of critical reviews by many of the foremost national experts, it constituted a valuable contemporary guide to statisticians working in many fields as well as a benchmark to which historians of the development of statistics in this country are likely to return again and again. The Social Science Research Council and the Society were both delighted when Professor Maunder came forward with the proposal that a revised version should be produced, indicating as well his willingness to take on the onerous task of editor. The two bodies were more than happy to act as co-sponsors of the project and to help in its planning through a joint steering committee. The result, we are confident, will be adjudged a worthy successor to the previous volumes by the very much larger 'statistics public' that has come into being in the intervening years.

Dr C. S. Smith
Secretary
Social Science Research Council
May 1977

E. M. L. Beale
Honorary Secretary
Royal Statistical Society
May 1977

MEMBERSHIP OF THE JOINT STEERING COMMITTEE

(May 1977)

Chairman: Professor Sir Roy Allen

Representing the Royal Statistical Society:
Dr W. R. Buckland
Miss S. V. Cunliffe
Dr S. Rosenbaum

Representing the Social Science Research Council:
Mr A. Noble
Mr T. S. Pilling
Dr W. Taylor

Secretary: Mr D. E. Allen

Introduction

The present volume, the seventh in the series, marks a distinct phase. On balance the users' interest is likely to be rather more in the economic than in the social side; this is a reversal of the position as compared with the previous volumes. It was, in fact, a deliberate aim to give priority to topics with an overt social interest in the first batch of reviews. Whenever 'social and economic' statistics are treated as a group there is a plainly evident tendency for the 'social' content to be subordinate to the 'economic' content, even though many sources may be relevant to both. Consequently, the initial emphasis in the series on social statistics has been an attempt to forestall this bias, and even though, in the long run, economic sources will dominate in quantity terms, it is an earnest of the intention that the needs of readers with other interests will not be submerged. In the present case, for example, although the most natural user may be the transport economist, it is to be hoped that the volume has much to offer also to the environmentalist.

The reviews in this volume form a closely related pair, both being concerned with road transport. There are two further volumes of reviews of data sources in the transport field currently in preparation, one on *Ports and Inland Waterways* and *Civil Aviation* and the other on *Rail* and *Sea Transport*. These three volumes devoted to the sources of transport statistics thus cover between them the major part of Order XXII of the Standard Industrial Classification. The omissions of consequence are, firstly, sources on the construction and operation of the road system as a whole and, secondly, postal services and telecommunications: it is hoped that work will start in the very near future on what would thus comprise a final fourth volume on the statistics of transport and communication.

The primary aim of this series is to act as a work of reference to the sources of statistical material of all kinds, both official and unofficial. It seeks to enable the user to discover what data are available on the subject in which he is interested, from where they may be obtained, and what the limitations are to their use. Data are regarded as available not only if published in the normal printed form but also if they are likely to be released to a bona fide enquirer in any other form, such as duplicated documents, computer print-out or even magnetic tape. On the other hand, no reference is made to material which, even if it is known to exist, is not accessible to the general run of potential users. The distinction, of course, is not clear-cut and mention of a source is not to be regarded as a guarantee that data will be released; in particular cases it may very well be a matter for negotiation. The latter caution applies with particular force to the question of obtaining computer print-outs of custom-specified tabulations. Where original records are held on magnetic tape it might appear that there should be no insuperable problem, apart from confidentiality, in obtaining any feasible analysis at a cost; in practice, it may well turn out that there are capacity restraints which override any simple cost calculation. Thus, what is requested might make demands on computer and programming resources to the extent that the routine work of the agency concerned would be intolerably affected.

The intention is that the sources for each topic should be reviewed in detail, and the brief supplied to authors has called for comprehensive coverage at the level of 'national interest'. This term does not denote any necessary restriction to statistics collected on a national basis (still less, of course, to national aggregates) but it means that sources of a purely local character, without wider interest in either content or methodology, are excluded. Indeed, the mere task of identifying all material of this latter kind is an impossibility. The interpretation of the brief has obviously involved discretion and it is up to the users of these reviews to say what unreasonable gaps become apparent to them. They are cordially invited to do so by communicating with me.

To facilitate the use of the series as a work of reference, certain features have been incorporated which are worth a word or two of explanation.

First, the text of each review is designed, in so far as varying subject matter permits, to follow a standard form of arrangement so that users may expect a similar pattern to be followed throughout the series. The starting point is a brief summary of the activity concerned and its organization, in order to give a clear background understanding of how data are collected, what is being measured, the stage at which measurements are made, what the reporting units are, the channels through which returns are routed and where they are processed. As a further part of this introductory material, there is a discussion of the specific problems of definition and measurement to which the topic gives rise. The core sections on available sources which follow are arranged at the author's discretion—by origin, by subject subdivision, or by type of data; there is too much heterogeneity between topics to permit any imposition of complete uniformity on all authors. The final section is devoted to a discussion of general shortcomings and possibly desirable improvements. In case a contrary expectation should be aroused, it should be said that authors have not been asked to produce a comprehensive plan for the reform of statistical reporting in the whole of their field. However, a review of existing sources is a natural opportunity to make some suggestions for future policy on the collection and publication of statistics within the scope concerned.

Secondly, detailed factual information about statistical series and other data are given in a Quick Reference List (QRL). The exact nature of the entries is best seen by glancing at the list and accordingly they are not described here. Again, the ordering is not prescribed except that entries are not classified by publication source since it is presumed that it is this which is unknown to the reader. In general, the routine type of information which is given in the QRL is not repeated verbally in the text; the former, however, serves as a search route to the latter in that a reference (by section number) is shown against a QRL entry when there is a related discussion in the text.

Third, a subject index to each review acts as a more or less conventional line of enquiry on textual references; however, it is a computerized system and, for an individual review, the only peculiarity which it introduces is the possibility of easily permuting entries. Thus an original entry in the index to the first review of the series is:

Average expenditure handicapped persons services,

which is also shown as:

Expenditure handicapped persons services, average, as

well as:

Handicapped persons services, average expenditure.

The object at this level is merely to facilitate search by giving as many variants as possible. In addition, individual review subject indexes are merged into a cumulative index which is held on magnetic tape and may possibly be used to produce a printed version from time to time if that seems desirable. Computer print-outs of the cumulative index to date are available on application to me at the Department of Economics, University of Exeter. In addition, selective searches of this index may be made by the input of key-words; the result is a print-out of all entries in which the key-word appears in the initial position in the subject index of any review. Like the cumulative index itself, this is a facility which may be of increasing help as the number of reviews in print grows.

Fourth, each review contains two listings of publications. The QRL key gives full details of the publications shown as sources and text references to them are made in the form [QRL serial number]; this list is confined essentially to data publications. The other listing is a general bibliography of works discussing wider aspects; text references in this case are made in the form [B serial number].

Finally, an attempt is made to reproduce the more important returns or forms used in data collection so that it may be seen what tabulations it is possible to make as well as helping to clarify the basis of those actually available. Unfortunately, there are severe practical limitations on the number of such forms that it is possible to append to a review and authors perforce have to be highly selective.

If all or any of these features succeed in their intention of increasing the value of the series in its basic function as a work of reference it will be gratifying; the extent to which the purpose is achieved, however, will be difficult to assess without 'feedback' from the readership. Users, therefore, will be rendering an essential service if they will send me a note of specific instances where, in consulting a review, they have failed to find the information sought.

As editor, I must express my very grateful thanks to all the members of the Joint Steering Committee of the Royal Statistical Society and the Social Science Research Council. It would be unfair to saddle them with any responsibility for shortcomings in execution but they have directed the overall strategy with as admirable a mixture of guidance and forbearance as any editor of such a series could desire. Especial thanks are due to the Secretary of the Committee who is an unfailing source of help even when sorely pressed by the more urgent demands of his other offices.

The authors join me in thanking all those who gave up their time to attend the seminar held to discuss the first drafts of their reviews and who contributed materially to improving the final versions. We are most grateful also to Philippa Stratton, of Heinemann Educational Books, for all her help, particularly during the vital production stages. The subject index entries for both reviews in this volume were compiled by Mrs Juliet Horwood who has also been responsible for many other aspects of the work. Our thanks go also to Mrs Gill Skinner, of the Social Studies Data Processing Unit at the University of Exeter, who has written the computer programs for the production of the subject indexes. Finally, we also wish to record our appreciation of the permission granted to us by the Controller of Her Majesty's Stationery Office to reproduce Crown copyright material.

University of Exeter W. F. Maunder
March 1976

Denys L. Munby
It is very sad to have to record that the first review in this volume is published posthumously; the death of Denys Munby occurred while on an archaeological tour in Turkey last year. His dedication and commitment to his special field are too well known to require comment by me but it is an opportunity to express my personal appreciation of the contribution he has made to this series. He took his responsibilities very seriously and in all ways, not least in his scrupulous regard for deadlines, he was one who made an editor's life easy. Denys Munby was more or less the first person I consulted when planning the group of reviews on Transport Statistics and this section of the series owes a great deal to the useful and sensible advice

which he gave in the formative stage and to the help which he always offered willingly whenever problems occurred during later developments.

For entirely independent reasons (in fact, arising from the financial exigencies of recent years) there has been an unfortunate delay in the publication of this volume which has imposed additional problems in dealing with the script in the final publication stages. It has been most fortunate that Anthony Watson has been able and willing to take on the brunt of this work; he has most generously spared the time to prepare not only the addenda on recent developments, but has inserted amendments in the text itself where updating seemed quite essential. Where the change is slight it has been made without comment, but in other, more substantial, instances it has been indicated by enclosing the remark in square brackets with an attribution to 'AW'. Amendments to the Quick Reference List have not been distinguished but, in fact, should be traceable fairly easily.

W. F. Maunder
April 1977

12
Road Passenger Transport

by
DENYS MUNBY

Contents

1 **Introduction**   11
  1.1 *Geography and Coverage*   11
  1.2 *Varieties of Passenger Movement*   12
  1.3 *Measurement of Passenger Movement*   13
  1.4 *Definitions*   14

2 **Organization of Passenger Transport**   15
  2.1 *Private Movement and Taxis*   15
  2.2 *Public Road Passenger Transport*   15

3 **Main Sources**   18
  3.1 *National Travel Survey*   18
  3.2 *Transportation Studies*   23
  3.3 *Road Censuses*   24
  3.4 *Traffic Commissioners*   25
  3.5 *'Passenger Transport in Great Britain'*   25
  3.6 *Reports of Undertakings*   27
  3.7 *Other Special Sources*   27
    3.7.2. Vehicle registration   27
    3.7.3. Family Expenditure Survey   27
    3.7.4. Census   28
    3.7.5. Rudd/Dawson expenditure estimates   28
    3.7.6 APPTO statistics   29
    3.7.7 Road Transport Industry Training Board reports   29
    3.7.8 Vehicle operating costs   29
    3.7.9 Motoring surveys   30

4 **Available Data**   31
  4.1 *Pedestrians*   31
  4.2 *Bicycles*   31
  4.3 *Private Cars, Motor-cycles and Taxis*   31
  4.4 *Public Passenger Transport*   33
  4.5 *Regional Statistics*   37
  4.6 *Northern Ireland*   39

5 **Comments and Suggestions**   41

  Quick Reference List: Table of Contents   47
  Quick Reference List   48
  Quick Reference List: Key to Publications   53

Bibliography	60
Appendix A: Index of Traffic and Transportation Surveys	62
Appendix B: Public Service Vehicles Returns	64
Appendix C: National Travel Survey Questionnaires	76
Appendix D: Long-Distance Travel Survey Questionnaires	126
Subject Index	135

Author's Foreword

The Author is most grateful to a number of people whom the Social Science Research Council brought together to discuss a first draft and who later took great trouble to bring to his attention errors of fact and judgment. This survey is much better than it would have been without their help, but of course the remaining errors are his, and he does not expect those who had helped him necessarily to share his views.

List of Abbreviations

AA	Automobile Association
APPTO	Association of Public Passenger Transport Operators
BB	Blue Book
BTC	British Transport Commission
E	England
FES	Family Expenditure Survey
LA	Local Authority
LT	London Transport
NBC	National Bus Company
NTS	National Travel Survey
PTA	Passenger Transport Authority
PTE	Passenger Transport Executive
PTGB	*Passenger Transport in Great Britain*
SELNEC	South-East Lancashire, North-East Cheshire
SIC	Standard Industrial Classification
STG	Scottish Transport Group
TC	Traffic Commissioners
THC	Transport Holding Company
TRRL	Transport and Road Research Laboratory
TS	*Transport Statistics Great Britain*
W	Wales

Reference Date of Sources Reviewed

This review is believed to represent the position, broadly speaking, as it obtained at August 1975. Later revisions have been inserted up to the proof-reading stage (April 1977) by Mr A. H. Watson, taking account, as far as possible, of any major changes in the situation.

Addendum on Recent Developments

The main statistical development since the text was written has been the appearance of *Transport Statistics Great Britain* [QRL 64]. This is the Department of Transport's new annual publication, covering comprehensively all modes of transport and travel. The first issue, covering the years 1964–74, was published in July 1976 and the second, for 1965–75, in March 1977.

The new annual includes the general range of data previously published in *Passenger Transport in Great Britain* [QRL 45] and *Highway Statistics* [QRL 34], and a very great deal more, including much that is relevant to the field of this review. There are, for example, tables on users' expenditure at market prices and factor cost, on the various forms of grants, subsidies and taxes, extensive data from the National Travel Survey on travel and car ownership, data on motor insurance, accidents, energy, employment, and offences relating to motor vehicles. Passenger transport by British Railways and London Transport is treated in detail, and there are tables on air transport and on international passenger movements. There are also sections devoted to forecasts, *inter alia* of vehicle numbers and mileage, car ownership and inland passenger traffic, and to international comparisons.

It is safe to say that the author would have welcomed the new annual with enthusiasm.

National Travel Survey
The author's text (3.1.2) notes briefly the publication in 1975 of a first report on the 1972/3 National Travel Survey. Since then two further volumes have been published by HMSO. The first report, in addition to customary analyses of numbers and mileage of journeys and of expenditure on public transport, includes a number of analyses of household vehicle availability, of drivers' driving experience and licence type, of car occupancy rates, of business mileage and form of expenses analysed by ownership of car, and of parking costs. The second volume includes further detailed analyses of journeys by households and individuals and of vehicle stages. The third volume is a comparison of the 1965 and 1972/3 surveys for a wide range of data. Results from the 1975/6 survey are expected to be published later this year.

National Traffic and Travel Survey 1976
In April 1976 the Minister for Transport announced a programme of home and roadside interview surveys in the English Regions, starting in the following month, designed to improve accuracy in assessing traffic demands on links of existing and projected road networks. There were to be 48,000 household interviews in selected areas in Greater London, other conurbations, large cities, medium and small towns and some rural areas, together with roadside interviews at sites on cordons surrounding these areas and others at sites on a series of screen-lines across the country. A map showing the locations involved was issued with the DOE Press Notice of 30 April 1976.

The data collected—on household characteristics, car ownership and travel trips the previous day (from household interviews) and on vehicle trips, trip origin and destination and purpose (from roadside interviews) were to be used primarily to calibrate and validate a regional highway traffic model and to establish a base year data-bank.

Much of the information obtained, and particularly on medium and longer distance travel flows on an origin/destination basis, would be of wide interest and it is to be hoped that the results will be adequately published in due course.

Transport Policy
For background on current transport problems and policies, as well as a data source, the Government's 1976 Consultation document, *Transport Policy* [B20] (HMSO) is useful. Volume 1 discusses the objectives of transport policy and the current situation, and reviews available policy options, posing questions as to possible courses of action. Volume 2 brings together a number of supporting technical papers, including papers on statistical trends and forecasts, on the distribution of public transport use by income groups, on traffic restraint in urban areas and public transport support. Much of the statistical content is available elsewhere, e.g. in *Transport Statistics Great Britain*, but there is much secondary analysis of interest and relevance to our field.

Transport Statistics for 1900–1970
Lastly, looking a little ahead, it is particularly fitting, in this addendum to Denys Munby's review, to record the impending appearance of a major contribution by him on transport statistics. For more than ten years he had been working on the compilation of a historical abstract of statistics of inland transport in Great Britain for the years 1900–1970. A first volume resulting from this work will be published by the Oxford University Press later this year.

This first volume deals with rail transport, public road passenger transport and London's transport. The last two are directly germane to the field of this review and the first deals with what was the main competing mode over the earlier part of the period. Figures on revenue account, working expenditure, capital investment, employment, earnings and wage rates, traffic, traffic revenue, fares, physical assets and operations will be found in detailed breakdown, together with very full notes on background, on sources, on definitions and coverage, on changes affecting comparability, and on details of further data available in the sources.

A. H. Watson
April 1977

I Introduction

1.1 Geography and Coverage

1.1.1 Movement takes place in space; geography is therefore important, and we need to define the area of our concern. Here we are concerned in principle with internal passenger movements within Great Britain, but not in fact with all of them. *Internal transport* would strictly exclude movements within Britain which are part of a continuous journey to or from some area outside Britain (e.g. movements of aircraft or ships on journeys to or from Britain on or over British 'space'), though the movements of passengers to or from the airport or the port *are* counted as internal transport.

1.1.2 The definition of Great Britain is clear, if not always well known to Englishmen; it includes England, Wales and Scotland, and when Northern Ireland is added becomes the United Kingdom. The Channel Islands and the Isle of Man form part of neither Great Britain nor the UK, and their treatment in official statistics gives rise to minor anomalies (see [B 13], p. 436). It requires only a little knowledge of geography to realize that Great Britain itself consists of a large number of islands the majority of which are not joined to the mainland by any fixed structure (the Isle of Wight, the Western Isles, the Orkneys, the Shetlands, etc.), though the population of these islands is very small in relation to the total and the journeys which they generate cannot be very great in total. Data about these journeys are very limited, as for all internal journeys by water.

1.1.3 This leads to the distinction between what we call *internal transport* and what is normally called *inland transport*. The Department of the Environment provides the main source of overall passenger statistics; it is called *Passenger Transport in Great Britain (PTGB)* [QRL 45] and describes itself as presenting statistics of 'passenger movement in Great Britain by all the main forms of inland transport—rail, public road transport, private road vehicles and air'. Table I (headed 'Total passenger transport in Great Britain') also includes air travel to Northern Ireland and the Channel Islands. Inland transport thus excludes all journeys by sea both to and from the various islands of Britain and coastwise round Britain, as well as all journeys by inland waterways. Rather inconsistently, but for obvious reasons, it includes air movements within the whole of Britain (and geographically rather more). [PTGB was superseded in 1976 by *Transport Statistics Great Britain (TS)* [QRL 64]—A.W.]

1.1.4 Transport internal to the UK would include, in addition, both inland transport in Northern Ireland and sea transport between Great Britain and Northern Ireland. Northern Ireland transport is entirely separate from that of Great Britain, and most information has to be sought in publications of the Northern Ireland government, only a few of which are available through HM Stationery Office, or catalogued in their invaluable lists. The only general sources that cover the whole of the UK are the National Income Blue Books (BB) [QRL 41], the Customs and Excise reports [QRL 57], the *Abstract of Regional Statistics* [QRL 18], and the *Family Expenditure Survey* (FES) [QRL 32]. A special subsection (4.6) briefly summarizes the main sources of Northern Ireland statistics.

1.1.5 This essay covers all inland transport on land in Great Britain except for railways. All the sources quoted relate to Great Britain, except where specified. It excludes data about the road system itself, and does not deal with data of a highway engineering nature (e.g. speed/flow relationships on parts of the system, and traffic control), or with accidents.

1.1.6 All movement is specific to particular areas or corridors, and perhaps most people's concern with transport is in fact with a set of particular movements in one area or corridor, or with comparison between one set of movements and another. Ideally we would like to have data on the whole matrix of movements of all kinds. In practice an enormous amount of information about particular local movements is collected by a host of different bodies, but this still remains a small part of the total matrix. A comprehensive survey of what data have been collected and are being collected in all the different areas of Great Britain would be a life's work. This essay is largely concerned with data that are national in coverage, though it also explains how far national data are generally available in the main sources for narrower areas or regions (see 4.5).

1.1.7 The main aim of the survey is to provide a summary guide to these main national sources with some detail of what may be found in them. To make proper use of them, a reader needs to be aware of the problems of describing and measuring passenger movement in general. Some of these problems are discussed in the rest of this section. The main text then follows in four sections. To understand the figures the user has to know something about the organizational framework, in particular that of the public road passenger industry, and this is dealt with in Section 2. The second main section, Section 3, discusses the main sources of road passenger statistics. Section 4 covers the main items of information in a systematic way under the six headings of pedestrians, bicycles, private cars, motor-cycles and taxis, public road transport, regional statistics, and Northern Ireland. The final section, Section 5, takes up a second aim of the survey with a commentary on the adequacy of the available statistics and some suggestions for improvement.

1.2 Varieties of Passenger Movement

1.2.1 The forms of transport are extremely varied and have many different dimensions. Firstly, people move on foot, and sometimes others move with them in prams and wheelchairs. People also move on bicycles. Then there are the various mechanical vehicles which move on public roads, motor-cycles, private cars, vans and lorries, taxis, and various sorts of buses; in all these cases people may move as drivers or as passengers. Mechanical vehicles also move in the air, on water and on railways; both in the air and on water they may move in private as well as in public vehicles. By *public* vehicles we mean those which are hired or let out for use by 'passengers' (e.g. buses and taxis), a self-drive hire car being treated as a *private* vehicle. (It is to be noted that movement on water may also be by non-mechanical means—rowing, sailing yachts, etc.)

1.2.2 A great deal of movement takes place within buildings or on sites off the public roads (including movement in lifts and on travelators, etc.). By convention and for convenience this movement is excluded. Similarly, the movement by drivers (and their assistants) on freight vehicles and on public vehicles is not counted as part of passenger transport.

1.2.3 The best overall summary of passenger transport movement is to be found in the data from the *National Travel Survey* (NTS) [QRL 42] which we describe later (in 3.1). This covers most, if not quite all, passenger transport movement. Unfortunately very little of the data has been published until recently.

1.3 Measurement of Passenger Movement

1.3.1 The commonest measure of passenger transport activity is the *journey*, the definition of which varies in the different sources. In the NTS [QRL 42] a journey is defined as 'a course of travel which has a single main purpose' and 'may be made by any combination of different means of transport or by one means only. A course of travel to the same destination for two different purposes counts only as one journey and is included under the main purpose of the journey. Circular trips which have no specific destination are split into two journeys, both having the same purpose, taking as the destination the place farthest away from the starting point.' A *journey stage* is defined as follows: 'each part of a journey which is made by a different means of transport or which requires a separate ticket is identified as a separate stage of that journey' [QRL 45, 1967]. By contrast in *PTGB* [QRL 45] (except for figures from NTS) and in most of the statistics of transport operators, a 'journey' means what is defined as a journey stage above. This follows from the fact that these statistics are collected from ticket counts, so that a person travelling on London Transport by bus to an Underground station, then on the Underground, and farther to his destination by another London Transport bus accounts for three London Transport journeys; he has of course in addition to make two journey stages on foot. Similarly, it is to be noted that while in early days the British Transport Commission counted as a British Rail journey a through-ticket journey beginning on British Rail and continuing on London Transport (and vice versa), later they counted them separately as two journeys, as naturally occurs in the statistics in the periods when the two organizations have been separated.

1.3.2 A passenger journey, however defined, has many dimensions. It varies in purpose, and purposes are multifold, as we shall discuss later with relation to the National Travel Survey. It varies in length, and this is perhaps the main reason why figures of the number of journeys (about which we know far more than about their other characteristics) are not very useful for most purposes. It varies in timing, and the time of the day, week and year is extremely important for the costs of any given journey. Different journey purposes have, of course, very different time patterns. The passenger journey also varies geographically, which is important in relation to two factors in particular, the density and distribution of population of the area in question (which affects the total stream of journeys, and hence their costs, along particular routes), and the nature of the infrastructure available in a given area (which determines the canalization of journeys and even whether they take place at all).

1.3.3 A more useful overall figure by which to measure passenger transport is the *passenger mile*. This again of itself is subject to all the variations to which journeys are subject. Passenger miles vary in purpose, timing and geography, and represent sums of journeys of different lengths. Furthermore, as journeys, passenger miles vary in quality. Each mode of transport has its own special characteristics of comfort, convenience, speed, etc. and not everyone values these characteristics in the same way, or in the same way at different times. There is, of course, a large literature on the valuation of travel time, and the Department of Transport provides guidance on standards to be adopted in cost-benefit analysis. Overall figures are provided by Transport and Road Research Laboratory publications on Motor Vehicle Costs [QRL 62] (*see* 4.3.4). Even if the passenger mile is the most useful available measure of passenger transport output, it is not satisfactory as a measure of either consumers' economic welfare or of producers' output. No attempts seem to have been made to construct any weighted measure of output, which might be equivalent to an index of shoe output which weighted the numbers produced by the value of different kinds of shoes. For limited purposes such an index might have value, but the enormous heterogeneity of journeys (particularly taking account of the geographical factors) would perhaps make such a measure of little general value. A factor of importance here is that the actual journey may differ in length (and cost) from the desired journey because of limitations of supply of infrastructure and transport provision. A person wishing to travel by train from Oxford to Cambridge may have to travel nearly twice as far in miles today as he once needed to; even if the cost (or time) has not increased correspondingly, it will have increased to some extent, and a statistically weighted index of output of the traditional kind is somewhat misleading (though not entirely different from the situation of a person who prefers a type of shoe once sold on a large scale and now having to be made specially for him). Briefly, people want to travel from A to B at a given time; they do not buy passenger miles except as a means to an end.

1.3.4 There are clearly great difficulties in measuring passenger miles (and passenger journeys) from the available data of money receipts and numbers of tickets sold (particularly with multiple ticket issues, and free and reduced fares). Tyson [B 9] suggested a simple method of estimating passenger mileage from passenger journeys and the fare scales. The actual methods London Transport uses are described in detail in an article by Baggaley [B 1], which sheds light on an otherwise not well-documented field.

1.3.5 From the producer's point of view, the passenger mile is a bad index of output where the means of transport is public. This is not because it is unimportant in relation to demand and profitability, but because it is not directly related to cost. For this the *vehicle mile* is a much better index. Apart from taxis and hire-cars where passenger miles and vehicle miles more or less correspond, the producer can only provide passenger miles if the utilization of the vehicle is adequate. His immediately escapable costs relate mainly to vehicle miles not to passenger miles, and this makes an important difference as compared with much production of goods, where escapable costs of materials and often of labour are related to the same units as are demanded by the public.

1.4 Definitions

1.4.1 There are many pitfalls of definition in this field. We have already discussed the not always precise definitions of a journey. One major question to ask of any set of data is whether all journeys are included or whether business journeys are excluded (see 4.3.1–3). Even with the apparently more precise counting of vehicles great confusion can arise. Firstly, there are motorized and other vehicles. Then there are 'business' and other vehicles, a distinction which may differ as between use and ownership. Thirdly, and particularly in the case of public service vehicles, there are the distinctions between vehicles owned, vehicles with road licences and vehicles with public service licences, as well as distinctions between vehicles running or in use in a period and vehicles in stock (see 4.4.7). In addition to all these there are the problems of numbers at a given date and numbers relating to a period; not all our sources are precise about this. We have mentioned the general problem of distinguishing British from English and Welsh and United Kingdom figures. There is also the general question of different years (calendar, financial, etc.). It is to be noted that the general distinction between internal and inland transport mentioned above is also relevant to transport flows within any area. Finally, it should be stated that EEC rules should not, it is believed, lead to any major changes in UK practice in this field.

2 Organization of Passenger Transport

2.1 Private Movement and Taxis

2.1.1 Little need be said about the organization of passenger movements other than those of the bus industry. All road users have to obey certain complicated (and often misunderstood) laws and regulations, with which we are not concerned here. All motor vehicles (except Crown vehicles) are subject to certain taxes both in general and in particular for making use of parts of the road system or its adjuncts. Certain parts of the road system are exclusively reserved for particular categories of vehicles (motorways, bus-only lanes, bicycle lanes, footpaths, access only, etc.). The road system itself is indeed a highly complex network, with the definition of which we are fortunately not concerned here.

2.1.2 Taxis, that is to say vehicles plying for hire, are subject to licensing by local authorities, and in particular the London taxi is subject to a rigid system of licensing and control by the Metropolitan Police, which there are apparently plans to extend throughout the country. Hire-cars are not subject to the same control.

2.2 Public Road Passenger Transport

2.2.1 The licensing system and the categories of licensed journeys are described below (under 3.4—Traffic Commissioners). Here we are concerned with the operational units which manage bus and coach services and their like, and for which statistics are available. The present framework is that laid down in the Transport Act, 1968, and the Transport (London) Act, 1969. There are six categories of operators: (1) Private operators; (2) Local authorities (LAs); (3) Passenger Transport Executives (PTEs); (4) London Transport (LT); (5) The National Bus Company (NBC); (6) The Scottish Transport Group (STG) (Scottish Bus Group).

2.2.2 (1) *Private operators*
These may be concerns which have their own vehicles for their own members (e.g. firms providing journeys to work for their employees, hospital or university bus services, etc.). In the 'public' sector they consist of private individuals or companies offering services to the public as licensed by the Traffic Commissioners. Since 1968 these last are a small part of the total industry, very small in the provision of regular scheduled services ('stage services'— 3.4.2 below), but providing for the major part of the tours and excursions field, and owning large numbers of vehicles (*see* 2.2.8).

2.2.3 (2) *Local authorities* (LAs)
These have been running bus services largely in urban areas for about seventy years, and trams for many years before that. The number of local authorities running bus services was reduced by the setting-up of the PTEs, but the Local Government Act, 1972, requires the new local authorities to co-ordinate passenger transport services in their area and gives them powers to reorganize undertakings within this area. One should also note that there are mixed municipal/National Bus Company undertakings, e.g. in Bristol.

2.2.4 (3) *Passenger Transport Executives* (PTEs)
These were established under the Transport Act, 1968, to reorganize and run the bus services in the major conurbations under Passenger Transport Authorities (PTAs) which were special bodies with local authority representation (and power to precept on the rates). They were required to plan

for transport as a whole in their areas. With the reform of local government under the Local Government Act, 1972, the special bodies were assimilated to the new metropolitan councils, much on the London pattern. Towards the end of 1969 PTEs were set up in the West Midland, Merseyside and South-East Lancashire/North-East Cheshire conurbations; Tyneside followed in January 1970, and Glasgow in June 1973. West Yorkshire and South Yorkshire were subsequently added.

2.2.5 (4) *London Transport* (LT)
Dating back to the creation of the London Passenger Transport Board in 1933 (with its near monopoly of all forms of passenger transport in London), this survived intact as a unit of the British Transport Commission (BTC) (1948-62) and as a separate nationalized industry (1963-9) with only minor changes in boundaries and responsibilities. From January 1970 it came under the control of the Greater London Council, but shorn of its country services (including Green Lines) which were handed over to the National Bus Company. Its bus services are only part of the total operation, which includes 'the Underground', that is to say a part of the total railway services serving the local London passenger (the division between its share and that of British Rail being largely a matter of history).

2.2.6 (5) *National Bus Company* (NBC)
The origins of this nationalized industry lie in the pre-war railway company bus services, and the sectors of the private bus industry bought by the BTC between 1948 and 1951. These were amalgamated with the Tilling and Scottish bus groups under the BTC, and then handed over to the Transport Holding Company (THC) from 1 January 1963. The THC (which had many other interests in road haulage, shipping, travel services, etc.) ran these bus services and others they acquired as separate undertakings, acting as a holding company, a form of organization also favoured by the large private company, British Electric Traction, which owned much of the private bus sector. The latter sold its interests to the THC in March 1968, thus setting the stage for the establishment of the NBC from 1 January 1969 under the Transport Act, 1968. The NBC has continued the holding company form of organization, and publishes minimal statistics about its operations as compared with its overall finances.

2.2.7 (6) *Scottish Transport Group* (STG) (Scottish Bus Group).
This was set up at the same time as the NBC to take over the old Scottish group of the BTC (see 2.2.6), which controlled the major part of the non-municipal bus operations in Scotland. Its bus operations are only part of its total activity.

2.2.8 An indication of the relative size of the various kinds of undertaking can be given in the simplest way by taking the figures for vehicles owned at the end of 1975 and vehicle miles and passenger journeys during the year.

Table 1

1975	Vehicles	Vehicle miles (m)	Passenger journeys (m)
Private	28,625	649	772
Municipal	6,160	162	1,180
PTE	11,020	329	2,257
LT	6,405	177	1,455
NBC	20,387	740	2,113
STG	4,301	149	392

Study of these figures by themselves (for example, a comparison of the relative positions of private, NBC and LA operations) can tell us practically the whole story of the different markets they serve and their relative importance. What other more detailed figures are available tell us little more. Thus the private sector had more buses than any other group, but its vehicles travelled fewer miles than those of the NBC, and it provided a very small number of passenger journeys. This reflects the high-quality long and high-value journeys of the tours and excursion sector. At the other extreme London Transport had the largest number of passenger journeys per bus (227,000), as compared with 27,000 in the private sector, about 100,000 in the rural areas (NBC and STG) and around 200,000 in the other urban areas (LA and PTE). As one would expect the denser the population the shorter the journeys. Similarly the passenger journeys per vehicle mile in the urban areas ranged around 7–8, as compared with around 3 in the rural areas and 1·2 for the private sector. Annual vehicle mileage per bus varied less, but, not unexpectedly, was highest in the rural areas (over 30,000 per bus), rather lower in the urban areas (under 30,000) and lowest of all in the private sector (23,000 vehicle miles per bus). These comparisons give some very rough indications of what one might expect the crucial load factor indices to look like, but without figures of passenger miles to compare with the vehicle mileage no exact conclusions can be drawn.

3 Main Sources

3.1 National Travel Survey (NTS) [QRL 42]

3.1.1 Very little was known of the travel habits of British people and in particular of their use of cars before the first household surveys made by the Government Social Survey for the Ministry of Transport in October 1961 [QRL 7]. Traditionally neither the railways nor the bus industry engaged in market research, London Transport being a partial exception to this rule (*see*, e.g. [QRL 4]); more recently, British Rail have embarked on such studies, but little has been published. The Social Surveys were on a quarterly basis (January, April, July and October) from October 1961 to January 1964 (excluding January 1962). They were confined to private motoring, and were followed by more comprehensive travel surveys (NTS) for 1964, 1965, 1966, 1972–3 and 1975/6 carried out by the Ministry [QRL 42]. The motoring surveys only covered England and Wales, the NTS Great Britain.

3.1.2 The results of the 1961–4 surveys were comprehensively published in a report by P. G. Gray [QRL 7], with preliminary results in *Economic Trends*, 1963 [QRL 43]. The later surveys have been quite inadequately published. The 1964 survey was published in two parts as a 'Preliminary report' (available from the Department) and some results of the 1965 survey were published in *Passenger Transport in Great Britain* (*PTGB*) [QRL 45] and *Highway Statistics* [QRL 34] (1967). The 1966 and 1972–3 surveys have not been published, except for some tables in *Social Trends* [QRL 58], discussed below (3.1.15). A two-page note on the 1965 and 1966 surveys is available from the Department (no reference number). Publication of the 1965 survey was promised 'towards the end of 1968' in [QRL 34] (1967), and *Statistical News*, ([B 16], May 1968, 1.30) and 'early in 1969' [QRL 45] (1967); these promises were not fulfilled. *Statistical News* (as above) stated that tables were available 'at reasonable cost' (i.e. for tables concerning households, vehicles, or individuals at about £3–7 per table, and about £35 for tabulations concerning journey characteristics). The 1972–3 survey is described in *Statistical News* ([B 16] February 1974, 24.20–1), where reference is made to intentions to publish about 100, out of the total of about 1,000 tables to be produced 'during the next two years'. (The first volume of forty-three tables was at last published in autumn 1975. [This was followed by two more volumes in 1976, one of them with detailed comparisons of 1972/3 data with 1965 data—A.W.]) Reference is there made to the address to which enquiries and requests for special tabulations should be made. All the data are stored on magnetic tape.

3.1.3 All these surveys were based on a random sample of households taken in the traditional manner from electoral registers. Households were both subjected to questionnaires and asked to fill in a travel record (and/or vehicle mileage book) for a week. A full description of the techniques used in the 1961–4 surveys is given in [QRL 7]; lesser details are given in the reports of the 1964 survey, and some information in [QRL 34, QRL 45] on the 1965 survey. *Statistical News* ([B 16] 24.20–1) gives a brief account of the 1972–3 survey. The 1961–4 surveys involved a basic sample of 3,282 households with 1,089 cars and 1,933 licence holders in England and Wales. The 1964 survey covered 5,013 households in Great Britain with 1,631 private cars, 290 goods vehicles, etc. and 385 motor-cycles and mopeds, etc. and with 2,857 licence holders for cars, etc. and 1,361 for motor cycles, etc. (also 439 provisional licences). It was conducted in three phases (January 29–March 14, May 30–July 11, October 13–December 3), and not all information was collected for every phase. The 1964 survey was 'largely experimental', while the 1965 survey (with a sample of 12,500 households and about 34,000 individuals and 7,000 vehicles) was regarded as 'the detailed base-line study against which subsequent changes will be measured'. The 1966 survey was on a smaller scale (5,000 households), while the 1972–3 survey yielded a sample of 7,000 households (20,000 individuals, 4,900 household vehicles and 233,000 journeys). The latter survey extended from April 1972 to March 1973. Each household kept records for a week, the weeks being evenly spread throughout the year and starting on different days of the week (*see* Appendix C).

3.1.4 The 1961–4 surveys were more limited in scope than the NTS, but the analysis was in much more detail. Thus, whereas journeys were only classified into to/from work, in the course of employment, and not connected with work, they were analysed for each half-hour round the clock for each day of the week during each of the quarters studied. Otherwise the analysis was much on the same lines as the later surveys.

3.1.5 The NTS covers practically all journeys made by households, but not those made by people living in institutions. It includes journeys for work purposes, but not those where the main purpose is to transport the vehicle (e.g. by bus drivers and conductors, lorry drivers, etc.). Information on times of journeys and details of short walks under one mile were only collected (1972–3) for the last day of each recording period (week). The basic data relate to households, persons, journeys and vehicles. The simplest way to outline the significance of the surveys is to describe the characteristics by which these categories are analysed, though the actual analysis may be somewhat different for the different surveys. Various cross-classifications of categories are available in the published tables in the form of totals and percentages, and more or less any cross-classifications are in principle available, at least for the 1972–3 survey. These characteristics are given below, as are also the areas for which data are available, the information about expenditure on public transport, and the special treatment of holiday travel. It is to be noted that information about certain characteristics is available for particular days of the week; also that for certain purposes categories are amalgamated in the published data.

3.1.6 (a) *Households*
These are characterized by number of persons (1, 2, 3, 4, 5 or more) and by various characteristics of the head of household. Households are also classified by income ranges (less than £8, £8–£13, £13–18, £18–23, £23–28, £28–33, £33–43, £43 and over), though the data on this proved much less reliable than for other items. A basic analysis is in terms of ownership of vehicles of various kinds (particularly car-owning households with 1 or 2 or more cars). Heads of households were classified by socio-economic group (employers, managers and professional; clerical workers; manual workers—supervisory and skilled; manual workers—semi-skilled and unskilled; farmers and own-account workers; retired; unoccupied housewife; others and unclassified). Households were also classified by number of driving-licence holders (1, 2, 3 or more).

3.1.7 (b) *Persons*
These were firstly characterized by sex and age (3–4, 5–10, 11–15, 16, 17–20, 21–9, 30–9, 40–9, 50–9, 60–4, 65 and over). Secondly, licence holders were classified (full licence for car or goods vehicles; full licence for motor-cycle, scooter and moped; provisional licence; no licence). Thirdly, some data were given relating to usual main drivers. Fourthly, personal income groups were distinguished for some purposes by region, based

on another simple question in the survey on this issue.

3.1.8 (c) *Journeys*
Journeys were treated in terms of journey stages (*see* 1.3.1 above), and many results were given in terms of both journeys and journey stages (or by 1, 2, 3 or more stages per journey). The basic characteristics of journey stages and journeys are described in terms of frequency and length, as follows:

Per week	Length in miles
0–under 1	under 1
1	1–under $2\frac{1}{2}$
2–4	$2\frac{1}{2}$–under 4
5–8	4–under 7
9–12	7–under 10
13–17	10–under 15
18–24	15–under 20
25 and over	20–under 30
or 18–29	30–under 60
30–49	60–under 100
50 and over	100 and over

Journey stages by public transport are analysed in ranges of none, 1–4, 5–10, 11–17 and 18 or more per week. From this it is clearly possible to build up a picture of total mileage by different types of vehicles and for different purposes. The mileage ranges for persons are none, under 10, 10 and less than 20, 20–30, 30–50, 50–100 and 100 and over; for vehicles they are less than 1, 1 and less than 50, 50–100, 100–150, 150–200, 200–300, 300–500, 500 and over.

3.1.9
Fundamental to this survey, and to all transportation surveys, is the analysis of journeys by mode of transport and journey purpose. The classification of these in the surveys follows a pattern which is more or less standard. The transport modes were:

Public transport
  Rail
    British Rail 1st class
    British Rail 2nd class
    London Transport Underground
  Local bus
    London Transport
    Other
  Long-distance bus
  Taxi or chauffeur-driven hire-cars
  Other public transport
Private transport
  Private bus
    Private tour or excursion bus
    Private works or school bus
  Car
    As driver
    As passenger in household car
    As passenger in non-household car
  Van (goods vehicle)
    As driver
    As passenger in household van
    As passenger in non-household van
  Motor-cycle, scooter, moped
    As driver
    As passenger
  Bicycle
  Other private transport (walking one mile or more, etc.)

(*Note:* to obtain this breakdown and others by area, London Transport buses were distinguished as between Central (Red), Country (Green) and Green Line.)

3.1.10
Journey purposes were classified as:
  In the course of work
  To/from work
  To/from school or college
  Other purposes:
    To/from shopping
      Regular purchases
      Occasional purchases
    Personal business (financial, medical, religious, etc.)
    To/from restaurants and public houses
    To/from sporting activities
    To/from places of entertainment

Pleasure trips
Visiting friends and relations
Accompanying or travelling to meet/set down other person

3.1.11 (d) *Vehicles*
These were classified as car taxed as private, goods vehicle taxed as private, goods vehicle taxed as dual purpose/goods, motor-cycle, moped or scooter, and pedal cycle. Many of the above classifications were related to vehicles as well as households or persons, but in particular vehicle occupancy was studied (1, 2, 3, 4, 5 or more persons per vehicle) and average mileage in relation to days of the week and time of year, as well as in terms of the range of mileages, journey purpose, etc. Some data are also given as to the number of vehicles owned by employers or other than the household itself. ([QRL 34] (1967) also gives details of cars by engine size, value and year of first registration.)

3.1.12 (e) *Areas*
The household's locality was classified by its density in terms of persons per acre, as many travel characteristics are affected by degrees of urbanization (less than 0·5, 0·5–less than 5, 5–10, 10–30, 30–50, 50 and over—persons per acre). Areas were classified into London Transport area, other conurbations, other urban areas, and non-urban areas, and for 1965 grouped into planning regions (with the GLC area and the rest of the South-East separately). Accessibility to various forms of public transport was also measured, but not published, as well as other area characteristics (but *see* 3.1.15).

3.1.13 (f) *Expenditure*
The survey confines itself to expenditure on public transport, and average figures are given per week and per year. These figures are given for each mode of public transport (express bus and taxi given separately) by journey length (less than 1 mile, 1–less than $2\frac{1}{2}$, $2\frac{1}{2}$–4, 4–7, 7–10, 10–15, 15–20, 20–30, and 30 and over). They are also analysed by whether paid by the informant, another person or a company (or organization), and by type of ticket (standard single or return, normal season, subsidized season, other reduced rate, free travel). Weekly household expenditure on public transport is given by the following ranges: none, 1d. to less than 2/6, 2/6 to 5/–, 5/– to 10/–, 10/– to 15/–, 15/– to 20/–, 20/– to 30/–, 30/– and over (1964).

3.1.14 (g) *Holiday travel*
The main 1964 analysis and the 1965 survey excluded holidays (and other trips of more than a few days away from home) other than short holidays taken during the actual survey period. A special analysis of annual holidays was made during phase III of the 1964 survey. The number and type of holiday taken by the various groups was recorded (touring in Great Britain; stayed at two places in Great Britain; stayed at one place in Great Britain; abroad). Mode of transport was analysed in terms of motor vehicles (household; borrowed or hired), train, bus and coach, and other, and mileages were recorded.

3.1.15 *1972–3 survey*
Social Trends [QRL 58] has published a number of tables based on the 1972–3 NTS. (a) The 1974 edition published a table of all journeys to work in 1973 by region of residence in terms of time and distance:

Minutes	*Distance (miles)*
under 15	under 1
15–30	1–2
30–60	2–5
over 60	5–10
	10–25
	over 25

(b) There was also a table of all journeys by purpose in 1973 by sex and various age-groups. (c) The means of transport used for all journeys, except walks of less than a mile, in 1972–3 (in terms of percentage of distance covered) is given by regions. (d) A final table gives for 1972–3 the time of journey to the nearest railway station by walking/bus for each region, the times being:

Minutes
6 or less (walking only)
7–13 (13 or less for bus)
14–26
27 or more

All these tables are given in terms of percentages, with the total sub-sample size given for (c) and (d). [Some of these data were repeated in the 1975 edition—A.W.]. In addition, it should be noted that the NTS, together with other surveys and sources of information, is used for the figures of passenger miles of travel and availability of cars to households published in *PTGB* [QRL 45] [and from 1964 in *Transport Statistics Great Britain* (*TS*) [QRL 64]—A.W.].

3.1.16 *Long-distance travel*

Other methods have been used to collect information on long-distance travel. From mid-1968 to mid-1969 a random stratified sample of individuals provided a continuing weekly record of journeys of twenty-five miles or more. The panel consisted of 600 members in the first year, and 783 thereafter, with a third of the members being replaced each year by a similar set of individuals ([QRL 45] (1971), p.v). Some results for the three years 1968/9–1970/1 were published in *PTGB* ([QRL 45] (1971), Table 7), giving the overall average annual number of journeys by car, bus/coach, rail and air for each of the years and by journey purpose (work or study, (excluding commuting); holiday and pleasure; and shopping, personal business, etc.). In 1973, the panel was superseded by a postal questionnaire addressed to a random sample of about 30,000 persons from each of the major conurbations (each with a population of about seven million), as described in *Statistical News* ([B 16] November 1974, 27.20). A response rate of over 70% has been achieved, and a sub-sample of non-respondents is interviewed. In addition, a sample of the 16–17 year olds in the households is sent postal questionnaires. These surveys cover journeys of more than twenty-five miles. 'Apart from the standard questions on origin and destination, travel method and journey purpose, respondents are asked to provide information for each journey on other topics such as the day of the week, the reason for choice of transport, the number of adults and children sharing the journey, the age, sex and occupation of the respondent, and whether a car was available to the household. A few further questions are included on regular journeys to work.' In 1973 Merseyside, SELNEC (South-East Lancashire, North-East Cheshire), West Yorkshire and South Yorkshire were surveyed. From July 1974 to June 1975 the new counties of West Midlands, Tyne and Wear, and Cleveland were covered, as well as the Glasgow and Edinburgh conurbations and the urban areas of Dundee and Aberdeen in Scotland. A national survey was also begun in July 1974 on similar lines to provide a framework for the detailed studies. No results seem to have been published, but information can be obtained from an address given in the above-mentioned note. (For some further information about holidays, *see* bibliography in Gordon and Edwards (1973) [B 3], and *Social Trends* (1974) [QRL 58], p 238 for the British Home Tourism Survey.) (*See* Appendix D.)

3.1.17 *The General Household Survey* [B 10] might be thought to be a natural source for further enquiries of the same kind as those initiated in the NTS. The first two years' surveys for 1971 and 1972 were (partially) published at the time of writing. The main travel questions asked were about journeys in the last two weeks, of 100 miles or over. These were classified in terms of the place of start and finish of the journey, type of transport used, purpose of the journey, and whether alone or with others (group or family). None of this information has been published. The

1972 survey also asked questions about numbers of cars available to members of households and this is published for 1/2 or more cars by region, house tenure and socio-economic group of head of household. *Social Trends* (1972 and 1973) [QRL 58] published from this survey tables of journey times of the journey to work of heads of household in 1971 and 1972 by region.

3.2 Transportation Studies

3.2.1 All the conurbations and many other towns have mounted major transportation surveys with a view to producing traffic plans for their areas. The models originated in the USA, and the first to be used in this country was for London [QRL 36]. By and large they follow a fairly standard methodology, though the complex computer packages involve many variations, known to the particular consultants involved, but not always to the general public and not always fully published (for commercial reasons). The standard basis of data collection is a combination of sample household surveys, road counts and measurements of journey times and costs. For these three elements of data input, special surveys have been mounted by consultants, and then combined together with other data from planning records, bus companies, railways and earlier local authority surveys. The basic units are zones as defined for each study area; these provide the origins and destinations of the strips detailed from the household sample surveys. These are then matched with the data from road counts, etc. and the flows assigned to particular parts of the areas' road network. At this stage the data may be adjusted in various ways to fit the model. From the point of view of passenger travel, the exercise results in a mass of information about journey from one zone to another by different modes of transport and for different journey purposes (mainly following the lines of the NTS; see 3.1.9–10 above). Pedestrian and bicycle journeys are often neglected, or only minimally considered.

3.2.2. The surveys are usually published by the consultants and/or the local authorities involved, often at great cost. These publications give varying amounts of information from the surveys; the London survey [QRL 36] is published in particular detail. We give references for typical surveys in Glasgow and West Midlands [QRL 33, QRL 63]. A useful summary of data from a considerable number of these surveys is to be found in a British Road Federation publication [QRL 17]. The Department of the Environment has compiled an index of surveys (and the topics they cover) carried out by all organizations outside central government. (See *Statistical News* [B 16], 22.31-2, and Appendix A.) For a summary of the techniques used in the surveys, see *Urban Traffic Engineering Techniques* (1965) [B 19], and *Traffic and Transport Plans* (Roads Circular 1/68) [B 17]; for a survey and critique *see* Bruton [B 2]. Regional plans may also include more broad-brush overall studies; *see* [QRL 59] for the South-East.

3.2.3 It would be pleasant to be able to summarize in some form the information available from all these reports or to provide the would-be reader with an easy guide to them. As suggested earlier (1.1.6), this is not possible. Unfortunately, more effort seems to have gone into deeper analysis of limited data, or into collecting more information from new surveys, than into making available on an overall and comparative basis the enormous mass of data already collected. Nor is it easy even to find one's way to the actual publications, which are only available from a host of local bodies throughout the country. The reader may be referred to a number of institutions with specialized libraries, which are likely to prove helpful: the Chartered Institute of Transport, the Town Planning Institute, the Transport and Road Research Laboratory, the Greater London Council (whose Department of Planning and Transportation produces a large number of survey and research reports). Above all, there is the Department of the Environment library at 2 Marsham

Street, SW 1, which provides admirable services. For those who want data on a particular subject, the simplest approach is to use the Department's index mentioned above to locate the surveys in which the information is to be found. More details of this index and the Department's service are given in Appendix A.

3.3 Road censuses [QRL 61]

3.3.1 Road censuses to measure traffic flows of different kinds at particular road sites have a long history. Since the early years of the century traffic in London has been measured at congested junctions and bridges. The purpose of these measurements has been to help in making decisions about road improvements. As a by-product they produce figures of vehicle movements which tell us about some aspects of passenger and goods movement. Earlier censuses were not scientifically based (see for example, *Road Fund Report* for 1953/4 [QRL 48] with figures for 1938, August 1950 and August 1953); they covered 5,753, 267 and 100 points on the road system in Great Britain, the later ones chosen from points included in the earlier samples; see also [QRL 50]. It is to be noted that counts at the same points over time, unless they represent a random sample of the whole road system, will not produce an unbiased estimate of the growth of *total* traffic, even if the road system itself is unchanged. One would expect traffic to expand faster on uncongested routes and more slowly on congested roads. In the past there was probably a tendency to choose points of heavy flow, where congestion would be most expected.

3.3.2 From 1956, flows have been measured each month at fifty selected points by automatic counters, the points being selected on a statistically random basis. These were supplemented by manual counts of each type of vehicle from 1958 during the daytime of one consecutive Friday, Saturday and Sunday each month, including pedal cycles, which do not actuate the automatic counters. In January 1966 the manual counts were expanded to over 200 points, including forty-five of the original fifty points. From these counts trends are measured, while the absolute level of traffic was measured in 1960, 1966 and autumn 1973–spring 1974 by means of short-period counts at 1,100 (1960) and 1,300 sites, which unlike the other counts included unclassified roads (see below). Motorways were not included in any of the counts until 1966. From May 1971, for reasons of economy, counting at non-motorway sites was reduced to two months in every three, with estimates for the remaining third of the sample.

3.3.3 The overall results of these counts are published in *Highway Statistics* from 1963 to 1973 [QRL 34] (and from 1974 in *TS* [QR 64]); formerly they were published in *Roads in England and Wales* [QRL 52] and the equivalent Scottish publications [QRL 35, QRL 55]. More detailed figures are given in various Transport and Road Research Laboratory reports [QRL 61]. Figures for previous periods to compare with the later surveys are given in MacNaughton-Smith and Tanner (1956) [B 5] and Scott and Tanner (1962) [B 6]. A summary account of the analysis is given in Chapter 2 of *Research on Road Traffic* (1965) [B 14] (see also [B 18]), and the methodology is discussed by Tanner (1957) [B 8].

3.3.4 From these counts hourly, daily, monthly and yearly traffic flows are estimated for different classes of vehicles and different types of road in different areas, though, because of the nature of the counts and small size of the samples, there cannot be a complete cross-classification for all types of data. Figures are given by engineering divisions of the Department and types of road. It is to be noted in the case of the latter that (a) the classification of types of road is administrative (trunk, classes I–III, unclassified), and, as the sample was based on the old classification prior to the April 1967 distinction between principal and other non-trunk roads, the figures follow the old classification; and that (b) the earlier figures exclude motorways, a fact not always made clear (e.g. *Highway Statistics*, 1965 [QRL 34], where the traffic is described as on 'all roads'). Care must also be taken in distinguishing figures for all motor vehicles, cars and taxis, and other types of road traffic.

3.4 Traffic Commissioners (TC) [QRL 19]

3.4.1 The reports of the Traffic Commissioners were, from 1931 to 1948, the main source of data for the bus industry. In 1949 they were largely superseded by the official *PTGB* reports [QRL 45]. But up to 1969/70 they still contained a useful analysis of undertakings by size (number of vehicles) in each of their control divisions. The reports also give some figures of licensed drivers and conductors representing the total stock of licences issued, many times greater than those actually in service (*see* 4.4.4), and administrative details of cases considered (fares, licence applications, etc.).

3.4.2 The Traffic Commissioners license all 'public service vehicles' and their drivers and conductors. The basic definitions are to be found in the Road Traffic Act, 1960, ss. 117–8 and 12th Schedule. 'A public service vehicle is a motor vehicle used for carrying passengers for hire or reward which either:

(a) is carrying passengers at separate fares, or

(b) is not carrying passengers at separate fares but is adapted to carry eight or more passengers.'

Public service vehicles can be 'stage carriages', 'express carriages' or 'contract carriages'. The last named is defined as 'not carrying passengers at separate fares'. A stage carriage is defined as 'a public service vehicle carrying passengers at separate fares, not being an express carriage'; an express service being defined in terms of the size of separate fares charged. But the exact distinctions are further refined in many complicated ways.

The final statistics are published in terms of stage services, express services, excursions and tours, and contract work (see *PTGB* [QRL 45] and *TS* [QRL 64]).

3.5 'Passenger Transport in Great Britain' (*PTGB*) [QRL 45]

3.5.1 We have already described the coverage of this source in 1.1.3. It has been the main source of publication of the 1965 NTS (*see* 3.1), and also brings together figures about railways and internal air movements from other sources, as well as general figures from the National Income Blue Book [QRL 41] and elsewhere. Historically, it is a continuation of a series on bus and tram statistics produced by the Ministry of Transport from 1949 to 1961–2; before that bus statistics were published by the Traffic Commissioners in their reports from 1931/2, while tramway returns go back to the nineteenth century. It is thus the primary publication source for bus and tram statistics.

3.5.2 We know of no detailed published explanation or analysis of the returns from operators of public service road vehicles (buses) which provide the basis for the data. Returns from London Transport seem to have been taken from their reports (*see* 1961/2 returns, p. 8). Returns from other operators are of three kinds (*see* Appendix B for details):

(1) Numbers of passengers carried, vehicle miles run, passenger receipts, employees and particulars of vehicle fleet from all operators for calendar years;

(2) Quarterly returns for the first three-quarters of each calendar year from large operators (with more than twenty-four vehicles), of vehicles, traffic and operations (published as they become available in the *Monthly Digest of Statistics*);

(3) Financial and statistical returns from large operators (with more than twenty-four vehicles) for their accounting years (up to 1970). In fact, as can be seen from the analysis below (*see* 4.4), there

is rather more information than this would seem to imply. Quarterly figures (since the middle of 1955) have been estimated from the returns from large operators; these accounted for 96% of passenger journeys outside London and 89% of passenger receipts in 1969 ([QRL 45] 1969).

3.5.3 Financial years vary. London Transport uses a calendar year. Local Authorities in England and Wales use a year ending on March 31, and in Scotland normally on May 15; it is to be noted that many transport statistics of LA operations for GB are described as for years ending on March 31, while in fact they represent an addition of the Scottish and English years, though this is rarely stated, and, of course, may not always be the case. The financial figures (as published up to 1970) are based on a consistent set of categories for all types of operators, but do not correspond with the analysis used in London Transport accounts, or in the accounts of municipal operators.

3.5.4 The road passenger transport tables in this source are clearly presented and summarize lucidly the data available from the various returns. With the establishment of the PTEs, a useful set of corrected figures back to 1960 was produced for the companies which constituted the new organizations, though the same has not been done for the London operations handed over to the NBC. Unfortunately, though the recent issues are very much better than the earlier ones, they are marred by continuous sloppiness in detail. The road passenger tables are indeed the most carelessly produced and in detail the most misleading we have come across in an extensive use of government economic statistics. On the whole, however, apart from misleading headings, the mistakes are small in quantity and need not deter the user who rounds the figures appropriately.

3.5.5 Explanation is sparse and unexplained changes are made in past figures. Tables are wrongly described in their headings, and two apparent versions of the same figure often appear in the same issue. Rounding is sloppy, and clerical mistakes are made in copying figures. Any user who wants accuracy would be well advised to ignore the last (or last two) digits, unless he prefers to engage in a rather tedious process of cross-checking. Part of this arises from the use of BTC and LT reports (not always properly understood) rather than the direct collection of returns from these organizations; but much is the result of sloppy presentation and inadequate supervision. The following examples, taken from the later and better returns, illustrate these rather severe strictures:

(a) Figures for passenger journeys were revised back to 1950–3 for different types of operators in the returns for 1958/9, 1959/60 and 1962 without explanation (though for good reasons). A useful summary table (No. 44 in the 1967 returns) returned to many of the earlier figures, and added a few further errors. The mistakes were corrected in the equivalent Table 30 of the 1968 returns (without explanation);

(b) Tables 27 and 28 of the 1969 returns only relate to buses and coaches, excluding trams and trolley-buses, though the heading belies this, and the equivalent tables in other years are comprehensive;

(c) The revised figures given for stage passenger journeys in 1969 in main urban and other areas in Table 39 of the 1970 returns (repeated in all later issues) do not seem to be consistent with the figures in Table 30 and those from London Transport;

(d) Two different figures are given in Tables 32 and 35 (1969) for the number of single- and double-deck buses in 1969;

(e) Table 39 in the 1973 returns (and other similar tables in earlier returns) headed 'receipts per passenger journey' does not make it clear whether the reference is to passenger receipts or total receipts.

3.6 Reports of Undertakings

3.6.1 The main national published reports relate to the BTC (1948–62) [QRL 24], London Transport (in BTC reports up to 1962, separately published by London Transport Executive from 1970) [QRL 37–8] and the Transport Holding Company and its successors, the NBC and STG [QRL 40, QRL 56]. The BTC and London Transport were traditionally great publishers of detailed statistics, while the THC followed the holding company tradition of minimal publication. The latter tradition has been followed by the NBC, which publishes minimal statistics about its operations, and none about the operations of the companies which are the actual operating units. The STG gives slightly more information, e.g. about total seating capacity of its fleet.

3.6.2 Apart from London Transport, the main use of the currently published set of reports is in the balance sheet information provided. Otherwise the information is to be found in more detail in *PTGB* [QRL 45] and *TS* [QRL 64].

3.7 Other Special Sources

3.7.1 This section deals rather summarily with certain official and non-official publications which include interesting information relevant to road passenger transport. The official sources discussed are the vehicle registration returns, the Family Expenditure Survey, the census, the Rudd/Dawson expenditure estimates, the Association of Public Passenger Transport Operators returns, and the Road Transport Industry Training Board reports. Non-official sources include sources for vehicle operating costs and some surveys of private motoring.

(1) OFFICIAL SOURCES

3.7.2 (a) *Vehicle registration*
The vehicle registration system is well known, and has been standardized since 1920. The major changes of recent years have been the substitution of a sample count of vehicles (since 1961) for the previous complete annual count, and the recent centralization of records in a computerized store. When the computerized system is fully working, the present sampling errors will be eliminated. The essential basis of the system remains, namely that vehicles are classified by excise categories, and therefore change when the basis of these changes (e.g. cars classified by horsepower under the old system, and those classified by cylinder capacity—since 1 January 1947; the former group are a small diminishing part of the whole). There are problems about Crown and exempt vehicles which have to be borne in mind. As we are not primarily concerned with the vehicle stock as such, we do not go into detail about these figures. Figures are available by regions and local authority areas for the various categories of vehicles, and new registration figures (based on complete counts) are published on a monthly basis. Fairly full summaries of all these figures (covering UK as well as GB) are published in *Highway Statistics* [QRL 34] (and from 1974 in *TS* [QRL 64]) though they were formerly (up to 1962) published separately in greater detail [QRL 49]. The main point to note is that, though there are long-standing figures of the stock (during the September quarter), and of new registrations, it is only since 1966 that data are available on date of first registration (two years combined for recent years).

3.7.3 (b) *Family Expenditure Survey* (FES) [QRL 32]
The Family Expenditure Survey (FES), (1953/4, 1957–annually) is well known, and does not need to be described. It is to be noted that it covers the UK as a whole. The transport information is in terms of average weekly expenditure on:

Net purchases of motor vehicles, spares and accessories.
Maintenance and running of motor vehicles.
Purchase and maintenance of other vehicles and boats.

Railway fares.
Bus and coach fares.
Other travel and transport.

Further details are given of the coverage of these categories.

This information is given for households of different income ranges, by income and household composition, by area (Greater London, provincial conurbations, other urban areas, rural areas) and by region (two years combined, except for transport as a whole). It is to be noted that where hire-purchase and credit sales are involved, expenditure is defined as instalments being paid at the date of interview, plus down-payments on commodities acquired within the preceding thirteen weeks (whereas in the Blue Book [QRL 41] consumption of, e.g. cars in a period is the purchase cost of the vehicle bought, regardless of when it is paid for). The survey has also collected (since 1969) information as to ownership of durable goods by households, and the numbers (and percentages) of those owning cars (1, 2, 3 or more) are given by regions. It is to be noted that, as with the Blue Book, business expenditure on transport is not included.

3.7.4 (c) *Census*

Though several earlier censuses collected information about the relation between workplaces and residence by local authority areas, the 1966 sample census [QRL 26] was the first to ask questions about the mode of travel to work (the categories being train, bus, car, goods vehicle, motor-cycle, pedal cycle, on foot, other, none and not stated). This is also related to households owning and not owning cars. The information is published for many, if not all, local authority areas in terms of a two-way classification by area of workplace and area of residence (i.e. for any given area the figures give numbers for each mode of travel for persons resident in the area and working in it, persons resident but working outside it, and persons working in the area but resident elsewhere, with the two resulting totals of persons resident in and working in the area). The 1971 census provides information of the same kind cross-classified as between areas of workplace and residence.

3.7.5 (d) *Rudd/Dawson expenditure estimates*

Rudd pioneered in the TRRL the first comprehensive estimates of expenditure on road transport in Great Britain for the years 1949 and 1950 [QRL 11]. They were continued by Dawson for 1960 [QRL 2] and annually up to 1969 [QRL 34] (1970). So far as road passenger transport is concerned, the items covered were:

Travel by bus, tram, etc.
Travel by taxi
Travel by private car or motor-cycle
Use of vehicles for the public service
Travel by pedal cycle

The estimates for the public services include both passenger and goods vehicles, and separate estimates for each were not possible. [QRL 34] combines the taxi figures with those for buses, etc. and pedal cycles with cars, etc.

Estimates for buses, etc. are from the receipts of undertakings, while the other figures are built up from items of outlay related to vehicles. For cars, etc. the items of expenditure are:

Licences
Garages and parking
Insurance
Fuel
Lubricants
Tyres
Maintenance and repairs
Depreciation
Retailing of used cars
Interest

Dawson (1960), but not Rudd (1949, 1950), gives detailed figures for taxis as above, but also including wages and profit. Hire-cars he includes with cars, whereas Rudd includes them with taxis. Rudd makes an estimate for interest for cars, etc. but excludes it from his total, whereas Dawson includes it. Dawson also gives separate figures for cars and motor-cycles, which Rudd does not. All these figures are at market prices and for total users' expenditure. There is some duplication in that, for example, business travel by tyre-making firms will be included in the expenditure on tyres; estimates of the extent of this are only made for the combined total of goods and passenger expenditure. The final figures thus differ from those in the Blue Book [QRL 41] in relating to GB (rather than UK), in including business travel and in the treatment of depreciation and interest (*see* 4.3.3 below).

3.7.6 (e) *APPTO statistics* [QRL 20]
The Association of Public Passenger Transport Operators publishes annually the accounts (and some other statistics) of the municipal and PTE bus and tram undertakings. The figures are not added up to make totals. The undertakings include Belfast and Douglas (Isle of Man). The accounts follow recommended standard forms (1950 or 1963 version), of which details are given below (4.4.3). Separate details are given for buses, trolleybuses and trams. The statistics published are for the standard items, i.e. mileage operated, passengers carried, and vehicles owned at the end of the year. Figures for one-man-operated mileage are given separately, and vehicles are broken down into single- and double-deck ones. These figures go back to 1959.

3.7.7 (f) *Road Transport Industry Training Board reports* [QRL 51]
This Training Board was established in September 1966, and covers a wide range of transport industries including road passenger transport. Because of its levy/grant arrangements and its overall obligations, one of its first needs was to establish a register of undertakings. Thus its work produces as a by-product not only information about employment, but also about establishments in the industry. From 1968/9 to 1971/2 the figures relate to all undertakings on the register, but from 1972/3 they only relate to 'leviable' employers, i.e. excluding those with a payroll of £7,500 or less, unless they wish to opt into the scheme. Taxi operators were exempt from the scheme in the middle of 1972, and soon after chauffeur-driven car hire also. Numbers of employers and employees are given at March 31 for each size group by numbers of employees (10 or less, 11-15, 16-30, 31-50, 51-250; also 1-5 up to 1971/2). The occupational breakdown of employees is also given up to 1971/2 (also by size of undertaking for 1969 and 1970). There are also figures of labour turnover (1968, 1972/3), recruits and leavers (1971/2, 1972/3), and numbers undergoing training, all by occupational group, as well as a mass of information about training schemes in different types of firms and occupations, and grants made for them.

(2) NON-OFFICIAL SOURCES

3.7.8 (a) *Vehicle operating costs*
Apart from the figures of consumers' running costs of motor vehicles in the Blue Book [QRL 41], and the figures from the accounts of bus undertakings in *PTGB* [QRL 45] and in their own reports (*see* 3.6), there are other sources for vehicle operating costs, the *Commercial Motor* for buses and the Automobile Association (AA) for private cars [QRL 27, QRL 21]. The first gives estimated figures for standing costs per week and running costs per mile for buses and coaches separately each year. Vehicles are classified by the number of seats, e.g. buses—14 seats (petrol buses); 31 and 41 seats (by petrol and diesel buses); 51, 70 and 80 seats (diesel buses); coaches—14, 31, and 41 seats (by petrol and diesel coaches), 51 seats (diesel coaches). Standing costs are in terms of licences, wages, rent and rates, insurance and interest; running costs in terms of fuel, lubricants, tyres, maintenance and depreciation, for different ranges of miles per week (200, 400 and 600). Total costs are given per mile and per week, and 'minimum charges' (i.e. to allow for profit) are suggested on

the same basis. The AA cost tables for private cars are on a similar basis for cars of different engine capacity, with more detail of such items as insurance, garage, servicing.

3.7.9 (b) *Motoring surveys*
We briefly mention two surveys of private motoring.

(1) The Birmingham University study, *People and the Motor Car* [QRL 46], was a household survey carried out by students in twelve cities with particular reference to types of residential development. The sample consisted of about 170 households in each city, chosen apparently by selected types of residential development. Household questionnaires were filled in by interviewees, and complete forms were obtained for 76-82% of households approached. Further individual questionnaires were left for members of households to fill in and between 50% and 67% of households completed all these, and a further 9-19% some of them. The report gives details of the questionnaires and forms, but does not specify the dates on which the surveys were undertaken (probably 1963). Much information is given about households, car ownership, travel to work, shopping habits, social visits and holidays. The fairly full treatment of parking and garaging throws light on a field for which there is not much information (see 4.3.5).

(2) *The Motorist Today* [QRL 39] a survey undertaken by Research Services for the AA in the first half of 1965, though no doubt more professional, is a slighter affair. Two thousand motorists were interviewed, the sample being taken from electoral registers. Unlike most of the other surveys here described, this included some questions on attitudes to motoring. An interesting classification is made by new car owners (since 1956), 'middle' car owners (i.e. only owning a car since between 1946 and 1955), and older car owners. There is information about travel to work, other uses of the car, holidays and annual mileages among other things. Not a great deal of data is published.

4 Available Data

4.1 Pedestrians

4.1.1 We do not know much about pedestrian journeys in general. Published figures from the NTS are only for walking journeys of one mile or more (*see* 3.1.5, etc.). But this clearly excludes the vast majority of pedestrian journey stages. A better indication of the importance of walking is provided by the 1966 sample census for journeys to work (*see* 3.7.4). 19% of total employees in E & W walked to work in that year.

4.1.2 A useful report from the Transport and Road Research Laboratory (1973) [QRL 10] brings together data from four sources about particular areas (London Traffic Survey area, Central London, Stevenage and Leamington). Some of the data is for work trips, some for all purposes; distributions by length of trip are given. A half of trips were for distances exceeding a range varying from 0·6 km in Leamington Spa to 1·27 km in Stevenage. (The report also gives similar data for cycle trips.)

4.2 Bicycles

4.2.1 Bicycle movement is not unimportant, some 4% of total inland passenger miles in 1961 and some 1% in 1973. *PTGB* [QRL 45] ignores it, though it includes air travel, which was less than a tenth of bicycle travel in 1961 and only just over two-thirds in 1973; the verdict is no doubt 'presumed dead', on the lines of Clough's new set of commandments. However *Highway Statistics* [QRL 34] gives the data (8% of total vehicle miles in 1961 and $1\frac{1}{2}$% in 1975).

4.2.2 The main source of overall data is the manual traffic counts (*see* 3.3). Movement on different types of road and by engineering areas is only available for 1960 and 1966; movement by hours of the day for 1968 and 1970 [QRL 61].

4.2.3 The use of the bicycle for the journey to work is documented in the 1966 census (*see* 3.7.4) and should be more fully documented in the 1971 results. Traffic surveys have often ignored bicycle movement (the London survey [QRL 36] defined a 'cycle' as a 'motor-cycle'). This is particularly important as the 1966 survey [QRL 61] shows that 70% of bicycle miles were on urban roads as compared with 55% of motor vehicle miles. The 1966 census [QRL 26] shows that $7\frac{1}{2}$% of journeys to work in England and Wales were made by bicycle. Other data about journey purposes are to be found in NTS [QRL 42] (*see* 3.1).

4.2.4 Expenditure on bicycles (together with prams, boats, etc.) is given in FES (*see* 3.7.3) [QRL 32], but in the Blue Book [QRL 41] it is lumped together with radio, electrical and other durable goods. Separate estimates are available for 1949, 1950 and 1960 from Rudd [QRL 11] and Dawson [QRL 2] (*see* 3.7.5).

4.3 Private Cars, Motor-cycles and Taxis

4.3.1 The main sources are the NTS ([QRL 42]; *see* 3.1) and the various road census (*see* 3.3). These provide the basic information about journeys by private car or other motor vehicles and the vehicle miles travelled under different circumstances. There are, however, certain limitations inherent in the two methods of collecting information. The former set of surveys is based on households, and does not cover people living in institutions. The other source being based on the road system gives very detailed information about the flow of vehicles (but cars and taxis, etc. are lumped together), from which overall estimates of vehicle miles can be calculated, but of its nature provides no information about the purpose of the journeys, but only of the quantity of movement by particular types of vehicle on particular types of road at particular times.

4.3.2 *Expenditure*

Information is available from the Blue Book [QRL 41] on consumers' expenditure in the UK on vehicles and running costs at current and fixed prices. Separate figures for licences, petrol and oil, and other running costs are given in the 1973 and 1974 Blue Books. The tax element is also estimated for all these. On the other hand, the Customs and Excise figures for fuel taxes [QRL 57] are not broken down by class of road user. It is to be noted that consumers' expenditure excludes business expenditure (*see* [B 12], p. 105). More detail is available from the FES ([QRL 32]; *see* 3.7.3) on a household basis, with some difference from the Blue Book in the definition of expenditure on vehicles (*see* 3.7.3).

4.3.3 The Rudd/Dawson estimates [QRL 2, QRL 11] are both more detailed in composition and more comprehensive (*see* 3.7.5). They cover both business and private car expenditure, though only for GB. Unlike the Blue Book, they treat cars as capital assets to be depreciated on which interest is to be charged, whereas BB includes the capital cost of the purchased car as consumers' expenditure in the year of purchase, and thus avoids the problem of depreciation. It can be seen that it is impossible by a simple comparison of the two sets of figures to estimate business expenditure on cars. For information on the purchase of cars by businesses and private persons one has to go to the motor transactions survey of 1971 (following on an earlier survey in 1962). This gives information as to expenditure, average cost of cars, type of car and hire-purchase arrangements for both new and used cars [QRL 43] (for the full survey, *see* [B 7]).

4.3.4 *Costs*

Overall costs for vehicles of different kinds (cars, vans, etc.) have been estimated by the Transport and Road Research Laboratory at intervals (1958, 1962, 1963, 1964, 1965, 1967, 1970, 1973) [QRL 62]. These include values attributed to non-working and working-time. They are given in terms of costs per vehicle mile (kilometre) at different (or given) speeds, and are used for cost benefit analyses of road improvement schemes. The basic data on out-of-pocket costs are derived from the *Commercial Motor* and AA tables, referred to in 3.7.8 [QRL 21, QRL 27]. Overall price indices for vehicles and running costs can be derived from the Blue Book tables [QRL 41]. The monthly index of retail prices ([QRL 28] and *Monthly Digest of Statistics*) includes an item for motoring and cycling combined.

4.3.5 *Vehicles*

The vehicle registration system gives great details of the stock of vehicles each year and monthly figures of new registrations ([QRL 34, QRL 49]; *see* 3.7.2). But these figures include, of course, all private cars owned and used by businesses. Cars used by private households are studied in detail in NTS ([QRL 42]; *see* 3.1), while *Highway Statistics* and *PTGB* [QRL 34, QRL 45] (and from 1974 *TS* [QRL 64]) publish annual estimates of the percentage of households with one and two or more cars (but, though the total number of households is given, the total number of cars is not—*see also* 3.1.17). A full census report on car availability in 1971 has also been published [QRL 26].

4.3.6 *Car parking*

This is an important aspect of the private car, which is not well documented nationally. Rudd and Dawson give estimates of garaging and parking expenditure in 1949, 1950 and 1960 (*see* 3.7.5). The only comprehensive surveys of car parking we know of are those carried out by the British Road Federation in 1961, September 1963 and the autumn of 1967 [QRL 25]. These were based on questionnaires sent to local authorities, and relate mainly to the number of publicly available parking spaces in towns of various types and sizes. The 1967 survey only related to central areas. Other questions were asked as to numbers of cars parked in the central area, and local authority plans and forecasts. But though comprehensive surveys have not been published, almost all local authorities will have undertaken some kind of survey, following on Ministry pressure since 1965 (*see* [B13]). Indeed this is a major part of all transportation surveys (*see* 3.2). [Public expenditure on car parking is given in *Highway Statistics* [QRL 34] and later in *TS* [QRL 64]—A.W.]

4.3.7 *Taxis*
Not a great deal is known about taxis and private hire cars. The stock of vehicles, and new registrations are known from the registration figures ([QRL 34, QRL 49]; *see* 3.7.2); and the detailed licensing system in London produces figures of vehicles and drivers licensed [QRL 47]. (Information on the controlled fares is available in the relevant Statutory Instruments.) But otherwise taxi operations are either lumped together with cars (as with figures from road censuses; *see* 3.3), or with other forms of passenger transport (see *Standard Industrial Classification* in 4.4.9). Thus numbers insured are not available since 1959 (*see* 4.4.4), though the 1951 and 1961 censuses give information [QRL 26], and the earnings surveys are not broken down into this amount of detail (*see* 4.4.5). Estimates of expenditure are, however, available for 1949, 1950 and 1960 (*see* 3.7.5).

4.3.8 *Forecasts*
Though these are strictly outside the limits of this survey, a brief mention should be made of the forecasts of vehicles and traffic, which are made by the TRRL and are the basis of traffic and road planning. The latest forecasts made in 1972 and 1974 follow on a continuous series which is mainly the work of Tanner [QRL 12, QRL 16]. They provide estimates of the numbers of vehicles of different kinds and vehicle-kilometres travelled in GB up to 2010. The basic car forecasts are founded on a logistic growth curve and a saturation level of cars per person, which are then related to car numbers by population forecasts. To these, assumptions about kilometres per car are added to give the traffic forecasts. For further details the reports are referred to. It is to be noted that whereas the earlier forecasts were based on a rather mechanical approach, the latest are related to assumptions about income growth and fuel prices. [*TS* [QRL 64] now includes a section with forecasts of vehicle numbers, car ownership and traffic—A.W.]

4.4 Public Passenger Transport
4.4.1 *Output*
The main measures of output are passenger journeys, passenger miles and vehicle miles (as discussed in 1.3); in addition there are money passenger receipts. The main source (*PTGB*) [QRL 45] gives information for passenger journeys, passenger receipts, vehicle miles and number of vehicles by a standard breakdown; (a) by type of operator (*see* 2.2.); (b) by type of service (stage services by main urban—London Transport and local authorities—and other areas, express services, etc.—*see* 3.4): not, of course, for vehicles; (c) by buses, trolleys and trams (not for vehicle miles; more detail was available for trolleys and trams in the past when they were more important; trolley-bus operations ceased in 1972). (*TS* [QRL 64] contains these series from 1974.) Quarterly figures for journeys and passenger receipts are also given by types of operator, but not in *TS*. Cross-classifications of (a) and (b) are given with more detail by size of operators (measured by numbers of vehicles; LAs and private up to 1972, LAs and National Bus Company groups in 1973 and also PTEs and Scottish Bus Group from 1974). Passenger mile figures have been estimated by LT for a long time and were published by BTC; overall figures, calculated by the Department from data on journeys, receipts and vehicle miles, also making

use of average journey length data from NTS (the detailed formulae have not been published), are available from 1951. Overall vehicle mile figures are also available from road censuses (see 3.3). Information about purpose of journey is only available from NTS (see 3.1) and transportation studies (see 3.2). Expenditure figures are also available in NTS [QRL 42], for total UK consumers in BB [QRL 41], and in FES [QRL 32] for certain types of families by regions. The BB figures exclude public authorities' and business expenditure (using data from NTS) and are revalued at constant prices using indices of estimated average receipts per passenger mile [B 12], pp. 173–4. For other expenditure figures see 3.7.5.

4.4.2 Costs

PTGB published (up to 1970) a full revenue account for types of undertakings for financial years ending between April 1 and March 31, according to a standard form. In the 1970 returns figures are given for London Transport, LAs and others (PTAs are not included); formerly figures were also given for the nationalized sector (see 3.6). The standard form is as follows:

> Receipts
>   From passengers
>   Stage services
>   Express services
>   Excursions and tours
>   Contract
>   Total passenger receipts
>   Parcels, mails, luggage, dogs, etc.
>   Advertising on vehicles and miscellaneous
>   From other operators for hire of vehicles
> Total receipts
> Expenditure
>   Wages of drivers and conductors (including National Insurance)
>   Petrol or other fuel or power for vehicles
>   Other expenditure
>   Wages, etc. of all other staff
>   Local Authority rates
>   Amounts paid out for repairs and maintenance, cost of tyres, spare parts and lubricating oil
>   Motor vehicle insurance
>   Other (excluding interest payments, capital expenditure and income and profits tax)
>   Total excluding depreciation
>   Provision for renewal and depreciation
>   Vehicles
>   Other assets
>   Total
>   Provision for redemption of debt by Local Authorities
>   Vehicles
>   Other assets
>   Total
> Total expenditure
>   Difference between total receipts and total expenditure
>   Add or deduct balance of receipts or payments under through and/or inter-operational agreements.
> Net difference between receipts and expenditure

It is to be noted that, though there is full detail of wage costs and depreciation (as well as repairs), there is no separate figure for the tax element in fuel costs, for which information does not seem to be available. BB [QRL 41] gives the total tax element (including subsidies) in consumers' expenditure on travel (rail, bus coach and tram, and other combined); the Customs and Excise accounts [QRL 57] do not give any breakdown of quantities of fuel or tax receipts by type of user. Standard cost figures are given in the *Commercial Motor* tables for specific types of vehicles [QRL 27]. Input–output tables are not helpful as they lump together road and rail transport or treat all road transport as a whole [B 11].

4.4.3 Another set of accounting figures is available for municipal and PTE undertakings from the APPTO returns [QRL 20] (see 3.7.6). The standard form is as follows:

> *Revenue accounts* (all given in £ and per vehicle mile)

Traffic revenue
Other revenue
    Total revenue
Traffic operation
Servicing vehicles and routes
Power
Repairs and maintenance
Alterations to buildings
Licences
Management and general expenses
Welfare and medical
Other items
    Total working expenses
Gross surplus or deficit
Net revenue and appropriation accounts
Total gross surplus or deficit (as per revenue a/c)
Income—
    Bank and other interests receivable
    Through and inter-operation
    Other income
Expenditure—
    Debt charges—Existing assets
                     Obsolete and displaced assets
    Depreciation
    Contribution to renewals and/or depreciation fund
    Bank and other interests payable
    Through and inter-operation
    Other expenditure
Net surplus or deficit
Net income/net loss available for appropriation
    Contribution to reserve fund
    Additional contribution to renewals and/or depreciation fund
    Revenue contribution to capital
    Contribution in aid of rates
    Other items
Contribution from rates
Balance brought forward
Balance carried forward

PTE accounts are given on a slightly different basis, with a less fine breakdown of items and some additional items to take account of their wide range of activities. For all the individual bus companies there is also a table of wages cost of drivers and conductors (including sick pay and holiday pay, but excluding National Insurance and superannuation).

4.4.4 *Labour*

PTGB [QRL 45] (and from 1974 *TS* [QRL 64]) gives the numbers employed by type of operator (also by size groups as above; *see* 4.4.1) and by male and female, for drivers, conductors and other staff at the end of the year. Figures for London with a greater amount of detail are given in LT reports [QRL 37, QRL 38]. Other figures are also available in the Road Transport Industry Training Board reports [QRL 51] (*see* 3.7.7). The standard Department of Employment figures are available for employees in employment and total employees (including unemployed) for both GB and UK [QRL 22, QRL 23, QRL 28]; but figures for tramway and omnibus services separately from other road passenger transport are not available after 1959. (These are according to the Standard Industrial Classification (SIC, *see* 4.4.9), which has only changed since 1948 in one small point, that irregular motor coach services (motor coach tours) were included with other road passenger transport (e.g. taxis, hire-cars, etc.) in 1948 and not after the 1958 reclassification.) The Census Industry figures follow the SIC and give in 1951 and 1961 separate figures for the two sectors, but not from 1966 [QRL 26]. The Occupation tables give separate figures for bus, etc. drivers and conductors (also drivers of other road passenger vehicles in 1971) but not otherwise for any relevant occupations separately distinguished for road passenger transport; long-run comparison is almost impossible because of the frequent and (from our point of view) irrational changes in definitions from one census to another. A final set of figures for licensed drivers and conductors appears in TC reports [QRL 19], giving both the total number of licences current and new licences granted in a year; but these figures bear no relation to the number employed in the industry (the total number of licences current are about twice the numbers employed as recorded by the Department), and must include those who have moved to other industries, the retired and perhaps the dead.

4.4.5 *Wages and earnings*
Wage rates for particular groups of drivers and conductors (and various categories of depot and garage workers and skilled maintenance workers) are given in *Time Rates of Wages and Hours of Labour* for the rates current on April 1 [QRL 60], and changes in wages and conditions are reported at intervals in the monthly supplement (*Changes in Rates of Wages and Hours of Work*) to the *Department of Employment Gazette* [QRL 28]. Earnings figures are available in the twice-yearly enquiries for men, women (full-time and part-time separately), youths and boys and girls, as well as hours worked [QRL 28]. Far more detail of the spread of earnings, etc. is available in the *New Earnings Surveys* [QRL 44]. Both these surveys follow the SIC definitions (*see* 4.4.9).

4.4.6 *Prices*
Derived indices of receipts per journey and per passenger mile can be obtained from the figures referred to in 4.4.1. (*PTGB* and *TS* give a table for receipts per passenger journey for London and for other undertakings by stage (LAs and PTA), and Other), and other types of service.) A price index of stage services for London, LA and PTA, and Other is available quarterly from 1954 (31 December 1953 = 100, up to the quarter ending 30 September 1969; and 31 December 1961 = 100, from 1962, quarterly from 1968). The index is based on the changes in fares on stage carriage services of all operators with 100 or more buses and coaches. When fares are changed the operators report to the Traffic Commissioners the estimated changes in their gross receipts which would result from the change in fare assuming no change in the volume or pattern of traffic. These changes are weighted by the operators' gross receipts from stage services in the preceding calendar year, or (1973) prior to the fare changes. (The item for fares in the monthly index of retail prices [QRL 28 and *Monthly Digest of Statistics*] combines rail and bus fares.)

4.4.7 *Vehicles*
There are abundant figures of the vehicle stock from different sources. Confusion can however arise if attention is not paid to the exact significance of any particular set of figures, with reference firstly to the date of the count, and secondly to their coverage. A distinction needs to be made between vehicles with ordinary excise licences and vehicles licensed as public service vehicles by the Traffic Commissioners (*see* 3.4). Not all vehicles owned may be licensed at any particular time, as there are seasonal fluctuations in traffic with the summer peak use, and it may pay to take out quarterly licences and keep the vehicles in stock. Buses and coaches may not always require a public service licence, e.g. work buses. There are also vehicles loaned from one undertaking to another, and vehicles used for training, etc. (a) The definitions used by *PTGB* [QRL 45] seem to relate to vehicles owned and licensed as public services vehicles, but do not always agree with BTC and LT figures [QRL 24, QRL 37, QRL 38], and some confusion seems to have crept in at times. They relate to the end of the calendar year, and are given by type of operator (*see* 4.4.1). The numbers of trams, trolley-buses, single- and double-deck buses are also given, and the figures are broken down by seating capacity. Total seating capacity is given for LT, other main urban areas (local authorities) and other areas. (b) The ordinary vehicle registration system produces counts of the stock of vehicles in the quarter ending September 30 [QRL 34, QRL 49]; for more details *see* 3.7.2. The figures relate to public transport vehicles, i.e. including taxis, and are given for both UK and

GB. Details for GB (excluding trams) are given by seating capacity and year of first registration; it is to be noted that there is a minor discrepancy in the ranges of seating capacity used here and in *PTGB*, the latter having one group for not over fourteen seats, the former having three ranges of not over fifteen seats. These figures are in principle available from the department for every registration county council, but details for public transport vehicles are only published for economic planning regions. (c) The same registration system produces figures of *new registration* which are published for calendar years on the same basis. Further details are available for the number of petrol and diesel public transport vehicles (not over eight seats and over eight seats). These figures are in principle available (from the department) monthly and in finer detail for every licensing authority. (d) Numbers of *undertakings* (by number of vehicles used) are given in *PTGB* [QRL 45] and TC's reports [QRL 19] (the latter up to 1969/70); these are two different series for years ending March 31 and December 31 (*see also* 1.4).

4.4.8 *Capital*
Figures for book values of capital, depreciation, investment, etc. are published (to varying degrees of detail) in the accounts of the major undertakings (*see* 3.6), but since 1962 with nothing of the detail to be found in the BTC reports [QRL 24]. The Blue Book [QRL 41] publishes its typical figures for gross and net fixed capital formation and capital stock for all road passenger transport (including taxis, etc.), and also for all buses and coaches. These figures relate of course to UK, and are republished in *PTGB* (giving separately the figures for capital formation in buses and coaches, on the one hand, and taxis and hire-cars on the other). (Before 1960, the figures for taxis, etc. were not included with road passenger transport.)

4.4.9 *Standard Industrial Classification* (SIC) [B 15]
The SIC definition of this sector is as follows (MLH No. 702):

Road passenger transport
1. Omnibus and tramway service.
   The operation of omnibus, motor coach, trolley-bus and tramway services.
2. Taxis and private-hire cars.
   The operation of taxi-cabs and private-hire cabs; owner-drivers are included. Car hire is also included.

It is to be noted that separate establishments engaged in the repair of vehicles are excluded, but ordinary and running repairs are included.

4.5 Regional statistics
4.5.1 We proceed first by analysing the regional information in terms of the main sources treated in Section 3 above and then discussing the publications dealing with regional statistics, finally making some general points. All references are to standard regions, unless other areas are specifically mentioned.

(1) MAIN SOURCES

4.5.2 *National Travel Survey* (3.1)
Data from the 1965 survey were published on a regional basis in *PTGB* [QRL 45] (1967). Two tables give the number and mileage of journey stages by mode of transport. More information is available, and some tables from the 1972/3 survey have appeared in *Social Trends* [QRL 58] (*see* 3.1.15). The long-distance travel surveys (*see* 3.1.16) will also produce important regional information for the areas covered.

4.5.3 *Road censuses* (3.3)
This information is collected by the nine departmental engineering divisions; *see*, for example, the maps in *Highway Statistics* [QRL 34] (1967) of the 1965 trunk road census. The Scottish figures were formerly published independently in detail in [QRL 35, QRL 55]. The information by engineering divisions was published in rather more detail

up to 1963 in *Roads in England and Wales* [QRL 52] than later [QRL 34, etc.]. Figures were then given for vehicle miles by type of vehicle for each division, but, as these were based on the 50-point census, they cannot have been very reliable. Later figures are only available for 1960 and 1966 based on 1,100 and 1,300 points [QRL 61]. What information is available for these by engineering division is summarized in the Quick Reference List (QRL) under 'area' in column 3. Similar information on a basis of standard regions could no doubt be easily reassembled.

4.5.4 *Traffic Commissioners* (TC) (3.4)
These have their own administrative areas (*see*, for example, map and definitions in 1968/9 report [QRL 19]). The number of operators by size group (vehicles) and the number of vehicles licensed are given for each of these divisions, up to 1969/70.

4.5.5 *Passenger Transport in Great Britain* (PTGB) (3.5)
No regional data are collected or published, except that the Scottish Transport Group figures are available separately [QRL 56]. These cover all the nationalized sector in Scotland and most of the road passenger transport outside cities. It would be perfectly possible to process the information from bus undertakings (at least for stage services) on an area basis, which could roughly correspond to the standard regions, though of course bus services operate often outside their 'own areas'. Even the National Bus Company publishes no breakdown of its figures (*see* 3.6.1).

4.5.6 *Vehicle registration* (3.7.2)
Figures of types of vehicle registered (both stock and new registrations) are regularly published by regions in the main source [QRL 34], as well as in the regional digests (*see* 4.5.10–12 below).

4.5.7 *Family Expenditure Survey* (FES) (3.7.3)
Figures for two years combined are regularly published by region for all the heads of expenditure (for transport and vehicles as a whole for each year), but not cross-classified by household or income characteristics. Numbers of households owning cars (1, 2, 3 or more) are also available by region. (*See also* 1971 census volume on car availability [QRL 26].)

4.5.8 *Census* (3.7.4, 4.4.4)
Regional figures are available both for those employed in road passenger transport and by occupation, as well as for the mode of travel to work in 1966.

4.5.9 *Employment* (4.4.4–5)
Figures of employees in employment by region are available for June each year by Minimum List Headings, i.e. giving figures for road passenger transport [QRL 28]. Earnings figures from the New Earnings Surveys are not given in such detail.

(2) PUBLICATIONS

4.5.10 The main source of regional statistics, the *Abstract of Regional Statistics* [QRL 18] only publishes two sets of tables relevant to our topic. The first is the registration figures of vehicles (stock and new registrations), by cars, goods and other vehicles; more detail is in fact given on a regional basis for the stock in *Highway Statistics* [QRL 34]. The second is the figures from the FES of expenditure on transport and vehicles as a whole (i.e. much less than the detail available in FES itself) and the percentage of households owning cars (one, two, three or more) from 1969.

4.5.11 *Scotland*
The *Scottish Abstract of Statistics* [QRL 54] replacing the biennial *Digest of Scottish Statistics* ([QRL 29]; the last number April 1971), follows much the same lines as the *Abstract of Regional Statistics* [QRL 18] (*see* 4.5.10), but with more detail. Vehicle figures (stock and new registrations) are

given in full by most categories, and there are also figures of net taxation receipts from vehicle and driving licences. FES information is given for each category of transport expenditure. There is also information about employees in employment for each Minimum List Heading of the SIC, thus giving the numbers for road passenger transport (by males and total). In addition, the volume publishes figures for the Scottish Transport Group (Scottish Bus Group) (vehicles by single- and double-deck, vehicle miles, passenger journeys and passenger receipts), and for the four main Scottish cities (vehicles, passenger journeys and revenue) [and more recently for the Glasgow PTE and for Lothian, Tayside and Grampian regions with more financial figures including revenue support, operating expenditure and net operating profit/loss—A.W.]. Details of traffic on Scottish roads were formerly published separately [QRL 35, QRL 55]. The Scottish census is also normally a separate publication (see [QRL 26]).

4.5.12 *Wales*

The *Digest of Welsh Statistics* [QRL 31] publishes the same figures as for Scotland (see 4.5.11) for vehicles and employees, but nothing about licence receipts. FES figures are only given for transport and vehicles as a whole. The 1971 volume publishes the occupation tables from the 1966 census in detail.

(3) SOME GENERAL POINTS

4.5.13 It is clear from the above that more regional information could be brought together from various other sources and published in the *Abstract of Regional Statistics* [QRL 18] or the country abstracts. It is also clear that information could fairly easily be assembled on a regional basis (or approximately so) from the Road censuses (see 4.5.3) and the returns from bus undertakings (see 4.5.5). The latter would be particularly valuable in view of the new duties of local authorities in respect of all passenger transport in their areas.

4.6 Northern Ireland

4.6.1 It is surprising how few figures, particularly in the transport field, cover the UK as a whole. Most cover GB, and separate Northern Ireland figures are not easy to come by (see 1.1.4). The National Income Blue Book, however, covers UK (but with no figures for GB) [QRL 41]; similarly with the Customs and Excise figures for fuel tax revenue [QRL 57].

4.6.2 There are a number of publications which give figures for Northern Ireland together with similar figures for Britain. The most notable is the *Abstract of Regional Statistics* [QRL 18], which gives the same figures for Northern Ireland, as for Wales, Scotland, and the English regions (see 4.5.10). But these figures are available elsewhere. The vehicle figures for UK and GB (and by subtraction Northern Ireland) are in *Highway Statistics* [QRL 34], in some detail for new registrations, though only by broad categories for the currently licensed stock. The other figures for household expenditure from the *Family Expenditure Survey* [QRL 32] are available there in as great detail for Northern Ireland as for British regions (see 4.5.7).

4.6.3 The APPTO reports [QRL 20] include Belfast with other municipal bus undertakings and give the same information as for the others (see 3.7.6 and 4.4.3). This is the only British source we know of which gives figures of Northern Ireland passenger transport, though the Department of Employment insurance figures are available for UK as well as GB for all road passenger transport employees (see 4.4.4). But the earnings surveys do not cover Northern Ireland.

4.6.4 It is not surprising, if regrettable, that British government departments, with their limited concerns, do not bother to publish statistics for an area for which they do not have administrative responsibility or direct access to the sources of information. It is, however, rather sad that neither the *General Household Survey (see*

3.1.17) nor the National Travel Survey (*see* 3.1) covers Northern Ireland.

4.6.5 Unfortunately the reader who looks for more information about the area in the *Digest of Statistics, Northern Ireland* [QRL 30] will not find much more relevant to our field. Employment figures are only given for transport and communication as a whole, and not by Minimum List Headings. Earnings and hours from the October survey (April and October up to 1969) are given for the same broad group; this is the one 'new' set of figures. The Family Expenditure Survey figures are published on the Welsh model (only for transport and vehicles as a whole). The vehicle registration figures give only as much detail for licences current as in *Highway Statistics* [QRL 34] for UK, and less detail for new registrations. There are no figures of vehicle flows or mileages, or of public service vehicle operations. For all these the reader will have to look to specialized local publications.

5 Comments and Suggestions

5.1 No one has ever brought together comprehensively all the available statistics on inland transport (until DOE in 1976). In its nearly fifty years of existence the Ministry of Transport never published an annual report or an overall statistical digest. The present situation cannot be understood without reference to its history. At its establishment in 1919, the Ministry inherited the meticulous nineteenth-century compilations of railway and tramway statistics from the Board of Trade. The Finance Act, 1920, and the Roads Act, 1920, established the Road Fund and the system of road vehicle registration. Section 3 (6) of the latter Act required an annual report to Parliament; hence the publication of road figures in these reports (*see* [QRL 48]). The Road Fund was abolished by the Miscellaneous Financial Provisions Act, 1955, from 1 April 1956, when roads in Scotland were devolved to the Secretary of State for Scotland; hence the continuation of these reports directly by the Ministry (still today 'presented to Parliament pursuant to Section 3 (6) of the Roads Act, 1920 as amended by Section 4 of the Miscellaneous Financial Provisions Act, 1955') [QRL 52]. Most figures in these reports have related simply to the areas for which the department has been responsible (today England). Similarly, vehicle registration figures were the inevitable outcome of the 1920 Acts. No attempt was made to collect statistics of the bus industry in the 1920s, and, when bus licensing was introduced in 1930, The Traffic Commissioners collected and published the relevant statistics. After the Second World War, the Ministry brought together the tram and bus statistics in its publication of statistics of *Public Road Passenger Transport in Great Britain (PTGB)* [QRL 45] (*see* 3.5 above). The Road Research Laboratory was then outside the department and continued so until the 1960s, with its own high-quality statistical publications. The position, at the end of the 1950s, as far as concerns our field, was summed up by the then Permanent Secretary (Sir Gilmour Jenkins) in the *Ministry of Transport and Civil Aviation* (1959), as follows:

> 'The collation of figures indicating the nation's transport resources and the nature of its employment is, of course, an essential prerequisite to the determination of policy.... On the inland transport side a number of returns are published—the annual census of vehicles, for example, and the annual booklet containing public road passenger transport statistics. Road accident statistics are compiled in great detail and variety with the aid of mechanical sorting equipment. ... Statistics on ... road transport are collected by the Statistics Division. The various operating Divisions then draw upon the results and use them for the formulation of policy. In other words the economic appraisement of the statistics produced is often the job of the operating division concerned' (pp. 205-7).

Precisely. The need is clearly stated and the failure to meet it is implicit in the facts as set out.

5.2 At the beginning of the 1960s a new broom appeared in the statistics field and swept away a few cobwebs. 'Apart from the summaries which are given in the *Monthly Digest of Statistics* and the *Annual Abstract of Statistics*, until the recent booklet (*Passenger Transport in Great Britain*, 1962) was issued by the Ministry of Transport no previous attempt had been made to bring together the detailed information concerning passenger transport in this country' (November 1963 [QRL 43]

(1), p. 159; it is to be noted that this article has some interesting (and not repeated) data on inputs into the public service vehicle industry in 1961). From this time onwards, *PTGB* included rail and some other passenger travel. At about the same period *Highway Statistics* [QRL 34] brought together the vehicle licensing figures and the road figures. The need was felt for more comprehensive information, and a large number of important new surveys (e.g. the conurbation traffic surveys and the motoring survey, later NTS) were initiated. No doubt shortage of skilled or trained staff inhibited proper publication.

5.3 A third stage began when the computer took over, and it seems to have been considered sufficient if the data was properly stored (if it always was) and available as required for particular purposes within the department. This is the modern version of the old system whereby each officer or branch of a department used different (often mutually inconsistent) figures calculated for his own purposes. In effect the Ministry of Transport as such had no statistical department and no objective of bringing together information on transport as a whole; indeed it may be doubted whether it was ever until perhaps its last few years a Ministry rather than a Stinnes-like conglomerate of specialist transport experts. The scattering of statistical centres and sources of supply of transport 'publications' of the Department of the Environment (*see* note to QRL key to publications) has its roots in a long past history.

5.4 In short, our first comment is quite simply that not enough is published, and that inadequately. These are two separate points. Publication may be entirely internal to the department and yet inadequate. Adequacy depends on there being available in some form a clear and detailed description of the sources, meaning and significance of the figures. Without such descriptions different administrators will be using different figures and maybe producing trend figures or complicated analyses based on incompatible sets of data. Inevitably mistakes in analysis are liable to occur, and perhaps mistakes in policy. As suggested above, this may be particularly dangerous where data are computerized. For example, A wants to do some work on the costs, receipts and employment of buses of different kinds in actual operations; he asks B for data on buses by types of operator. B provides him with data on buses owned, not buses in service, because this is how the computer programme is set up. Both A and B are too busy to spend a long time discussing exactly what is needed and available. A does not know about the computer programme or the sources of the figures, B is not familiar with the particular research in question. If A wants to find out exactly what the figures relate to, he has to ask B about the details of the computer programme, and to find a copy of the questionnaire from C. He may in fact rely on a brief paper written by D, which has the merit of giving a clear description of the data, though it happens to be both out of date and not completely accurate, as D wrote it at a particular time to serve a particular purpose of his own. The production of the kind of clear, detailed and up-to-date descriptions we have in mind is a somewhat dreary and time-consuming matter. A, B and D have much more important and interesting things to do, and C has plenty to do supervising the data collection. But lack of the clear description may invalidate the work done by A, B and D. The description needs to be easily available to all in some standard form which everyone knows how to find. It may be suspected that the lack of such common descriptions available even within the department has been a major cause of the slap-dash statistics we have had occasion to refer to.

5.5 The simplest and most straightforwardly available description of the kind we have in mind is to be found in printed form. Departments, like the old Board of Trade, Ministry of Labour or General Registry Office, which regularly published in this way (whether in the substantive reports, in special works on definitions, or in their regular journals), have tended to produce the most accurate and careful statistics. They have also served the needs of outside researchers at the same time. The lack of such guides to *Highway Statistics* and *PTGB* has been a great nuisance. In this respect the former is rather better in its definitions than the latter.

5.6 The importance of independent research, not sponsored by departments, does not need stressing. For this purpose publication in the full sense is obviously desirable. As a second-best the availability of unpublished material from the department is important, and the department has done much in this respect. As a third-best the availability of data, as in the case of the National Travel Survey, is extremely useful, but, unless people know what data are available, they cannot make full use of the opportunity. The delays in publishing the National Travel Survey might be thought to be somewhat scandalous. At the time of writing, only the first part of a report on the 1972/3 survey has been published, to be followed by two further parts (published in 1976).

5.7 It may be that too many data have been collected in too many different ways. One may suspect a tendency to initiate new surveys before old ones have been fully absorbed. The proliferation of overlapping surveys, aided and abetted by computers, may be neither cheap nor wise. The extent of overlapping between the transportation surveys, the census, the National Travel Survey, the General Household Survey, the Family Expenditure Survey and the Long-Distance Travel Survey is somewhat frightening. None of these, except for the census, the Family Expenditure Survey, and many transportation surveys, have been fully published. We have already commented (3.2.3) on the lack of any detailed comparative studies of the transportation surveys.

5.8 Nevertheless, it can still be claimed that we do not know enough about the passenger transport field as a whole. There has never been a census of transport, whether on the passenger or on the goods side, so that the role of transport (or road passenger transport) in the economy as a whole cannot be properly measured and assessed. We know the total of consumers' expenditure on road passenger transport, and on another basis, from Rudd and Dawson (3.7.5), total expenditure on the same, and we also have the total receipts of the public service undertakings. We know about business spending on new vehicles. But we do not know the total of business spending on passenger transport. We do not have a full picture of inputs into the whole sector. We know about employment in public road passenger transport, but not about other employment involved (e.g. to take a related subject, there are no figures of the numbers employed in maintaining the road system). And so on. In other words 'an essential prerequisite to the determination of policy' is 'the collection of figures indicating the nation's transport resources and the nature of its employment'. Perhaps a start might be made in the late 1970s in rethinking whether this work could be begun.

5.9 There is also an important point about standardization of definitions and coverage. There is no need to believe in standardization as a panacea. Different purposes require different definitions. Roadside traffic censuses must rely on appearance of vehicles, while licensing figures can be classified according to use. But where data are collected locally, as with transportation surveys, the central department has a role in ensuring that they are comparable. It has for example been reasonably suggested that there should be a standard form of local traffic census which would enable continuous trends of traffic flow as a whole to be monitored in different areas. This would be the local equivalent of the sample national traffic surveys. Similarly, standard accounting procedures and cost breakdowns for bus undertakings would be helpful (*see* 4.4.2–3), and so would standardization of data about public service vehicles.

5.10 Now for some particular details. We clearly need to bring together more coherently the available data about walking and bicycling, if not to collect more. The road-biased collection of statistics has tended to write these off as out-of-date activities; it is not irrelevant that *PTGB* omits bicycle use of roads (*see* 4.2.1). Even in America people (occasionally) walk.

5.11 We need to be able to assess changes in people's travel habits, and the continuation of the NTS (or similar surveys) at intervals is essential and obviously crucial for knowledge of private motoring behaviour. Traffic counts alone cannot provide the information required. An alternative source of information might be provided by greater use of the census. It is almost certain that the cost of extracting the journey-to-work data at a level of disaggregation equivalent to the zones used in local traffic surveys would be less than the cost of the less adequate information provided by the latter. To make use of the census in this way would also suggest that it might be expanded to ask more questions about transport. Local transportation surveys of course provide a great deal more than data about origins and destinations of journeys, but their very large cost does not seem to have resulted in equivalent (acceptable) results. Perhaps the large-scale transportation surveys have had their day. If not, it is at least a question to be asked whether central government could not provide more comprehensive data more cheaply.

5.12 In the public field, perhaps the biggest gap is in our knowledge of taxis and private hire cars. There seems to be no comprehensive knowledge of the industry's turnover or activities, or even of the numbers employed (except in some censuses in a general way).

5.13 The basic framework of figures about public service vehicle operation is adequately published. It is, however, regrettable that the figures of costs from the accounts have not been published for recent years. Now that a very large part of the bus industry is in the public sector, it ought not to be too difficult for all this sector to have its accounts (with some basic statistics) published for each separate undertaking, as was done for the old tram undertakings before the Second World War. What we have in mind is a publication like the APPTO reports (3.7.6) for all municipal and PTE, National Bus Company, Scottish Transport Group (Scottish Bus Group), etc. undertakings.

5.14 As we suggested at the beginning, the passenger mile is a key statistic. And yet we only have passenger mile statistics for the country as a whole and for London Transport. Some further breakdown of these figures would be very helpful, even if it is not possible to expect every undertaking, even in the public sector, to produce such figures. Could not a start be made with the larger undertakings? Passenger miles are not only the best indicators of demand for transport, but divided by vehicle miles give us the load factor, which is perhaps the most important single indicator of performance and financial success. As it is, local authorities who have to decide what subsidies to give for local transport must be largely in the dark in assessing these on a rational basis.

5.15 The other important figure for assessing bus operations is the journey length. We do not know the average for particular types of operator or service, much less the distribution of lengths. The NTS produces these figures for the population as a whole, or by regions, or purposes. But this is not of course the same as the experience of particular operators. Should there be some standard form of sample survey for collection of these data by operators?

5.16 To sum up. Consumers' expenditure in 1973 on all travel and purchase of cars totalled £5,731m, or 13% of total consumption. It was greater than expenditure on fuel and light and clothing combined; it was nearly 70% of expenditure on food. Can it be said that the two main publications on the subject, *Passenger Transport in Great Britain* and *Highway Statistics* (the latter of which covers a wider field than we are concerned with), have given an adequate picture of a set of activities of such importance? We look forward to the new annual publication, which is to combine the two.

Quick Reference List—Table of Contents

Output   48
  (1) *Passenger miles*   48
  (2) *Passenger journeys*   48
  (3) *Vehicle miles*   49

Expenditure   50

Prices   50

Costs   50

Labour   51

Wages and earnings   51

Vehicles   51
  (1) *Stock*   51
  (2) *Additions to stock*   51
  (3) *Availability*   51
  (4) *Occupancy*   51
  (5) *Ownership*   51

Capital   52

Quick Reference List

Subject	Breakdown	Area (if not GB)	Frequency	Publication (see QRL key)	Text reference
Output					
(1) *Passenger miles*					
Walking	Journey purpose; household characteristics, etc.		1964, 1965, 1966, 1972/3, 1975/6	[QRL 42]	3.1.1–12
Bicycles	Journey purpose; household characteristics, etc.		1964, 1965, 1966, 1972/3, 1975/6	[QRL 42]	3.1.1–12
	Type of road; area		1960, 1966	[QRL 61]	3.3, 4.2.2
	Hours of the day; urban/rural		1968, 1970	[QRL 61]	3.3, 4.2.2
	All		1938. Annual from 1949	[QRL 34], [QRL 61]	3.3, 4.2
Motor-cycles	Journey purpose; household characteristics, etc.		1964, 1965, 1966 1972/3, 1975/6	[QRL 41]	3.1.1–12
Private cars	Journey purpose; household characteristics, etc.	E & W	1961–4 (quarterly)	[QRL 7]	3.1.1–4
—	Journey purpose; household characteristics, etc.		1964, 1965, 1966, 1972/3, 1975/6	[QRL 42]	3.1.1–12, 14–17
Cars and taxis	All		Annual from 1952	[QRL 45]	3.3, 4.3.1
Public road transport	Journey purpose; household characteristics, etc.		1964, 1965, 1966, 1972/3, 1975/6	[QRL 42]	3.1.1–12 14–17
—	All		Annual from 1951	[QRL 45]	3.5, 4.4.1
(2) *Passenger journeys*					
Walking	All (or journey to work). Trip length	London, Stevenage, Leamington Spa	Various (1962–5)	[QRL 10]	4.1.2
—	Journey to work; LA areas		1966, 1971	[QRL 26]	3.7.4, 4.1.1
—	Journey purpose; household characteristics, etc.		1964, 1965, 1966, 1972/3, 1975/6	[QRL 42]	3.1.1–12, 4.1
Bicycles	Journey purpose; household characteristics, etc.		1964, 1965, 1966, 1972/3, 1975/6	[QRL 42]	3.1.1–12, 4.1
	Journey to work; LA areas		1966, 1971	[QRL 26]	3.7.4, 4.2.3
Motor-cycles	Journey purpose; household characteristics, etc.		1964, 1965, 1966, 1972/3, 1975/6	[QRL 42]	3.1.1–12
Private cars	Journey to work; LA areas		1966, 1971	[QRL 26]	3.7.4
	Journey purpose; household characteristics, etc.	E & W	1961–4 (quarterly)	[QRL 7]	3.1.1–12

Quick Reference List

Category	Detail	Area	Period	Source	Section
—	Journey purpose; household characteristics, etc.		1964, 1965, 1966, 1972/3, 1975/6	[QRL 42]	3.1.1-12, 14-17
—	Journey to work; LA areas		1966, 1971	[QRL 26]	3.7.4
Public road transport	Journey to work; LA areas		1966, 1971	[QRL 26]	3.7.4
—	Journey purpose; household characteristics, etc.		1964, 1965, 1966, 1972/3, 1975/6	[QRL 42]	3.1.1-12, 14-17
	Type of operator; type of service; type of vehicle		Quarterly	[QRL 45]	2.2, 3.5, 4.4.1
	Municipal undertakings and PTEs	UK	Annual	[QRL 20]	3.7.6
(3) Vehicle miles					
Bicycles	*See passenger miles*				
Motor-cycles	Journey purpose; household characteristics, etc.		1964, 1965, 1966, 1972/3, 1975/6	[QRL 42]	3.1.1-12
	Type of vehicle; type of road; area		1960, 1966	[QRL 61]	3.3
	Hours of the day; urban/rural motorways		1968, 1970	[QRL 61]	3.3
	All; months by weekdays, Saturdays, Sundays; urban/rural/motorways by months		Annual (1938, 1949—)	[QRL 34], [QRL 61]	3.3
Private cars	Journey purpose; household characteristics, etc.	E & W	1961-4 (quarterly)	[QRL 7]	3.1.1-12
	Journey purpose; household characteristics, etc.		1964, 1965, 1966, 1972/3, 1975/6	[QRL 42]	3.1.1-12, 14-17
Cars and taxis	Type of road; area		1960, 1966	[QRL 61]	3.3, 4.3.1
	Hours of the day; urban/rural motorways		1968, 1970	[QRL 61]	3.3, 4.3.1
	All; months by weekdays, Saturdays, Sundays; urban/rural/motorways by months		Annual (1938, 1949—)	[QRL 34], [QRL 61]	3.3, 4.3.1
Public road transport	Journey purpose; household characteristics, etc.		1964, 1965, 1966, 1972/3, 1975/6	[QRL 42]	3.1.1-12, 14-17
	Type of operator; type of service; type of vehicle		Annual	[QRL 45]	2.2, 3.5, 4.4.1
	Type of road; area		1960, 1966	[QRL 61]	3.3
	Hours of the day; urban/rural motorways		1968, 1970	[QRL 61]	3.3
	All; months by weekdays, Saturdays, Sundays; urban/rural/motorways by months		Annual (1938, 1949—)	[QRL 34], [QRL 61]	3.3
All motor vehicles	Municipal undertakings and PTEs	UK	Annual	[QRL 20]	3.7.6
	Type of road; days of each month		Annual (1956—)	[QRL 61]	3.3

Subject	Breakdown	Area (if not GB)	Frequency	Publication (see QRL key)	Text reference
Expenditure					
Private motor vehicles (consumers)	Purchase of vehicles; running costs	UK	Annual	[QRL 41]	3.7.3, 4.3.2
—(all)	All vehicle costs		1949, 1950, 1960–9	[QRL 2], [QRL 11]	3.7.5
—(households)	Households; areas	UK	Annual	[QRL 32]	3.7.3, 4.3.2
Public road transport (households)	Journey purpose; household characteristics, etc.		1964, 1965, 1966, 1972/3, 1975/6	[QRL 42]	3.1.1–13
—(households)	Type of household; areas	UK	Annual	[QRL 32]	3.7.3
—(passenger receipts)	Type of operator; type of service; type of vehicle		Quarterly	[QRL 45]	2.2, 3.5, 4.4.1–3
—(traffic receipts)	Municipal undertakings and PTEs	UK	Annual	[QRL 20]	3.7.6
—(consumers)	All	UK	Annual	[QRL 41]	4.4.1
Prices					
Private motor vehicles (consumers)	Vehicles; running costs	UK	Annual	[QRL 41]	4.3.2
Public road transport (consumers)	All	UK	Annual	[QRL 41]	4.3.4
—(fares)	London; local authorities (PTAs); other		Quarterly	[QRL 45]	4.4.6
Costs					
Private motor vehicles (per vehicle mile)	Class of vehicle; speed		1958, 1962–5, 1967, 1970	[QRL 62]	4.3.3
—(running costs)	Class of vehicle		Occasional	[QRL 21]	3.7.8, 4.3.3
Public road transport (per vehicle mile)	Speed		1958, 1962–5, 1967, 1970	[QRL 62]	4.3.3
—	Class of vehicle; running and standing costs		Annual	[QRL 27]	3.7.8, 4.3.3
—(accounts)	Type of operator		Annual	[QRL 45]	2.2, 4.4.2–3
—(accounts)	Municipal undertakings and PTEs	UK	Annual	[QRL 20]	3.7.6
Petrol duties		UK	Annual	[QRL 57]	4.3.2

Labour

Road passenger transport (insured)	Tramway and omnibus; other		Annual to 1959	[QRL 22] [QRL 23] [QRL 28]	4.4.4
—	All		Annual	[QRL 22] [QRL 23] [QRL 28]	4.4.4
—(employees)	Categories of staff; sex; type of operator; size of operator		Annual from 1964	[QRL 45]	4.4.4
—(employees)	Occupations; size of undertakings		Annual from 1967	[QRL 51]	3.7.7
—	Industry; occupation		1951, 1961, 1966, 1971	[QRL 26]	4.4.4

Wages and earnings (Public road transport)

Wages	Categories of workers	UK	Annual (and when changes occur)	[QRL 60] [QRL 28]	4.4.5
Earnings	Sex; adults/youths; part-time women	UK	Biennial	[QRL 28]	4.4.5
—	Range of earnings; various categories	GB	Annual (April) from 1970	[QRL 44]	4.4.5

Vehicles

(1) Stock

Motor vehicles licensed	Type of vehicle (road licence category); date of first registration	GB, UK	Annual	[QRL 49], [QRL 34]	3.7.2, 4.3.4, 4.4.7
Public road transport (public service vehicles)	Type of operator; type of vehicle; seating capacity; size of undertaking		Annual	[QRL 45], [QRL 19]	2.2, 2.4, 4.4.7
—	Municipal undertakings and PTEs	UK	Annual	[QRL 20]	3.7.6
Taxis	All	London	Annual	[QRL 47]	4.3.5

(2) Additions to stock

Motor vehicles licensed (new registrations)	Type of vehicle (road licence category)	GB UK	Monthly	[QRL 49], [QRL 34]	3.7.2, 4.3.4, 4.4.7

(3) Availability

Households	Vehicle types; household characteristics; weekly mileage; planning regions		1972/3	[QRL 42]	3.1.1–3.1.15 Addendum

(4) Occupancy

Persons	Private vehicles; journey purpose; length of stage; planning region; type of area		1972/3	[QRL 42]	3.1.1–3.1.15 Addendum

(5) Ownership

Firms/household members etc.	Characteristics of car; business mileage; form of business expenses received		1972/3	[QRL 42]	3.1.1–3.1.15 Addendum

Subject	Breakdown	Area (if not GB)	Frequency	Publication (see QRL key)	Text reference
Capital					
Vehicles (consumers' expenditure)	All	UK	Annual	[QRL 41]	3.7.3, 4.3.2
Vehicles, ships and aircraft (capital account expenditure)	Industries; sectors	UK	Annual	[QRL 41]	3.7.3, 4.3.2
Vehicles (capital account expenditure)	Buses and coaches; other road vehicles	UK	Annual	[QRL 41]	3.7.3, 4.3.2
Road passenger transport (fixed capital)	Vehicles (buses and coaches; taxis and hire cars); plant and machinery; new buildings and works	UK	Annual	[QRL 41], [QRL 45]	4.4.8
Public road transport (accounts)	Various undertakings		Annual	[QRL 24], [QRL 37], [QRL 38], [QRL 40], [QRL 56]	3.6, 4.4.8

Quick Reference List: Key to Publications

Government departments are designated by their latest title in the case of continuous publications. The same applies to the precise title of a continuous publication which may have changed over time.

Department of Transport: formerly Department of the Environment, Ministry of Transport, Ministry of Transport and Civil Aviation, etc.

Department of Employment: formerly Department of Employment and Productivity and Ministry of Labour.

General Register Office, Scotland: formerly General Registry Office, Scotland.

Office of Population Censuses and Surveys: formerly General Register Office.

Scottish Development Department: formerly Scottish Home Department.

Traffic Commissioners: formerly (1947–56) Licensing Authorities for Public Service Vehicles.

Transport and Road Research Laboratory (TRRL) (Department of the Environment): formerly Road Research Laboratory (Department of Scientific and Industrial Research, etc.).

Welsh Office: formerly Home Office, Ministry of Housing, etc.

It is to be noted that there has been a trend over time (particularly marked for transport statistics) to down-grade publications. Parliamentary publications (e.g. Command papers and House of Commons papers) become Departmental publications (HMSO; *see* annual and monthly catalogues); Departmental publications cease to be published by HMSO, and are available (free or at a price) from the Department itself. But, though most users are aware of the difficulties of obtaining publications from HMSO, not all readers may be aware of the hazards of trying to obtain publications from a Department such as the DOE. There are probably more points from which they are issued than the HMSO has bookshops and (so-called) agents throughout the United Kingdom (40). There are a 'DOE Publication Department' and a 'Directorate of Information'; credat Iudaeus Apella: they are only to be approached with prior knowledge of their activities. Fortunately, the DOE Library Services (Room P3/178, 2 Marsham Street, London SW1P 3EB) produced in February 1973 a *DOE Annual List of Publications 1971* (not HMSO; available free) giving full information of *all* publications and the building and room from which they can be obtained. Lists for 1972 and 1973 have also been published, and are available on request.

Note. The date of the latest issue of a publication used in the text is given in the last **column**. This date is that of the title (and contents), not the date of publication.

Quick Reference List Key to Publications

Reference number	Author, and/or Organization responsible	Title	Publisher	Frequency or date of publication	Remarks
[QRL 1]	Buckley, S. Commercial Motor	'Commercial Motor' Tables of Operating Costs for Goods and Passenger Vehicles	See [QRL 27]	—	
[QRL 2]	Dawson, R. F. F. Royal Statistical Society	'Estimated Expenditure on Road Transport in Great Britain' 1960, (JRSS, Series A, 1962, 125, 462)	Royal Statistical Society, London	1962	
[QRL 3]	Dawson, R. F. F. Department of the Environment	Vehicle Operating Costs in 1962, 1973, etc. (1973 with P. Vass)	See [QRL 62]	—	
[QRL 4]	Dawson, R. F. F. and Wardrop, J. G. Department of Scientific and Industrial Research	Passenger Mileage by Road in Greater London. (Road Research Technical Paper, No. 59)	HMSO, London	1962	
[QRL 5]	Dunn, J. B. Department of the Environment	Traffic Census Results for 1969–1972, etc.	See [QRL 61]	—	
[QRL 6]	Dunn, J. B. and Hutchings, I. J. Department of the Environment	The Distribution of Traffic in Great Britain through the 24 hours of the Day in 1968	See [QRL 61]	—	
[QRL 7]	Gray, P. G. Government Social Survey	Private Motoring in England and Wales (SS329)	HMSO, London	1969	
[QRL 8]	Gyenes, L. Department of the Environment	The Distribution of Hourly Volumes of Traffic at Fifty Sites in 1970	See [QRL 61]	—	
[QRL 9]	Gyenes, L. Department of the Environment	Fifty-Point Traffic Census: The Automatic Processing of Hourly Flows	See [QRL 61]	—	
[QRL 10]	Mitchell, C. B. B. Department of the Environment	Pedestrian and Cycle Journeys in English Urban Areas (LR 497)	TRRL, Crowthorne	1973	On request
[QRL 11]	Rudd Ernest Royal Statistical Society	'Estimates of Expenditure on Road Transport in Great Britain,' (JRSS, Series A, 1952, 115, 179)	Royal Statistical Society London	1952	

Quick Reference List: Key to Publications   55

[QRL 12]	Tanner, J. C. Department of the Environment	*Forecasts of Vehicles and Traffic in Great Britain: 1974 Revision* (LR 650)	TRRL, Crowthorne	1974	On request
[QRL 13]	Tanner, J. C., Johnson, H. D. and Scott, J. R. Department of Scientific and Industrial Research	*Sample Survey of the Roads and Traffic of Great Britain* (Road Research Technical Paper, No. 62)	See [QRL 61]	—	
[QRL 14]	Tanner, J. C. and Scott, J. R. Department of Scientific and Industrial Research	*50-Point Traffic Census: the First 5 Years* (Road Research Technical Paper, No. 63)	See [QRL 61]	—	
[QRL 15]	Timbers, Janice A. Ministry of Transport	*Traffic Survey at 1300 Sites* (LR 206)	See [QRL 61]	—	
[QRL 16]	Tulpule, A. H. Department of the Environment	*Forecasts of Vehicles and Traffic in Great Britain: 1972 Revision* (LR 543)	TRRL, Crowthorne	1973	On request
[QRL 17]	Voorhees, Alan M., and Associates Ltd. British Road Federation	*Traffic in the Conurbations*	British Road Federation, London	n.d. [1970?]	
[QRL 18]	Central Statistical Office	*Abstract of Regional Statistics* (1965–)	HMSO, London	Annual	
[QRL 19]	Department of the Environment	*Annual Reports of the Traffic Commissioners to the Minister of Transport* (1931/2– 1937/8, 1947/8–) (TC)	Department of the Environment, London (from 1969/70)	Annual	On request
[QRL 20]	Association of Public Passenger Transport Operators (Inc.)	*Association of Public Passenger Transport Operators. Annual Summary of Accounts and Statistical Information*	Association of Public Passenger Transport Operators, Friars House, 6 Parkway, Chelmsford, Essex	Annual	
[QRL 21]	Automobile Association	*Automobile Association. Schedule of Estimated Running costs based on New Car Values*	Automobile Association, London	Occasional	
[QRL 22]	Department of Employment	*British Labour Statistics, Historical Abstract, 1886–1968*	HMSO, London	1971	
[QRL 23]	Department of Employment	*British Labour Statistics, Yearbook* (1969–)	HMSO, London	Annual	
[QRL 24]	—	*British Transport Commission. Annual Report and Accounts* (1948–62) (BTC)	HMSO, London	Annual House of Commons Paper	
[QRL 25]	British Road Federation	*Car Parking*	British Road Federation, London	1961, 1964, 1968	

Reference number	Author/ and/or Organization responsible	Title	Publisher	Frequency or date of publication	Remarks
[QRL 26]	Office of Population Censuses and Surveys, and General Register Office, Scotland	*Census* (1)*Census 1961.* (a) *England and Wales. Industry tables* (b) *England and Wales. Occupation Tables* (c) *Scotland. Vol. 6. Occupation, Industry and workplace* (2) *Sample Census 1966.* (a) *Great Britain. Economic Activity Tables* (b) *England and Wales. Workplace and Transport Tables* (c) *Scotland/ Workplace and Transport tables* (3) *Census 1971.* (a) *Availability of Cars* (b) *Economic Activity/ Parts II, III*	HMSO, London HMSO, London HMSO, Edinburgh HMSO, Edinburgh and London HMSO, London HMSO, Edinburgh HMSO, London HMSO, London	1966 1966 1966 1968 1968 1968 1974 1975	
[QRL 27]	*Commercial Motor*	'Commercial Motor' Tables of Operating Costs for Goods and Passenger Vehicles, by S. Buckley	IPC Transport Press Ltd. London	Annual	
[QRL 28]	Department of Employment	*Department of Employment Gazette*	HMSO, London	Monthly	
[QRL 29]	Scottish Development Department	*Digest of Scottish Statistics* (April 1953–April 1971)	HMSO, Edinburgh	April, October	
[QRL 30]	Department of Finance Belfast	*Digest of Statistics, Northern Ireland*	HMSO, Belfast	March, September	
[QRL 31]	Welsh Office	*Digest of Welsh Statistics* (1954–)	HMSO, Cardiff	Annual	
[QRL 32]	Department of Employment	*Family Expenditure Survey* (FES)	HMSO, London	Annual	
[QRL 33]	Glasgow Corporation	*Greater Glasgow Transportation Study*, Vols 1, 2, 3, 4	Glasgow Corporation	1967, 1968, 1971	
[QRL 34]	Department of the Environment	*Highway Statistics* (1963–1973)	HMSO, London	Annual	
[QRL 35]	Scottish Development Department	*Industry and Employment in Scotland and Scottish Roads Report* (1960–1, 1961–2)	HMSO, Edinburgh	Cmnd. 1391, 1727	
[QRL 36]	Greater London Council	*London Traffic Survey*, Vols 1, 2	Greater London Council, London	1964, 1966	
[QRL 37]	—	*London Transport Board, Annual Report and Accounts* (1963–9) (LT)	HMSO, London	Annual	House of Commons Paper
[QRL 38]	London Transport Executive	*London Transport Executive. Annual Report and Accounts* (1970——) (LT)	London Transport Executive, London	Annual	

Quick Reference List: Key to Publications 57

[QRL 39]	Automobile Association	*The Motorist Today. (Some Findings of General Interest from a Survey Commissioned by the Automobile Association)*	Automobile Association, London	1966
[QRL 40]	National Bus Company	*National Bus Company, Annual Report and Accounts* (1969–). (Main successor to Transport Holding Company buses; reports for 1962–8)	National Bus Company, London	Annual
[QRL 41]	Central Statistical Office	*National Income and Expenditure* (Blue Book—BB).	HMSO, London	Annual
[QRL 42]	Department of the Environment	*National Travel Survey (NTS) 1964* (Preliminary Report) Part I—Household Vehicle Ownership and Use. Part II—Personal Travel by Public and Private Transport. (Some results from the 1965 survey are published in the 1967 issues of [QRL 34] and [QRL 45].) *National Travel Survey 1972/3* (1) *Cross Sectional Analysis of Passenger Travel in Great Britain* (2) *Number of Journeys per Week by Different Types of Households, Individuals and Vehicles* (3) *A Comparison of 1965 and 1972/73 Surveys*	Department of the Environment HMSO, London HMSO, London HMSO, London	1967 1975 1976 1976
[QRL 43]	Central Statistical Office	*New Contributions to Economic Statistics.* (1) (Third Series): *Motor Car Ownership and Use* (pp. 139–48); *Passenger Transport in Great Britain* (pp. 159–65). (2) (Seventh Series): *The Motor Transactions Survey, 1971*.	HMSO, London	Occasional (Reprints from *Economic Trends*) 1964, 1975
[QRL 44]	Department of Employment	*New Earnings Survey* (1968–)	HMSO, London	Annual
[QRL 45]	Department of the Environment	*Passenger Transport in Great Britain (PTGB)* (1949–1973)	HMSO, London	Annual
[QRL 46]	University of Birmingham	*People and the Motor Car: A Study of the Movement of People Related to their Residential Environment.* Vol. 1. Report. Vol. 2. Tables.	Department of Transportation and Environmental Planning, University of Birmingham, Birmingham	1964
[QRL 47]	Home Office	*Report of the Commissioner of Police of the Metropolis for the Year ....*	HMSO, London	Annual Command Paper

58 Road Passenger Transport

Reference number	Author/ and/or Organization responsible	Title	Publisher	Frequency or date of publication	Remarks
[QRL 48]	Ministry of Transport	*Report on the Administration of the Road Fund* (1953/4)	HMSO, London	HMSO, London	
[QRL 49]	Ministry of Transport	*Road Motor Vehicles* (to 1962)	HMSO, London	Five returns per year, 1946-56 Annual, 1957-62	
[QRL 50]	Ministry of Transport	*Road Traffic Census, 1950*	HMSO, London	1952	
[QRL 51]	Department of Employment	*Road Transport Industry Training Board, Report and Statement of Accounts* (1966/7–)	Road Transport Industry Training Board, Wembley (from 1972/3)	Annual	
[QRL 52]	Ministry of Transport	*Roads in England and Wales* (1956/7–1964/5)	HMSO, London	Annual House of Commons Paper	
[QRL 53]	Office of Population Censuses and Surveys	*Sample Census, 1966*	See [QRL 26]	—	
[QRL 54]	Scottish Office	*Scottish Abstract of Statistics* (1971–)	HMSO, Edinburgh	Annual	
[QRL 55]	Scottish Development Department	*Scottish Development Department Report for . . .* (1962–6)	HMSO, Edinburgh	Annual Command Papers	
[QRL 56]	Scottish Transport Group	*Scottish Transport Group Annual Report and Accounts* (1969–) *(see under [QRL 24 and QRL 40])*	Scottish Transport Group, Edinburgh	Annual (House of Commons Papers, 1969, 1970)	
[QRL 57]	Customs and Excise	*Sixty-fifth Report of the Commissioners of Her Majesty's Customs and Excise for the year ended March 31, 1974*	HMSO, London	Annual Command Paper	
[QRL 58]	Central Statistical Office	*Social Trends*	HMSO, London	Annual	
[QRL 59]	Department of the Environment	*Strategic Plan for the South-East: Studies. Vol. 3. Transportation*	HMSO, London	1971	
[QRL 60]	Department of Employment	*Time Rates of Wages and Hours of Labour*	HMSO, London	Annual	
[QRL 61]	Department of the Environment Tanner, J. C., Johnson H. D. and Scott, J. R.	*Traffic Censuses* (1) *Sample Survey of the Roads and Traffic of Great Britain* (Road Research Technical Paper, No. 62)	HMSO, London	1962	
	Tanner, J. C. and Scott, J. R.	(2) *50-Point Traffic Census—the first 5 Years* (Road Research Technical Paper, No. 63)	HMSO, London	1962	
	Timbers, Janice A.	(3) *Traffic Survey at 1300 Sites* (LR 206)	TRRL, Crowthorne	1968	On request

	Dunn, J. B. and Hutchings, I. J.	(4) *The Distribution of Traffic in Great Britain through the 24 Hours of the Day in 1968* (LR 295)	TRRL, Crowthorne	1969	On request
	Dunn, J. B.	(5) *Traffic Census Results for 1969, 1970, 1971, 1972* (LR 371, 428, 548, 618) (For earlier reports, see references in LR 371)	TRRL, Crowthorne	Annual	On request
	Gyenes, L.	(6) *The Distribution of Hourly Volumes of Traffic at Fifty Sites in 1970* (LR 549)	TRRL, Crowthorne	1973	On request
	Gyenes, L.	(7) *50-Point Traffic Census: the Automatic Processing of Hourly Flows* (LR 558)	TRRL, Crowthorne	1973	On request
[QRL 62]	Department of the Environment	*Vehicle Operating Costs* by R. F. F. Dawson (1) 1962. *Traffic Engineering and Control*. 1963, 4 (9), 498–9, 514	Printerhall Ltd., London	1963	
		(2) 1963. *Research on Road Traffic*, Chap. 15.	HMSO, London	1965	
		(3) 1964. *The Economic Assessment of Road Improvement Schemes* (Road Research Technical Paper, No. 75)	HMSO, London	1968	
		(4) 1970, 1973. *Vehicle Operating Costs in 1970, 1973*. (1973 with P. Vass). (LR 439, 661) (See bibliography for other unpublished reports)	TRRL, Crowthorne	Occasional	On request
[QRL 63]	West Midlands Transport Study, Technical Committee	*West Midlands Transport Study, Vols. 1, 2, 3*	West Midlands Transport Study, Birmingham	1968	
[QRL 64]	Department of Transport	*Transport Statistics Great Britain* (TS 1974–)	HMSO, London	Annual	

Select Bibliography

[B 1] Baggaley, D. A., 'Passenger miles computation in London Transport'. To be published in *Journal of Transport Economics and Policy*.

[B 2] Bruton, M. J., *Introduction to Transport Planning*, London, Hutchinson, 1970.

[B 3] Gordon, I. R. and Edwards, S. L. 'Holiday trip generation', *Journal of Transport Economics and Policy*, 1973, 7, p. 153.

[B 4] Hillman, M., Henderson, I. and Whalley, A., *Personal Mobility and Transport Policy* (Political and Economic Planning, 1973).

[B 5] MacNaughton-Smith, P. and Tanner, J. C. 'Trends in traffic flow in Great Britain from 1938 to 1955', *Surveyor*, 1956, 115, p. 1029.

[B 6] Scott, J. R. and Tanner, J. C. 'Traffic trends in vehicle-miles in Great Britain, 1938–60', *Surveyor*, 1962, 121, p. 645.

[B 7] Sirker, A. K., *Motor Transactions Survey, 1971*, Social Survey Division, Office of Population Censuses and Surveys. 55726. London, HMSO, 1975.

[B 8] Tanner, J. C., 'The sampling of road traffic', *Applied Statistics*, 1957, 6, p. 161.

[B 9] Tyson, W. J., 'An analysis of trends in bus passenger miles', *Journal of Transport Economics and Policy*, 1974, 1, p. 40.

[B 10] Office of Population Censuses and Surveys, Social Surveys Division, *The General Household Survey: Introductory Report, and 1972*, London, HMSO, 1973 and 1975.

[B 11] Central Statistical Office, *Input–output Tables for the United Kingdom, 1963, 1968, 1970, 1971*, London, HMSO, 1970, 1973, 1975.

[B 12] Central Statistical Office. *National Accounts Statistics, Sources and Methods,* London, HMSO, 1968.

[B 13] Ministry of Housing and Local Government, etc. *Parking in Town Centres*, Planning Bulletin No. 7, London, HMSO, 1965.

[B 14] Department of Scientific and Industrial Research, Road Research Laboratory, *Research on Road Traffic*, London, HMSO, 1965.

[B 15] Central Statistical Office, *Standard Industrial Classification*, London, HMSO, 1968.

[B 16] Central Statistical Office *Statistical News*, London, HMSO. Quarterly.

[B 17] Ministry of Transport, *Traffic and Transport Plans*, Roads Circular No. 1/68, London, HMSO, 1968.

[B 18] Department of the Environment, Transport and Road Research Laboratory, *Transport and Road Research* (1974), London, HMSO, 1975. Annual.

[B 19] Ministry of Transport/Scottish Development Department, *Urban Traffic Engineering Techniques*, London, HMSO, 1965.

[B 20] Department of the Environment, *Transport Policy, A Consultation Document* (2 vols), London, HMSO, 1976.

Appendices

Appendix A	The Index of Traffic and Transportation Surveys (compiled by the Department of the Environment)—A press notice of 30 October 1973 [*see* 3.2.2 of text]	62
Appendix B	Returns from operators of Public Service Road Vehicles	64
	(a) Calendar year return for 1974	64
	(b) Quarterly returns	68
	(c) Financial and statistical returns	72
	[*see* 3.5.2 of text]	
Appendix C	National Travel Survey Questionnaires	76
	(a) For 1972/3	
	Household schedule	76
	Individual schedule	78
	Motor vehicle schedule	82
	Record of journeys	87
	(b) For 1975/6	
	Contact sheet	107
	Individual sheet	109
	Vehicle sheet	114
	Journey sheet	120
	Household sheet	122
	[*see* 3.1.3 of text]	
Appendix D	Long-Distance Travel Survey Questionnaires	126
	(a) Continuing postal survey	126
	(b) Conurbation postal survey	130
	[*see* 3.1.6 of text]	

Appendix A

Department of the Environment
Index of Traffic and Transportation Surveys
A press notice of 30 October 1973

An index of traffic and transportation surveys has been compiled by the Department of the Environment for use as a source of reference by government departments, local authorities, universities and all other organizations concerned with transport policy or research.

The Index was started six years ago when organizations sponsoring surveys were asked to complete, in respect of each survey carried out during the preceding two years, a detailed questionnaire about the survey methods used and the subject-matter of the research. Details were received for some 500 surveys.

The Index has been brought up to date by a fresh approach to sponsoring organizations and there are now details of over 1,000 surveys stored on microfilm. The use of an 'optical feature card' system assists in the identification of surveys which have covered a particular topic or used particular techniques in sampling or analysis. Where access to survey results is required enquiries will be referred to the organization responsible for the work. Results will be issued at the discretion of that organization.

The Index has been set up by the Department as a service to all interested organizations and to assist them in identifying areas of interest. It is hoped that the Index will be fully used and requests for lists of feature headings and details of surveys, which should include mention of feature headings of particular interest, should be sent to Mrs J. S. Andrews, Department of the Environment, Statistics Transport 'A' Division, Room 1324, Thames House South, Millbank, London SW1P 4HQ. Tel: 01-834 9020, Ext 1695.

List of Main Feature Headings

SECTION A. GENERAL INFORMATION

Type of survey
Area covered
Dates of fieldwork
Size of sample
Size of population
Sampling technique
Geographical zone codes
Zoning system
Number of businesses
Type of businesses
Method of analysis
Tabulations

Form of storage for basic data
Programming language used
Availability of reports
Further studies

SECTION B. SURVEYS OF VEHICLE MOVEMENTS

Traffic volumes
Transportation inventories
Speed of flow
Public passenger transport
Freight transport fleets
Vehicle classifications
Vehicle movements

SECTION C. SURVEYS OF PERSON MOVEMENTS

Where and how information was obtained
Mode of transport
Journey purpose
Times of journeys
Cost of journeys
Origins and destinations
Additional data

SECTION D. SURVEYS OF FREIGHT MOVEMENTS

Commodity classification
Individual freight consignments
Other details of journey
Pipelines
Air
Inland waterways
Coastal shipping
Non-coastal shipping
Road
Rail

SECTION E. PARKING SURVEYS

Facilities
Type of parking
Characteristics (duration, usage, etc.)
Operation (public/private)
Survey method

Department of the Environment
Directorate of Statistics R/101
Albion Court, 197 Marlowes, Hemel Hempstead, Herts HP1 1BN

Telephone Hemel Hempstead 2561-7 Ext. 314
(STD 0442)

SPECIMEN

January 1975

Dear Sir

PUBLIC SERVICE VEHICLES CALENDAR YEAR STATISTICAL RETURN FOR 1974 FORM STATS 32

The purpose of this enquiry is to obtain regular and up-to-date information on the activities and resources of the public passenger transport industry. The resulting statistics enable Government to formulate policy in the light of both overall and detailed trends in passenger transport.

I should like to ask for your co-operation in this enquiry by completing the accompanying form according to the notes, ensuring that the figures are clear and in the correct columns ready for computer processing. The status of the person signing the declaration should be shown. Please return the form in the enclosed 'official paid' envelope by 28 February 1975, keeping one copy of the form as a record in case of queries.

The information provided by you will be used solely for statistical purposes and will be treated as strictly confidential. Statistics which are published or made publicly available will be prepared in such a way that particulars relating to any individual operation will not be disclosed unless the operator concerned gives written consent.

This enquiry has statutory authority: as an operator of public service vehicles you are required under the Road Traffic Act 1960 to submit an annual statistical return to this Department. Section 157 of the Act states:—

(i) It shall be the duty of a person carrying on the business of operating public service vehicles to keep such accounts and records in relation thereto and to make to the Minister such financial and statistical returns, and in such manner and at such times, as the Minister may from time to time require.

(ii) If a person fails to comply with the requirements of the foregoing sub-section, he shall be liable on summary conviction to a fine not exceeding twenty pounds, and in the case of a continuing offence to a fine not exceeding five pounds for every day during which the offence continues.

If you have any difficulties in completing the form, please write or telephone the Department at the above address.

Yours faithfully

G. Penrice

G PENRICE
Director of Statistics

NOTES ON COMPLETION OF THE FORM *Appendix B*

General

1   If you held public service vehicle licences but did not use them, you should still complete section 1. If you think that any section, or even the whole form, is no longer applicable to you please use the back of the form to explain the circumstances. In general if exact figures are not available in some sections reasonable estimates will be acceptable.

SECTION 1   VEHICLES

2   The entries in this section should cover all vehicles (including those with a passenger seating capacity less than 8) for which public service vehicle licences were held on 31 December, whether owned, being acquired by hire purchase or out on hire to another operator.

3   'One man operated' vehicles means those which have been certified by the Traffic Commissioners as equipped for automatic fare collection or fare collection by the driver on stage or express services.

SECTION 2   TRAFFIC

4   Traffic information should relate to work done at any time during the year. Include use of vehicles hired in (with or without driver) from another operator, as well as vehicles owned or on hire purchase; exclude use of vehicles hired out to another operator. Thus any services run on behalf of another operator should be accounted for in that operator's return.

5   Do not include work for which a public service vehicle licence was not needed, even though such a licence is held for the vehicle in question. For work in connection with foreign tours, include figures only for that part of a journey within Great Britain.

6   Traffic information should be entered against the type of operation on which the vehicles were used. Where bus or coach operations occur under a 'road service licence', issued (in addition to the public service vehicle licences) to authorise stage services, express services, excursions or tours the work done should be entered on one of the first three lines as appropriate.

7   Information relating to all other operations requiring public service vehicle licences, but not needing road service licences, should be given on the fourth line, i.e. contract, private hire and own account . This will include contract work for transporting particular groups of people, e.g. school children and, in particular, work under section 118(2) of the Road Traffic Act 1960 (where separate fares may be paid). The use of vehicles under public service vehicle licences for the benefit of the operator's own business should also be included.

8   Number of Passengers: Give the total number of passengers carried during the year on each type of service. Children and persons travelling at concessionary fares or free should be counted as full passengers. All such passengers should be included e.g. old age pensioners, disabled persons, employees or other privileged persons travelling free whether or not issued with tickets or passes. If some category of passenger cannot possibly be included please say so and show the corresponding receipts (if any) separately. Where basic information is in terms of tickets sold an adjustment should be made to obtain the best estimate of passenger journeys.

9   A passenger issued with a return ticket or a ticket for a round trip (out and home) should be reckoned as two passengers, as should a passenger carried out and home on contract or private hire. Passengers issued with weekly or monthly tickets should be counted as 12 passengers or 50 passengers respectively, unless more accurate information is available from surveys. A passenger with a ticket for a period of longer than a month

should be reckoned at the rate of 50 passengers per month. Each passenger travelling to or from a port or airport in Great Britain should be counted as one passenger, and one with a ticket for an extended tour in Great Britain not exceeding 14 days should be treated as a weekly ticket and reckoned as 12 passengers. Any such tickets longer than 14 days should be dealt with as monthly tickets and reckoned as 50 passengers.

10 Vehicle miles: State against the appropriate type of service the number of vehicle miles (loaded and empty) run during the time the vehicles were in use for the purpose of conveying passengers. Miles run to and from a depot should be included with the type of service to which such empty running mainly relates.

11 Passenger receipts: For each type of service give the gross amounts paid by or in respect of the passengers shown, including commission paid to booking agents but excluding amounts for meals, hotel accommodation etc, and any commission to booking agents for such items. Include any receipts from local authorities in respect of concessionary fares and also show this receipt separately on the back of the form. For foreign tours work include only a sum representing the charge for that part of the journey (excluding accommodation) taking place within Great Britain, if necessary using estimates. Exclude receipts from parcels, mails, luggage, dogs, etc.

SECTION 3 EMPLOYMENT

12 Give the numbers employed as at the end of the year. Where a person is employed on more than one type of work, for example maintenance and driving, include that person in the type of work on which he is mainly engaged (except for 'working proprietors', see below).

13 Include as 'other staff' all maintenance, cleaning, administrative, etc staff and also all 'working proprietors'. Working proprietors are persons engaged in the business covered by this return, who are regarded as self-employed for National Insurance purposes, and members of their families who work in the business without receiving any fixed wages or salaries. Exclude persons who work less than half the normal number of working hours on public service vehicle operations. Include directors working in the business irrespective of whether they are in receipt of a definite wage, salary or commission but exclude part-time directors paid by fee only.

14 Where the public service vehicle operations are a minor ancillary part of business operations not otherwise concerned with passenger transport, it may be that no person is concerned for as much as half-time. In this case enter '0' against each heading of section 3, but where several persons contribute in part, enter a figure in 'other staff' approximating to the total manpower involved.

NB The information which you provide will be processed by computer. Please write or type each entry at the right hand side of the appropriate group of boxes, as in this example:

			3	1	2	6	8	4

Department of the Environment

PLEASE KEEP THIS PAGE

PUBLIC SERVICE VEHICLES CALENDAR YEAR STATISTICAL RETURN FOR 1974
Road Traffic Act 1960 - Section 157

Ref No. [For Official Use: 1 2 3 4 5 6 7 8 9 10 11 12 13]

SECTION 1 – VEHICLES (SEE NOTES)

Passenger seating capacity of vehicles (excluding driver)	Number of vehicles as at 31st December			
	Single Decker		Double Decker	
	One man operated	Other	One man operated	Other
1 Not over 14 seats	15 16 17 18	19 20 21 22	23 24 25 26	27 28 29 30
15 – 48	31 32 33 34	35 36 37 38	39 40 41 42	43 44 45 46
49 – 72	47 48 49 50	51 52 53 54	55 56 57 58	59 60 61 62
Over 72	63 64 65 66	67 68 69 70	71 72 73 74	75 76 77 78

2 Total passenger seating capacity of the above vehicles	15 16 17 18 19 20
Total passenger capacity including permitted standing room	21 22 23 24 25 26

SECTION 2 – TRAFFIC (SEE NOTES)

Type of Service	Total number of passengers carried during year	Total number of vehicle miles run during year	Total passenger receipts during the year to nearest £
	16 17 18 19 20 21 22 23 24	26 27 28 29 30 31 32 33 34	35 36 37 38 39 40 41 42 43
3 1 Stage			
3 2 Express			
3 3 Excursions and tours			
3 4 Contract, private hire and own account			

SPECIMEN

SECTION 3 – EMPLOYMENT (SEE NOTES)

	Number employed as at 31st December	
	Male	Female
4 Drivers	15 16 17 18 19	20 21 22 23 24
Conductors	25 26 27 28 29	30 31 32 33 34
Other staff	35 36 37 38 39	40 41 42 43 44

Name and address of operator (and trading name if different)

....
....
....
....

DECLARATION
I hereby certify that to the best of my knowledge and belief, the information given is true and correct and has been compiled in accordance with the explanatory notes.

Signed ....

Status ....

Tel. no. ....

Date ....

Directorate of Statistics
Department of the Environment
Room 101
Albion Court
197 Marlowes
Hemel Hempstead HP1 1BN
Herts.

Date as postmark

PUBLIC SERVICE VEHICLES
QUARTERLY STATISTICAL RETURN

Dear Sir/Madam

As a holder of a Public Service Vehicle licence, you are Statutorily required under Section 157 of the Road Traffic Act 1960 to submit a Quarterly Statistical return to the Department of the Environment covering details of your Public Service Vehicle Operations during the Preceding Quarter. I would be grateful if you will complete the appropriate part of the Form and return it to me as soon as possible in the enclosed pre-paid envelope while retaining the other part for your own records.

The notes overleaf should be carefully studied before completing the return. If you have any query regarding the completion of the form you should contact Mrs A MacDougall at the above address by letter or telephone. Tel. 0442 2561 extn. 314 or 239.

Your cooperation on this matter is appreciated.

Yours faithfully

G. PENRICE
Director of Statistics

Stats 31

Appendix B 69

Please keep this copy

Road Traffic Act 1960 — Section 157

PUBLIC SERVICE VEHICLES
QUARTERLY STATISTICAL RETURN

(exclusive of Tramcars and Trolleybuses)

Section 157—(1) It shall be the duty of a person carrying on the business of operating public service vehicles to keep such accounts and records in relation thereto and to make to the Minister such financial and statistical returns, and in such manner and at such times, as the Minister may from time to time require.

(2) If a person fails to comply with the requirements of the foregoing subsection, he shall be liable on summary conviction to a fine not exceeding twenty pounds, and in the case of a continuing offence is a fine not exceeding five pounds for every day during which the offence continues.

Return for Three Months Ended ....

To be completed and returned by the end of the month following the end of the quarter.

Name and address of person(s) ....
carrying on the business
(See Note 1)

....

PLEASE READ THE NOTES CAREFULLY

....

Telephone No. ....

Section 1 — Vehicles *(See Notes 2 & 3)*

(i) Number of vehicles for which you held public service vehicle licences at the end of the quarter.

....

(ii) Number of above public service vehicles for which you held excise licences at the end of the quarter.

....

Section 2 — Traffic During the Quarter *(See Notes 4 to 8)*

(i) Number of passengers carried. ....

(ii) Number of vehicle miles run. ....

(iii) Receipts (to nearest pound) from passengers. £ ....

DECLARATION

I hereby certify that to the best of my knowledge and belief the information given above is true and correct, and has been compiled in accordance with the explanatory notes.

Signed ....
(See Note 1)

Date .... Status ....

Notes on Completion of Return

GENERAL

1. The quarters in respect of which returns should be rendered are those ending on 31st March, 30th June, 30th September. Insert the appropriate date and below it give the trade name, if any, of the business and the full names of the person(s) owning it. The return should be signed by the owner, or in the case of a partnership by one of the partners, or in the case of a body corporate (such as a local authority, statutory company, or limited liability company) by a duly authorised person. The status of the person signing should be shown below his signature.

SECTION 1 VEHICLES

2. The entries in this section should relate to the last day of the quarter, and should cover all vehicles for which you held public service vehicle licences, whether owned, being acquired by hire purchase or on hire to another operator. Exclude any vehicles which you operated for which public service vehicle licences were not held.

3. The entry in (ii) should relate to those of the vehicles recorded in (i) which were licensed under the Vehicles (Excise) Act, 1949, at the end of the quarter.

SECTION 2 TRAFFIC

4. The information to be shown in this Section should relate to all vehicles operated by the person carrying on the business, whether owned, being acquired by hire purchase, or on hire from another undertaking, but should exclude work done by vehicles while on hire to other operators. Where it is uncertain which of the two operators is to be considered the operator of a hired vehicle the two persons concerned should arrange between themselves which of them should include details of the trip. Exclude the work of taxis and private hire cars (vehicles seating less than eight passengers) unless it was performed under a road service licence. For work in connection with foreign tours include only figures for that part of the journey within Great Britain.

5. If no work has been carried out by the vehicles shown in Section I, or the vehicles have been hired out to another person during the whole of the quarter, the words "not operated" or "vehicles hired out", whichever applies, should be inserted in Section II.

6. Passengers carried.—Children are to be counted as full passengers. A passenger who was issued with a return ticket for a round trip (out and home) should be reckoned as two passengers, as should a passenger carried out and home on contract or private hire. A passenger to whom a monthly ticket was issued should be reckoned as fifty passengers, and a passenger to whom a ticket for a period longer than a month was issued should be reckoned at the rate if fifty passengers per month. Each passenger travelling to or from a port or airport in Great Britain should be counted as one passenger.

7. Vehicle miles run:— Give the aggregate number of vehicle miles (both loaded and empty) run during the hours the vehicles are in service for the purposes of conveying passengers. Only vehicle miles run in Great Britain should be included.

8. Receipts from passengers:—Give the gross amounts paid by or in respect of the passengers accounted for in (i) (including commission paid to booking agents), but exclude amounts for meals, hotel accommodation, etc., and any commission to booking agents for such items. For foreign tours work include only a sum representing the charge for the part of the journey (excluding accommodation), taking place within Great Britain, if necessary on an estimated basis. Exclude receipts from parcels, mails, luggage, dogs etc.

Appendix B

Form Stats 31   Ministry Ref. No. ....

Road Traffic Act 1960 – Section 157

PUBLIC SERVICE VEHICLES
QUARTERLY STATISTICAL RETURN

(exclusive of Tramcars and Trolleybuses)

Section 157—(1) It shall be the duty of a person carrying on the business of operating public service vehicles to keep such accounts and records in relation thereto and to make to the Minister such financial and statistical returns, and in such manner and at such times, as the Minister may from time to time require.

(2) If a person fails to comply with the requirements of the foregoing subsection, he shall be liable on summary conviction to a fine not exceeding twenty pounds, and in the case of a continuing offence to a fine not exceeding five pounds for every day during which the offence continues.

Return for Three Months Ended ....
To be completed and returned by the end of the month following the end of the quarter.

Name and address of person(s) ....
carrying on the business
(See Note 1)   ....

PLEASE READ
THE NOTES
CAREFULLY   Telephone No. ....

Section 1 – Vehicles *(See Notes 2 & 3)*

    (i) Number of vehicles for which you held public service vehicle licences at the end of the quarter.   ....

    (ii) Number of above public service vehicles for which you held excise licences at the end of the quarter.   ....

Section 2 – Traffic During the Quarter *(See Notes 4 to 8)*

    (i) Number of passengers carried.   ....

    (ii) Number of vehicle miles run.   ....

    (iii) Receipts (to nearest pound) from passengers. £...

DECLARATION

I hereby certify that to the best of my knowledge and belief the information given above is true and correct, and has been compiled in accordance with the explanatory notes.

For Office Use Only
Carded ....
Ent. ....
Chk. ....

Signed ....
(See Note 1)

Date ....   Status ....

72   Road Passenger Transport

Telephone enquiries—
Waterloo 7999 Extn. 2619

Ministry of Transport,
Statistics Division,
St. Christopher House,
London, S.E.1.

Sir,

Public Service Vehicles—Annual Financial and Statistical Return

I am directed by the Minister of Transport to inform you that by virtue of the powers under Section 157 of the Road Traffic Act, 1960, you are required, as a person carrying on the business of operating public service vehicles, to complete this form in respect of your financial year which ended .... It should be returned to this address as soon as possible but in any case not later than ....

The return will be treated as confidential as explained in paragraph 2 of the notes.

You should read the notes overleaf before completing the form; if you have any difficulty in completing it enquiries may be made by letter, or by telephone to the number and extension given above.

May I ask for your co-operation in completing your return as soon as possible? It should be completed as soon as figures are available without waiting for your annual accounts to be audited; if in any section you cannot give precise figures you should give the best estimate you can.

I am, Sir,

Your obedient Servant,

A. H. Watson,

Chief Statistician

ANNUAL FINANCIAL AND STATISTICAL RETURN TO BE MADE PURSUANT TO SECTION 157 OF THE ROAD TRAFFIC ACT, 1960

Section 157—(1) *It shall be the duty of a person carrying on the business of operating public service vehicles to keep such accounts and records in relation thereto and to make to the Minister such financial and statistical returns, and in such manner and at such times, as the Minister may from time to time require.*

(2) *If a person fails to comply with the requirements of the foregoing subsection, he shall be liable on summary conviction to a fine not exceeding twenty pounds, and in the case of a continuing offence to a fine not exceeding five pounds for every day during which the offence continues.*

Name and address of
person carrying on
the business (Note 1)
(BLOCK LETTERS)

Telephone No. ....

Financial year ended .... 196......

Declaration (see note 1)

I hereby certify that to the best of my knowledge and belief the information given above and overleaf is true and correct, *and has been compiled in accordance with the explanatory notes.*

Signed ....   Date ....

Status in business ....

(1)

Appendix B 73

PUBLIC SERVICE VEHICLES
ANNUAL FINANCIAL AND STATISTICAL RETURN

SECTION I. TRAFFIC

1. State the number of vehicles for which you held public service vehicle licences at the end of the period (note 3)

2. State the total number of passengers carried and vehicle miles run during the year under each type of service (notes 4, 5, and 6) :—

	Passengers	Vehicle miles
Services operated under road service licences		
(a) Stage		
(b) Express		
(c) Excursions and tours		
Services not operated under road service licences		
(d) Contract and private hire work		
TOTAL		

SECTION II. REVENUE ACCOUNT (Note 7)

3. RECEIPTS :   £
   (a) From traffic (note 8) :
      (i) Passengers
         Services operated under road service licences : Stage ...
         Express ...
         Excursions and Tours ...
         Services not operated under road service licences : Contract (to include private hire work)
      (ii) Parcels, mails, luggage, dogs, etc. ...
   (b) From advertising on vehicles, and miscellaneous ...
   (c) From other operators for hire of vehicles...

   Total Receipts ... ...£

4. EXPENDITURE :
   (a) Gross wages of drivers and conductors (including employers share of national insurance contributions) ...
   (b) Fuel excluding lubricating oil ...
   (c) Provision for renewals and depreciation (note 9) :
      (i) Vehicles ...
      (ii) Other assets ...
   (d) (*Local Authorities only*). Provision for redemption of debt (note 10) :
      (i) Vehicles ...
      (ii) Other assets ...
   (e) Other expenditure
      (i) Gross wages and salaries of staff other than those included under 4(a) (note 11)
      (ii) Local authority rates ...
      (iii) Amounts paid out for repairs and maintenance and cost of tyres, spare parts and lubricating oil (note 12) ...
      (iv) Motor vehicle insurance (note 13) ...
      (v) Other (note 14) ...

   Total Expenditure ... ...£

5. DIFFERENCE BETWEEN TOTAL RECEIPTS AND TOTAL EXPENDITURE ...

6. Add or deduct BALANCE OF RECEIPTS OR PAYMENTS UNDER THROUGH AND/OR INTER-OPERATION AGREEMENTS (Note 15) ...

   NET RECEIPTS ... ...£

Stats 33 (For office use only. Cdd. _____ Ckd. _____)

(2)

NOTES ON COMPLETION OF THE RETURN

GENERAL

(1) Give on page 1 the trade name, if any, of the business and the full name of the person(s) owning it. The declaration should be signed by the owner or by a duly authorised person.

(2) All the information you give will be treated as strictly confidential ; the results of this annual inquiry are prepared and published in a way which does not reveal particulars relating to any individual undertaking.

SECTION I. TRAFFIC

(3) The number of vehicles for which you hold public service vehicle licences should include all vehicles which are owned by you (or being acquired by hire purchase) even though they may be on hire to other operators.

(4) The figures of passengers and vehicle miles should relate to all vehicles operated by the undertaking making the return, whether owned or on hire from another undertaking ; they should exclude details of work done by vehicles on hire to other operators. The work of taxis and private hire cars (vehicles seating less than 8 passengers) should also be excluded unless performed under a road service licence. For work in connection with foreign tours only figures for that part of the journey within Great Britain should be included.

(5) Children should be counted as full passengers and a passenger who was issued with a return ticket or a ticket for a round trip, or who was carried out and home on contract or private hire should be reckoned as two passengers. In the case of season ticket holders a weekly ticket should be reckoned as 12 passengers and tickets of a month or longer should be reckoned as 50 passengers per month.

(6) The number of vehicle miles run should include those run during the time the vehicles are in service for the purpose of conveying passengers whether the vehicles are loaded or empty.

SECTION II. REVENUE ACCOUNT

(7) Only figures relating to the operation of public service vehicles should be entered in this return. Operators engaged in other businesses in addition to the operation of public service vehicles should divide their receipts and expenditure between public service vehicles and the other businesses, as far as possible on an actual basis. In cases where this cannot be done the proportion applicable to public service vehicles should be estimated. Receipts and expenditure for meals, hotel accommodation and similar items for passengers, and, in the case of foreign tours, for that portion of journeys made outside Great Britain should be excluded from the return.

(8) The gross receipts from the operation of services by vehicles owned or hired to the operator should be shown against the appropriate type of service under item 3(*a*)(i). Amounts received by the operator in respect of vehicles hired to other operators should be included in item 3(*c*).

(9) The amount set aside for renewals or depreciation during the year should be shown against the appropriate sub-head of item 4(*c*).

(10) Interest and contributions to capital expenditure should be excluded from item 4(*d*).

(11) Include in item 4(*e*)(i) wages and salaries paid to operating, maintenance and administrative staff. Reasonable remuneration for directors working in the business may also be included but directors' fees should not be included in this return. Superannuation contributions should be included in this item.

(12) Only amounts **paid out** in respect of repairs and maintenance should be included in item 4(*e*)(iii) ; the cost of maintenance and repair work done by the operators' own staff should be excluded. All purchases of tyres and spare parts should be included, also any payments made under contract in respect of tyre maintenance.

(13) The amount shown under 4(*e*)(iv) should relate to motor vehicle insurance only ; all other insurances relating to the business, including fire, burglary, employers' liability, etc., should be included in item 4(*e*)(v).

(14) Show in item 4(*e*)(v) all expenditure not already included in items 4(*a*) to 4(*e*)(iv), including commission to booking agents, but excluding interest payments, contributions to capital expenditure, and income and profits tax payments.

(15) Item 6 applies only to those operators who are parties to through and/or inter-operation agreements, and should be the balance (plus or minus) of the receipts from and payments to the other parties.

ANNUAL FINANCIAL AND STATISTICAL RETURN TO BE MADE PURSUANT TO SECTION 157 OF THE ROAD TRAFFIC ACT, 1960

Section 157—(1) *It shall be the duty of a person carrying on the business of operating public service vehicles to keep such accounts and records in relation thereto and to make to the Minister such financial and statistical returns, and in such manner and at such times, as the Minister may from time to time require.*

(2) If a person fails to comply with the requirements of the foregoing subsection, he shall be liable on summary conviction to a fine not exceeding twenty pounds, and in the case of a continuing offence to a fine not exceeding five pounds for every day during which the offence continues.

Name and address of person carrying on the business (Note 1) (BLOCK LETTERS) ....

Telephone No. ....

Financial year ended .... 196......

Declaration (see note 1)

I hereby certify that to the best of my knowledge and belief the information given above and overleaf is true and correct, *and has been compiled in accordance with the explanatory notes.*

Signed .... Date ....

Status in business ....

Appendix B 75

PUBLIC SERVICE VEHICLES
ANNUAL FINANCIAL AND STATISTICAL RETURN
Duplicate—To be Retained by Operator

SECTION I. TRAFFIC

1. State the number of vehicles for which you held public service vehicle licences at the end of the period (note 3)

2. State the total number of passengers carried and vehicle miles run during the year under each type of service (notes 4, 5, and 6) :—

	Passengers	Vehicle miles
Services operated under road service licences		
(a) Stage		
(b) Express		
(c) Excursions and tours		
Services not operated under road service licences		
(d) Contract and private hire work		
TOTAL		

SECTION II. REVENUE ACCOUNT (Note 7)

3. RECEIPTS : £
   - (a) From traffic (note 8) :
     - (i) Passengers
       - Services operated under road service licences : Stage ... ...
       - Express ... ...
       - Excursions and Tours ... ...
       - Services not operated under road service licences : Contract (to include private hire work)
     - (ii) Parcels, mails, luggage, dogs, etc. ... ...
   - (b) From advertising on vehicles, and miscellaneous ... ...
   - (c) From other operators for hire of vehicles... ... ...
   - Total Receipts ... ...£

4. EXPENDITURE :
   - (a) Gross wages of drivers and conductors (including employers share of national insurance contributions) ... ...
   - (b) Fuel excluding lubricating oil ... ...
   - (c) Provision for renewals and depreciation (note 9) :
     - (i) Vehicles ... ...
     - (ii) Other assets ... ...
   - (d) (*Local Authorities only*). Provision for redemption of debt (note 10) :
     - (i) Vehicles ... ...
     - (ii) Other assets ... ...
   - (e) Other expenditure
     - (i) Gross wages and salaries of staff other than those included under 4(a) (note 11)
     - (ii) Local authority rates ... ...
     - (iii) Amounts paid out for repairs and maintenance and cost of tyres, spare parts and lubricating oil (note 12) ... ...
     - (iv) Motor vehicle insurance (note 13) ... ...
     - (v) Other (note 14) ... ...
   - Total Expenditure ... ...£

5. DIFFERENCE BETWEEN TOTAL RECEIPTS AND TOTAL EXPENDITURE ... ...

6. Add or deduct BALANCE OF RECEIPTS OR PAYMENTS UNDER THROUGH AND/OR INTER-OPERATION AGREEMENTS (Note 15) ... ...

NET RECEIPTS ... ...£

Stats 33.

Road Passenger Transport

OPCS
Social Survey Division

HOUSEHOLD SCHEDULE

NATIONAL TRAVEL SURVEY

S 494

INTERVIEWERS' NAME .... AUTH NO. ....

Recording period started:

Date [Day][Month]

Sampling Area code [ ][ ] Serial number [ ][ ] H/H number [ ]

Day of week on which recording started
RING: Sun Mon Tue Wed Thu Fri Sat
        1   2   3   4   5   6   7

Date of H/H interview [Day][Month]

HOUSEHOLD COMPOSITION

Per. No.	Relationship to HOH	Off use	H/W	Sex M / F	Age last birth-day	Marital Status M / S / Wid Sep Div	Working Status *F / 10+ to 30 / Up to incl 10 / N
1	HOH	O	1	1 2		1 2 3	1 2 3 4
2			1	1 2		1 2 3	1 2 3 4
3			1	1 2		1 2 3	1 2 3 4
4			1	1 2		1 2 3	1 2 3 4
5			1	1 2		1 2 3	1 2 3 4
6			1	1 2		1 2 3	1 2 3 4
7			1	1 2		1 2 3	1 2 3 4
8			1	1 2		1 2 3	1 2 3 4
9			1	1 2		1 2 3	1 2 3 4
10			1	1 2		1 2 3	1 2 3 4
off use					off use		

SPECIMEN

PLACING INTERVIEW - GO TO Q.1

PERSON NOS OF THOSE SEEN AT PLACING CALL(S)(AGED 11+) [ ][ ][ ]

COMPLETE AFTER COLLECTION INTERVIEW
complete (a) and (b) for all household members except children under 3
complete (c) for all main drivers

Per. No	(a) Completed Record Book		(b) Individual Schedule			Inft is main driver	(c) Motor Vehicle Schedule — Enter vehicle number in line with main driver	
	Achieved	Not* achieved	Achieved	Not* achieved	DNA under 16		Achieved Vhls	Not achieved*Vhls
1	1	3	1	2	3	1		
	1	3	1	2	3	1		
	1	3	1	2	3	1		
	1	3	1	2	3	1		
	1	3	1	2	3	1		
	1	3	1	2	3	1		
	1	3	1	2	3	1		

*WHEN SCHEDULES CODED "NOT ACHIEVED" FULL DETAILS SHOULD BE RECORDED ON THE "CALLS AND CONTACT" SHEET, <u>NOT</u> ON THE INTERVIEW SCHEDULES.

Appendix C 77

ASK Q.1 AT PLACING INTERVIEW

SHOW PROMPT CARD A

1(a) Would you look at this card and tell me if anyone in the household owns or has the regular use of any of these types of vehicle?

(b) Is anyone in the household likely to own or have the regular use of any of these types of vehicle before (end of recording period)?

	1(a)	1(b)

"REGULAR" MEANS FOR DURATION OF RECORDING PERIOD AT LEAST

ENTER NUMBER OF VEHICLES IN LINE WITH TYPE

Cars (including estate and 3-wheelers)
Motorcycle with sidecar attachment
Motorcycles, scooters, mo-peds
Vans, lorries etc
Other
(specify) ....

ENTER TOTAL MOTOR VEHICLES ⟶

NO MOTOR VEHICLES   0   0

                                             ask (i)

ENTER TOTAL NUMBER OF BICYCLES ⟶

NO BICYCLES   0   0

(i) Who uses the bicycles?

ENTER PERSON NUMBERS ⟶

MOTOR VEHICLE SUMMARY

VEHICLE NO.					
PERSON NO. OF MAIN DRIVER					
INT. USE					

ASK AT PLACING OR COLLECTION INTERVIEW TO HOH ONLY WHEN THERE IS NO MOTOR VEHICLE IN THE HOUSEHOLD, AND HOH IS UNDER 65, OR IF HOH 65+ ASK OLDEST MALE/FEMALE IN NEXT GENERATION AGED 16-64.

2. Is there any particular reason why you don't have a motor vehicle?

No/None 0

THIS QUESTION ANSWERED BY (PERSON NO.) ⟶

DNA AT LEAST ONE MOTOR VEHICLE IN THE HOUSEHOLD/HOH 65 OR OVER/NO INFORMANT 16-64 IN NEXT GENERATION 1
QN ASKED AT PLACING INTERVIEW 2
QN ASKED AT COLLECTION INTERVIEW 3
QN APPLIES BUT NOT ASKED BECAUSE HOH DID NOT CO-OPERATE/NOT AVAILABLE/OTHER INFORMANT NOT AVAILABLE/DID NOT CO-OPERATE 4

Road Passenger Transport

NATIONAL TRAVEL SURVEY   S 494

8/72   INDIVIDUAL SCHEDULE

Interview carried out:
    at placing call 1
    at collection call .. 2

           Area   Serial   Hld   Person

ASK ALL AGED 16 AND OVER

1. Do you hold a driving licence at present?   Yes .... 1 ask(a)&(b)
                                                      No .... 2 go to Q2

    (a) What type of vehicle is covered by your licence?
        PROMPT AS NECESSARY AND
        CODE ALL THAT APPLY IN COL (a)

FOR EACH CODE 1 RINGED AT (a) ASK

    (b) Is the licence for that type of vehicle full or provisional?

	(a)	(b) Full	(b) Prov
Car	1	2	3
Motor Cycle	1	2	3
Any other vhl	1	2	3

        CODE IN COL (b)

IF FULL LICENCE HELD (CODE 2 AT (b)) ASK

    (c) How long have you held a full licence for any motor vehicle?
          Less than 1 year .... 0 ⎫ go to
          1–5 years (ENTER NUMBER) .....   ⎬ Q3
          6 or more years .... 6 ⎭

2. Did you ever hold a full driving licence?   Yes .... 1 ask (a)
    IF YES   No .... 2 go to Q3

    (a) When did you give it up? ENTER YEAR ....

3. Do you (or any of your children) hold a current season ticket for any form of transport?   Yes .... 1 ask(a-h)
                                                            No .... 2 go to Q4

ENTER DETAILS OF SEASON TICKET(S) HELD BY INFORMANT (AND CHILDREN IF APPLICABLE) AT (a)-(f) IN GRID BELOW, THEN ASK (g-h) FOR EACH TICKET

Ticket	a) Per No.	b) Mode of transport	c) Ticket from	d) Ticket to	e) Full price paid £ p	f) Period covered
1						
2						
3						

    (g) Did anyone outside the household pay anything towards the cost of this ticket?
        CODE IN BOX BELOW
        IF 'YES' OBTAIN AND ENTER DETAILS OF WHO PAID AND AMOUNT

    (h) How many journeys do you (does ....) normally make each week on this season ticket? RECORD BELOW, AS SINGLE JOURNEYS

Ticket	g) Anyone outside household pay? No	g) Anyone outside household pay? Yes	IF YES, DETAILS OF SUBSIDY Who paid	IF YES, DETAILS OF SUBSIDY Amount of subs £ p	h) No. of single journeys normally made in week (ENTER NO. OR RANGE)
1	1	2			
2	1	2			
3	1	2			

Appendix C 79

4. DNA - Informant not able to use public transport
       because of disability, age, etc. .... 1 go to Q7
    (FROM OBSERVATION; OR INFORMATION VOLUNTEERED BY INFORMANT; OR
    BACK CODED FROM (a) BELOW)

RING ONE CODE ONLY
IN EACH COLUMN

(a) How long does it take you to walk from your home to your <u>nearest</u> bus stop?

(b) How long would it take you to walk from your home to your <u>nearest</u> operating railway (or tube) station?
    IF 7 MINS OR OVER AT (b)
    (4-7 or 8) ASK (c)

(c) How long - on average - would/does it take you to travel from your home to ...(station) if you used public transport to get there?

    INCLUDE ALL WAITING TIME ETC.

Time taken	(a)	(b)	(c)
Less than 2 mins	1	1	1
2 - 3	2	2	2
4 - 6	3	3	3
7 - 13	4	4	4
14 - 26	5	5	5
27 - 43	6	6	6
44 or longer	7	7	7
Don't know	8	8	8
Not possible to get to the station by public transport	-	-	9
No bus service	9	-	-
No train service	-	9	-

IF ABSOLUTELY NO SERVICE: BUS - RING CODE 6 AT 5(a) AND ASK 5(c)
                           TRAIN - RING CODE 6 AT 6(a) AND ASK 6(c)

2

I should like to ask you something about your views on public transport in this locality. How good do you personally find the local services?

5. (a) On the whole, do you think that the local bus services are

RUNNING PROMPT
- very good 1
- fairly good .... 2 } ask (b)
- rather poor 3
- or very poor? 4

SPONTANEOUS ANSWERS
- don't know/never use services 5
- no local bus service .... 6 ask (c)
- qualified answers (SPECIFY) .... 7 ask (b)

(b) In what ways are the local bus services <u>not</u> good?

None 0

IF NO LOCAL BUS SERVICE:
(c) Is there anything you would like to say about this?

6. (a) On the whole, do you think that the local train services are

RUNNING PROMPT
- very good 1
- fairly good .... 2 } ask (b)
- rather poor 3
- or very poor? 4

SPONTANEOUS ANSWERS
- don't know/never use services 5
- no local train service .... 6 ask (c)
- qualified answers (SPECIFY) .... 7 ask (b)

(b) In what ways are the local train services <u>not</u> good?

None 0

IF NO LOCAL TRAIN SERVICE:
(c) Is there anything you would like to say about this?

3

Appendix C

7. Working details

    Full-time work (30+ hours a week) 1
    Part-time work (over 10 up to and including 30 hours a week) 2
    Part-time work (up to and including 10 hours a week) .... 3 } ask (a)&(b)

    Unemployed (either looking for work or would be if not
            temporarily sick) 4
    Retired 5
    Student 6

    Housewife unoccupied 7
    Other not working 8

IF CODED 1 - 5 AT MAIN QUESTION ASK FOR

(a) Occupation: _

              _

(b) Industry: _

            _

TO SELF EMPLOYED OR MANAGERIAL ONLY

(c) Self employed:
           with employees .... 1 ask (i)
           with NO employees 2

    Employed   with supervision of staff .... 3 } ask (i)
    manager   with NO supervision of staff 4

    (i) Number of employees in the establishment ....

EXPLAIN CAREFULLY WHY INCOME DETAILS ARE NEEDED

8. Gross income - from all sources

	Annual £	Weekly £	
	0 - under 500	0 - under 10	1
	500 - " 750	10 - " 15	2
	750 - " 1000	15 - " 20	3
	1000 - " 1250	20 - " 25	4
	1250 - " 1500	25 - " 30	5
	1500 - " 1750	30 - " 35	6
	1750 - " 2000	35 - " 40	7
	2000 - " 2500	40 - " 50	8
	2500 - " 3000	50 - " 60	9
	3000 - " 4000	60 - " 80	10
	4000 - " 5000	80 - " 100	11
	5000 and over	100 and over	12
	Refusal/DK		13

FOR EVERY HOH, CHECK THAT YOU HAVE COMPLETED AN INDIVIDUAL SCHEDULE
       WITH THEM. FAILING THIS, QNS 7 & 8 SHOULD BE COMPLETED
       WITH SOMEONE SUITABLY RELATED TO THEM <u>UNLESS</u> THE HOH
       HAS REFUSED COOPERATION.

       IF QNS 7 & 8 CANNOT BE ASKED AT ALL BECAUSE THE
       HOH REFUSES COOPERATION, RING CODE 0 BELOW.

            Q's 7 & 8 not asked - HOH refused 0

82 Road Passenger Transport

MOTOR VEHICLE SCHEDULE   S 494

TO THE MAIN DRIVER OF A VEHICLE CODED A.
ELIGIBLE AT Q.1 OF HOUSEHOLD SCHEDULE

| Sampling area code | Serial number | H/H No. | V/HL | Main driver Per No |

I understand you own/have the regular use of (vehicle)? IF 'NO' DISCONTINUE
May I check that you are the main driver (EXPLAIN) of this vehicle. IF NOT
MAIN DRIVER CARRY OUT INTERVIEW WITH PERSON WHO IS.

1. What type of motor vehicle is it?
   - Wheel van or lorry 1
   - 4 wheel car: saloon .... 2 ⎫
   -         : estate .... 3 ⎬ ask (a)&(b)
   -         : convertible .... 4 ⎭
   - 3 wheel vehicle 5
   - Scooter/M cycle with sidecar 6
   - Motor cycle 7
   - Scooter 8
   - Moped 9
   - Other (SPECIFY) 0

   IF 4 WHEEL CAR (MAIN CODED 2-4):
   (a) What is the make and model of your car?
   ....
   (b) And when was it first registered?
   ....

2. What is the engine capacity? RECORD IN C.C.'s ....

   IF CAR, VAN OR LORRY (Q.1 CODED 1-5):

3. Does your vehicle have seat belts, including any for a child?
   Yes .... 1 ask (a)-(d)
   No .... 2 go to Q4

   (a) Are any of these belts specially made for children?
   (CHECK THAT THEY ARE ANCHORED TO THE CAR)
   Yes 1
   No 2

   (b) (Including belts for children)
   what types of belt do you have?   Lap only 1
   RUNNING PROMPT   Diagonal only 2
                                       Lap and diagonal 3
   .... or some other type (SPECIFY) 4

   (c) And which seats are fitted with belts (including childrens)?

   (ENTER '0' IF NECESSARY)
   Front Seats Enter No. ——→ ....
   Rear Seats   Enter No. ——→ ....

   (d) Are the belts:

	Yes	No
in one fixed position	1	4
or do the straps recoil to allow the passenger free movement	2	5
or are they some other type? (SPECIFY)	3	6

   INDIVIDUAL PROMPT (INERTIA REEL) — CODE ALL THAT APPLY

Appendix C 83

4. What taxation class is your vehicle?

| IF INFORMANT SAYS BOTH PRIVATE & GOODS CHECK TAX. IF MORE THAN £9.15 4-MONTHLY or £25 ANNUALLY ANSWER IS 'GOODS' |

Private ONLY 1
Goods ONLY 2
Motor cycle/mo-ped 3
Invalid car 4
Hackney Carriage 5
Other (SPECIFY) 6

5. How is the vehicle registered? Is it in the name of yourself or some other person in this household, or is it registered outside this household?

EXPLAIN IF NECESSARY: "NAME ON LOG BOOK"

Registered by this household .... 1 ask (a)
Registered outside this household .... 2 ask (b)

(a) Is the vehicle used for business purposes or in the course of work at all, that is excluding journeys to and from the usual place of work?

Yes .... 1 ask (i)
No .... 2 go to Q6

IF VEHICLE USED IN COURSE OR WORK (PART (a) CODED 1):

(i) On average, how often is it used for business purposes or in the course of work?
....

go to Q6

(b) Is it registered by another private household, by the employer of someone in this household, or by some other body?

PROBE TO FIND OUT IF HIRED OR BORROWED ON SHORT TERM BASIS (i.e. LESS THAN 1 YR) & NOTE ON SCHEDULE

Registered by another private household 1
Registered by employer 2
Other (SPECIFY) 3

2

TO HOUSEHOLDS CONTAINING WORKERS (WORKING STATUS CODED 1, 2 OR 3) ON
HOUSEHOLD SCHEDULE   DNA - No workers in H/H .... 0 go to Q7

6. Does anyone in your household ever use this (vehicle) for journeys
    to and from their usual place of work?
                                            Yes ....1 ask (a)
                                            No ....2 go to (b)

    > DO NOT COUNT IF VEHICLE USED FOR
    > PART OF JOURNEY ONLY

    (a) (i) On average how often is the vehicle used for these
             journeys? Would it be
                                     most days (every day) 1
             RUNNING PROMPT   1-3 days a week 2
                                     or less often? 3

        (ii) Where is the vehicle usually parked while the driver is
             at work? Is it
                                     in the street 1
                                     at the firm's premises or
             RUNNING PROMPT   in the firm's car park etc ......2 ⎫ ask (iii)
                                     in a public car park ....3 ⎬
                                     or somewhere else? (SPECIFY) ....4 ⎭

        (iii) What does it usually cost to park the (vehicle) while the
              driver is at work? (DAILY charge) ....
                                     No charge/nothing 0

    IF NO (MAIN Q CODED 2) AND MAIN DRIVER WORKING
              DNA (Main driver not working/works at home) ....0 go to Q7

    (b) Would it be possible for you to park your (vehicle) at or
        near your usual place of work?
                                                            ask (i)
                                     Yes ....1 & (ii)
                                     No ....2 ⎫
                                     Don't know never tried ..3 ⎬ go to Q7
                                     No usual place of work ..4 ⎭

        (i) Would that be in the
                                     street 1
                                     at the firm's premises or in the
             RUNNING   firm's car park etc ....2 ⎫ ask (ii)
             PROMPT   in a public car park ....3 ⎬
                                     or somewhere else? (SPECIFY) ....4 ⎭

        (ii) What do you think it would cost you to park your
             (vehicle) there while you were at work? (DAILY CHARGE) ...
                                     No charge/nothing 0

7. Where do you usually keep your (vehicle) at night?
                                     In garage/covered carport 1
                                     Uncovered parking space on own premises ...2
                                     In the street 3
                                     Other (SPECIFY) 4

    > AT NIGHT EQUALS
    > WHEN INFORMANT
    > SLEEPS FOR
    > SHIFTWORKERS

Appendix C 85

	DNA (Vehicle hired or borrowed on short term basis) ...	0 go to Q.10

8. (a) What is the annual mileage of the vehicle? RECORD (ESTIMATE) FOR VEHICLES WHICH HAVE BEEN IN THE HOUSEHOLD LESS THAN ONE YEAR ASK: What do you think the annual mileage of the vehicle will be? RECORD

   ....

   ....

   (b) Could I just check, is all this mileage private driving (that is including any journeys to or from the usual place of work), or is <u>any</u> of the driving done for business purposes, or in the course of work?

   All PRIVATE mileage ....1 ⎫ go to Q.9
   All BUSINESS/COURSE OF WORK mileage ....2 ⎬
   Includes BUSINESS/COURSE OF WORK AND PRIVATE MILEAGE 3   ask (i) then Q9

   (i) Approximately how much of the annual mileage is business (or course of work) mileage? (NEAREST ESTIMATE) ....

9. Do you or anyone else in the household receive any payment from an employer, or any tax concession which reduces your total motoring costs for (this particular vehicle) such as:

		YES	NO
	Mileage expenses based on the number of miles covered ..	1 ask(a)	2
	A fixed payment made at periodic intervals	1 ask(b)	2
INDIVIDUAL	Free petrol (payments for petrol refunded)	1	2
PROMPT	Road tax and insurance	1	2
	The whole of the initial cost of the vehicle	1 ask(c)	2
	or part of the initial cost of the vehicle	1	2
	Bills for servicing and repairs paid....................	1	2
	(SELF-EMPLOYED INFORMANT) tax relief allowed	1	2
	Any other payment (SPECIFY)	1	2

IF MILEAGE EXPENSES RECEIVED
(a) You told me that mileage expenses are paid in respect of this vehicle. What rates are paid? FOR EACH RATE: How much of the annual mileage (AS AT Q8(a)) is paid for at this rate?

	Rate		
	......p a mile	......p a mile	......p a mile
Up to 25%	1	1	1
26 - 50%	2	2	2
51 - 75%	3	3	3
76 - 100%	4	4	4
MORE PRECISE EST. IF POSS-IBLE			

ENTER ⟶

IF FIXED PAYMENT RECEIVED
(b) What payment do you receive? ENTER AMOUNT ...
                                   AND PERIOD ....

IF WHOLE INITIAL COST PAID
(c) Does your employer actually own the (vehicle) or do you own it yourself?

Employer owns 1
Informant owns . ..2

DNA (this schedule being asked at collection interview) ..0 go to Q.11

10. Has the vehicle a mileometer in working order?

MILEOMETER WORKING 1
MILEOMETER NOT WORKING <u>OR</u>
NO MILEOMETER 2
COMPLETE REMAINDER OF SCHEDULE AT COLLECTION INTERVIEW

86 Road Passenger Transport

COMPLETE THIS PAGE AT COLLECTION INTERVIEW

FROM MAIN DRIVERS'
BOOK, ENTER
READINGS FROM ──────▶ END OF RCDG P'D ....
                          AND START OF RCDG P'D ....

ENTER DIFFERENCE (TOTAL MILEAGE DONE DURING RECORDING PERIOD ──────▶
(IF NO MILEOMETER READING ENTER ESTIMATED MILEAGE)
....
None ....0 go to Q13

11. I see that ... miles were done in this (vehicle) during the week you kept the record. Did anyone other than yourself drive the vehicle during that week?
    Yes ....1 ask (a)
    No ....2 go to Q12

    (a) Who drove the vehicle?
        Other driver(s) within household (Enter P. No's)   ask (i)

        Non household drivers ....0 ask (i) & (ii)

    (i) How many of these miles were done in all by:
        PROMPT AS NECESSARY
        Drivers from your household (other than yourself)
        RECORD ──────────────────────▶   ....
        Drivers from outside of household RECORD ──────▶ ....

    (ii) Were any of these miles done when the car was being serviced or repaired; or MOT tested? (or when it was being driven to the garage etc. for this purpose)
        Yes .....1 ask (A)
        No ......2 go to Q12

        (A) About how many miles were driven for these purposes? ──▶ ....go to Q12

12. Was any mileage done in the vehicle (solely) for the purpose of delivering goods?
    Yes ....1 ask (a)
    No ....2 go to Q14

    (a) About how many miles were driven for this purpose? ──────▶ ....go to Q14

                                    TOTAL MILEAGE of use

13. Why was the vehicle not used during the week you kept the record?

    DO NOT PROMPT.
    CODE ALL THAT
    APPLY

    vehicle under repair/servicing 1
    driver sick/on holiday 2
    driver disqualified 3
    No occasion to use vehicle 4
    Other (SPECIFY) 5

    (a) Was the vehicle taxed during the week you kept the record?
        Yes 1
        No 2

14. CHECK YOU HAVE COMPLETED EITHER THE INDIVIDUAL SCHEDULE WITH THE HOH, OR FAILING THIS, PAGE 4 OF THE INDIVIDUAL SCHEDULE WITH SOMEONE IN SUITABLE RELATIONSHIP, UNLESS THE HOH HAS REFUSED CO-OPERATION.

Appendix C   87

NATIONAL TRAVEL SURVEY

Ref. no. ☐☐☐☐
Area

☐☐
Serial

☐
H

☐
P

IN CONFIDENCE

All the particulars you give on this form will be treated in STRICT CONFIDENCE. Please do not put your name and address on it.

SPECIMEN

OPCS, Social Survey Division
Atlantic House
Holborn Viaduct
London EC1 N 2PD

RECORD OF JOURNEYS

DON'T include short walks (under 1 mile).*

DON'T include journeys you make as driver, pilot, etc., of a passenger or goods vehicle.

*Except on last day (see separate instruction sheet).

DRIVERS only:

Mileometer reading at START of recording period ....

Mileometer reading at END of recording period ....

HOW TO FILL UP THIS BOOKLET

PART 1   Should be filled in for all journeys (except walks of less than 1 mile).

PART 2   Should be filled in for stages of a journey made by PUBLIC TRANSPORT only (e.g. RAIL, BUS, TAXI, etc.). Include any journeys made as a passenger in a firm's or school bus.

PART 3   Should be filled in for stages of a journey made by a PRIVATE MOTOR VEHICLE only (that is, a car or other motor vehicle belonging or available throughout the recording week to a private person (who may or may not be a member of your household)).

WALKING and BICYCLE journeys need only be recorded in PART 1.

NOTES ON THE QUESTIONS

PART 1

Purpose of journey: Just a short description will do. A few examples are: "To go shopping", "To visit friends", "To go to work", "To take child to school", "To have a drink at the pub", etc.

How did you travel: Enter the means of travel, e.g. Bus, Train, Bicycle, Walked, Taxi, etc.

If the journey involved more than one way of travelling, then enter on the first line how you travelled for the first part of the journey (that is, the first stage). Then on the second line write your means of travel for the next stage (part) of the journey, and so on until you have recorded all the different stages of your journey.

Number of miles covered: For each stage of the journey, enter the number of miles covered.

If you do not know the exact distance, please put down an approximate figure.

Appendix C   89

NOTES ON THE QUESTIONS (continued from previous page)

PART 2

Cost of your own ticket (fare): Write what it cost for your ticket alone. If the journey was by taxi divide the total cost, excluding any tip, equally among the people travelling in it. If you bought a return, put down the full cost both times.

PART 3

Were you in a vehicle from your own household: Answer "Yes" if the vehicle was owned by someone in your household, or if it was available to them for the whole week. Otherwise answer "No".

PLEASE WRITE ONLY ON THE DOTTED LINES. DON'T WRITE IN THE BLANK COLUMNS.

An example showing how to enter journey details:

FOR ALL JOURNEYS	S T A G E	PART 1 — ALL STAGES		PART 2 — For stages made by PUBLIC TRANSPORT			PART 3 — For stages made by PRIVATE MOTOR VEHICLE		
What was the purpose of the journey?		How did you travel? (Was it by bus, train, car, etc.)	How far did you travel? (Number of miles)	What was the cost of your own ticket or fare?	Was it a single or return ticket? (Write in 'Single', 'Return', 'Season', etc.)	Did you, or your firm, or someone else pay for the ticket? (Write in 'Self' or 'Other')	Were you in a vehicle from your own household? (Write in 'Yes' or 'No')	Were you the DRIVER or a PASSENGER? (Write in 'Driver' or 'Passenger')	DRIVERS only: How many people were in the vehicle?
JOURNEY 1 To go to work	1	Friend's Car	2½				No	Passenger	
	2	British Rail	11	42p	Return	Self			
	3								
	4								
	5								
JOURNEY 2 To return home from work	1	British Rail	11	42p	Return	Self			
	2	Bus	2	5p	Single	Other			
	3								
	4								

RECORD OF JOURNEYS MADE ON THE FIRST DAY   DAY OF WEEK.............. DATE..............

FOR ALL JOURNEYS	STAGE	PART 1 — ALL STAGES		PART 2 — For stages made by PUBLIC TRANSPORT			PART 3 — For stages made by PRIVATE MOTOR VEHICLE		DRIVERS only
What was the purpose of the journey?		How did you travel? *(Was it by bus, train, car, etc.)*	How far did you travel? *(Number of miles)*	What was the cost of your own ticket or fare?	Was it a single or return ticket? *(Write in 'Single', 'Return', 'Season, etc.)*	Did you, or your firm, or someone else pay for the ticket? *(Write in 'Self' or 'Other')*	Were you in a vehicle from your household? *(Write in 'Yes' or 'No')*	Were you the DRIVER or a PASSENGER? *(Write in 'Driver' or 'Passenger')*	How many people were in the vehicle?
JOURNEY 1	1								
	2								
	3								
	4								
	5								
JOURNEY 2	1								
	2								
	3								
	4								
	5								
JOURNEY 3	1								
	2								
	3								
	4								
	5								
JOURNEY 4	1								
	2								
	3								
	4								
	5								

SPECIMEN

Appendix C 91

RECORD OF JOURNEYS MADE ON THE FIRST DAY   DAY OF WEEK............ DATE............

FOR ALL JOURNEYS	STAGE	PART 1 — ALL STAGES		PART 2 — For stages made by PUBLIC TRANSPORT			PART 3 — For stages made by PRIVATE MOTOR VEHICLE		
What was the purpose of the journey?		How did you travel? *(Was it by bus, train, car, etc.)*	How far did you travel? *(Number of miles)*	What was the cost of your own ticket or fare?	Was it a single or return ticket? *(Write in 'Single', 'Return', 'Season', etc.)*	Did you, or your firm, or someone else pay for the ticket? *(Write in 'Self' or 'Other')*	Were you in a vehicle from your household? *(Write in 'Yes' or 'No')*	Were you the DRIVER or a PASSENGER? *(Write in 'Driver' or 'Passenger')*	DRIVERS only: How many people were in the vehicle?
JOURNEY 5	1								
	2								
	3								
	4								
	5								
JOURNEY 6	1								
	2								
	3								
	4								
	5								
JOURNEY 7	1								
	2								
	3								
	4								
	5								
JOURNEY 8	1								
	2								
	3								
	4								
	5								

SPECIMEN

RECORD OF JOURNEYS MADE ON THE SECOND DAY

DAY OF WEEK .... DATE ....

FOR ALL JOURNEYS	STAGE	PART 1 — ALL STAGES		PART 2 — For stages made by PUBLIC TRANSPORT		PART 3 — For stages made by PRIVATE MOTOR VEHICLE		DRIVERS only:
What was the purpose of the journey?		How did you travel? *(Was it by bus, train, car, etc.)*	How far did you travel? *(Number of miles)*	What was the cost of your own ticket or fare?	Was it a single or return ticket? *(Write in 'Single', 'Return', 'Season', etc.)*	Did you, or your firm, or someone else pay for the ticket? *(Write in 'Self' or 'Other')*	Were you in a vehicle from your household? *(Write in 'Yes' or 'No')*	Were you the DRIVER or a PASSENGER? *(Write in 'Driver' or 'Passenger')*	How many people were in the vehicle?
JOURNEY 1	1								
	2								
	3								
	4								
	5								
JOURNEY 2	1								
	2								
	3								
	4								
	5								
JOURNEY 3	1								
	2								
	3								
	4								
	5								
JOURNEY 4	1								
	2								
	3								
	4								
	5								

SPECIMEN

Appendix C 93

RECORD OF JOURNEYS MADE ON THE SECOND DAY   DAY OF WEEK.......... DATE..........

FOR ALL JOURNEYS	S T A G E	PART 1 — ALL STAGES		PART 2 — For stages made by PUBLIC TRANSPORT			PART 3 — For stages made by PRIVATE MOTOR VEHICLE		DRIVERS only:
What was the purpose of the journey?		How did you travel? *(Was it by bus, train, car, etc.)*	How far did you travel? *(Number of miles)*	What was the cost of your own ticket or fare?	Was it a single or return ticket? *(Write in 'Single', 'Return', 'Season', etc.)*	Did you, or your firm, or someone else pay for the ticket? *(Write in 'Self' or 'Other')*	Were you in a vehicle from your household? *(Write in 'Yes' or 'No')*	Were you the DRIVER or a PASSENGER? *(Write in 'Driver' or 'Passenger')*	How many people were in the vehicle?

JOURNEY 5: stages 1–5
JOURNEY 6: stages 1–5
JOURNEY 7: stages 1–5
JOURNEY 8: stages 1–5

(SPECIMEN)

RECORD OF JOURNEYS MADE ON THE THIRD DAY

DAY OF WEEK............ DATE............

SPECIMEN

FOR ALL JOURNEYS	STAGE	PART 1 — ALL STAGES			PART 2 — For stages made by PUBLIC TRANSPORT			PART 3 — For stages made by PRIVATE MOTOR VEHICLE		
What was the purpose of the journey?		How did you travel? *(Was it by bus, train, car, etc.)*	How far did you travel? *(Number of miles)*		What was the cost of your own ticket or fare?	Was it a single or return ticket? *(Write in 'Single', 'Return', 'Season', etc.)*	Did you, or your firm, or someone else pay for the ticket? *(Write in 'Self' or 'Other')*	Were you in a vehicle from your household? *(Write in 'Yes' or 'No')*	Were you the DRIVER or a PASSENGER? *(Write in 'Driver' or 'Passenger')*	DRIVERS only: How many people were in the vehicle?
JOURNEY 1	1									
	2									
	3									
	4									
	5									
JOURNEY 2	1									
	2									
	3									
	4									
	5									
JOURNEY 3	1									
	2									
	3									
	4									
	5									
JOURNEY 4	1									
	2									
	3									
	4									
	5									

Appendix C   95

RECORD OF JOURNEYS MADE ON THE THIRD DAY   DAY OF WEEK.............. DATE..............

FOR ALL JOURNEYS	STAGE	PART 1 — ALL STAGES		PART 2 — For stages made by PUBLIC TRANSPORT			PART 3 — For stages made by PRIVATE MOTOR VEHICLE		DRIVERS only:
What was the purpose of the journey?		How did you travel? *(Was it by bus, train, car, etc.)*	How far did you travel? *(Number of miles)*	What was the cost of your own ticket or fare?	Was it a single or return ticket? *(Write in 'Single', 'Return', 'Season', etc.)*	Did you, or your firm, or someone else pay for the ticket? *(Write in 'Self' or 'Other')*	Were you in a vehicle from your household? *(Write in 'Yes' or 'No')*	Were you the DRIVER or a PASSENGER? *(Write in 'Driver' or 'Passenger')*	How many people were in the vehicle?
JOURNEY 5	1								
	2								
	3								
	4								
	5								
JOURNEY 6	1								
	2								
	3								
	4								
	5								
JOURNEY 7	1								
	2								
	3								
	4								
	5								
JOURNEY 8	1								
	2								
	3								
	4								
	5								

SPECIMEN

Road Passenger Transport

RECORD OF JOURNEYS MADE ON THE FOURTH DAY   DAY OF WEEK............   DATE............

FOR ALL JOURNEYS	STAGE	PART 1 — ALL STAGES		PART 2 — For stages made by PUBLIC TRANSPORT		PART 3 — For stages made by PRIVATE MOTOR VEHICLE		DRIVERS only
What was the purpose of the journey?		How did you travel? *(Was it by bus, train, car, etc.)*	How far did you travel? *(Number of miles)*	What was the cost of your own ticket or fare?	Was it a single or return ticket? *(Write in 'Single', 'Return', 'Season', etc.)*	Did you, or your firm, or someone else pay for the ticket? *(Write in 'Self' or 'Other')*	Were you in a vehicle from your household? *(Write in 'Yes' or 'No')*	Were you the DRIVER or a PASSENGER? *(Write in 'Driver' or 'Passenger')*	How many people were in the vehicle?
JOURNEY 1	1								
	2								
	3								
	4								
	5								
JOURNEY 2	1								
	2								
	3								
	4								
	5								
JOURNEY 3	1								
	2								
	3								
	4								
	5								
JOURNEY 4	1								
	2								
	3								
	4								
	5								

SPECIMEN

Appendix C   97

RECORD OF JOURNEYS MADE ON THE FOURTH DAY

DAY OF WEEK............   DATE............

FOR ALL JOURNEYS	STAGE	PART I — ALL STAGES		PART 2 — For stages made by PUBLIC TRANSPORT			PART 3 — For stages made by PRIVATE MOTOR VEHICLE		
What was the purpose of the journey?		How did you travel? (Was it by bus, train, car, etc.)	How far did you travel? (Number of miles)	What was the cost of your own ticket or fare?	Was it a single or return ticket? (Write in 'Single', 'Return', 'Season', etc.)	Did you, or your firm, or someone else pay for the ticket? (Write in 'Self' or 'Other')	Were you in a vehicle from your household? (Write in 'Yes' or 'No')	Were you the DRIVER or a PASSENGER? (Write in 'Driver' or 'Passenger')	DRIVERS only: How many people were in the vehicle?
JOURNEY 5	1 2 3 4 5								
JOURNEY 6	1 2 3 4 5								
JOURNEY 7	1 2 3 4 5								
JOURNEY 8	1 2 3 4 5								

SPECIMEN

RECORD OF JOURNEYS MADE ON THE FIFTH DAY

DAY OF WEEK .... DATE ....

FOR ALL JOURNEYS	STAGE	PART 1 — ALL STAGES		PART 2 — For stages made by PUBLIC TRANSPORT			PART 3 — For stages made by PRIVATE MOTOR VEHICLE		DRIVERS only:
What was the purpose of the journey?		How did you travel? (Was it by bus, train, car, etc.)	How far did you travel? (Number of miles)	What was the cost of your own ticket or fare?	Was it a single or return ticket? (Write in 'Single', 'Return', 'Season', etc.)	Did you, or your firm, or someone else pay for the ticket? (Write in 'Self' or 'Other'.)	Were you in a vehicle from your household? (Write in 'Yes' or 'No'.)	Were you the DRIVER or a PASSENGER? (Write in 'Driver' or 'Passenger'.)	How many people were in the vehicle?
JOURNEY 1	1								
	2								
	3								
	4								
	5								
JOURNEY 2	1								
	2								
	3								
	4								
	5								
JOURNEY 3	1								
	2								
	3								
	4								
	5								
JOURNEY 4	1								
	2								
	3								
	4								
	5								

SPECIMEN

Appendix C 99

RECORD OF JOURNEYS MADE ON THE FIFTH DAY   DAY OF WEEK............ DATE............

FOR ALL JOURNEYS	STAGE	PART 1 ALL STAGES		PART 2 For stages made by PUBLIC TRANSPORT			PART 3 For stages made by PRIVATE MOTOR VEHICLE		
What was the purpose of the journey?		How did you travel? *(Was it by bus, train, car, etc.)*	How far did you travel? *(Number of miles)*	What was the cost of your own ticket or fare?	Was it a single or return ticket? *(Write in 'Single', 'Return', 'Season', etc.)*	Did you, or your firm, or someone else pay for the ticket? *(Write in 'Self' or 'Other')*	Were you in a vehicle from your household? *(Write in 'Yes' or 'No')*	Were you the DRIVER or a PASSENGER? *(Write in 'Driver' or 'Passenger')*	DRIVERS only: How many people were in the vehicle?
JOURNEY 5	1								
	2								
	3								
	4								
	5								
JOURNEY 6	1								
	2								
	3								
	4								
	5								
JOURNEY 7	1								
	2								
	3								
	4								
	5								
JOURNEY 8	1								
	2								
	3								
	4								
	5								

SPECIMEN

Road Passenger Transport

RECORD OF JOURNEYS MADE ON THE SIXTH DAY   DAY OF WEEK............   DATE............

FOR ALL JOURNEYS	STAGE	PART 1 — ALL STAGES		PART 2 — For stages made by PUBLIC TRANSPORT		PART 3 — For stages made by PRIVATE MOTOR VEHICLE		DRIVERS only:
What was the purpose of the journey?		How did you travel? (Was it by bus, train, car, etc.)	How far did you travel? (Number of miles)	What was the cost of your own ticket or fare?	Was it a single or return ticket? (Write in 'Single', 'Return', 'Season', etc.)	Did you, or your firm, or someone else pay for the ticket? (Write in 'Self' or 'Other')	Were you in a vehicle from your household? (Write in 'Yes' or 'No')	Were you the DRIVER or a PASSENGER? (Write in 'Driver' or 'Passenger')	How many people were in the vehicle?
JOURNEY 1	1								
	2								
	3								
	4								
	5								
JOURNEY 2	1								
	2								
	3								
	4								
	5								
JOURNEY 3	1								
	2								
	3								
	4								
	5								
JOURNEY 4	1								
	2								
	3								
	4								
	5								

SPECIMEN

Appendix C 101

RECORD OF JOURNEYS MADE ON THE SIXTH DAY   DAY OF WEEK............   DATE............

FOR ALL JOURNEYS	PART 1 — ALL STAGES		PART 2 — For stages made by PUBLIC TRANSPORT			PART 3 — For stages made by PRIVATE MOTOR VEHICLE		
What was the purpose of the journey?	How did you travel? *(Was it by bus, train, car, etc.)*	How far did you travel? *(Number of miles)*	What was the cost of your own ticket or fare?	Was it a single or return ticket? *(Write in 'Single', 'Return', 'Season', etc.)*	Did you, or your firm, or someone else pay for the ticket? *(Write in 'Self' or 'Other')*	Were you in a vehicle from your household? *(Write in 'Yes' or 'No')*	Were you the DRIVER or a PASSENGER? *(Write in 'Driver' or 'Passenger')*	DRIVERS only: How many people were in the vehicle?

(SPECIMEN)

JOURNEY 5 — stages 1, 2, 3, 4, 5
JOURNEY 6 — stages 1, 2, 3, 4, 5
JOURNEY 7 — stages 1, 2, 3, 4, 5
JOURNEY 8 — stages 1, 2, 3, 4, 5

RECORD OF JOURNEYS MADE ON THE LAST DAY

DAY OF WEEK .... DATE ....

What was the purpose of your journey?	FOR ALL JOURNEYS				S T A G E	PART I — ALL STAGES		
	Where did your journey begin and end?	What time did your journey begin?	How long did the journey take, door to door?			How much time did you spend on each stage, NOT including waiting?	How did you travel? *(Was it by bus, train, car, etc.)*	How far did you travel? *(Number of miles)*
JOURNEY 1	Journey BEGAN at: .... ENDED at:	....	....		1	....	....	....
					2	....	....	....
					3	....	....	....
					4	....	....	....
					5	....	....	....
JOURNEY 2	Journey BEGAN at: .... ENDED at:	....	....		1	....	....	....
					2	....	....	....
					3	....	....	....
					4	....	....	....
					5	....	....	....
JOURNEY 3	Journey BEGAN at: .... ENDED at:	....	....		1	....	....	....
					2	....	....	....
					3	....	....	....
					4	....	....	....
					5	....	....	....
JOURNEY 4	Journey BEGAN at: .... ENDED at:	....	....		1	....	....	....
					2	....	....	....
					3	....	....	....
					4	....	....	....
					5	....	....	....

SPECIMEN

We should like a little extra information about journeys made on this day.

Please fill in the usual details, and also complete the additional columns as far as you are able.

If you are not certain what to put down, the interviewer will help when she calls.

IF YOU DID MORE THAN 4 JOURNEYS, PLEASE CONTINUE OVERLEAF.

Appendix C 103

RECORD OF JOURNEYS MADE ON THE LAST DAY   DAY OF WEEK............ DATE............

What was the purpose of your journey?	FOR ALL JOURNEYS		How long did the journey take, door to door?	STAGE	PART I — ALL STAGES		
	Where did your journey begin and end?	What time did your journey begin?			How much time did you spend on each stage, NOT including waiting?	How did you travel? *(Was it by bus, train, car, etc.)*	How far did you travel? *(Number of miles)*
JOURNEY 5	Journey BEGAN at: .... ENDED at:	....	....	1 2 3 4 5	....	....	....
JOURNEY 6	Journey BEGAN at: .... ENDED at:	....	....	1 2 3 4 5	....	....	....
JOURNEY 7	Journey BEGAN at: .... ENDED at:	....	....	1 2 3 4 5	....	....	....
JOURNEY 8	Journey BEGAN at: .... ENDED at:	....	....	1 2 3 4 5	....	....	....

SPECIMEN

PART 2 — For stages made by PUBLIC TRANSPORT

S T A G E	What was the cost of your ticket or fare?	Was it a single or return ticket? (Write in 'Single,' 'Return,' 'Season,' etc.)	Did you, or your firm, or someone else pay for the ticket? (Write in 'Self' or 'Other')
1			
2			
3			
4			
5			
1			
2			
3			
4			
5			
1			
2			
3			
4			
5			
1			
2			
3			
4			
5			

PART 3 — For stages made by PRIVATE MOTOR VEHICLE

Were you in a vehicle from your household? (Write in 'Yes' or 'No')	Were you the DRIVER or a PASSENGER? (Write in 'Driver' or 'Passenger')	DRIVERS only: How many people were in the vehicle?

THE INTERVIEWER WILL COMPLETE THIS SECTION WHEN SHE CALLS

Seats used	Frequency				
	5 or more times a week	2-4 times a week	Once a week	1-3 times a month	Less often
1 4 2 5 3 6	5	4	3	2	—
1 4 2 5 3 6					
1 4 2 5 3 6					
1 4 2 5 3 6					
1 4 2 5 3 6					
1 4 2 5 3 6	5	4	3	2	—
1 4 2 5 3 6					
1 4 2 5 3 6					
1 4 2 5 3 6					
1 4 2 5 3 6					
1 4 2 5 3 6	5	4	3	2	—
1 4 2 5 3 6					
1 4 2 5 3 6					
1 4 2 5 3 6					
1 4 2 5 3 6					
1 4 2 5 3 6	5	4	3	2	—
1 4 2 5 3 6					
1 4 2 5 3 6					
1 4 2 5 3 6					
1 4 2 5 3 6					

SPECIMEN

Appendix C   105

		PART 2			PART 3			THE INTERVIEWER WILL COMPLETE THIS SECTION WHEN SHE CALLS				
		For stages made by PUBLIC TRANSPORT			*For stages made by* PRIVATE MOTOR VEHICLE					Frequency		
S T A G E		What was the cost of your ticket or fare?	Was it a single or return ticket? *(Write in 'Single', 'Return', 'Season', etc.)*	Did you, or your firm, or someone else pay for the ticket? *(Write in 'Self' or 'Other')*	Were you in a vehicle from your household? *(Write in 'Yes' or 'No')*	Were you the DRIVER or a PASSENGER? *(Write in 'Driver' or 'Passenger')*	DRIVERS only: How many people were in the vehicle?	Seats used	5 or more times a week	2-4 times a week	Once a times a week	1-3 times a month	Less often
	1							1 2 3 4 5 6	5	4	3	2	1
	2							1 2 3 4 5 6	5	4	3	2	1
	3							1 2 3 4 5 6					
	4							1 2 3 4 5 6					
	5							1 2 3 4 5 6					
	1							1 2 3 4 5 6	5	4	3	2	1
	2							1 2 3 4 5 6					
	3							1 2 3 4 5 6					
	4							1 2 3 4 5 6					
	5							1 2 3 4 5 6					
	1							1 2 3 4 5 6	5	4	3	2	1
	2							1 2 3 4 5 6					
	3							1 2 3 4 5 6					
	4							1 2 3 4 5 6					
	5							1 2 3 4 5 6					
	1							1 2 3 4 5 6	5	4	3	2	1
	2							1 2 3 4 5 6					
	3							1 2 3 4 5 6					
	4							1 2 3 4 5 6					
	5							1 2 3 4 5 6					

SPECIMEN

Please do NOT write anything here.

MAIN DRIVER of:	v	/ v	/ v
JOURNEYS in which no stage done in any household vehicle:			
Day	Journey No.		

At end of recording period, please tick 'Yes' or 'No'.

During the recording period, did you either acquire or dispose of a motor vehicle?

YES......
NO.......

SPECIMEN

Appendix C   107

CENTRE FOR SAMPLE SURVEYS LTD.
16 Duncan Terrace, London N1 8BZ.   01-278 2061

Office Use Only — Project 4 0 0 — Record
June '75 — Card 1

(P.400)   **NATIONAL TRAVEL – CONTACT SHEET**

Surname(s) _____   0 0 0 0 0 0

Listed Address _____   Area [ ][ ]   Address [ ]

No. of Households at address ⟶ [ ]   If more than one ⟶ This Household (A, B or C) ⟶ [ ]

A.   ADDRESS PRODUCTIVITY ⟶ IF ADDRESS IS ELIGIBLE (i.e. traced and contains household(s)) TICK BOX AND CONTINUE WITH PART B ⟶ [ ]

No trace of address 0
Vacant (habitable) premises 1
Derelict, demolished premises 2
Business, industrial premises only . . . 3
Institution premises - (no eligible residents) 4

GIVE NON-RESPONSE DETAILS

B.   HOUSEHOLD PRODUCTIVITY (final summary)

No contact with household adult at placement   5
Total refusal at placement (including illness and language) 6
Agreed initially, ... at pick-up stage . . . 7
Agreed initially, unable to contact anyone at pick-up stage 8
Partially productive household 9
Fully productive household . . . . . . Y

GIVE NON-RESPONSE DETAILS

SPECIMEN

C.   CALL SUMMARY (placement & pick-ups)

i) Circle col. no. of 1st successful placement and 1st successful pick-up

Time	1	2	3	4	5	6	7	8	9	10	11	12
Noon or before	1	1	1	1	1	1	1	1	1	1	1	1
1201-1400	2	2	2	2	2	2	2	2	2	2	2	2
1401-1700	3	3	3	3	3	3	3	3	3	3	3	3
1701-1900	4	4	4	4	4	4	4	4	4	4	4	4
1901 or later	5	5	5	5	5	5	5	5	5	5	5	5

ii)
	1	2	3	4	5	6	7	8	9	10	11	12
Weekday	1	1	1	1	1	1	1	1	1	1	1	1
Weekend	2	2	2	2	2	2	2	2	2	2	2	2

Date of first visit to address _____
Date of first successful placement contact _____
Total no. of placement visits ⟶ [ ]

O.U.O. [ ][ ][ ][ ][ ][ ]

D.   TRAVEL WEEK

Start day: (WRITE IN) ____   OFFICE USE ONLY
Date: (WRITE IN) ____

E.   INTERVIEWER

Name _____ (WRITE IN)
Interviewer No. ⟶ [ ][ ]

OFFICE USE ONLY

Project 4 0 0   Card 0   Area [ ][ ]   Placements [ ]
          Day   Productivity   Address [ ]   Pick-ups [ ]
Date [ ][ ][ ]   Time   Intv.

BASIC CLASSIFICATION

Do not approach neighbours for any of this information

COMPLETE AT PLACEMENT STAGE FOR ALL CO-OPERATIVE HOUSEHOLDS AND REFUSALS TO MAIN SURVEY (Codes 6-Y at B)

PART F CAN ALSO BE COMPLETED BY OBSERVATION FOR NON CONTACT HOUSEHOLDS AT PLACEMENT (Code 5 at B)

F. ACCOMMODATION TYPE

Whole house/ Bungalow/ or Cottage
- detached 1
- semi-detached 2
- terraced (including ends) 3

Purpose-built flat/maisonette 4
Converted flat/maisonette 5
Room(s) (or flat) - not self-contained . . 6
Caravan 7
Other (WRITE IN) 8

Not possible to obtain information 9

G. HOUSEHOLD STRUCTURE

No. of infants less than 3 years . . .
No. of children aged 3-15 years
No. of adults 16-59 . . . .
No. of adults 60 years and over .

TOTAL NO. IN HOUSEHOLD
(including respondent)

H. CAR OWNERSHIP

No. of cars or light vans for regular use of household, including business owned vehicles
- None 0
- One 1
- 2 or more 2
- No information 3

I. RESPONDENT'S STATUS

(Priority Code)
- Head of H/Hold 1
- Housewife 2
- Other adult member of h/hold 3
- Other (STATE) 4

J. WORKING STATUS (Head of Household)

Working full time (over 30 hours) 1
Part time (over 10 up to 30 hours) . . . 2
Part time (10 hours or less) 3
Unemployed, temporarily sick (seeking work) 4
Retired (including permanently sick) . . . 5
Semi-retired (i.e. retired but working part time) 6
Full-time student 7
Non-working housewife 8
Other non-working (STATE) 9
No information 0

K. OCCUPATION (previous main occ. for codes 4, 5 or 6.)
o.u.o.

Job title and description

Skill, training experience and qualifications

Supervision and management responsibilities

Industry, business or profession of employer

- Self employed 1
- Employed manager 2
- Other employee 3

No. of employees in est.
- None (or family only) 0
- 1-24 1
- 25 or more 2

Name of respondent:

Appendix C 109

CENTRE FOR SAMPLE SURVEYS LTD.
16 Duncan Terrace, London, N1 8BZ. 01-278 2061

(P.400)

NATIONAL TRAVEL – INDIVIDUAL

Office use only — Record
Project 400 (1-3) (4-8)
June 75 — Card 6 (9)

Area ☐☐ Address ☐☐ 0 (10)

Identification Reference of Respondent _____ PERSON NO. ☐☐ (11-12)   000 (13-15)

COMPLETE THIS PAGE FOR EACH INDIVIDUAL 3 YEARS AND OVER		

1 Do you (does ..child..) have any kind of travel token or special pass, other than a season ticket that allows you (him/her) to travel on buses or trains (including the underground) either free or at reduced rate?   Yes 1   No 2 → Q2   (16)

IF 'YES' – GIVE DETAILS

Issued by:
Reason for concession:
Nature of concession:
Cost to respondent of tokens/pass:

2 Do you (does ..child..) have any current season ticket for use on buses or trains (including the underground)?   Yes 1   No 2   (17)

SPECIMEN

IF 'YES' – GIVE DETAILS

	TICKET 1	TICKET 2
Mode(s) of transport:		
Ticket starts from: (PLACE NAMES) and ends at:		
Period covered:		
Normal no. of single journeys per week with tickets:		
Full cost of ticket:	£ p	£ p
Amount of ticket cost paid by person/organisation outside household (enter nil if none)	£ p	£ p
Nature of person/organisation subsidising ticket:	Private individual 1 Business/organisation 2	Private individual 1 Business/organisation 2

CHILDREN AGED 3 15 END
ADULTS AGED 16+ → Q3

COMPLETE AT PICK-UP FOR EACH INDIVIDUAL (3 YRS +)

TRAVEL DAY

	First						Last
Enter Travel days →							
Number of journeys recorded							
No journey made	00	00	00	00	00	00	00
No details of journeys	98	98	98	98	98	98	98
Method of completion { Mainly from diary	1	1	1	1	1	1	1
Mainly from memory	2	2	2	2	2	2	2

(18-20)(21-23)(24-26)(27-29)(30-32)(33-35)(36-38)

Make one entry for each day, making sure that the entry coincides with journey record sheets for the individual.

Also make one entry per day.

TOTAL ☐
RECORDED JOURNEYS
(39-40)

110 Road Passenger Transport

THE REMAINDER IS COMPLETED ONLY FOR THOSE 16 YRS +

3	Fares on buses and trains have increased during the past 2 years. a) Have fare increases caused you to do anything different as regards journeys you made by bus or train?	Yes .... No .... Can't remember	(41) 1 2 3	} → Q4
	IF 'YES' ASK (b) & (c) b) What journeys or parts of journeys which you made were affected? Was it .... [READ OUT PRECODES, MORE THAN ONE CODE MAY BE RINGED] .... or	journeys to work, school or college? journeys to shops ....? other kinds of journeys ....?	(42) 1 2 3	
	c) What sort of changes did you make?	(PROBE FULLY)	(43) (44)	
4a)	ASK ALL AGED 16+ Have there been any cuts or major alterations in the bus or train service in this area during the past 2 years that you are aware of?	Yes, have been cuts .... No, Don't know .... Not lived here long enough	(45) 1 2 3	} → Q5
b)	IF 'YES' Did any of these cuts or alterations cause you to do anything different as regards journeys you made by bus or train?	Yes .... No .... Can't remember....................	(46) 1 2 3	} → Q5
c)	IF 'YES' ASK (c) & (d) What journeys or parts of journeys which you made were affected? Was it .... [READ OUT PRECODES, MORE THAN ONE CODE MAY BE RINGED] .... or	journeys to work, school or college? journeys to shops ....? other kinds of journeys ....?	(47) 1 2 3	
d)	What sort of changes did you make?	(PROBE FULLY)	(48) (49)	

			(50)
5a)	ASK ALL AGED 16+	Yes	1
	Do you hold a full driving licence, valid in this country, to drive either a car or to drive a motorcycle, scooter or moped?	No	2
			(51)
b)	ASK ALL AGED 16+	Yes - car	1
	Do you (also) hold a provisional driving licence for a car, motorcycle, scooter or moped?	Yes - motorcycle etc.	2
		Yes - invalid vehicle only	3
		No provisional licence held	4

	ASK ALL WITH FULL DRIVING LICENCE(S) - (Code 1 at Q5a, remainder to Q7)		(52)
6a)	How long have you held any kind of full driving licence?	Less than 1 year	0
		1-5 years (ENTER NO.) →	☐
		6 years or more	6
			(53)
b)	Is your current licence a British licence?	Yes	1
		No	2
			(54)
c)	Is it a full licence for a car only a motorcycle only or for both?	Both car and motorcycle	1
		Car only	2
		Motorcycle only	3
		Invalid vehicle only	4
			(55)
d)	Do you have a licence to enable you to drive a heavy good or public services vehicle?	Yes	1
		No	2

		Probe for correct precode	(56-57)
	ASK ALL AGED 16+		
7	Are you in paid employment?		
	Full-time work (over 30 hrs. a week)		01
	Part-time work (over 10, up to and including 30 hours a week)		02
	Part-time work (up to and including 10 hours a week)		03
	Unemployed, temporarily sick (seeking work)		04) Skip to back page
	Retired (including permanently sick)		05)
	Semi-retired (i.e. retired but now working part-time)		06
	Full time student (those also with part-time job code 02 or 03 as well)		07) Skip to income which should be left to pick-up.
	Non-working housewife		08)
	Other non-working (STATE)		09)

CONTINUE FOR THOSE WORKING FULL OR PART TIME (Codes 01-03, 06)

FOR THOSE CODED 04 or 05 GO TO BACK PAGE AND COMPLETE OCCUPATION (AND INCOME) DETAILS

FOR THOSE CODED 07, 08 or 09 YOU SHOULD END QUESTIONAIRE HERE AND COMPLETE INCOME QUESTION AT PICK UP

Road Passenger Transport

ASK ALL WORKING FULL TIME OR PART TIME (Codes 01-03 and 06 at Q7)

PRIORITY CODE (58)

8a) When you go to work do you .... go to the same place every time — 1) Defines usual place or work

[READ OUT CODES
USE PAST MONTH IF PATTERN
VARIES]

.... go to the same place on at least 2 days running each week — 2)

.... go to different places — 3) Go to
.... work at home — 4) Back page

ASK ALL WITH USUAL PLACE OF WORK (Codes 1 and 2 at 8a) (59)

b) Is that workplace .... in the centre of a large town or city — 1

Give Town Name: _____

[READ OUT CODES]

.... in an urban area outside a town centre — 2
.... in the country or a rural area — 3
.... or somewhere else (STATE) — 4

c) What is the most usual method you use to travel to work? (60)

Driver of household vehicle — For Entire Journey — 1
Passenger of household vehicle — 2
Other method (including only part of journey in household vehicle) — 3 → Q10

Household Vehicle Ref. No. ☐

ASK ALL WHO USE HOUSEHOLD VEHICLE FOR ENTIRE JOURNEY (Codes 1 and 2 at 8c) (61)

9a) On how many days a week do you usually use .... (vehicle identity) .... to get to work?

Most days (every day) — 1
1-3 days a week — 2
Less often — 3

ASK ALL (62)

b) Assuming you are not able to use that vehicle how do you or would you get there?

Another household vehicle — 1
Non-household private vehicle — 2
Public transport — 3
Walk, cycle — 4
Other (STATE) — 5   Ring code
Not able to specify alternative — 6 → 5 at (c)

c) Does it (or would it) take you less time, about the same time or longer to get to work by that method?
IF 'LONGER' PROBE HOW MUCH LONGER (and Code 3 or 4) (63)

Less time — 1
About same time — 2
Longer — 3
Very much longer (i.e. 50% increase) — 4
Not able to specify alternative — 5
Go to Back page

FOR ALL NOT USING HOUSEHOLD VEHICLE (Code 3 at 8c) (64)

Summary Code
→ Household has no car/van — 1) Go to
→ Individual has no full licence for car/van — 2) Back page
→ Individual does not usually use household vehicle — 3

IF CODE 3 IS RINGED (65)

10a) Suppose you used a car to get to your place of work. Where would you be most likely to leave it when you got there?

In the street — 1
In firm's car park or on firms premises — 2
In public car park — 3
Somewhere else (STATE) — 4
Nowhere to park at all — 5 → Q11

IF PARKING POSSIBLE (Codes 1-4) (66-68)

b) How much per day would that cost you?   ENTER IN PENCE → ☐☐☐

[COSTS ACTUALLY PAID BY SOMEONE ELSE ARE ALSO INCLUDED]

No charge — 000
Don't know — 888

Appendix C 113

11. OCCUPATION DETAILS (Codes 01-06 at Q7)   O.U.O.
                                                          ☐☐ (69-70)

    Job title &
    description _____

    Skills, training,
    experience & qualifications. _____

    Supervision &
    Management responsibilities. _____

    Industry, business or
    profession of employer _____

                                  No. of employees in establishment
    Self employed   1   ⎡None (or family workers only) .... 0⎤
    Employed manager   2 ──▶   │1-24 .... 1⎬
    Other employee   3   ⎣25 or more .... 2⎦

GIVE COMPARABLE OCCUPATION DETAILS OF
SEMI-RETIREDS CURRENT OCCUPATION, A
RETIREDS PREVIOUS OCCUPATION IF HE IS NOW
WORKING FULL TIME AND STUDENTS PART TIME
WORK. (NOTING WHETHER VACATIONAL OR NOT).

SPECIMEN

---

12. INCOME (ASK ALL INDIVIDUALS 16 YEARS AND OVER)   Enter Code
                                                          for Income
    Into which of the groups on this card does your own gross
    income come - before any deductions for income tax, national   ☐☐ (71-72)
    insurance or pension contributions, but not including money
    received from other members of your household.

    SELF EMPLOYED   That is your income in the last 12 months for   Nil   00
                         which you can give a figure from your business
                         (practice etc.) together with any pension or   Refused   98
                         private source of income.

    OTHER INDIVIDUALS   That is your income from your job (including
                         bonuses and overtime) or from a pension or
                         from a private source of income.

FOR HEADS OF H/HOLD NOT COMPLETING INDIVIDUAL Q'NAIRE		(73)
NOTE: An individual questionaire should be returned for every head of household	Q. 7, 11 & 12 completed by proxy	1
Questions 7, 11 and 12 (only) should be completed by suitable proxy if H. of H. has not refused.	Q7, 11 & 12 not attempted as H. of H. refused	2

CENTRE FOR SAMPLE SURVEYS LTD.
16 Duncan Terrace, London N1 8BZ. 01-278 2061

P400 **NATIONAL TRAVEL - VEHICLE**

Area ☐☐☐   Address ☐☐

Project	400	1 – 3
Record		4 – 8
Card	4	9

Identification
Reference of Vehicle _____ Vehicle Reference No. ☐ (10) 11 ☐☐☐☐☐ 15

1. May I check that you are the household member who usually drives most miles per year in (vehicle identity)?

   IF NOT MAIN DRIVER REDIRECT TO MAIN DRIVER

   MAIN DRIVER PERSON NO. ☐ (16)

2. What type of vehicle is it?

   (17)
   - Van or lorry (4 wheel or more) — 1
   - 4 wheel car → saloon — 2
   - → estate — 3
   - → convertible — 4
   - 3 wheel vehicle — 5
   - Motorcycle (or scooter) with side car — 6
   - Motorcycle — 7
   - Scooter — 8
   - Moped — 9
   - Other (STATE) — X

   SPECIMEN

3. **COMPLETE DETAILS FOR ALL VEHICLES**

   IF REGISTRATION DOCUMENT NOT AVAILABLE, ASK AS QUESTIONS

   (18)
   - Registration document seen — 1
   - Registration document not seen — 2

   REGISTRATION DETAILS

   CARS ONLY (codes 2 – 4) (at Q.2)

   a) Make: _____
   b) Model: _____
   c) Date of 1st registration: MONTH ____ YEAR 19 ____   (19) ☐ (20 – 21)
   (INCLUDING PERIOD WITH PREVIOUS OWNER(S))

   ALL VEHICLES:
   d) Taxation class:

   TO DISTINGUISH PRIVATE FROM GOODS, CHECK TAX LAST PAID. FOR PRIVATE
   OLD: £25 or £9.15
   NEW: £40 or £14.65

   (22)
   - Private only — 1
   - Goods only — 2
   - Motorcycle, scooter or moped — 3
   - Invalid car(riage) — 4
   - Hackney carriage — 5
   - Other (STATE) — 6

   e) Engine Capacity: ENTER c.c.'s _____   (23-24)

   IF VAN/LORRY, CODE UNLADEN WEIGHT INSTEAD

   (25)
   - Up to 1½ tons (30 cwt.) — 1
   - Over 1½ tons (30 cwt.) — 2

Appendix C 115

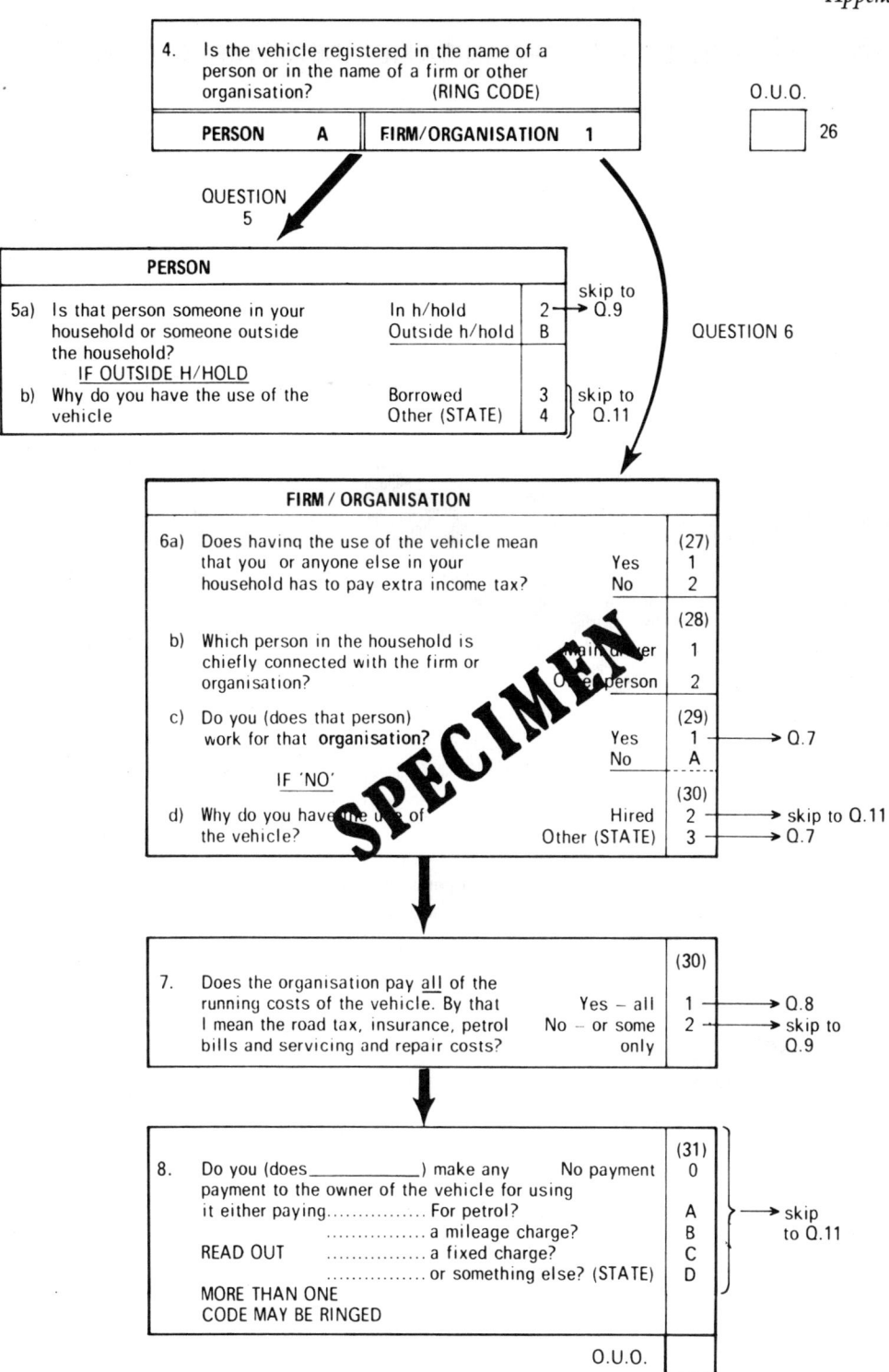

HOUSEHOLD REGISTERED AND ORGANISATION REGISTERED (N.F.S.)

9a)	Some drivers are able to claim some of the purchase or the running costs of their vehicle against their income tax. Does this apply to your vehicle?		Yes	(33) 1	
			No	2 → Q.10	
			Don't know	3 → Q.10	
	IF 'YES'		Yes	No	
	b) What does that tax allowance cover? Is any of it for .... purchase/depreciation costs?		1	2	(34)
	........................,........................... running costs?		1	2	(35)
	READ OUT (MULTI-CODE) No details known			3	

				(36)
10a)	Some drivers have some of the costs of their vehicle paid by their firm or other organisation. Are the <u>purchase costs</u> of your vehicle paid for in this way either fully or partly?	Yes – fully	1	
		Yes – partly	2	
		No – not at all	3	

			Yes	No	
b)	And what about <u>running costs</u>, are all or some of the following paid for by a firm or organisation? .... Road tax		1	2	(37)
	..... Insurance		1	2	(38)
	.... parking/garaging		1	2	(39)
	........Servicing and repairs		1	2	(40)
	READ OUT (MULTI-CODE) Fixed allowance – Unspecified		4		
	No details known			3	

			Yes	No	
c)	And what about mileage that you do either for your firm (organisation) or for any other purposes. Do you get .... Any of your petrol paid for (free)		1	2	(41)
	.... a mileage allowance		1	2	(42)
	.... mileage paid for as part of a fixed allowance		1	2	(43)
	READ OUT (MULTI-CODE) No details known			3	

				(44)	
d)	Is there any other way in which the cost of purchasing or running the vehicle is reduced?		Yes	1	
			No →	2	Q.11
	IF 'YES' – GIVE FULL DETAILS				
				(45)	

O.U.O.

Appendix C

11	**ASK ALL**		(46)	
a)	Petrol prices have gone up several times during the past 2 years Have these price increases caused you to do anything different as regards the use of this vehicle	Yes No Can't remember	1 2 3	⎫ ⎬ ➔ Q.12 ⎭
	IF 'YES' (ask (b) and (c)			
	b) What journeys or parts of journeys which you made were affected? Was it.....	Journeys to work/school/college	1	(47)
	⎡READ OUT PRECODES. MORE ⎤ ⎢THAN ONE CODE MAY BE ⎥ ⎣RINGED ⎦	Journeys to shops	2	(48)
		Other kinds of journeys	3	(49)

	c) What sort of changes did you make?
	  PROBE: **What other sorts of changes?**
	         UNTIL FINAL 'NONE' - RECORD FULLY
			(50)
			
			(51)
			
			(52)	

SPECIMEN

12	**ASK ALL** Where do you usually keep this vehicle at night? ⎡FOR SHIFTWORKERS ⎤ ⎣NIGHT SLEEPING HOURS ⎦	Garage/covered carport Uncovered parking space on premises In the street (on verge etc.) Other (STATE)	(53) 1 2 3 4	
13a)	During the last four weeks has this vehicle been serviced or repaired or had any replacements fitted?	Yes No	(54) 1 2 ➔ Q.14	
	IF 'YES' ask (b) and (c) b) What was the total cost of this? **ENTER AMOUNT** £_____	None – under guarantee/warranty Amount not known	(55–57) 888 998	
	c) Was all or part of this work done by a garage or someone who was employed to do it?	Yes – all or part No – none	(58) 1 2	

Road Passenger Transport

ASK ALL

14 I would like to get a figure for the approximate annual mileage of the vehicle, however rough and ready your estimate might be.

FILTER
If vehicle is borrowed/hired (Q.5 or Q.6) Check whether for...... (59)
Less than 1 year   0 → Q.17
1 year or more   1
If less than one year (code 0) skip to back page

First can you tell me the total miles the vehicle is driven in a year?

TOTAL... miles   (60 – 62)

ESTIMATE FORWARD IF DRIVEN FOR LESS THAN ONE YEAR

15 If any of the remaining questions apply also to someone else in your household driving this vehicle, can you include the miles they <u>drive</u> with your mileage

FILTER
(63)
If no workers in H'hold ring code → 0 → Q.17 and skip to back page

a) First, about how many of the total annual miles are <u>driven</u> by you in getting to or from your usual place of work either all the way or part of the way?

COMMUTING............................... miles   (64 – 66)

b) And leaving aside those journeys, how many of the vehicle miles are <u>driven</u> by you <u>in the course of your work?</u>

IN COURSE OF WORK................................. miles   (67 – 69)

c) So that means that the vehicle is driven about .... miles a year for journeys other than getting to work and back or for journeys made in the course of work?

OTHER............................ miles   (70 – 72)

CHECK ADDITION OF 3 CATEGORIES TO TOTAL AND RE-DO IF NECESSARY

16a) Is the vehicle driven by you to get to or from your usual place of work, by that I mean <u>all</u> the way.

(73)
Yes   1
No   2 → Q.17

IF 'YES'

b) When the vehicle is driven to or from work, where is it normally left whilst you are at work?

(74)
In the street   1
In firm's carpark or on firm's premises   2
In public carpark   3
Somewhere else (STATE)   4
Vehicle not left there   5

c) How much per day does it cost you to leave the vehicle there?

ENTER IN PENCE ☐☐   (75 – 77)
No charge   000

d) Does anyone from outside the household normally travel in the vehicle when it is used to get to or from work, either for all or part of the journey?

(78)
YES (ENTER NO.) ☐
(of people)
(outside H/hold)   No   0

Appendix C 119

– 6 –

				(16)
Office Use Only (1 – 8) As Card 4	Card 5 (9)	(10 – 15) As Card 4		
17	Has the vehicle a mileometer in working order?		Mileometer working	1
			Mileometer not working	2
			No mileometer	3

COMPLETE REMAINDER AT PICK-UP INTERVIEW

Mileometer broken during period — 2

18a) MILEOMETER READINGS

END OF PERIOD MILES _____ mls.
START OF PERIOD MILES _____ mls.

[ESTIMATES IF NECESSARY]

MILEAGE IN PERIOD [____] mls. (17 – 20)

No mileage driven 0000 → Q.20

b) I see that .... (miles) ...... were done in this vehicle during the travel week.

How many of those miles were driven by .... You .... mls. (21 – 24)
[READ OUT] .... other member(s) of h/hold _____ mls. (25 – 28)
.... someone outside household _____ mls. (29 – 32)

ENTER PERSON REFERENCE No's (Don't include main driver)

CHECK MILES ADD TO CORRECT TOTAL

19a) Was any of the mileage during the travel week in this vehicle made either

[READ OUT] .... for carrying goods in the course of work _____ mls. (33 – 36)
.... or miles travelled as part of this vehicle's service or repair including getting there and back _____ mls. (37 – 40)

b) So that leaving aside those categories, the remaining mileage of the vehicle was .... (Interviewer to calculate) _____ mls. (41 – 44)

			(45)
IF VEHICLE WAS NOT USED DURING TRAVEL WEEK		Vehicle not insured	0
20a)	Why was the vehicle not used during the travel week?	.... Vehicle repair/service	1
		.... Driver sick/on holiday	2
	DO NOT PROMPT	.... Driver disqualified	3
		.... Other (STATE)	4
			(46)
b)	Was the vehicle taxed during the travel week?	Yes	1
		No	2

Office use only   47 [ ][ ][ ][ ] 51

120 Road Passenger Transport

[Specimen form: "NATIONAL TRAVEL — JOURNEY SHEET", Centre For Sample Surveys Ltd., 16 Duncan Terrace, London N1 8BZ 01-278 2061, P400, June 1975, Project 400, Card 7. The page shows two copies of a blank specimen journey sheet overstamped "SPECIMEN".]

The journey sheet is divided into the following sections:

(A) JOURNEY DETAILS: Journey No, Day (Mon 1, Tue 2, Wed 3, Thur 4, Fri 5, Sat 6, Sun 7; Is this Final Day? Yes 1 / No 2), Purpose From / To (Home 01, Work 02, In course of work 03, Education 04, Shopping 05, Personal business 06, Eat/Drink 07, Social 08, Entertainment 09, Sport-participate 10, Sport-watch 11, Holiday 12, Day trip/just walk 13, Escorting 14, Other (STATE) 15), Start Time (24 hour clock).

(B) ALL STAGES — Method of Travel: Walk 01, Bicycle 02, Works school bus 03, Car, m/cycle combination 04, M/cycle, scooter, moped 05, Van, lorry 06, Other private (STATE) 07, PUBLIC BUS (ordinary) 08, London Transport 09, Elsewhere 10, PUBLIC BUS (express) 11, Taxi 12, LT Underground 13, B R Train (1st class) 14, B R Train (2nd class) 15, Other Public (STATE). Distance Travelled (miles). Stage 2, Stage 3, Stage 4.

(C) PRIVATE STAGES (04-07): Whose Vehicle? — H/H Vehicle (Ref No.), Borrowed 7, Hired 8, Other (STATE) 9. Driver or Passenger? — Driver 1, Passenger 2. Number in Vehicle? (include driver).

(D) PUBLIC STAGES (08-15): Ticket Type? — Ordinary 1, Single 1, Return 2, Season 3, Free 4, Other (STATE) 5. Total Cost? Who Paid? — Self 1, H/Hold member 2, Other person 3, Company/organisation 4.

(E) ALL FINAL DAY STAGES: Total Journey Time (Door to door), Walking Time (Preceding), Travelling Time (Exclude walking waiting) mins. N.B. 1 mile walked in 20 mins. Final walk at end of journey should be entered as separate stage.

Duplicated Journeys (Not to be used for same or final day)
1) If exact replica of previous journey for same person enter previous journey no
2) If respondent was accompanying other person on exact replica journey which you have already recorded (for driver) Enter person No and journey No

Appendix C   121

(Specimen of the National Travel — Journey Sheet form, Centre For Sample Surveys Ltd., 16 Duncan Terrace, London N1 8BZ 01-278 2061, P400, June 1975, Card 7, Project 400.)

NATIONAL TRAVEL — JOURNEY SHEET

The form is divided into sections (A) through (E), repeated twice on the sheet:

(A) JOURNEY DETAILS: Journey No, Day (Mon 1, Tue 2, Wed 3, Thur 4, Fri 5, Sat 6, Sun 7), Is this Final Day? (Yes 1 / No 2), From / To purpose codes (Home 01, Work 02, In course of work 03, Education 04, Shopping 05, Personal business 06, Eat/Drink 07, Social 08, Entertainment 09, Sport-participate 10, Sport-watch 11, Holiday 12, Day trip just walk 13, Escorting 14, Other (STATE) 15), Start Time (24 hour clock).

(B) ALL STAGES: Method of Travel — Walk 01, Bicycle 02, Works school bus 03, Car, m/cycle combination 04, M/cycle, scooter, moped 05, Van, lorry 06, Other private (STATE) 07, PUBLIC BUS (ordinary) 08, London Transport 09, Elsewhere 10, PUBLIC BUS (express) 11, Taxi 12, L T Underground 13, B R Train (1st class) 14, B R Train (2nd class) 15, Other Public (STATE). Distance Travelled (miles). Stages 2, 3, 4.

(C) PRIVATE STAGES (04–07): Whose Vehicle? — H/H Vehicle (Ref No →), Borrowed 7, Hired 8, Other (STATE) 9. Driver or Passenger? — Driver 1, Passenger 2. Number in Vehicle (include driver).

(D) PUBLIC STAGES (08–15): Ticket Type? — Ordinary 1, Single 1, Return 2, Season 3, Free 4, Other (STATE) 5. Total Cost? Who Paid? — Self 1, H. Hold member 2, Other person 3, Company/organisation 4.

(E) ALL FINAL DAY STAGES: Total Journey Time (Door to door) mins. Walking Time (Preceding) mins. Travelling Time (Exclude walking waiting) mins. Final walk at end of journey should be entered as separate stage. N.B. 1 mile walked in 20 mins.

Duplicated Journeys (Not to be used for final day):
1) If exact replica of previous journey for same person enter previous journey no.
2) If respondent was accompanying other person on exact replica journey which you have already recorded (for driver) Enter person No and journey No.

122 Road Passenger Transport

CENTRE FOR SAMPLE SURVEYS LTD.
16 Duncan Terrace, London N1 8BZ.   01-278 2061

(P.400) **NATIONAL TRAVEL – HOUSEHOLD**

Office Use Only — June '75
Project 4 0 0
Record
Card 2

Area [ ][ ][ ]   Address [ ][ ]   0 0 0 0 0

[0]   [1][ ]

PERSON NUMBER (only include 3 years and over)

		1	2	3	4	5	6	7	8	9	10
A. RELATIONSHIP (to Head of Household) (Specify above dotted line)	O.U.O. [ ] Housewife / Other member	H of H ① A B	A B	A B	A B	A B	A B	A B	A B	A B	A B
B. SEX	Male / Female	1 2	1 2	1 2	1 2	1 2	1 2	1 2	1 2	1 2	1 2
C. AGE (last birthday)		-- --	-- --	-- --	-- --	-- --	-- --	-- --	-- --	-- --	-- --
D. MARITAL STATUS	Married / Single / Widowed/Divorced/Separated	1 2 3	1 2 3	1 2 3	1 2 3	1 2 3	1 2 3	1 2 3	1 2 3	1 2 3	1 2 3
E. WORKING STATUS	Full-time (over 30 hours)	1	1	1	1	1	1	1	1	1	1
	Part-time (10 up to 30)	2	2	2	2	2	2	2	2	2	2
	Part-time (10 hours or less)	3	3	3	3	3	3	3	3	3	3
	No paid employment	4	4	4	4	4	4	4	4	4	4

F. PLACEMENT PRODUCTIVITY

		1	2	3	4	5	6	7	8	9	10
Not taking part at all. (No indv. q'naire)	refused / language, sickness etc. / absent throughout	0 1 2	0 1 2	0 1 2	0 1 2	0 1 2	0 1 2	0 1 2	0 1 2	0 1 2	0 1 2
Not taking part in travel record (indv. q'naire only)	refused travel info. / language, sickness etc. / later absence	3 4 5	3 4 5	3 4 5	3 4 5	3 4 5	3 4 5	3 4 5	3 4 5	3 4 5	3 4 5
Not seen but assumed co-operative / Agreed to take part (by proxy if under 11 yrs.)		6 7	6 7	6 7	6 7	6 7	6 7	6 7	6 7	6 7	6 7

G. PICK-UP PRODUCTIVITY (Code 6 or 7 at F)

	1	2	3	4	5	6	7	8	9	10
Totally refused at pick-up interview	1	1	1	1	1	1	1	1	1	1
Too sick for pick-up interview	2	2	2	2	2	2	2	2	2	2
Away during pick-up period	3	3	3	3	3	3	3	3	3	3
Unable to contact at pick-up stage	4	4	4	4	4	4	4	4	4	4
Individual questionnaire completed only	5	5	5	5	5	5	5	5	5	5
Took part fully in giving individual and travel details	6	6	6	6	6	6	6	6	6	6

Office Use Only   3+ [ ][ ] I [ ][ ] T [ ][ ]   [ ][ ]

Appendix C 123

(1-8) AS CARD 1 | CARD 3 · 0 0 0 0 0 0

			Col./Code	Skip to
1a)	Is your accommodation owned or being bought by your household or is it rented?	Owned/buying......	1 →	Q2
		Rented..........	2	
	[OWNERSHIP APPLIES TO FREEHOLD, LONG LEASE, FEUHOLD AND BUYING THROUGH HOUSING ASSOCIATION]	Rent free........	3	
	IF RENTED/RENT FREE			
b)	Is it rented from a Council or New Town Corporation, from a housing association or from a private landlord?	Council/New Town..	1 →	Q2
		Private landlord.. (inc. housing ass'n.)	2	
	[PRIVATE LANDLORD APPLIES TO A PERSON, FIRM OR "COST-RENT" HOUSING ASSOCIATION]			
	IF PRIVATE LANDLORD			
c)	Is the accommodation rented fully furnished, partly furnished or unfurnished?	Fully furnished...	1	
		Partly furnished..	2	
		Unfurnished.......	3	

2a)	**ASK ALL** About how long would it take me to walk from your home to the nearest bus-stop? It is the nearest one I am interested in even if that isn't the main one you use.	**BEST ESTIMATE**		
		6 minutes or less	1	
		7-13 minutes	2	
		14-26 minutes	3	
		27-43 minutes	4	
		44 or longer	5	
		Don't know	6	
	SHOW CARD A	**PRIORITY CODE**		
b)	Would you look at this card and tell me how often I would be able to get a bus from there during the day?	Could not get one every day	1	
		There are several per day	2	
		There is at least one every hour	3	
		There is at least one every ½ hour	4	
	[IF 'VARIES' TAKE OFF PEAK FREQUENCY]	They run more frequently than every ½hr.	5	
		Don't know	6	

			(a) BY BUS	(b) WALKING
3.	Now I want you to tell me about your nearest railway or underground station. Again it is the nearest one I am interested in, even if that isn't the main one or the one you use.	**BEST ESTIMATE**		
		6 minutes or less	1	1
		7-13 minutes	2	2
		14-26 minutes	3	3
a)	First, how long would it take me to get there by bus from here, including walking to the bus stop?	27-43 minutes	4	4
		44 or longer	5	5
		No buses to station	6	-
b)	And how long would it take me if I walked from here to the station?	No station within 50 mls.	7	-
		Don't know	8	8
	SHOW CARD A	**PRIORITY CODE**		
c)	And again from this card, how often would I be able to get a train from the station during the day? It doesn't matter where the trains go.	Could not get one every day	1	
		There are several per day	2	
		There is at least one every hour	3	
		There is at least one every ½ hour	4	
		They run more frequently than every ½hr.	5	
		Don't know	6	

[FOR RANGE ESTIMATES OF FREQUENCIES (Q2, 3 AND 6) e.g. 25-30 MINUTES, CODE INTO LOWEST GROUP i.e. CODE 3]

4. What are the main difficulties (if any) of travelling by bus in this area?
   PROBE ONCE ONLY. RECORD ANSWER FULLY

5. What are the main difficulties (if any) of travelling by train (or by underground) in this area?
   PROBE ONCE ONLY. RECORD ANSWER FULLY

6. How long would it take me to get from your home to each of the following places ..... first by bus and then by walking all the way?

   READ EACH IN TURN. RING CODES ON EACH LINE, ONE FOR THE BUS TIME AND ONE FOR THE WALKING TIME. THEN GO TO NEXT LINE. CODE BEST ESTIMATES.

READ OUT	BY BUS							BY WALKING					
	6 mins or less	7-13 mins	14-26 mins	27-43 mins	44 mins or longer	NOT PRACTICABLE BY BUS	Don't know	6 mins or less	7-13 mins	14-26 mins	27-43 mins	44 mins or longer	Don't know
The doctor's surgery	1	2	3	4	5	6	7	1	2	3	4	5	6
The nearest post office	1	2	3	4	5	6	7	1	2	3	4	5	6
The nearest chemist to get a prescription	1	2	3	4	5	6	7	1	2	3	4	5	6
The nearest shop selling groceries	1	2	3	4	5	6	7	1	2	3	4	5	6
The nearest store like Woolworths	1	2	3	4	5	6	7	1	2	3	4	5	6
The nearest general hospital	1	2	3	4	5	6	7	1	2	3	4	5	6

SPECIMEN

Appendix C 125

7a. Does the household have any bicycles which are used on the public roads?   Write in Number [ ] → Yes   1
   No   2→Q8

b. Who uses it (them)?   Person Ref. No's → [ ] [ ] [ ] [ ]

SHOW CARD B

8a. Would you look at this card and tell me if anyone in the household owns or has the regular use of any of these motor vehicles?

[REGULAR AVAILABLE DURING TRAVEL WEEK]

If 'Yes' → Enter Number of motor vehicles → [ ]
No, none   0

b. (Apart from that/those vehicles) Is anyone in the household likely to have one of the vehicles on this card between now and (last recording day)?

[INCLUDE VEHICLES WHICH WILL BECOME A H/HOLD VEHICLE DURING TRAVEL WEEK]

If 'Yes' → Enter Number of motor vehicles → [ ]
No, none   0

c. Who usually drives the most mileage in the _____ (vehicle identity) _____ taken over the year as a whole?

SPECIMEN

		1	2	3	4	5	6
(i)	Ring Vehicle Reference No.		2	3	4	5	6
(ii)	Identity Reference						
(iii) TYPE	Car (incl. estate & 3 wheeler)	1	1	1	1	1	1
	M.cycle/scooter, with sidecar	2	2	2	2	2	2
	Motorcycle, scooter, moped	3	3	3	3	3	3
	Van, lorry, jeep, landrover	4	4	4	4	4	4
	Other (Write in)	5	5	5	5	5	5
(iv)	Main Driver Person Reference No.						
(v)	available at placement (8a)	1	1	1	1	1	1
	anticipated before recording ends (8b)	2	2	2	2	2	2
(vi) PICK-UP	disposed of during travel week	1	1	1	1	1	1
	acquired before recording ends	2	2	2	2	2	2
(vii)	For vehicles disposed of or acquired enter no. of days during travel week on which vehicle was available for use by the household						

CHECK AT PICK-UP (record in (vi))   Office Use: | 1 | 2 | 1 | 2 | 1 | 2 | 1 | 2 | 1 | 2 | 1 | 2 |

May I just check whether you have got rid of any motor vehicles I noted last time. And have you aquired any new ones?

IF DISPOSALS OR ACQUISITIONS HAVE OCCURRED ADD DETAILS IN VEHICLE GRID. DON'T INCLUDE PART HIRINGS

OPINION RESEARCH CENTRE
TRAVEL SURVEY

This questionnaire is part of a survey being conducted in connection with the planning of travel facilities.

This travel survey includes journeys made in the course of work and for holidays and leisure during the past 14 days, no matter how unusual this fortnight might have been. Please complete this questionnaire yourself (as the person to whom it was addressed) and only include journeys you have made — do not include any journeys made by other members of your household.

TRAVEL TO WORK OR COLLEGE — the following questions are about travel to and from your place of work or study (including regular voluntary or unpaid work).

Q.1 Do you usually make a regular journey to work or college? (By regular we mean on at least 2 days a week)

- Yes [ ]
- No [ ] Go to Q.6

Please mark one

Q.2 On which days did you make this work/college journey in the last 14 days?

Write in total number [ ]

and also tick days on which journeys made to work/college.

Mon	Tue	Wed	Thur	Fri	Sat	Sun	Mon	Tue	Wed	Thur	Fri	Sat	Sun

Q.3 How far from your place of residence is the place where you work or study?

- More than 25 miles [ ]
- 25 miles or less [ ]

Please mark one

Q.4a Where do you normally start this journey from?
Please give as much detail as possible

District/Area _____
Town _____
County _____

Q.4b Where is your place of work or college?
Please give as much detail as possible

District/Area _____
Town _____
County _____

Q.5 What is the main method of travel you use on your normal journey to and from the place where you work or study?

Please mark one

- Taken by employer's bus, lorry or car [ ]
- Bus [ ]
- Train [ ]
- Car/van (driver) [ ]
- Car/van (passenger) [ ]
- Motorcycle/moped [ ]
- Pedal cycle [ ]
- On foot [ ]
- Other method (write in) _____ [ ]

SPECIMEN

Appendix D   127

OTHER JOURNEYS OF OVER 25 MILES MADE WITHIN GREAT BRITAIN (EXCLUDING NORTHERN IRELAND) WITHIN THE LAST 14 DAYS

> **Note** — a journey is to a place. When you come home again or go on to another place that counts as another journey please don't count any journeys you have made driving or as a member of the crew of, long or short distance lorries, trains, buses, taxis and aircraft.

Q.6 Have you made any journeys of <u>over 25 miles</u> of the following types within the last 14 days? — Journeys to do with holidays, leisure, business and personal life.   Yes ☐
(Do not count regular journeys to or from work or college which have been covered already)   No ☐ Go to last page

Please give details of each journey <u>over 25 miles</u> made in the last 14 days. <u>A return journey counts as a separate journey</u>. If any trip included travel overseas please record only the part travelled in Great Britain, providing this was over 25 miles.

Q.7 How many of these journeys have you made in the last 14 days?
Write in number of journeys. _____

If you made more than 6 journeys of over 25 miles please give details of the first 6 journeys. If you have made no journeys please turn to the last page.

Q.8 Please write in the: —	First Journey	Second Journey	Third Journey	Fourth Journey	Fifth Journey	Sixth Journey
Date of journey						
Day of week of journey	Mon ☐ Tues ☐ Wed ☐ Thur ☐ Fri ☐ Sat ☐ Sun ☐	Mon ☐ Tues ☐ Wed ☐ Thur ☐ Fri ☐ Sat ☐ Sun ☐	Mon ☐ Tues ☐ Wed ☐ Thur ☐ Fri ☐ Sat ☐ Sun ☐	Mon ☐ Tues ☐ Wed ☐ Thur ☐ Fri ☐ Sat ☐ Sun ☐	Mon ☐ Tues ☐ Wed ☐ Thur ☐ Fri ☐ Sat ☐ Sun ☐	Mon ☐ Tues ☐ Wed ☐ Thur ☐ Fri ☐ Sat ☐ Sun ☐

Q.9 What was the <u>main</u> purpose of the journey?

> Note — If you were returning home — please mark the activity from which you were returning.

Please mark one for each journey:

	First	Second	Third	Fourth	Fifth	Sixth
Appointment or call in course of work	☐	☐	☐	☐	☐	☐
Shopping/personal business	☐	☐	☐	☐	☐	☐
(To/from) Holiday/forces leave	☐	☐	☐	☐	☐	☐
Sport/entertainment	☐	☐	☐	☐	☐	☐
Visiting friend/relations	☐	☐	☐	☐	☐	☐
Pleasure trip	☐	☐	☐	☐	☐	☐
Other (Please write in)	☐	☐	☐	☐	☐	☐

Q.10 What was the <u>main</u> method of travel used?

Please mark one for each journey:

	First	Second	Third	Fourth	Fifth	Sixth
Train	☐	☐	☐	☐	☐	☐
Ordinary bus/express bus	☐	☐	☐	☐	☐	☐
Coach excursion or tour (for which ticket is required)	☐	☐	☐	☐	☐	☐
Privately hired bus or coach	☐	☐	☐	☐	☐	☐
Taxi/chauffeur-driven car hire	☐	☐	☐	☐	☐	☐
Car/van (driver)	☐	☐	☐	☐	☐	☐
Car/van (passenger)	☐	☐	☐	☐	☐	☐
Motorcycle/moped	☐	☐	☐	☐	☐	☐
Pedal cycle	☐	☐	☐	☐	☐	☐
*Aircraft	☐	☐	☐	☐	☐	☐
Other (Please write in)	☐	☐	☐	☐	☐	☐

* Note: only tick aircraft if the complete aircraft journey was within Great Britain.

	First Journey	Second Journey	Third Journey	Fourth Journey	Fifth Journey	Sixth Journey
Q.11a Where did you start this journey from?						
District/area						
Town						
County						
Q.11b What was the town and district of your final destination?						
District/area						
Town						
County						
Q.12 Was any part of this trip outside Great Britain? IF YES What was the main country you visited? (Write in)						
Q.13 Were you travelling alone, or were you travelling with any of your family, friends relatives etc., whom you had arranged to travel with?						
Alone						
With others						
Please mark in number for each journey.						
Q.14 How many others were there with you?						
Of these						
a) How many were under 14?						
b) How many were 14 or 15?						
c) How many were 16 or 17?						
d) How many were 18 or over?						

Appendix D   129

Everyone please answer, whether or not you have made any journeys.

This section includes questions about yourself and it is, like everything else, strictly confidential. Answers are used only in combination with others to provide statistical analysis or travel information and cannot be individually identified.

Your Sex:—   Male   [ ]
              Female   [ ]

Your Age:—   16 – 17   [ ]
              18 – 19   [ ]
              20 – 24   [ ]   **Please mark one**
              25 – 34   [ ]
              35 – 44   [ ]
              45 – 54   [ ]
              55 – 64   [ ]
              65 +   [ ]

What is your occupation?
(please give as much detail as possible including the industry)
(if retired, state previous occupation.)

Write in _____

_____

_____

What is your position in the household?

Head of the household .... [ ]
Housewife .... [ ]
Son/daughter of head of household .... [ ]
Parent/parent-in-law of head of
   household .... [ ]
Other (write in) _____ [ ]

What is the occupation of the head of the household?

Note — If you are the head of the household write in "as before".

(if retired, state previous occupation)

_____

_____

_____

Does your household have use of a car?   Yes [ ]
                                          No [ ]

Do you have a current motor car driving   Yes [ ]
licence?   No [ ]

How many members (including yourself) of the household are there aged:

Please mark number of

Aged	Males	Females
0 – 4	1 2 3 4 5	1 2 3 4 5
5 – 13	1 2 3 4 5	1 2 3 4 5
14 – 15	1 2 3 4 5	1 2 3 4 5
16 – 17	1 2 3 4 5	1 2 3 4 5
18 – 19	1 2 3 4 5	1 2 3 4 5
20 – 24	1 2 3 4 5	1 2 3 4 5
25 – 34	1 2 3 4 5	1 2 3 4 5
35 – 44	1 2 3 4 5	1 2 3 4 5
45 – 54	1 2 3 4 5	1 2 3 4 5
55 – 64	1 2 3 4 5	1 2 3 4 5
65 or over	1 2 3 4 5	1 2 3 4 5

We would be interested to hear any comment you may have about the public transport service? (write in)

_____

_____

_____

Thank you for your help, please return this to us in the stamped return envelope supplied.

SPECIMEN

OPINION RESEARCH CENTRE
TRAVEL SURVEY

This questionnaire is part of a survey being conducted in connection with the planning of travel facilities.

This travel survey includes journeys made in the course of work and for holidays and leisure during the past 14 days, no matter how unusual this fortnight might have been. Please complete this questionnaire yourself (as the person to whom it was addressed) and only include journeys you have made — do not include any journeys made by other members of your household.

TRAVEL TO WORK OR COLLEGE — the following questions are about travel to and from your place of work or study (including regular voluntary or unpaid work).

Q.1 Do you usually make a regular journey to work or college? (By regular we mean on at least 2 days a week)
Yes ☐
No ☐ — Go to Q.7
Please mark one

Q.2 On which days did you make this work/college journey in the last 14 days?
Write in total number ☐
and also tick days on which journeys made to work/college.

M	T	W	T	F	S	S	M	T	W	T	F	S	S
o	u	e	h	r	a	u	o	u	e	h	r	a	u
n	e	d	u	i	t	n	n	e	d	u	i	t	n
			.										

Q.3a Do you start your regular journey to work or college from this address or from somewhere else?
From this address ☐
From another address ☐
Please mark one

Q.3b How far from your place of residence is the place where you work or study?
More than 25 miles ☐
25 miles or less ☐
Please mark one

Q.4a Where do you normally start this journey from?
Please give as much detail as possible
Street _____
District/Area _____
Town _____
County _____

Q.4b Where is your place of work or college?
Please give as much detail as possible
Street _____
District/Area _____
Town _____
County _____

Q.5 What is the <u>main</u> method of travel you use on your normal journey to and from the place where you work or study?
Please mark one

Taken by employer's bus, lorry or car ☐
Bus ☐
Train ☐
Car/van (driver) ☐
Car/van (passenger) ☐
Motorcycle/moped ☐
Pedal cycle ☐
On foot ☐
Other method (write in) _____ ☐

Q.6a If your main method is TRAIN where do you get <u>on</u> the train?
Please give as much detail as possible
Town _____
or Station _____

Q.6b And where do you get <u>off</u> the TRAIN?
Please give as much detail as possible
Town _____
or Station _____

OTHER JOURNEYS OF OVER 25 MILES MADE WITHIN GREAT BRITAIN (EXCLUDING NORTHERN IRELAND) WITHIN THE LAST 14 DAYS

Note — a journey is to a place. When you come home again or go on to another place that counts as another journey — please don't count any journeys you have made driving or as a member of the crew of, long or short distance lorries, trains, buses, taxis and aircraft.

Q.7 Have you made any journeys of <u>over 25 miles</u> of the following types within the last 14 days? — Journeys to do with holidays, leisure, business and personal life.   Yes ☐
(Do not count regular journeys to or from work or college which have been covered already)   No ☐ — Go to last page

Please give details of each journey <u>over 25 miles</u> made in the last 14 days. <u>A return journey counts as a separate journey.</u> If any trip included travel overseas please record only the part travelled in Great Britain, providing this was over 25 miles.

Q.8 How many of these journeys have you made in the last 14 days?
Write in number of journeys. _____

If you made more than 6 journeys of over 25 miles please give details of the first 6 journeys. If you have made no journeys please turn to the last page.

Q.9 Please write in the:—

	First Journey	Second Journey	Third Journey	Fourth Journey	Fifth Journey	Sixth Journey
Date of journey	_____	_____	_____	_____	_____	_____
Day of week of journey	Mon ☐ Tues. ☐ Wed. ☐ Thur. ☐ Fri. ☐ Sat. ☐ Sun. ☐	Mon ☐ Tues ☐ Wed. ☐ Thur. ☐ Fri. ☐ Sat. ☐ Sun. ☐	Mon ☐ Tues. ☐ Wed. ☐ Thur. ☐ Fri. ☐ Sat. ☐ Sun. ☐	Mon ☐ Tues. ☐ Wed. ☐ Thur. ☐ Fri. ☐ Sat. ☐ Sun. ☐	Mon ☐ Tues. ☐ Wed. ☐ Thur. ☐ Fri. ☐ Sat. ☐ Sun. ☐	Mon ☐ Tues ☐ Wed. ☐ Thur. ☐ Fri. ☐ Sat. ☐ Sun. ☐

Q.10 What was the <u>main</u> purpose of the journey?

Note — If you were returning home — please mark the activity from which you were returning.

Please mark one for each journey

	First	Second	Third	Fourth	Fifth	Sixth
Appointment or call in course of work	☐	☐	☐	☐	☐	☐
Shopping/personal business	☐	☐	☐	☐	☐	☐
(To/from) Holiday/forces leave	☐	☐	☐	☐	☐	☐
Sport/entertainment	☐	☐	☐	☐	☐	☐
Visiting friend/relations	☐	☐	☐	☐	☐	☐
Pleasure trip	☐	☐	☐	☐	☐	☐
Other (Please write in)	☐	☐	☐	☐	☐	☐

Q.11 What was the <u>main</u> method of travel used?

Please mark one for each journey

	First	Second	Third	Fourth	Fifth	Sixth
Train	☐	☐	☐	☐	☐	☐
Ordinary bus/express bus	☐	☐	☐	☐	☐	☐
Coach excursion or tour (for which ticket is required)	☐	☐	☐	☐	☐	☐
Privately hired bus or coach	☐	☐	☐	☐	☐	☐
Taxi/chauffeur-driven car hire	☐	☐	☐	☐	☐	☐
Car/van (driver)	☐	☐	☐	☐	☐	☐
Car/van (passenger)	☐	☐	☐	☐	☐	☐
Motorcycle/moped	☐	☐	☐	☐	☐	☐
Pedal cycle	☐	☐	☐	☐	☐	☐
*Aircraft	☐	☐	☐	☐	☐	☐
Other (Please write in)	☐	☐	☐	☐	☐	☐

* Note: only tick aircraft if the complete aircraft journey was within Great Britain.

	First Journey	Second Journey	Third Journey	Fourth Journey	Fifth Journey	Sixth Journey
Q.12 What was the main reason for your choosing this method of travel? *Mark one for each journey.*						
Cheapest	☐	☐	☐	☐	☐	☐
Speed	☐	☐	☐	☐	☐	☐
Most comfortable	☐	☐	☐	☐	☐	☐
No choice	☐	☐	☐	☐	☐	☐
Organised trips	☐	☐	☐	☐	☐	☐
Most convenient	☐	☐	☐	☐	☐	☐
Other (write in)	☐	☐	☐	☐	☐	☐
Q.13a Where did you start this journey from?						
District/Area						
Town						
County						
Q.13b What was the town and district of your final destination?						
District/Area						
Town						
County						
Q.13c Was this journey to or from your place of residence?						
Yes	☐	☐	☐	☐	☐	☐
No	☐	☐	☐	☐	☐	☐
Q.14 Was any part of this trip outside Great Britain? IF YES What was the main country you visited? (Write in)						
Q.15a If your main method of travel was TRAIN or AIRCRAFT, where did you get on the train or aircraft?						
Town						
Station or Airport						
Q.15b And where did you get off the TRAIN or AIRCRAFT?						
Town						
Station or Airport						
Q.16 Were you travelling alone, or were you travelling with any of your family, friends, relatives etc., whom you had arranged to travel with?						
Alone	☐	☐	☐	☐	☐	☐
With others	☐	☐	☐	☐	☐	☐

'ALONE' go to Q.18

Appendix D   133

	First Journey	Second Journey	Third Journey	Fourth Journey	Fifth Journey	Sixth Journey
Please mark in number for each journey.						
Q.17 How many others were there with you?						
Of these						
a) How many were under 14?						
b) How many were 14 or 15?						
c) How many were 16 or 17?						
d) How many were 18 or over?						
Q.18 How many nights did you spend away from home on the trip which includes this journey? Write in number:—						

This section includes questions about yourself and it is, like everything else, strictly confidential. Answers are used only in combination with others to provide statistical analysis or travel information and cannot be individually identified.

Your Sex:— Male ☐   Female ☐

Your Age:—
- 16 – 17 ☐
- 18 – 19 ☐
- 20 – 24 ☐   Please mark one
- 25 – 34 ☐
- 35 – 44 ☐
- 45 – 54 ☐
- 55 – 64 ☐
- 65+ ☐

What is your occupation?
(please give as much detail as possible including the industry)
(if retired, state previous occupation)
Write in _____

What is your position in the household?
- Head of the household ☐
- Housewife ☐
- Son/daughter or head of household ☐
- Parent/parent-in-law of head of household ☐
- Other (write in) _____ ☐

What is the occupation of the head of the household?

Note — If you are the head of the household write in "as before".

(if retired, state previous occupation.)

_____

Does your household have use of a car?   Yes ☐   No ☐

Do you have a current motor car driving licence?   Yes ☐   No ☐

How many members (including yourself) of the household are there aged:

Please mark number of

Aged	Males (1 2 3 4 5)	Females (1 2 3 4 5)
0 – 4	☐ ☐ ☐ ☐ ☐	☐ ☐ ☐ ☐ ☐
5 – 13	☐ ☐ ☐ ☐ ☐	☐ ☐ ☐ ☐ ☐
14 – 15	☐ ☐ ☐ ☐ ☐	☐ ☐ ☐ ☐ ☐
16 – 17	☐ ☐ ☐ ☐ ☐	☐ ☐ ☐ ☐ ☐
18 – 19	☐ ☐ ☐ ☐ ☐	☐ ☐ ☐ ☐ ☐
20 – 24	☐ ☐ ☐ ☐ ☐	☐ ☐ ☐ ☐ ☐
25 – 34	☐ ☐ ☐ ☐ ☐	☐ ☐ ☐ ☐ ☐
35 – 44	☐ ☐ ☐ ☐ ☐	☐ ☐ ☐ ☐ ☐
45 – 54	☐ ☐ ☐ ☐ ☐	☐ ☐ ☐ ☐ ☐
55 – 64	☐ ☐ ☐ ☐ ☐	☐ ☐ ☐ ☐ ☐
65 or over	☐ ☐ ☐ ☐ ☐	☐ ☐ ☐ ☐ ☐

We would be interested to hear any comment you may have about the public transport service? (write in)

_____

_____

_____

Thank you for your help, please return this to us in the stamped return envelope supplied.

Subject Index

APPTO, *See* Association of Public Passenger Transport Operators
Association of Public Passenger Transport Operators, 3.7.6, 4.4.3, 4.6.3
Automobile Association, 3.7.8, 3.7.9, 4.3.4
Bicycles, 3.1.9, 3.2.1, 3.3.2, 3.7.4, 4.2, 5.10
Bicycles, expenditure on, 4.2.4
Blue Book, National Income, 1.1.4, 3.5.1, 3.7.3, 3.7.5, 3.7.8, 4.2.4, 4.3.2, 4.3.3, 4.3.4, 4.4.1, 4.4.2, 4.4.8, 4.6.1
British Electrical Traction, 2.2.6
British Home Tourism Survey, 3.1.16
British Road Federation, 4.3.6
British Transport Commission, 1.3.1, 2.2.5, 2.2.6, 3.6.1
Bus Company, National, 2.2.1, 2.2.5, 2.2.6, 2.2.8, 3.6.1
Bus drivers' and conductors' licences, 3.4.1, 3.4.2, 4.4.4
Bus industry data, 3.4.1, 3.5.1
Business journeys, 1.4

Capital, public transport, 4.4.8
Car parking, 3.7.5, 3.7.9, 4.3.6
Carriages, contract, 3.4.2
Carriages, express, 3.4.2
Carriages, stage, 3.4.2
Cars, private, 4.3
Census of population, regional data from, 4.5.8
Census of population transport data, 3.7.4, 4.5.8
Census-road, counting methods, 3.3.2
Census-road, publication of results, 3.3.3
Census-road, regional data in, 4.5.3
Censuses, road, 3.3, 4.5.3
Channel Islands, 1.1.2, 1.1.3
Chartered Institute of Transport, 3.2.3
Circular trips, 1.3.1
Commercial Motor, 3.7.8, 4.3.4, 4.4.2
Computer data, 5.3
Contract carriages, 3.4.2
Cost of fuel, 3.7.5, 3.7.8, 4.4.2
Cost of insurance, 3.7.5, 3.7.8, 4.4.2
Cost of licences, 3.7.5, 3.7.8
Cost of lubricants, 3.7.5, 3.7.8, 4.4.2
Cost of maintenance and repairs, 3.7.5, 3.7.8, 4.4.2
Cost of tyres, 3.7.5, 3.7.8, 4.4.2
Cost of wages, 4.4.2, 4.4.3
Costs, vehicle operation, 1.3.3, 3.7.3, 3.7.5, 3.7.8, 4.3.4, 4.4.2, 4.4.3
Criticism of existing data, 5
Customs and Excise reports, 1.1.4

Dawson expenditure estimates, Rudd, 3.7.5, 4.2.4, 4.3.3
Definition of a public service vehicle, 1.2.1, 3.4.2, 4.4.7
Definition of journey, 1.3.1, 1.4

Definition of journey stage, 1.3.1
Definitions, standardization of, 5.9
Department of Employment, 4.4.4
Department of Environment library, 3.2.3
Department of the Environment, 1.1.3, 1.3.3, 3.2.3, 5.3
Depreciation of vehicles, 3.7.5, 3.7.8, 4.3.3, 4.4.2
Diesel public transport vehicles, 4.4.7
Drivers, usual, main, 3.1.7
Driving licence holders, 3.1.6, 3.1.7

Earnings in public transport, wages and, 4.4.5
Earnings Survey, New, 4.4.5
Employer-owned vehicles, 3.1.11
Employment data, regional, 4.5.9
Employment in public transport, 3.7.7, 4.4.4, 4.5.9
European Economic Community rules, 1.4
Excise reports, Customs and, 1.1.4
Excursions, tours and, 2.2.2, 2.2.8, 3.1.9, 3.4.2, 4.4.2
Executives, Passenger Transport, 2.2.1, 2.2.4, 2.2.8, 3.5.4, 3.7.6
Expenditure estimates for road transport, 3.7.5
Expenditure estimates, Rudd/Dawson, 3.7.5, 4.2.4, 4.3.3
Expenditure in NTS, 3.1.13
Expenditure on bicycles, 4.2.4
Expenditure on vehicles, 3.7.5, 3.7.8
Expenditure, private transport, 4.3.2, 4.3.3
Expenditure, Public transport, 3.7.5, 4.4.1, 4.4.2
Expenditure Survey, Family, 1.1.4, 3.7.3, 4.2.4, 4.3.2, 4.5.7, 4.6.2
Expenditure, tax element in transport, 4.4.2
Expenditure, total, travel, 5.16
Express carriages, 3.4.2
Express services, 3.4.2, 4.4.1, 4.4.2

Family Expenditure Survey, 1.1.4, 3.7.3, 4.2.4, 4.3.2, 4.5.7, 4.6.2
Family Expenditure Survey, Regional data from, 4.5.7, 4.5.10
Fares, 3.4.1, 3.7.3, 4.4.6
FES, *see* Family Expenditure Survey
Finance Act 1920, 5.1
Forecasts of vehicles and traffic, 4.3.8
Fuel, cost of, 3.7.5, 3.7.8, 4.2.2

Garaging, 3.7.5, 3.7.9, 4.3.6
General Household Survey, 3.1.17, 4.6.4
Government Social Surveys, 3.1.1, 3.1.2
Green-line, 2.2.5, 3.1.9

Head of household, socio-economic group of, 3.1.6, 3.1.17
Hire cars, 1.2.1, 2.1.2, 3.1.9, 3.7.5, 4.3.7, 5.12
Hire purchase arrangements, 3.7.3, 4.3.3
History of inland transport statistics, 5.1
Holiday travel in NTS, 3.1.14, 3.1.16

Household, socio-economic group of head of, 3.1.6, 3.1.17
Household Survey, General, 3.1.17, 4.6.4
Household surveys, 3.1.1, 3.1.2, 3.1.4
Households in NTS, 3.1.5, 3.1.6

Improvements, suggested, 5
Income Blue Book, National, 1.1.4, 3.5.1, 3.7.3, 3.7.5, 3.7.8, 4.2.4, 4.3.2, 4.3.3, 4.3.4, 4.4.1, 4.4.2, 4.4.8, 4.6.1
Index of traffic and transportation surveys, 3.2.2, 3.2.3
Index, price, 4.4.6
Industrial Classification, Standard, 4.3.7, 4.4.5, 4.4.9
Inland transport, 1.1.3, 1.1.5
Inland transport statistics, history of, 5.1
Institute of Transport, Chartered, 3.2.3
Institute, Town Planning, 3.2.3
Insurance, cost of, 3.7.5, 3.7.8, 4.4.2
Interest on vehicles, 3.7.5, 3.7.8, 4.3.3
Internal transport, 1.1.1, 1.1.3
Isle of Man, 1.1.2

Journey, definition of, 1.3.1, 1.4
Journey frequency in NTS, 3.1.8
Journey, length of, 3.1.8, 5.15
Journey, passenger, 1.3.2, 1.3.4, 2.2.8, 4.4.1
Journey, purpose of, 3.1.9, 3.1.15, 3.2.1, 4.4.1
Journey stage, definition of, 1.3.1
Journey stages in NTS, 3.1.8
Journey in NTS, 3.1.5, 3.1.8, 3.1.9, 3.1.10

Laboratory, Transport and Road Research, 1.3.3, 3.2.3, 3.7.5, 4.1.2, 4.3.4, 4.3.8, 5.1
Labour, public transport, 3.7.7, 4.4.4
Length of journey, 3.1.8, 5.15
Library, Department of Environment, 3.2.3
Licence holders, driving, 3.1.6, 3.1.7
Licences, bus drivers' and conductors', 3.4.1, 3.4.2, 4.4.4
Licences, cost of, 3.7.5, 3.7.8
Load factor, 2.2.8, 5.14
Local authorities, 2.2.1, 2.2.3, 2.2.8
Local Government Act 1972, 2.2.3, 2.2.4
London Passenger Transport Board, 2.2.5
London Transport, 2.2.1, 2.2.5, 2.2.8, 3.1.1, 3.1.9, 3.5.2, 3.6.1
Long distance travel, 3.1.16
Lubricants, cost of, 3.7.5, 3.7.8, 4.4.2

Main drivers, usual, 3.1.7
Maintenance and repairs, cost of, 3.7.5, 3.7.8, 4.4.2
Measurement of passenger movement, 1.3
Methodology in transportation studies, 3.2.1
Mile, passenger, 1.3.3, 1.3.4, 1.3.5, 4.4.1, 5.14
Mile, vehicle, 1.3.5, 2.2.8, 4.3.1, 4.4.1, 5.14
Ministry of Transport, 3.1.1, 3.5.1, 5.1, 5.2, 5.3
Miscellaneous Financial Provisions Act 1955, 5.1
Mode of transport, 3.1.9, 3.1.15, 3.1.17, 3.2.1
Motor-cycles, 4.3
Motor transactions survey, 4.3.3
Motoring surveys, 3.1.1, 3.1.2, 3.1.4
Motorist Today, 3.7.9
Movement, measurement of passenger, 1.3

Movement on sites, 1.2.2
Movement, private, 2.1.1, 2.2.8
Movement, public, 2.2
Movement within buildings, 1.2.2
Movement, varieties of, passenger, 1.2

National Bus Company, 2.2.1, 2.2.5, 2.2.6, 2.2.8, 3.6.1
National Income Blue Book, 1.1.4, 3.5.1, 3.7.3, 3.7.5, 3.7.8, 4.2.4, 4.3.2, 4.3.3, 4.3.4, 4.4.1, 4.4.2, 4.4.8, 4.6.1
National Travel Survey, 1.2.3, 1.3.1, 1.3.2, 3.1, 4.5.2, 4.6.4
National Travel Survey, see also, NTS
New Earnings Survey, 4.4.5
Northern Ireland transport, 1.1.4, 4.6
NTS areas, 3.1.12
NTS data availability, 3.1.2
NTS, expenditure in, 3.1.13
NTS, holiday travel in, 3.1.14, 3.1.16
NTS, households in, 3.1.5, 3.1.6
NTS, journey frequency in, 3.1.8
NTS, journey stages in, 3.1.8
NTS journeys in, 3.1.5, 3.1.8, 3.1.9, 3.1.10
NTS, persons in, 3.1.5, 3.1.7
NTS, regional data in, 4.5.2
NTS results, publication of, 3.1.2, 3.1.15
NTS, ticket type in, 3.1.13
NTS, vehicle classification in 3.1.4, 3.1.11

Operation costs, vehicle, 1.3.3, 3.7.3, 3.7.5, 3.7.8, 4.3.4, 4.4.2, 4.4.3
Operational units, public transport, 2.2
Organization of passenger transport, 2
Output, passenger transport, 1.3.3, 1.3.5, 4.4.1

Parking, car, 3.7.5, 3.7.9, 4.3.6
Passenger journey, 1.3.2, 1.3.4, 2.2.8, 4.4.1
Passenger mile, 1.3.3, 1.3.4, 1.3.5, 4.4.1, 5.14
Passenger movement, measurement of, 1.3
Passenger movement, varieties of, 1.2
Passenger receipts, 4.4.1, 4.4.6
Passenger Transport Authority, 2.2.4
Passenger Transport Executives, 2.2.1, 2.2.4, 2.2.8, 3.5.4, 3.7.6
Passenger Transport in Great Britain, 1.1.3, 1.3.1, 3.1.2, 3.1.15, 3.1.16, 3.4.1, 3.5, 3.6.2, 4.2.1, 4.4.1, 4.4.2, 4.4.4, 4.4.6, 4.4.7, 4.4.8, 4.5.2, 4.5.5, 5.1, 5.2, 5.5, 5.16
Passenger transport in Great Britain, see also PTGB
Passenger transport, organization of, 2
Passenger transport output, 1.3.3, 1.3.5, 4.4.1
Pedestrians, 3.1.5, 3.2.1, 3.7.4, 4.1, 5.10
People and the Motor Car, 3.7.9
Persons in NTS, 3.1.5, 3.1.7
Petrol public transport vehicles, 4.4.7
Planning, traffic and road, 3.2.1, 4.3.8
Price index, 4.4.6
Prices, public transport, 4.4.6
Private cars, 4.3
Private movement, 2.1.1, 2.2.8
Private operators, 2.2.1, 2.2.2
Private transport expenditure, 4.3.2, 4.3.3
PTGB, accuracy of, 3.5.4, 3.5.5

Subject Index 137

PTGB, regional data from, 4.5.5
PTGB, returns for, 3.5.2
PTGB-financial years in, 3.5.3
Public movement, 2.2
Public Passenger Transport Operators, Association of, 3.7.6, 4.4.3, 4.6.3
Public service vehicle, definition of a, 1.2.1, 3.4.2, 4.4.7
Public transport capital, 4.4.8
Public transport, employment in, 3.7.7, 4.4.4, 4.5.9
Public transport expenditure, 3.7.5, 4.4.1, 4.4.2
Public transport labour, 3.7.7, 4.4.4
Public transport operational units, 2.2
Public transport prices, 4.4.6
Public transport receipts, 4.4.2
Public transport undertakings, reports of, 3.6
Public transport undertakings, vehicles owned by, 2.2.8
Public transport undertakings, relative size of, 2.2.8
Public transport vehicles, diesel, 4.4.7
Public transport vehicles, petrol, 4.4.7
Public transport, wages and earnings in, 4.4.5
Publication of NTS results, 3.1.2, 3.1.15
Publication of road census results, 3.3.3
Publication of transportation studies, 3.2.2
Purpose of journey, 3.1.9, 3.1.15, 3.2.1, 4.4.1

Receipts, passenger, 4.4.1, 4.4.6
Receipts, public transport, 4.4.2
Regional data from census of population, 4.5.8
Regional data from Family Expenditure Survey, 4.5.7, 4.5.10
Regional data from *PTGB*, 4.5.5
Regional data from Traffic Commissioners, 4.5.4
Regional data from vehicle registration, 4.5.6
Regional data in road census, 4.5.3
Regional data in NTS, 4.5.2
Regional employment data, 4.5.9
Regional statistics, 4.5
Register of transport undertakings, 3.7.7
Registration, regional data from vehicle, 4.5.6
Registration, vehicle, 3.7.2, 4.3.5, 4.4.7, 4.5.6, 4.5.10, 5.1
Repairs, cost of maintenance and, 3.7.5, 3.7.8, 4.4.2
Reports of public transport undertakings, 3.6
Retailing of used cars, 3.7.5
Returns for *PTGB*, 3.5.2
Road censuses, 3.4, 4.5.3
Road Federation, British, 4.3.6
Road fund, 5.1
Road Fund Report, 3.3.1
Road planning, traffic and, 3.2.1, 4.3.8
Road Research Laboratory, Transport and, 1.3.3, 3.2.3, 3.7.5, 4.1.2, 4.3.4, 4.3.8, 5.1
Road system, 1.1.5, 2.1.1
Road Transport Industry Training Board, 3.7.7
Road, types of, 3.3.4
Roads Act 1920, 5.1
Rudd/Dawson expenditure estimates, 3.7.5, 4.2.4, 4.3.3

Scottish Bus Group, *see* Scottish Transport Group
Scottish transport data, 4.5.5, 4.5.11
Scottish Transport Group, 2.2.1, 2.2.7, 2.2.8, 3.6.1

Self-drive hire car, 1.2.1
Services, express, 3.4.2, 4.4.1, 4.4.2
Services, stage, 2.2.2, 3.4.2, 4.4.1, 4.4.2
Sites, movement on, 1.2.2
Social Surveys, Government, 3.1.1, 3.1.2
Socio-economic group of head of household, 3.1.6, 3.1.17
Stage carriages, 3.4.2
Stage services, 2.2.2, 3.4.2, 4.4.1, 4.4.2
Standard Industrial Classification, 4.3.7, 4.4.5, 4.4.9
Standardization of definitions, 5.9
Stock of vehicles, 3.7.2, 4.3.5, 4.4.7, 4.5.10
Suggested improvements, 5
Survey, British Home Tourism, 3.1.16
Survey data overlapping, 5.7
Survey, Family Expenditure, 1.1.4, 3.7.3, 4.2.4, 4.3.2, 4.5.7, 4.6.2
Survey, General Household, 3.1.17, 4.6.4
Survey, motor transactions, 4.3.3
Survey, National Travel, 1.2.3, 1.3.1, 1.3.2, 3.1, 4.5.2, 4.6.4
Survey, New Earnings, 4.4.5
Surveys, Government Social, 3.1.1, 3.1.2
Surveys, household, 3.1.1, 3.1.2, 3.1.4
Surveys, index of traffic and transportation, 3.2.2, 3.2.3
Surveys, motoring, 3.1.1, 3.1.2, 3.1.4
Surveys, independent motoring, 3.7.9
Tax element in transport expenditure, 4.4.2
Taxis, 1.3.5, 2.1.2, 3.1.9, 3.7.5, 4.3.7, 5.12
Ticket type in NTS, 3.1.13
Time, valuation of travel, 1.3.3
Tours and excursions, 2.2.2, 2.2.8, 3.1.9, 3.4.2, 4.4.2
Town Planning Institute, 3.2.3
Traffic and road planning, 3.2.1, 4.3.8
Traffic and transportation surveys, index of, 3.2.2, 3.2.3
Traffic Commissioners, 2.2.2, 3.4, 3.5.1, 4.5.4
Traffic Commissioners, regional data from, 4.5.4
Traffic flow, 3.3.2, 3.3.4, 4.3.1
Traffic, forecasts of vehicles and, 4.3.8
Traffic levels, 3.3.2
Training Board, Road Transport Industry, 3.7.7
Transport Acts, 2.2.1, 2.2.4, 2.2.6
Transport and Road Research Laboratory, 1.3.3, 3.2.3, 3.7.5, 4.1.2, 4.3.4, 4.3.8, 5.1
Transport, Chartered Institute of, 3.2.3
Transport Holding Company, 2.2.6, 3.6.1
Transport statistics, history of inland, 5.1
Transport undertakings, register of, 3.7.6
Transportation studies, 3.2, 4.3.6
Transportation studies, methodology in, 3.2.1
Transportation studies, publication of, 3.2.2
Transportation studies, zones in, 3.2.1
Transportation surveys, index of traffic and, 3.2.2, 3.2.3
Travel expenditure, total, 5.16
Travel Survey, National, 1.2.3, 1.3.1, 1.3.2, 3.1, 4.5.2, 4.6.4
Travel time, valuation of, 1.3.3
Trips, circular, 1.3.1
Types of road, 3.3.4
Tyres, cost of, 3.7.5, 3.7.8, 4.4.2

Underground, 2.2.5, 3.1.9
Undertakings, register of transport, 3.7.7

Undertakings, reports of public transport, 3.6
Undertakings, vehicles owned by public transport, 2.2.8
Undertakings, public transport, relative size of, 2.2.8
Used cars, retailing of, 3.7.5

Valuation of travel time, 1.3.3
Vehicle classification in NTS, 3.1.5, 3.1.11
Vehicle mile, 1.3.5, 2.2.8, 4.3.1, 4.4.1, 5.14
Vehicle operation costs, 1.3.3, 3.7.3, 3.7.5, 3.7.8, 4.3.4, 4.4.2, 4.4.3
Vehicle registration, 3.7.2, 4.3.5, 4.4.7, 4.5.6, 4.5.10, 5.1
Vehicle registration, regional data from, 4.5.6
Vehicles and traffic, forecasts of, 4.3.8

Vehicles, depreciation of, 3.7.5, 3.7.8, 4.3.3, 4.4.2
Vehicles, diesel public transport, 4.4.7
Vehicles, expenditure on, 3.7.5, 3.7.8
Vehicles owned by public transport undertakings, 2.2.8
Vehicles, petrol public transport, 4.4.7
Vehicles, stock of, 3.7.2, 4.3.5, 4.4.7, 4.5.10

Wages and earnings in public transport, 4.4.5
Wages, cost of, 4.4.2, 4.4.3
Welsh transport data, 4.5.12

Zones in transportation studies, 3.2.1

13
Road Goods Transport

by
ANTHONY WATSON

Contents

1 **Introduction** 9
   1.1 *Scope* 9
   1.2 *Characteristics and Organization* 9
   1.3 *Licensing and Regulation* 10
   1.4 *Trade Associations* 11
   1.5 *Importance relative to Other Transport* 12
   1.6 *Statistical Reporting* 12

2 **Usage, Definitions, Coverage and Measurement** 14
   2.1 *Usage, Definitions, Coverage* 14
   2.2 *Measurement* 16

3 **Sources** 18
   3.1 *Introduction* 18
   3.2 *Vehicle Registration and Excise Licensing* 18
   3.3 *Annual Reports of Area Licensing Authorities* 19
   3.4 *The MOT, DOE and DTp Road Goods Sample Surveys* 20
   3.5 *The Goods Vehicle Index (1962) and the Goods Vehicle List (1972)* 27
   3.6 *TRTA Survey of C-Licensed Vehicles* 28
   3.7 *The Small Firm in the Road Haulage Industry* 29
   3.8 *Study on the Road Haulage Industry since 1968* 29
   3.9 *Reports of Undertakings* 30
   3.10 *Trade Tables of Operating Costs in Publications* 30
   3.11 *Road Haulage Association Cost Reports* 31
   3.12 *Rudd/Dawson Estimates of Expenditure on Road Transport* 31
   3.13 *Survey of Operating Costs in Road Freight Transport* 32
   3.14 *Censuses of Production and Distribution* 34
   3.15 *Survey of Transport from Manufacturing Establishments* 35
   3.16 *Other Surveys of Industry's Use of Transport* 36
   3.17 *Dept. of Employment Publications* 37
   3.18 *Annual Reports of the Road Transport Industry Training Board* 38
   3.19 *The National Accounts* 38
   3.20 *Input–Output Analyses* 40
   3.21 *Road Traffic Censuses and Counts* 41
   3.22 *Traffic and Transportation Studies and Surveys* 44
   3.23 *Road Accidents* 44
   3.24 *Studies of Environmental Effects* 45
   3.25 *Digest of Energy Statistics* 46

Road Goods Transport

   3.26 *Prices and Charges*   47
   3.27 *Goods Vehicle Roll-on/Roll-off Traffic at Ports*   47
   3.28 *DTp Roll-on/Roll-off Goods Survey*   48
   3.29 *EEC Statistical Requirements*   48
   3.30 *Highway Statistics*   49
   3.31 *Transport Statistics, Great Britain*   50
   3.32 *CSO Monthly Digest and Annual Abstract*   50
   3.33 *Basic Road Statistics*   51
   3.34 *Publications by International Organizations*   51

4 **Regional Statistics**   53
   4.1   *The Regional Abstracts and Digests*   53
   4.2   *Other Sources*   53

5 **Modelling and Forecasts**   54

6 **Comments and Suggestions**   55

   Quick Reference List   59
   Quick Reference List Key to Publications   67
   Bibliography   75
   Appendix A: DTp Index of Traffic and Transportation Surveys   78
   Appendix B: Copies of Forms   93
   Subject Index   123

Author's Foreword

The author is much indebted to a number of experts for many useful comments and suggestions made on his first draft. He is also grateful to staff of the DTp Headquarters Library and of the Library of the Scottish Office, Edinburgh, for their efficient assistance; and to Mr J. A. Rushbrook for the trouble he took, on his behalf, in clearing a considerable number of questions in various quarters at the London end, to Professor Maunder for guidance and patience, and to his assistant Mrs Juliet Horwood, particularly for compiling the Subject Index.

Edinburgh

A. H. Watson
April 1977

List of Abbreviations

BM	*Business Monitor* (publication)
BRB	British Railways Board
BRF	British Road Federation
BRS	British Road Services
BSO	Business statistics office
BTC	British Transport Commission
CAPS	Cost and Productivity Scheme
CIC	Centre for Interfirm Comparisons
CSO	Central Statistical Office
CSTE	Commodity Classification for Transport Statistics in Europe
DE	Department of Employment
DOE	Department of the Environment
DTp	Department of Transport
DVLC	Drivers and Vehicles Licensing Centre (Swansea)
ECE	Economic Commission for Europe (within United Nations)
ECMT	European Conference of Ministers of Transport
EEC	European Economic Community
Ec Pl	Economic Planning (Regions)
FH	For hire or reward
f.g.v.	Farmers' goods vehicles
FTA	Freight Transport Association
GDFCF	Gross Domestic Fixed Capital Formation
GDP	Gross Domestic Product
g.g.v.	General goods vehicles
g.v.	Goods vehicles
GVI	Goods Vehicle Index
GVL	Goods Vehicle List
HGV	Heavy Goods Vehicle
HS	*Highway Statistics* (publication)
IEA	Institute of Economic Affairs
LTO	Local Taxation Office
MLH	Minimum List Heading (in SIC)
MOT	Ministry of Transport
NBPI	National Board for Prices and Incomes
NFC	National Freight Corporation
NPC	National Ports Council
NST	Nomenclature for Statistics of Transport (EEC classification)
OA	Own account

PTGB	*Passenger Transport in Great Britain* (publication)
RE	Railway Executive (of BTC)
RHA	Road Haulage Association
RHE	Road Haulage Executive (of BTC)
RRL	Road Research Laboratory
RSS	Royal Statistical Society
RTITB	Road Transport Industry Training Board
SIC	Standard Industrial Classification
SMMT	Society of Motor Manufacturers and Traders
SN	*Statistical News* (publication)
TRRL	Transport and Road Research Laboratory
TRTA	Traders' Road Transport Association
TS	*Transport Statistics Great Britain* (publication)
v.v.	vice versa

Reference Date of Sources Reviewed

This review is believed to represent the position, broadly speaking, as it obtained at January 1976. Later revisions have been inserted up to the proof-reading stage (April 1977) taking account, as far as possible, of significant changes in the situation including the separation of the Department of Transport from the Department of the Environment.

I Introduction

1.1 Scope

1.1.1 This review discusses the sources of information on the service activity, road goods transport, embracing

(a) carriage for hire or reward
(b) carriage 'on own account', i.e. by undertakings in connection with a firm's own business.

1.1.2 The relevant Minimum List Headings in the 1968 Standard Industrial Classification (SIC) [B 39] are

MLH 703—Road haulage contracting for general hire or reward

MLH 704—Other road haulage—comprising cartage and haulage undertakings of all types mainly engaged in carrying goods in connection with another business operated under common ownership or control, e.g. separate road haulage subsidiaries of large undertakings.

A small proportion of 'own-account' transport units or departments which qualify as separate establishments because a full range of economic census information can be supplied are also classified to MLH 704: some others, not qualifying as establishments, if at separate addresses, may also for limited purposes only, e.g. for geographical analysis of employment, be treated as 'local units' and classified to MLH 704—*see* paras 8 and 9 of [B 39].

1.1.3 The great bulk of 'own-account' activity is by units which do not qualify as establishments, so that the activity is classified to the MLH appropriate to the main business concerned. This must always be remembered in using SIC-classified data, e.g. in national income tables and employment statistics.

1.1.4 In the 1958 version of the SIC [B 38] there was only one MLH for road haulage, MLH 703—Road haulage contracting. The rules for defining establishments were also somewhat different.

1.1.5 Separate establishments engaged in repair of vehicles are not regarded as part of road goods transport either for the purposes of official statistics on road transport or in the SIC—they are in MLH 894—but ordinary maintenance and running repairs done by an operator are treated as part of the transport or other main activity.

1.2 Characteristics and Organization

1.2.1 Road goods transport uses (end 1975) some 1·7 million goods vehicles. The great majority of these, some 1·5 million, are owned and used mainly on own-account work by undertakings across the whole range of industries and services, but predominantly by distribution and construction, which together account for some two-thirds of the total own-account fleet. Of this 1·5 million vehicles, about 1·1 million are light vans used for local delivery work, maintenance and service functions of many kinds, and in various roles ancillary to the main business of the owners.

1.2.2 Some 200,000 are used by the professional hauliers in hire and reward operations of many kinds, including, for example, long-distance 'trunk' services for container and other traffic, local general haulage, parcels services, furniture removals, tanker and refrigerated services, tipping and other kinds.

1.2.3 The professional hauliers, with, in general, larger and more intensively used vehicles, account for about half the total tonnage of goods carried, and for nearly two-thirds of the total ton-mileage; their share of the total has been rising steadily.

1.2.4 The activity is highly fragmented. Apart from the million or so light vans, many of them owned in ones and twos by small retail and other businesses, the 560,000-plus larger vehicles now subject to Operators' Licensing (see 1.3.5 below) are in the hands of well over 100,000 operators: in both the public haulage and own-account fields, while there are a number of large fleets of 100 vehicles or more, about 70% of the operators have either one or two vehicles.

1.2.5 The nationalized element comprises a number of companies, owning altogether some 25,000 vehicles, providing a variety of general haulage and specialized services. They include British Road Services Ltd., BRS Parcels Ltd., National Carriers Ltd. and Freightliners Ltd. They operate, as Companies' Act companies, as subsidiaries of the National Freight Corporation (NFC) set up under the 1968 Transport Act [B 47]. See also the White Paper *The Transport of Freight* [B 50], and for a detailed examination, the Report from the Select Committee on Nationalized Industries [QRL 99].

1.2.6 There is no organized road haulage market, not surprisingly in view of the immense variety of service and the countrywide dispersion of users and operators. Charges are a matter for negotiation between trader and haulier: there is free and often intense competition in rates and quality of service not only within the industry, but also, in some sectors, with the railways and the Post Office. The Road Haulage Association (RHA), the trade association of the 'for hire' operators, provides guidance to its members on operating costs and their trends and, on a confidential basis, on rates, but this is not necessarily adhered to closely, if at all. Some operators publish tariffs, but these are generally to be regarded more as bases for negotiation than as actual prices in force.

1.3 Licensing and Regulation

1.3.1 For most of its lifetime, the industry has operated under the licensing system set up by the 1933 Road and Rail Traffic Act [B 35]. This distinguished four types of carriers' licences—A, Contract A, B and C licences. Vehicles operated on an A licence could be used for the carriage of goods for hire and reward; those on 'Contract A' were vehicles whose operator was under contract for a continuous period of at least a year, to carry goods for another firm in connection with its trade or business, other than road haulage; B-licensed vehicles could be used for carrying goods either in connection with the business of the licensee, or for hire or reward. C-licensed vehicles could be used only for the carriage of goods in connection with the trade or business, other than road haulage, of the licensee.

1.3.2 This system of 'quantity' licensing was administered by eleven Area Licensing Authorities appointed by the Minister of Transport. C licences were freely available, subject to good behaviour, but applicants for A or B licences had to prove need against objections from existing licence holders and the railways. If granted, B licences were subject to restrictions, e.g. in the areas served and commodities carried. Holders of A licences had to operate within the definition of 'normal user', i.e. the main work intended for the vehicles which had to be declared at the time of application (see para 2.30 of [QRL 57]).

1.3.3 The system was suspended during the Second World War, modified during the period from 1947 to 1953 when long-distance haulage was nationalized, and restored by the Transport Act of 1953 [B 45] with changes in criteria directed towards more liberality in the granting of licences. The main change was that considerations of the interests of trade and industry as users of transport were to have priority over those of the providers of transport. The Act continued in force until 1968.

1.3.4 The licensing system and its categories strongly influenced both content and methodology of the statistical surveys carried out between 1952 and 1968.

1.3.5 *The present system*
Under the present system of 'quality' licensing introduced by the Transport Act, 1968 [B 47] following recommendations of the Geddes Committee on carriers' licensing [QRL 57]

1. Operators of small goods vehicles—those not over $1\frac{1}{2}$ tons unladen weight (if unplated) or $3\frac{1}{2}$ tons gross plated weight (*see* 2.1.10)—need no carriers' licence.
2. Operators of other goods vehicles must hold Operators' Licences. An Operator's Licence may be obtained by satisfying the licensing authorities for each area where the operator has a base, that he is a fit person to hold a licence, that he has made satisfactory arrangements for complying with road transport laws, and has sufficient financial resources at his disposal to maintain satisfactorily the number of vehicles he wishes to operate.
3. Every holder of an Operator's Licence, and every small goods vehicle operator may carry goods for hire or reward, or on his own account, or both, without constraint as to goods carried or areas served.

For more detail, *see* the 'popular' guide [B 27].

1.3.6 A provision of the 1968 Act, enabling the Minister of Transport to introduce a system of 'quantity' licensing for 'large goods vehicles'—those over 16 tons when loaded—doing trips of over 100 miles or carrying certain bulk goods over shorter distances, with the NFC and the British Railways Board (BRB) having the right to object if the proposed service could be provided wholly or partly by rail, remains (early 1977) in abeyance.

1.3.7 For a full account of the earlier licensing system and its working over the various periods of its life, *see* the Report of the Geddes Committee *Carriers' Licensing* [QRL 57]. *The Small Firm in the Road Haulage Industry* [QRL 2] has a compact account of carriers' licensing from 1933 onwards, and discusses its influence on the growth and structure of the industry. See also *Road and Rail* [B 23] particularly for the 1920s and 1930s, *European Transport* [B 3], and *The Road Haulage Industry Since 1968* [QRL 1].

1.3.8 Operators must comply with a variety of regulations, largely under the Road Safety Act, 1967 [B 36], aimed at safety. These provide, *inter alia*, for annual testing at Ministry stations of vehicles over $1\frac{1}{2}$ tons unladen weight, for operators to have adequate systems of inspection and maintenance, for maximum permitted loading of vehicles and for maximum working hours for drivers. Drivers of Heavy Goods Vehicles (in this context vehicles over 3 tons unladen weight) must undergo tests and hold special licences: between 1939 and 1967, these were not required.

1.3.9 EEC regulations imposing more stringent limitations on drivers' hours, and requiring the fitting of tachographs, providing a continuous record of distance, speed, driving time and stationary time, to vehicles over $3\frac{1}{2}$ tonnes gross weight were due to come into force for domestic operations on 1 January 1976, but the date for implementation has been postponed.

1.4 Trade Associations
1.4.1 The principal trade associations are the Road Haulage Association for the 'for hire'

operators (already mentioned) and the Freight Transport Association (FTA), founded in 1969 and merging the Traders Road Transport Association (TRTA) and some other traders' organizations. The British Road Federation (BRF) is a national organization representing varied interests, including operators, private motorists, road constructors, vehicle manufacturers and ancillary trades. Its objectives are stated as including the promotion of road development and of a constructive national transport policy. It publishes a useful annual—*Basic Road Statistics* [QRL 51]—*see* 3.33.

1.5 Importance relative to Other Transport

1.5.1 Taking a broad perspective it may be observed that in 1975, in domestic freight transport—

> road goods transport accounted for 85% of total tonnage, and 67% of total ton-mileage; rail had 10 and 17% respectively, and coastal shipping 2 and 13%;

on the roads—

> goods transport used 1·7 million of the total of 17·5 million vehicles licensed, and accounted for about 17% of total vehicle-mileage run;

users spent (at market prices) approximately—

> £8,800 million on road goods transport, £7,400 million on private motoring, £1,050 million on other road passenger transport and £860 million on rail freight and passenger services together.

Broad data of this type are to be found in the *Annual Abstract* [QRL 47], and with many detailed breakdowns in *Transport Statistics* (TS) [QRL 108]. *See also*, e.g., reports of road goods surveys by the Ministry of Transport (MOT) [QRL 24, QRL 25, QRL 103], *The Transport Needs of GB in the next 20 years* [B 49], the 1967 White Paper [B 50], the Consultation Document, *Transport Policy* [B 55], *European Transport* [B 3] and studies of expenditure [QRL 12, QRL 13, QRL 31].

1.5.2 Data on the importance of road goods transport in the UK economy are less easy to find. It is not legitimate (though it is sometimes done) to express users' expenditure (as in 1.5.1) as a share of gross domestic (or gross national) product (GDP), since the former is in gross expenditure terms and the latter in net output or value-added terms. The 1965–75 Blue Book [QRL 78] shows net output for UK transport as an 'industry' at some 6·2% of GDP in 1975, but this is not broken down by modes, and it excludes the great bulk of the contribution from own-account road transport which is probably some $3\frac{1}{2}$ to 4 percentage points. From a MOT survey on operators' costs in 1965 [QRL 23], the total contribution to GDP of road goods transport was estimated at some $5\frac{1}{2}\%$, of which professional haulage accounted for rather less than $1\frac{1}{2}$ percentage points (*see* (3.13.14)). No comparable up-to-date estimate has been published. *See also*, N. Rubra, *Transport and Communication in GB* [B 21] which discusses data sources on transport and communication, in less detail than the present review, but with an emphasis on the economic framework and on applications of the published data, and which includes a section on the difficulties and possibilities of using net output and other data in evaluating the importance of transport in the economy.

1.6 Statistical Reporting

1.6.1 There are no statutory obligations on the industry for regular statistical reporting on operations or output. Provisions of the Road and Rail Traffic Act of 1933 [B 35] and of the Road Traffic Act of 1960 [B 37], which lapsed with the passing of the 1968 Act, requiring licensed operators to keep records of journeys, district served, types of goods and maximum load carried, were for enforcement purposes and could not be used to require statistical reporting.

1.6.2 The various statistical enquiries conducted by the Ministry of Transport and later the Department of the Environment (DOE) and the Department of Transport (DTp) have all been sample surveys carried out under powers given by the Statistics of Trade Act 1947 [B41].

1.7 The next section deals with some matters of usage, definitions, coverage and measurement. Section 3 deals with primary and secondary sources of statistics and Section 4 with what is available on a regional basis. Section 5 gives some references to published work on use of available data for modelling and forecasting. In Section 6 some comments are made on what is at present available and on some gaps, and suggestions made for future development. Annexed are:

A Quick Reference List of statistical data arranged in subject order
A Quick Reference List Key to publications (QRL) given as sources
A general bibliography
Appendices with forms of return
A subject index

References in the text to publications given as, e.g., [QRL 8] refer to the QRL Key.

2 Usage, Definitions, Coverage and Measurement

2.1 Usage, Definitions, Coverage

2.1.1 Road transport for hire or reward is most commonly referred to as 'public haulage' or 'professional haulage' and its providers as public hauliers or professional hauliers. The term 'road haulage' is sometimes used in this sense—the Road Haulage Association's membership are the professional hauliers—but often in a wider sense, e.g. in the SIC, and sometimes in the sense of road goods transport as a whole. In this review, to minimize confusion, usage will as far as possible follow the SIC; 'road haulage' will refer to the combined activity of the MLH industries 'Road haulage contracting' and 'Other road haulage', which taken together will be referred to as the 'road haulage industry', or 'the industry'. Own-account transport, not in MLH 704, and thus treated in the SIC as ancillary activity within other industries will be referred to simply as 'own-account' transport.

2.1.2 Since the term 'public' can have the connotation of state-owned or operated, the short term 'for hire' is often preferred, particularly in international usage, to denote public haulage operation. It will be used here where the sense permits, but 'public haulage' or 'professional haulage' will also be used especially where reference to sources makes this appropriate. 'Public' will not be used to denote nationalized. FH and OA will be used as abbreviations for 'for hire' and 'on own-account'.

2.1.3 While the great majority of operators provide only FH or only OA services, a small proportion undertake both, and some of these operators' vehicles (under the pre-1968 licensing system those with B-licences) are used from time to time for both. In aggregate statistics with an FH/OA split, the output of these vehicles has customarily been classified as FH with the aggregate sometimes labelled 'mostly FH'. It is however planned by DOE (end 1975) to change to a new basis of classifying individual journeys, by purpose, as FH or OA.

2.1.4 *Goods vehicles*
In official statistics on road goods transport, the term *goods vehicle* is used with different meanings according to context.

2.1.5 In the context of vehicle excise licensing and registration, the term is restricted to mean a vehicle taxed to carry goods in connection with a trade or business, on public roads. It excludes vehicles not used on public roads, most vehicles belonging to the armed Forces, Crown vehicles—those owned by Government Departments, and other exempt vehicles. See *Transport Statistics Great Britain* (*Transport Statistics* or *TS* for short) [QRL 108], Notes and Definitions, and schedules to the Vehicles (Excise) Acts of 1962 [B 53] and 1971 [B 54] for more detail.

2.1.6 The excise licence class, goods vehicles (g.v.), includes vehicles licensed to draw trailers and has two subclasses, 'Farmers' (or Agricultural) Goods Vehicles' (f.g.v.) registered in the name of a person engaged in agriculture and used on roads solely for carrying the produce of, and requisites for, his agricultural land (71,000 in GB, 1975), and 'General Goods Vehicles' (g.g.v.)—the rest (1,703,000 in 1975), which for convenience includes tower wagons other than for lighting and showmen's goods vehicles (1,000 and 3,000 respectively in 1974 but not distinguished from

1975), and which also includes cars, e.g. estate cars, licensed to carry goods. Note that about 40,000 vehicles were transferred from Crown vehicles after the GPO's change in status in 1969; and for some changes in classification of farmers' vehicles see Notes in HS and TS [QRL 70, QRL 108].

2.1.7 In the context of traffic on the roads, as measured by roadside censuses and counts, vehicles are classified by enumerators according to their general appearance, and not by excise taxation status. In official statistics from these sources, vehicles with more than three wheels are classified as

'cars', which include taxis and light vans with side windows
'buses or coaches', and
'goods vehicles'

Here 'goods vehicles' is a sweeping-up category covering not only goods vehicles as normally understood, but also agricultural tractors and a variety of specialized vehicles like excavators, mobile cranes and mowing machines (all told about 420,000 vehicles in GB, 1975), as well as about 80,000 other vehicles in the 'Crown' and 'Exempt' excise classes, and some Forces' vehicles. Most of these additional 'goods vehicles' make comparatively little use of public roads—see HS and TS [QRL 70, QRL 108], Notes and Definitions.

2.1.8 In road accident reporting, the coverage of 'goods vehicles' is somewhere between that in the excise licensing and the road census contexts. Vehicles are classified according to their construction and not according to excise category or use at the time of the accident. Goods vehicles in this context exclude estate and other cars being used for the carriage of goods, but include vans that may be licensed as private vehicles, as well as Crown or Forces vehicles corresponding to normal commercial vehicles. See *Stats 20—Instructions for the Completion of Road Accident Reports* [B 43].

2.1.9 *Vehicle weights*
Classification of goods vehicles by *unladen weight* is enshrined in the excise licensing legislation and has naturally been used both in statistical series on vehicle stock and new registrations, and for vehicle classification in statistical survey work. For many purposes classification by *gross weight* or *maximum carrying capacity* is more meaningful.

2.1.10 *Gross weight* is the maximum authorized loaded weight. From 1968, under provisions of the Road Safety Act, 1967 [B 36], maximum gross weights, axle weights and where applicable total tractor plus trailer weights (train weights) are assigned at a vehicle's first annual examination and testing. They are indicated on plates fixed to vehicles and are referred to as *plated weights*. Before its first examination a vehicle is classified on the manufacturer's recommended gross weight. *Maximum Carrying Capacity* is the difference between unladen weight and gross weight. The ratio between carrying capacity and unladen weight varies considerably—*see*, e.g. tabulations in [QRL 103] Part 1, [QRL 104] and [QRL 25].

2.1.11 The term 'heavy goods vehicle' is generally used to cover all goods vehicles other than those in the light category, i.e. those with unladen weight over $1\frac{1}{2}$ tons or gross weight over $3\frac{1}{2}$ tons, and ranging up to the really heavy vehicles of over 30 tons gross weight. The term is thus far from being a synonym for 'Juggernaut'. Exceptionally in the context of special licensing for goods vehicle drivers (*see* 1.3.8 above) it refers to vehicles over 3 tons unladen weight.

2.1.12 *Coverage of road goods transport*
For conventional and practical reasons, the coverage of Road Goods Transport in all official

statistical enquiries beginning in 1952 has been limited to the activity of operating *General Goods Vehicles* for the carriage of goods on public roads in Great Britain. Thus it excludes the operation of farmers' goods vehicles, and of Crown and Exempt vans and lorries and Forces' vehicles. It also excludes all operations off the public roads, e.g. on construction sites and industrial sites. The Post Office Mail Services, including parcels service, are excluded, and there may be shifts between unrecorded and recorded road transport, e.g. of mail order houses' traffic, from parcel post to road haulage.

2.1.13 *Domestic and international road goods transport*
The term *domestic road goods transport* refers to operations by national operators between points wholly within national territory. *International road goods transport* is that undertaken by vehicles in journeys crossing national frontiers, whether by land or water crossings.

2.1.14 The statistics of the total output of road goods transport undertakings in Great Britain include both their output on domestic road goods transport, and also that on the parts of their international operations which are on the British road system. It takes no account of the operations of foreign carriers on the parts of their international journeys which are on British roads.

2.1.15 Statistics of traffic on the roads derived from roadside censuses (*see* 3.21 below) on the other hand *include* the movements of foreign-registered vehicles, which are not separately distinguished by the enumerators.

2.2 Measurement

2.2.1 The common measures of physical output of road goods transport are tonnage carried, ton-mileage, and vehicle-mileage (and metric equivalents).

2.2.2 *Tonnage* serves as a measure of the quantity of goods loaded (and unloaded) and transported. It has deficiencies. For many types of commodity, for example, furniture and livestock, weight is not a normal unit of quantity. For some types, and particularly low-density goods, e.g. furniture again, which may fill a vehicle before it is loaded to its full weight-carrying capacity, the cubic dimensions or the number of items may be more important to the carrier. In much OA transport, for example in local delivery work, in construction, and in maintenance and servicing work, records may not always be kept of the quantities of goods carried, let alone their weight. But no better common measure than weight is available and for the purposes of statistical enquiries operators are usually willing, given advance notice, to estimate weights of traffic where they are not otherwise recorded. The estimates may of course be rough and ready.

2.2.3 Tonnage data, however, reflect nothing of an essential dimension of transport—the distance moved. *Ton-mileage*, that is the weight of each consignment or load multiplied by the distance it is carried—is a better measure of work done. But although it incorporates a distance element, it is not very revealing as an aggregate. Thus, a total of 5,000 ton-miles could represent 1,000 local journeys averaging 5 miles with a 1 ton load, ten 10-ton loads carried 50 miles, or a single 10-ton load carried 500 miles—alternatives with very different operational, economic and environmental implications.

2.2.4 *Vehicle-mileage* is a useful measure from the point of view of the operator, of the work done by a vehicle, or fleet of vehicles, in providing the transport service, and a good measure also of the use of the road system. But as with ton-mileage, a given vehicle-mileage aggregate can represent many alternative collections of journeys—a single trip of 500 miles and back yielding the same number of vehicle-miles as 100 local trips of 5 miles each. And it takes no account of vehicle size or load capacity.

2.2.5 At best these measures take account of only one or two dimensions: it must always be borne in mind that transport output has many dimensions or attributes—weight, loadability, distance carried, origin, destination, commodity, size and type of vehicle used, transit time, convenience, reliability and other aspects of service quality, and others—affecting cost to the producer and price or value to the consumer or user. Great care is often necessary in interpreting and using apparently simple aggregate statistics. For a discussion of aggregate output measures in transport for index and other purposes *see* Bayliss and Hebden [B 4]. Deakin and Seward [QRL 15] also discuss this in their study of productivity in transport, and Munby in [B 18]. *See also* Glover [QRL 24].

2.2.6 The multidimensionality and great variety of product makes it desirable that data on output be collected at a stage which permits adequate analysis and cross-analysis. In collecting output data from operators, usually in respect of a sample of vehicles over a sample period, the basic record is normally a separate record of journey and load details for each vehicle journey. Data obtained from users may include records for individual consignments.

2.2.7 The computation of ton-mileage from the basic record involves a difficulty in respect of journeys with several, sometimes many, intermediate stops for unloading or loading, and often of a circular nature. These far outnumber end-to-end journeys in OA operations and account for an appreciable proportion in FH operations. The problem is to obtain a reasonably accurate result without involving the operator in an excessive recording burden. Various approaches have been used over the years, and are described in the methodological sections of the various survey reports. The current method sums the actual tonnage x mileage on each stage for journeys of fewer than five stops; for those of five or more stops, estimates are made from the total tonnage collected and/or delivered, and the numbers of stops for collection and delivery.

3 Sources

3.1 This section reviews the sources of data, in source order, grouped broadly by contexts, as follows:

   The vehicle and carriers' licensing systems (3.2–3.3)
   Operators' output and fleet structure (3.4–3.9)
   Operating costs, expenditure on road goods transport (3.10–3.13)
   Industries' use of road goods transport (3.14–3.16)
   Manpower and earnings (3.17–3.18)
   National Accounts and Input–Output analyses (3.19, 3.20)
   Goods transport as traffic on the roads (3.21–3.23)
   Road goods transport and the environment (3.24)
   Energy statistics (3.25)
   Prices and charges (3.26)
   International traffic and EEC statistics (3.27–3.29)
   Regular statistical publications (3.30–3.34)

There is necessarily some overlap between the groups, partly because of the number of different topics covered by some enquiries.

THE VEHICLE AND CARRIERS' LICENSING SYSTEMS

3.2 Vehicle Registration and Excise Licensing

3.2.1 Since 1920, vehicle licensing and registration have been functions of Local Authorities—including, until the recent reorganization, County, County Borough and Burgh Councils. From late 1974, the DOE (now DTp) computerized Driver and Vehicle Licensing Centre (DVLC) at Swansea took over new registrations and began the process of taking over re-licensing of existing vehicles: over a period of years it will progressively work back from the newest to the oldest vehicles by year of first registration. (See *Statistical News* (*SN*) 28.18 [B 42]).

3.2.2 Statistics of vehicles currently licensed have been based on an annual examination of licence files at the Local Taxation Offices (LTO). In years before 1961 and in 1966 a full count of vehicles was made. In 1961–5 and from 1967, the count has been based on a sample of licence files, generally one-tenth, but on a full count in LTOs with smaller numbers of files. See *HS* [QRL 70], Introduction, and *TS* [QRL 108] for details and note on sampling errors. Until all vehicles are registered centrally, a 10% sample on records remaining at LTOs will be combined with a complete census on vehicles transferred to DVLC.

3.2.3 For practical reasons the count in LTOs cannot be taken on a single day. The figures actually relate to all vehicles with a licence current in the quarter ending September 30 and hence contain some element of duplication or overstatement—they could, for example, include both a vehicle scrapped in the first month and its replacement.

3.2.4 It should be noted that, although licences must normally be taken out with the local authority in whose area they are kept, vehicles not ordinarily kept in any one area may be licensed with the authority of the area in which the holder lives or of that for his place of business. Owners of fleets normally license all vehicles with one authority. Thus numbers of vehicles licensed with a particular local authority may differ from those of numbers kept or operated in its area.

3.2.5 The current licence, or 'stock', figures for all excise licence classes and for exempt vehicles are published annually by DTp from 1974 in *TS* [QRL 108] which gives for the latest year,

(a) for general goods vehicles (g.g.v.) separately, stock by unladen-weight groups (also eleven-year series), stock by years of first registration by unladen-weight groups, stock by Economic Planning Regions (Ec Pl Regions) by unladen weight groups,

(b) for total goods vehicles (g.v.) (i.e. including f.g.v. and not distinguishing g.g.v., stock by registration and licensing authorities).

There are also series for total g.v. going back to 1930 annually, and by intervals back to 1903 for GB, and back to 1926 annually for UK. (The figures pre-1920 are highly questionable estimates by the Society of Motor Manufacturers and Traders (SMMT) made in 1935.)

3.2.6 From 1963 to 1973, the current licence figures were published annually in *HS* [QRL 70], and before 1963, in *Road Motor Vehicles* [QRL 92]. It may be noted that analyses of goods vehicle stock by registration and licensing authorities, and of g.g.v. stock by Ec Pl Regions, appeared first in *HS* 1966; and that analyses by years of first registration appeared first in *HS* 1969.

3.2.7 *New registrations*
Figures for GB derived from monthly tabulations from DVLC Swansea, and before late 1974 from monthly returns made by LTOs are published monthly in a *Business Monitor* (*BM*)—code M1 [QRL 76], and annually in *TS* [QRL 108] from 1974, and in *HS* [QRL 70] (1963 to 1973) and *Road Motor Vehicles* [QRL 92] before 1963.

3.2.8 *BM* gives latest month figures for g.g.v. by unladen-weight groups by fuel used, with year-to-date figures by unladen-weight groups. *TS* gives eleven-year series, and *HS* nine-year series, for g.g.v. by unladen-weight groups: *TS* has similar series by type of fuel used. Both *HS* and *TS* give annual series back to 1950 and month-by-month figures for the latest year, but only for g.v., without distinguishing g.g.v. More detailed analyses, by type of fuel and size of vehicle, and by Licensing Authority are available for an annual fee (see *TS*).

3.2.9 The Society of Motor Manufacturers and Traders' (SMMT) *Monthly Statistical Review* [QRL 100] also publishes figures of new registrations distinguishing used vehicles registered for the first time, and of vans and goods vehicles newly subject to hire-purchase agreements. The SMMT annual publication *The Motor Industry of Great Britain* [QRL 74] contains both new registration and current licence data. It gives some figures for the Isle of Man and Channel Islands (not in the GB figures) and some data on new registrations by make and nationality. Summary figures for new registrations and current licences of total g.v. are also published in *Basic Road Statistics* [QRL 51]—see 3.33 below.

3.3 Annual Reports of the Area Licensing Authorities

3.3.1 The reports [QRL 49] of the eleven Area Licensing Authorities, first appointed to administer the carriers' licensing provisions of the Road and Rail Traffic Act, 1933, are the main source of data about the working of the provisions for the regulation of the carriage of goods by road and about the licensing of drivers of Heavy Goods Vehicles (HGVs). Details of the licensing system set up by the 1933 Act and of the provisions for Operators' Licences which replaced it in 1968 have been given in 1.3 above. For details of the Authorities' Areas—the 'Traffic Areas' in England and Wales, *see* map in *TS* [QRL 108].

3.3.2 The reports from 1935 to 1969, with a gap between 1938 and 1945, give statistics at

September of each year (at December before 1951) of vehicles with each category of licence (A, B, C) and corresponding figures of operators, or rather licence holders—one operator might hold more than one category of licence. The vehicle figures are given for a range of unladen-weight groups.

3.3.3 In the collected reports for 1972 and subsequent years, there are summary statistics by Areas and in total for the number of operators holding Operators' Licences and of the vehicles operated thereunder, divided into tractor units and rigid vehicles. There is no breakdown by size of vehicle, and it is to be noted that the grand total for operators contains some duplication, since an operator must have a licence for each Area in which he has a base.

3.3.4 The individual Area reports also contain statistics of applications for licences, of objections received and of the numbers of cases heard at Public Inquiry; of suspensions, revocations and curtailment of licences; of prosecutions and convictions for offences relating e.g. to Operators' Licences, hours and records regulations, and to *The Motor Vehicles (Construction and Use) Regulations* [B 31], including the overloading of vehicles, plating and testing; of vehicle examinations and prohibitions, noise and smoke checks; of applications, issue, suspension and revocations of HGV Drivers' Licences.

3.3.5 It is to be noted that in 1961, the series for A, Contract A, and B vehicles were revised with effect back to 1946 after an overdue weeding of records. The series for C licence vehicles was also revised with effect back to 1951, to conform with the basis used from 1961 onwards, of estimating the number of C licence vehicles as the difference between the A and B figures and the total number of goods vehicles (excluding farmers' vehicles) shown in the annual censuses. *Basic Road Statistics* [QRL 51] for 1970 gives the 1938 figures and the complete series from 1946 to 1969.

3.3.6 Statistics of the total number of vehicles in each carriers' licensing class were also published in *HS* [QRL 70] from 1963 to 1968, but the 1969 to 1973 issues gave no data for vehicles under Operators' Licences. However, *TS* [QRL 108] gives an analysis of operators, or strictly, of holders of Operators' Licences, by fleet size and also reproduces the summary table referred to in 3.3.3 above.

3.3.7 *TS* also includes statistics on the heavy goods vehicle testing scheme by Traffic Areas and GB total and of visual checks of heavy goods vehicle exhaust smoke, by Traffic Areas.

OPERATORS' OUTPUT AND FLEET STRUCTURE

3.4 The MOT, DOE and DTp Goods Sample Surveys

3.4.1 The primary source of statistics on output, both in terms of the use made of vehicles and of the traffic carried, is the series of sample surveys carried out by the Ministry of Transport in 1952, 1958, 1962 and 1967/8, and the continuing quarterly sample survey started in 1970.

3.4.2 *The 1952 survey*
The pioneer survey carried out by Glover and Miller was based on a stratified random sample of about 8,000 vehicles drawn from a frame consisting of the complete vehicle index with a sheet for every vehicle operated under carrier's licence or by the British Transport Commission's (BTC's) Road Haulage Executive (RHE) and Railway Executive (RE). The main two-way stratification was by the six vehicle categories—A, Contract A, B and C licences, BTC (RHE) and BTC (RE)—and by seven unladen-weight groups: within each cell the sampling fraction was held constant between licensing Areas.

3.4.3 A form was sent to the operators of each of the selected vehicles asking them to state the unladen weight and carrying capacity of the vehicle, the type of carrier's licence, fuel used and year of manufacture. Operators were also asked to state, for each journey made in a specified coming week, the nature of the goods carried, and, for the purpose of estimating ton-mileage, the mileage run loaded over 50% of capacity, loaded under 50% and empty, and the maximum load carried at any point on the journey. The week chosen was the fourth week in September which it was hoped would not be seriously disturbed by seasonal influences.

3.4.4 The legal powers used, as for each of the succeeding surveys, were those conferred by the Statistics of Trade Act, 1947 [B 41].

3.4.5 Some 7,200 usable forms were returned, and these were processed and tabulated manually. Details of the methodology and the results were published in a paper read before the Royal Statistical Society in April 1954 [QRL 25]. Most of the resulting data are presented in the form of cross-analyses, for the seven vehicle unladen-weight groups and the six categories A, Contract A, B, C licence, BTC (RHE) and BTC (RE). Data so presented include:

mean carrying capacity,
age of vehicles (proportions manufactured pre-1939, 1940–5, 1946–52),
proportion using diesel fuel,
mean days spent idle for various reasons,
proportions of vehicles engaged wholly or mainly in carrying certain commodities (fourteen groups),
proportions of vehicles running different numbers of loaded journeys per week,
mean weekly vehicle-mileage,
vehicle-mileage, loaded and empty,
mean weekly tonnage carried per vehicle,
mean weekly ton-mileage per vehicle,
range of mean lengths of haul.

The standard error of mean weekly vehicle mileage and ton-mileage for most cells of the two-way stratification was generally within the range of 4 to 5% and 5 to 7% respectively.

3.4.6 Estimates of weekly aggregate tonnage and ton-mileage for all vehicles were obtained by grossing up to the vehicle population, and including estimates for unsampled cells. Also, with due recognition of the hazards, but with some confidence in view of the close relationship between the index of industrial production for the month and the year, the weekly aggregates were grossed up to obtain estimated annual aggregates for vehicle-miles, tonnage and ton-mileage.

3.4.7 The report includes detailed discussion on the indications yielded about the structure of the fleet, about the pattern of operations and nature of the goods carried and how they varied between vehicle categories and sizes.

3.4.8 The final table, giving corresponding annual figures for rail, inland waterways and coastal shipping, gives the earliest informed perspective of the place of road goods transport in the domestic carriage of goods.

3.4.9 *The 1958 Survey*
The second survey in the series was undertaken in April 1958. Since 1952 there had been, *inter alia*, a large increase in the goods vehicle fleet, a structural change in the industry due to denationalization and the removal of radius restrictions on A and B licence operators, and an increase in the speed limit for heavy goods vehicles.

3.4.10 Methodology was very similar to that of the 1952 survey as was also the sample size—some 7,400 vehicles. The data was again processed manually. A major difference was that, following denationalization, the remaining BTC vehicles were not treated separately, but included both in the sampling frame and in the analysis of results in accordance with the category of licence they now held.

3.4.11 Apart from this, a more sophisticated method was used for estimating the whole year's output from the data for the sample week. This made use of the indications, from the system of 50-point traffic counts (*see* 3.21 below) of monthly variations in the goods vehicle traffic on the country's road system, together with special counts made during the week of the enquiry.

3.4.12 The results were published in 1959 in *The Transport of Goods by Road* [QRL 106]. The range of data presented is very similar to that in the 1952 survey report, and the later report again includes an extensive discussion of the indications yielded about the structure of the industry, the pattern of operations and the nature of the goods carried, and highlights changes since 1952 in the shares of road and rail in the total domestic goods transport. OA operations are discussed in detail and pitfalls in attempting deductions about their efficiency are exemplified.

3.4.13 It should be noted that the tonnage and ton-mileage estimates for 1958 were revised upwards in 1963 by about 6 and 9% respectively (*see* 3.4.25 below).

3.4.14 Some of the data are also reproduced in a paper by Glover to the Royal Statistical Society in January 1960, *Statistics of the Transport of Goods by Road* [QRL 24]. He discusses the theoretical and methodological considerations underlying the choice of commodity classification and includes a classification of C licence vehicles according to SIC Order of the operator's business.

3.4.15 The paper goes on to a detailed discussion of the possibilities and snags in using bench-mark data from the 1958 survey in combination with the 50-point and other road traffic census data which yield good estimates of vehicle-mileage to give reliable indications of

(a) monthly or quarterly variations in goods ton mileage by road,
(b) annual changes.

It is reasoned that load factors are unlikely to vary much, though there may be slow changes, e.g. in the ratio of carrying capacity to unladen weight and in the mix of traffic by types of road, time of the day or week, which would make it desirable to modify or re-base the series from time to time.

3.4.16 Using figures published by the Road Research Laboratory in *Road Research 1958* [QRL 93] of trends in vehicle traffic flow in Great Britain from 1938 to 1958, the 1958 bench-mark figures are projected annually back to 1951 and to a crude estimate for 1938 and set against figures for goods ton-mileage by rail.

3.4.17 The short- and long-period series are also compared with corresponding series for the CSO's Index of Industrial Production and there is a valuable discussion on the development of relationships between measures of transport output and of economic activity and their possibilities for forecasting output.

3.4.18 The monthly series for goods ton-mileage by road was instituted and used as an input to a new CSO Monthly Index of Inland Goods Transport—road, rail and total—with 1958 = 100, described in [B 40].

3.4.19 *The 1962 survey*
Following the 1958 survey, estimates of tonnage and ton-mileage output were made by reference to changes in goods vehicle mileage estimates from road census data. Because of the recognized limitations of the method for longer-term application, a third sample survey was undertaken in 1962 to provide more reliable estimates of the trend of goods transport by road. Other objectives were to obtain for the first time reasonably good estimates of the movements between regions of Great Britain and subdivisions on an origin/distribution basis; and to obtain more detailed data on commodities carried. The survey was accordingly on a much larger scale than its predecessors. It was

spread over four weeks between April 1962 and January 1963 and involved a total sample of some 40,000 vehicles making 700,000 journeys in the survey weeks.

3.4.20 The methodology is very fully described in the *Methodological Report* [QRL 103]. The stratification scheme was the same as before but the sampling frame for all except C licence vehicles was a new Goods Vehicle Index (GVI), linked to an Operators' Index, constructed at Ministry HQ, instead of the set of separate indexes maintained at each Area office which had become unreliable through accumulation of 'dead' entries. For details of the GVI *see* 3.5 below.

3.4.21 Additional information was sought, notably on nature of business of C licence operators, on vehicle body types and on length of loaded journeys. Processing was by Hollerith punched-card machinery. [QRL 103] includes a full account of sampling and other possible errors and reproduces the questionnaires used.

3.4.22 The results of the survey are published in three booklets [QRL 103]:

Final Results—Part 1
Final Results—Commodity Analysis
Final Results—Geographical Analysis

These contain over 200 tables and a number of maps. In general the data, except averages, are in grossed-up form relating to the total vehicle population and its aggregate operations in 1962.

3.4.23 [QRL 103] *Part 1* contains analyses

(a) on vehicle numbers by 1, licence category; 2, unladen weight; 3, type of fuel used; 4, carrying capacity; 5, body type; 6, year of first registration; 7, nature of business of operator of C vehicles (SIC Orders with some MLH breakdown); 8, main type of work for C vehicles (8 types by land use of destination)

with cross-analyses by 1×2, $3 \times 1 \times 2$, $4 \times 1 \times 2$, $5 \times 1 \times 4$, $6 \times 1 \times 2$, 7×2 and 8×7.

(b) on transport operations
  number of journeys
  tons carried
  ton mileage
    all by type of journey (end to end/intermediate) × length of haul × licence category × unladen weight
  vehicle-mileage
    by loaded/unloaded × type of journey × licence category × unladen weight
  average annual tons carried, ton-mileage, mileage per vehicle
    all by licence category × unladen weight
  tons carried, ton-mileage and vehicle-mileage by C vehicles
    by type of work and (except vehicle-mileage) by nature of business of operator.

3.4.24 There are also analyses of the numbers of vehicles idle (by reasons), on site work and on non-transport work, of ton-mileage FH and OA by B licence vehicles and of ton-mileage by quarters of the year.

3.4.25 There is a full commentary with further derived statistics, comparisons with 1952, and with revised figures for 1958 resulting partly from revisions of the vehicle population after a purging of the vehicle index (*see* p. 21 of *Part 1*). The most noticeable revisions of the 1958 figures were increases of 6% in total tonnage, 13% in ton-mileage by C vehicles, 9% in total tonnage by C vehicles, and a reduction of 8% in ton-mileage by A contract vehicles. Revised series for eleven years up to 1962 for goods vehicle numbers by unladen weight by licence category are also given.

3.4.26 For the [QRL 103] *Commodity Analysis* the classification used is based on that recommended by the Unite Nations Economic

Commission for Europe (ECE) for use for transport purposes (CSTE) with subdivision of some headings of the latter's condensed twenty-heading classification desirable in the road transport context. For details of CSTE *see* [B 26] which shows CSTE and other main classifications in parallel: *see also* article in *Statistical News* 24.5 [B 15] for a review of commodity classifications and codings.

3.4.27 Figures are given for thirty-four commodity groups, of tonnage and ton-mileage by A and B vehicles, C vehicles in the distributive trades and other C vehicles. Comparative figures for rail and other inland transport in Great Britain are given, though classification differences make difficulties. There are also:

> an analysis, for each commodity, of proportions moved in the four seasons; and
> cross-analyses, for C licence operators, of tonnage and ton-mileage by commodities and nature of business of operator (MLH groups).

3.4.28 In the [QRL 103] *Geographical Analysis* the main analysis is in terms of the ten standard regions of England and Wales, as defined by the Registrar-General—*see* [B 12], and Scotland. For some purposes the regions were subdivided into a total of 107 zones, normally following county and other administrative boundaries, but with some subdivisions of large urban areas. Details were not published but are available from DTp Directorate of Statistics.

3.4.29 For the purpose of origin-destination matrices 'intermediate journeys' (those involving setting down and/or picking up goods at several points in the journey—*see* 2.2.7 above) were treated as comprising two end-to-end journeys with the farthest point from base being taken as outward destination. This results in some inflation of length of haul of intermediate traffic. On the other hand, because operators of C-licensed vehicles of unladen weight 1 ton and less—not 3

tons and less as stated in Chisholm and O'Sullivan [QRL 7], *see below*—were not asked to provide information on individual journeys: their journeys and the tonnage carried were allocated arbitrarily to the intra-zonal category on the basis of the vehicle's garage address. Resulting understatement of inter-zonal and inter-regional flows is probably very slight, because the vehicles concerned are mainly used for local delivery purposes.

3.4.30 The [QRL 103] *Geographical Analysis* gives for each of the Standard Regions of Great Britain plus Scotland:

(1) estimates of numbers of journeys and tonnage moved *within* the region, analysed by length of haul (0–24, 24–49, 49–99, over 99 miles)
(2) estimates of the number of journeys and tonnage moved, *outwards to* and *inwards from* each other region. The tonnage figures are by length of haul ranges
(3) estimates of the tonnage moved within, to and from each other region analysed by commodity (ten groups).

The introduction includes an appropriate warning about the considerable sampling errors attaching to the figures for the relatively smaller flows.

3.4.31 There are also maps of the main flows between pairs of zones in the 107 × 107 zone matrix. These are the flows of over 250,000 tons per annum (total, both directions): they account for 80% of the tonnage moved between zones in 1962 by road transport.

3.4.32 Tabulations for the 107 × 107 zone matrix were not published. However, magnetic tapes were produced for the purposes of further analysis—*MOT Mathematical Advisory Unit Note 101* [QRL 89] describes them—and tabulations from them have been made available to a number of researchers. They were in two forms—(i) tabulations of the 1962 data for each of fifteen commodity classes in 107 × 107 zone matrices;

(ii) tabulations of the 1962 data adjusted to 1964 levels by references to changes in industrial output, and regrouped using thirteen commodity classes and seventy-eight zones, together with corresponding data for rail traffic in 1964 collected by the British Railways Board. Data in both forms were used by Chisholm and O'Sullivan in examining approaches to modelling flows of freight traffic in Great Britain, exploring models for estimating traffic generated and attracted by zones, its distribution and modal split—*see* their book *Freight Flows and Spatial Aspects of the British Economy* [QRL 7]. This includes, *inter alia*, tables (i) of data for each of the seventy-eight zones, with zone centroid; population; employment; tons, ton-miles and mean haul inward and outward, road and total; (ii) of the results of various regression analyses. *See also* Heyman, *Initial Attempts at Modelling Road Freight Flows* [B 8].

3.4.33 *The 1967/68 survey*
The fourth in the series was carried out over a period of twelve months from June 1967 to May 1968. This time one-twelfth of the total sample of 46,000 vehicles was used each month. The completed questionnaires were this time processed by Agency computer: many severe problems were experienced. A report *Survey of the Transport of Goods by Road 1967/68* [QRL 104] was published by DOE in 1971.

3.4.34 The sampling frame was a combination of the Department's Goods Vehicle Index, which contained records of all goods vehicles on carriers' licences except for C vehicles not over 3 tons unladen weight, and licensing records at the Traffic Area Offices for the latter vehicles. Stratification was again by licence class, unladen weight and Traffic Area. An account of the methodology was published in *Statistical News* (*SN*) No. 9 [B 9].

3.4.35 The range of information sought was similar to that of the 1962 survey with additional questions on:

nature of other business of B licence operator
weight of tractor unit of articulated vehicle
plated weight (if allocated)—*see* 2.1.10
number of axles of vehicle
type of terminal at origin or destination
whether journey extended overnight
length of container if used
whether change-over or shunt drivers used.

A copy of the questionnaire is reproduced in Appendix B of this Review.

3.4.36 The report [QRL 104] includes a selection of tables of results, less extensive than those published for the 1962 survey. Further tables covering more specialized topics and in a more detailed form, some on microfilm, are retained at DOE. Details are available on request and information from them can be obtained at cost subject to availability of resources to prepare it. A computer tape containing grossed-up data on origins and destinations of freight flows in a detailed analysis by geographical zones and types of commodities is also offered—*see SN* 9.6 [B 9].

3.4.37 The tables in the report include analyses
(a) on vehicle numbers,
by 1, licence category (FH/OA); 2, unladen weight; 3, type of fuel used; 4, carrying capacity; 5, body type; 6, nature of business of C vehicle operator (SIC Orders in twelve groups); 7, deployment in survey week (idle by reasons, sitework, on public roads carrying and not carrying goods); with cross-analyses $1 \times 2 \times 4$, $4 \times 1 \times 3$, $5 \times 1 \times 2$, $5 \times 1 \times 4$, 2×4, 7×1, 7×2.
(b) on transport operations,
vehicle-miles run empty/loaded
tons carried
ton-mileage
all by FH/OA $\times$ unladen weight, FH/OA $\times$ carrying capacity
average annual tons carried, ton-mileage and vehicle-mileage per vehicle
all by FH/OA $\times$ unladen weight

tons, ton-miles × commodities × length of haul
ton-miles by region, within, outwards and inwards
tons by region of origin × region of destination.

The commentary includes comparisons of fleet composition and transport operations with previous years.

3.4.38 The estimates of aggregate tonnage and ton-mileage by road goods transport in 1968 obtained from the survey were about 9% higher than previously available estimates made by extrapolating on road traffic census data. [QRL 104] gives revised series for the years 1963 to 1969.

3.4.39 *The continuing survey*
The continuing survey on a quarterly basis was started in 1970 to meet the need for more timely and reliable estimates of the trend in output than had been provided by the extrapolation method.

3.4.40 The same basic method of obtaining journey-by-journey details of a week's work for a sample of vehicles is used. With the vehicles no longer having ABC licence categories, the operator is asked whether the vehicle is used wholly for hire or reward, wholly on contract work for a single customer, wholly on OA, or partly FH, partly OA.

3.4.41 Samples of vehicles are drawn every quarter, and one-thirteenth used every week. Initially the sample size was 3,000 vehicles a quarter but it was increased to 6,000 a quarter in 1973 because *inter alia* the initial sample size was inadequate for the degree of detail likely to be required by the EEC in statistics on domestic road goods transport (*see* 3.29 below).

3.4.42 For the first two years the sampling frame used was the Goods Vehicle Index, but this had become progressively so unreliable that it was superseded at the beginning of 1972 by a new computerized Goods Vehicle List (GVL) containing, for each goods vehicle on Operator's Licence, some 560,000 in all in 1974, the following details:

unladen weight; plated weight; vehicle registration number; rigid or articulated vehicle; body type; tipper or non-tipper; year of registration; Operator's Licence no. and address of vehicle owner; area in which licensed.

3.4.43 For stratification purposes, the categories of the old carriers' licences were no longer available and experiment was necessary. Initially a simple scheme of three unladen-weight groups for rigid, and three for articulated vehicles was tried. This was changed in 1972 to a scheme with eight unladen-weight groups for rigid and four for articulated vehicles, and in 1973 to one with eight *plated-weight* groups for rigid and four *plated-weight* groups for articulated vehicles.

3.4.44 Initially, as in previous surveys, the sampling fraction was constant within each cell between Traffic Areas. In 1973, however, in order to reduce sampling errors in the estimates of the smaller inter-regional flows, the sampling fractions for the vehicles licensed in the Northern, Eastern, South Wales, Western and Scottish Traffic Areas were raised so as to increase the sample of vehicles and hence the number of inter-regional journeys made, by a factor of about four.

3.4.45 The information is processed by computer quarterly and grossed up to produce estimates of the work done by road goods vehicles on Excise licence. An adjustment is made to take account of the unsampled weight groups (mainly goods vehicles less than $3\frac{1}{2}$ tons gross weight). The adjustment factor was derived from results of the 1967/8 survey and, subsequently, from information obtained in 1974 from a special *ad hoc* survey of small goods vehicles (results not published, but those of repetitions should appear in *TS* [QRL 108]). Although the unsampled vehicles are large in number, they do not contribute much to work done, and this approximate method of accounting for these vehicles is considered by DOE to be adequate.

3.4.46 Results for the first three years were published in a DOE press notice, *The Transport of Goods by Road 1970–1972* [QRL 107]—*see SN 21.23* [B 42]. This gave quarterly and annual figures of tonnage and ton-mileage together with analyses for the year 1972:

(a) of tonnage and ton-mileage by FH/OA and vehicle unladen weight (3 groups);
(b) of average length of haul also by FH/OA and unladen weight;
(c) of proportions of tonnage for eighteen groups of commodities.

Details of methodology were given in Appendices.

3.4.47 The quarterly changes in the estimates were noted as being in most cases within the margin of sampling errors—given as $\pm 5.8\%$ on tonnage and $\pm 4.2\%$ on ton-mileage for 95% confidence. They corresponded fairly well, however, with quarterly changes in vehicle mileage from traffic counts. The increase in sample size from 1973 will of course have reduced the sampling errors.

3.4.48 The quarterly ton-mileage estimates derived are now used as the basis for the CSO *Monthly Digest* [QRL 73] quarterly series in index form, but no other quarterly figures are published at present.

3.4.49 Annual figures from the survey were published in HS [QRL 70] up to 1973, in the same detail as in (a), (b) and (c) of 3.4.46 above, except that the tonnage analysis at (a) is omitted. Defects in the sampling frame, changes to another frame and other teething troubles in the first two or three years were reflected in substantial revisions of the tonnage and ton-mileage series back to 1969 appearing in HS 1973 [QRL 70], regrettably without an explanatory footnote.

3.4.50 With the appearance of the first issue of *Transport Statistics* [QRL 108] for 1964–74, the results of the continuing survey are published in greater detail, *and in metric units* (other than for vehicle weights and length of haul, still given in tons and miles). TS gives, for the latest year,

tonnes carried
tonne-kilometres
  by 1, FH/OA; 2, rigid/articulated vehicle; 3, vehicle gross weight; 4, unladen weight; 5, length of haul; 6, commodity carried (fifteen groups—tonnes only)
with cross-analyses $1 \times 2 \times 3$, 1×4, 1×5, 6×5, and 3×5.

There are also eleven-year series for tonnes and tonne-kilometres by FH/OA.

3.4.51 The 1975 figures were made available first in a note *The Transport of Goods by Road in Great Britain 1975* [QRL 107]. This gave more information than TS on average lengths of haul, analyses with vehicle weight ranges in metric as well as imperial tons, and quarterly summary figures of tonnes and tonne kilometres by FH/OA and length of haul for 1974 and 1975.

3.5 The Goods Vehicle Index (1962) and the Goods Vehicle List (1972)

3.5.1 An analysis of fleet size structure for public haulage operators, as at 31.12.63, derived from the 1962 GVI (3.4.20 refers), was published in 1964 [QRL 81]. This gave for Great Britain as a whole and for each Traffic Area the numbers of operators and numbers of vehicles, analysed by fleet size (1, 2, 3, 4, 5 and by 9 graduated groups to over 200 vehicles). In addition, for Great Britain only, analyses by fleet size were given of the numbers of operators of A or Contract A vehicles only, B vehicles only and mixed fleets.

3.5.2 This analysis was reproduced in *HS 1964* [QRL 70] together with a similar analysis for operators of C licence vehicles over 3 tons unladen weight, as at 30.9.64. Analyses of fleet size structure in 1966 based on the same indexes were given in the report on the *Survey of Operating Costs* [QRL 23] (3.13 below) and for 1969, in percentage terms only, in *HS 1969*. However, deterioration over time due to the accumulation of 'dead entries' relating to vehicles scrapped or sold and operators going out of business frustrated hopes that the indexes could be used for a continuing source of statistics on the vehicle fleet and its structure.

3.5.3 The difficulties of maintaining any large register of vehicles in a usable state by limiting deadwood are discussed in an article in *SN 20* [B 10] which outlines solutions and describes the GVL—details in 3.4.42 above—set up in 1972. With improved purging methods, this register is now expected to provide the needed continuing source of statistics on the vehicle fleet used under Operators' Licences, as well as an efficient sampling frame for the continuing survey of road goods transport.

3.5.4 A number of analyses derived from the GVL as at September 1975 are published in *TS 1975* [QRL 108]. There are analyses of vehicle numbers

> by 1, rigid/articulated vehicles 2, gross weight (nine groups) 3, type of body (eight types) 4, year of first registration (pre-1966, 1966 by years to 1974) 5, size of fleet (1, 2, 3, 4, 5 and by 9 graduated groups to 200 and over) with cross analyses $1\times2\times3$, $1\times2\times4$, $1\times3\times4$, $1\times3\times5$.

There is also an analysis of numbers of operators by size of fleet.

3.6 TRTA Survey of C-Licensed Vehicles

3.6.1 A survey was made in 1958 by the Traders Road Transport Association (TRTA), then the national organization representing C licence holders, to provide in some respects a fuller picture of C licence operation than emerged from the MOT's 1952 and 1958 sample surveys covering all types of road goods transport.

3.6.2 The survey was on a voluntary basis, addressed to all TRTA members. Some 4,840 completed questionnaires covering 98,300 vehicles —about 9% of C-licensed vehicles, though as many as 59% were over 5 tons unladen weight. This was not a random or systematic sample, and of course did not include any of the many C-licensed vehicles operated by non-members.

3.6.3 Respondents were asked to state the nature of their business, total number of C vehicles operated analysed by unladen weight, whether load-carrying or not, body type, extent to which loaded on average on return journeys, and whether used on journeys beyond 75-mile radius. Members were also asked to indicate the six most important reasons for using their own vehicles in preference to hired road haulage and rail transport respectively. No information on output was sought.

3.6.4 The completed questionnaires were sent to an independent agency for analysis and tabulation and the results were published by the TRTA in October 1959 in a booklet *Survey of C licensed vehicles* [QRL 102], in which it is stated that the document has been checked by an independent statistician as a precaution against bias, selectivity, inaccuracy or lack of reasonable statistical argument.

3.6.5 The results are given mainly in the form of aggregate tables for the operators responding and their vehicles with analyses of:

> 1, fleet size; 2, type of vehicle—non-load carriers (service, representatives', other)—load carriers by body type; 3, vehicle unladen weight;

4, nature of business (sixteen groups); 5, return load factor (empty, less than 50%, 50% or more, on circular delivery and on average empty for less than 25% of trips); 6, whether operated beyond 75-mile radius; 7, numbers of operators and numbers weighted by vehicles owned, quoting specified reasons for using own vehicles in preference to FH road and rail transport (twelve reasons)

together with various 2, 3 and 4 way cross-analyses. There is a commentary on some of the main implications.

3.7 The Small Firm in the Road Haulage Industry: Bayliss [QRL 2]

3.7.1 This is a Research Report commissioned by the Committee of Inquiry on Small Firms. The study is confined to FH operators and is concerned with the existence and predominance in terms of numbers of the small operator and the reasons therefor. It examines growth and structure in terms of distribution of fleet size from the 1930s until the early 1970s and reviews the regulation of the FH industry over this period and its effect on its structure.

3.7.2 The author draws largely on published statistics, but he also describes and uses a method of obtaining data on the structure of the industry and how it changes, by analysing details in the South-Eastern Area Licensing Records, of applications for A licences, of the Authority's decisions and of changes over a period of 1963 to 1968 in the licences held, for a sample of operators. Information from the Authority's records also yielded data on the structure of the industry in 1932. The data resulting are set out and discussed in some detail in [QRL 2]. In addition to the tabular analysis of the 1953 to 1968 data on fleet size structure, details are also given of a multiple regression analysis used to throw light on the growth of firms over the period.

3.7.3 The author also analyses the effects of returns to scale and the level of investment on operating costs and on the structure of the industry, drawing on the data and findings of the survey discussed in 3.13 below.

3.8 Study on the Road Haulage Industry since 1968 [QRL 1]

3.8.1 The purpose of this study by Bayliss for DOE was to provide information on developments in the structure, operations and financial aspects of road goods transport, under the operators' licensing system established by the *Transport Act 1968* [B 47] in place of the previous system of carriers' licensing (*see* 1.3 above).

3.8.2 The investigation involved four sample surveys addressed

(1) to 2,000 former holders of A or B licences—to obtain information on fleet size and composition, type of work and operating costs for comparison with results of the 1966 cost survey;

(2) to 2,200 former holders of C licences—to obtain information on the extent to which they were now working for hire or reward;

(3) to 2,500 new entrants to the industry—to obtain information on fleet structure and nature of work;

(4) to 1,100 operators of fleets in which all vehicles are under $3\frac{1}{2}$ tons gross weight (those no longer needing Operators' Licences)—to obtain information on proportions working other than OA.

3.8.3 The study also made use of data on investment in capital equipment by a sample of FH operators, derived from an annual enquiry carried out by the Business Statistics Office (*see* 3.19.9), and of information from Licensing Authorities on reasons for surrender of Operators' Licences.

3.8.4 Part 1 of [QRL 1] analyses changes in the structure of the industry and gives data on:

the extent of FH carriage by former OA operators, analysed by fleet size;

the fleets and FH operations of new entrants, by size of fleet;

the reason for exits from the industry;

fleet size and composition, and operations by type of work for former A, B licence operators still working FH.

Part 11 analyses operating costs of professional hauliers and gives data, for various fleet sizes, of

expenditure by categories;

costs and receipts per mile, per ton of fleet unladen weight, and per ton carried, and by category of work;

profits as a proportion of net assets.

Comparisons are made with results of the 1965 survey and data given on investment in capital equipment annually from 1967 to 1970 by the sample of hauliers mentioned in 3.8.3.

3.8.5 An appendix gives an account of methodology of the surveys (but without details of questionnaires).

3.9 Reports of Undertakings

3.9.1 The annual reports of the British Transport Commission and its successors, the British Railways Board and the Transport Holding Company and latterly the National Freight Corporation, give some statistical information about the nationalized sector.

3.9.2 The early BTC Reports [QRL 55] give figures on the numbers of different types of vehicles owned by British Road Services, classified by tonnage capacity, and by the railway collection and delivery services (including horse-drawn vehicles until the mid 1950s). Figures of total BRS receipts, but no tonnage, or ton-mileage data, though data on tonnage and numbers of parcels carried by the railway collection and delivery services were given.

3.9.3 The four-weekly *British Transport Commission: Transport Statistics* [QRL 56] gives only receipts from road transport divided into collection and delivery and others.

3.9.4 The Annual Reports of the National Freight Corporation [QRL 77] give operating account and balance sheet information in consolidated form and for three groups of subsidiary companies:

General haulage and container companies, including Freightliners Ltd. (49% owned by BRB);

Parcels companies, including National Carriers Ltd., which, *inter alia*, operate the former rail collection and delivery services;

Special traffics companies, including heavy haulage, removals, bulk liquid and other companies.

For the three groups of companies there is an approximate percentage analysis of working expenses and there are statistics of staff numbers, of goods vehicles, and their aggregate tonnage capacity, of additional trailers and containers, and of total vehicle mileage. But, as also in the period of the Transport Holding Company, there are no figures of tonnage carried, or ton-mileage.

3.9.5 The 1972/3 *Report of the Select Committee on Nationalised Industries* [QRL 99] which gives very full background on the National Freight Corporation and its forbears, commented unfavourably on the paucity of information about physical performance published by the Corporation.

OPERATING COSTS, EXPENDITURE ON ROAD GOODS TRANSPORT

3.10 Commercial Motor Tables of Operating Costs [QRL 60]
Motor Transport Tables of Operating Costs [QRL 75]

3.10.1 These compilations are published annually by the journals and give estimated costs of operating vehicles of various capacities and types. The figures are based on samples (size unknown) of vehicles carried out at a base year and updated for price and wage increases. The wages element included aims at an average picture and excludes overtime and other special payments. Standing costs and running costs are itemized and resulting total operating costs per mile and per week for a range of assumed mileage run per week or per annum are tabulated. The *Commercial Motor* tables exclude overheads and profits: 'minimum charges' allowing for both are suggested. The *Motor Transport* tables include a profit allowance of 20% over costs.

3.10.2 Harrison [QRL 26] analysed the *Commercial Motor* tables for 1948/9 to 1964, deriving trends for four types of vehicle at various weekly mileages and discussing reasons for the trends and the implications of changes in the make-up of the total vehicle fleet.

3.10.3 For application of the data in estimating total expenditure on road goods transport, *see* 3.12 below. They have also been used by the Transport and Road Research Laboratory (TRRL) since 1958 as an input to specialized vehicle operating cost formulae for use in economic assessments—these include value of vehicle occupants' time, and fuel taxation is largely excluded. *See* Dawson [QRL 14] for recent versions and earlier references.

3.11 Road Haulage Association Costs Reports

3.11.1 The monthly *Road Way* [QRL 96]—the RHA's journal—occasionally includes reports on the make-up and trend of operating costs. Reports by the Centre for Interfirm Comparisons (CIC), based on data submitted by RHA members subscribing to a Cost and Productivity Scheme (CAPS) appeared in May 1970, February 1971 and April 1972. CAPS in the third of these gave

(a) vehicle and other operating costs by detailed headings, and financial charges, for years 1968/9, 1969/70, 1970/1 and 1971/2 all expressed in index form with 1967/68 = 100;
(b) indications of revenue increases needed for example to yield a given return, or to cover cost increases; and
(c) productivity indices for the same periods
  mileage per vehicle
  payload capacity per vehicle
  mileage per driver
all by vehicle size and type of operation.

3.11.2 The CAPS scheme has since been replaced by a new vehicle-costing scheme (*Road Way* [QRL 96] September 1973 refers), also operated as a subscription service by the CIC. Summarized results from this scheme may be the basis for more recent analyses, e.g. in *Road Way* for April 1975, which sets out cost changes, under detailed headings, in percentage terms.

3.11.3 The size and character of the samples of operators involved and the methods used by CIC are not indicated in the reports.

3.12 Rudd/Dawson Estimates of Expenditure on Road Transport

3.12.1 The earliest comprehensive estimates of expenditure in Great Britain on road transport by all modes were made by Rudd of the Road Research Laboratory (RRL) in 1949 and 1950. Dawson, also of RRL, followed up with a similar exercise in 1960. The method used, in each study, for the road goods transport component, was essentially to apply costs per mile derived from tables of vehicle-operating cost data given in *Commercial Motor* [QRL 60] (*see also* 3.10 above) to annual vehicle-mile data derived either from traffic counts or from the MOT's survey of road goods transport for 1958, checked, adjusted and supplemented by data from various other sources. The results were set out in papers to the Royal Statistical Society (RSS) [QRL 31 and 12].

3.12.2 Extrapolations from these and from repetitions by Dawson in 1965 and 1966 [QRL 13] were published in summary form in *HS* [QRL 70] until 1969, but were not regarded as very reliable. *TS* [QRL 108] 1974 introduces a new series of estimates using the same general method, for United Kingdom instead of Great Britain, and going back to 1964, with corresponding data for other modes.

3.12.3 Estimates by this method must be regarded as subject to a considerable margin of error, particularly at a time when costs are rising rapidly. The formula derivation and unchanging notional profit element are likely to be particularly shaky. The series is likely to be a better indicator of medium- or long-term trends than of actual levels and year-to-year changes.

3.12.4 Estimates of total expenditure on goods transport at factor cost (i.e. users' expenditure less taxes plus subsidies) for road and rail in 1964 and 1974 are given in *Transport Policy*, Vol. 2, Paper 1 [B 55].

3.13 Survey of Operating Costs in Road Freight Transport

3.13.1 This survey, carried out for the MOT in 1966, is the only large-scale survey of operators' costs to have been undertaken. Information was collected, both on FH and OA operations, on the costs of operating whole fleets and specific vehicles within those fleets. The costs of 2,150 A or B licence fleets and 2,100 C licence fleets were analysed, together with those of 4,000 specific vehicles in A or B fleets and 6,000 specific vehicles in C fleets. With the sampling frames available it was necessary to restrict most of the analysis for C licence fleets to those containing at least one vehicle over 3 tons unladen weight. A detailed account of methodology is given in the report on the survey, *Operating Costs in Road Freight Transport* [QRL 23].

3.13.2 The study was aimed at establishing total expenditure in road goods transport in 1965, and how costs vary with respect to such factors as fleet size and vehicle size. Information was also obtained on numbers employed and the nature of their work, on self-employment and on aspects of fleet structure and utilization.

3.13.3 The data collected included:

cost items in about twenty headings
receipts (FH only)
numbers of drivers and attendants, maintenance and other staff full-time and part-time on transport work as such
capital expenditure and disposals
vehicle and fleet characteristics
mileage and hours run
tonnage carried.

The report includes very full analysis and discussion with many detailed tables. The main topics are now outlined.

3.13.4 *Expenditure on road goods transport*
The report gives the first and to date the only estimate of total expenditure on road goods transport in Great Britain directly derived from data obtained from the industry. The estimated total expenditure in 1965 is broken down by cost categories and by public hauliers, C operators with at least one vehicle over 3 tons unladen weight, and other C operators.

3.13.5 The estimated labour cost included for C licence transport makes no allowance for the time spent by drivers on non-transport activities, such as installation of equipment delivered, repair work, collection of cash or orders or other work associated with the main activity of the firm. Rudd [QRL 31] and Dawson [QRL 12] made arbitrary deductions of 50% and 10% respectively from drivers' wages on this account. The present report discusses the problem but makes no adjustment.

The estimated total labour costs given therefore overstate somewhat the manpower resources devoted to transport of goods as such.

3.13.6 The results also inevitably reflect the allocations of joint costs in various areas which the operators had to make in providing the data.

3.13.7 *Fleet structure*
Distributions are given of the numbers of operators with fleets of different sizes and the number of vehicles in each size group. Number of vehicles by unladen weight groups, average tonnage carried per vehicle, tonnage per ton unladen weight and mileage per vehicle are all analysed by size of fleet and there are also analyses by carrying capacity and type of body, and of night running.

3.13.8 *Fleet-operating costs* are analysed in great detail for fleets of 1, 2, 3, 4, 5 vehicles and successive groups of larger numbers. Unit costs per mile, per ton unladen weight, receipts and profits per mile in public haulage and gross and net investment figures are given for each fleet size, and the indications as to economies of scale discussed.

3.13.9 *Vehicle-operating costs* per annum per mile, per hour and per ton carried are analysed by carriers' licence category and by unladen weight and by carrying capacity.

3.13.10 The determinants of vehicle-operating costs and total fleet costs, and receipts in public haulage, were also examined by regression models, and the results are discussed both in lay terms and, in an appendix, in technical detail.

3.13.11 Cost-per-mile figures derived in the survey are compared with *Motor Transport* cost tables [QRL 75] for vehicles of various carrying capacities, separately for running costs, standing costs (including drivers' wages) and in total. Running costs from the survey were in general higher than in the cost tables: probable reasons are discussed. Standing costs were in general very close to those in the cost tables.

3.13.12 *Employment in road transport*
From the manpower data obtained, estimates were made of total numbers employed, full-time and part-time, in road goods transport in 1965. They may be understated by the exclusion of staff, e.g. clerical workers, employed in fleets with large C vehicles, who were neither drivers, attendants, nor maintenance staff.

3.13.13 It must be emphasized that the coverage of these estimates of the total manpower engaged in public haulage is very different from that of the Department of Employment (DE) statistics (*see* 3.17.3 below) for employees in the 1958 SIC MLH 703 for 'road haulage contracting'. The DE statistics exclude self-employed persons and part-time employees and classify some full-time employees with other SIC industries—e.g. the then railway collection and delivery staff with *rail transport* and probably many coal merchants with B licences with *distribution*. The report discusses these differences as well as a large difference between the total estimated number of drivers and the much smaller number giving their occupation in the *1961 Population Census* [QRL 58] as 'driver of goods vehicles'. Many or possibly most drivers of light OA vans regard their main occupation as, e.g., that of service personnel or salesman.

3.13.14 The report also, in Appendix 3, gives estimates for FH and OA operation separately and in total

(a) of inputs, i.e. purchases from other industries and indirect taxes
(b) of net output, or value added
(c) of capital expenditure.

(N.B. the heading to Table 1 should be £ million, not £000.) These imply contributions to GDP of 1·4% for public haulage and of 5·5% for road goods transport as a whole.

INDUSTRIES' USE OF ROAD GOODS TRANSPORT

3.14 Censuses of Production and Distribution

3.14.1 Reports on the Board of Trade's Censuses of Production undertaken in 1963, 1968, 1970, 1971 and 1972 [QRL 85] contain information on establishments' expenditure on road goods transport. In earlier censuses, the only expenditure information was on purchased transport and for all modes together (see [B 18]), but the 1963 census reports gave in addition information on expenditure by establishments on their own C or B licence fleets, broken down into wages and salaries of persons mainly engaged on road transport, fuel, insurance, vehicle licences, depreciation and payments to others for repairs and maintenance. Costs of inward delivery are excluded except as covered by own account transport. The industries covered are mining, manufacturing, construction, gas, electricity and water supply.

3.14.2 The 1963 data were analysed by Edwards in *Transport Cost in British Industry* [QRL 20] and in *Regional Variations in Freight Cost* [QRL 18]. The former reproduces, for each MLH industry the figures for

 expenditure on transport—bought, own and total;
 net output; and
 various ratios.

Coverage, definitions and results are discussed, with inter-industry comparisons under main headings of

 expenditure on transport;
 share of transport in total production costs;
 transport unit costs (per ton and per ton-mile for C licence vehicles);
 trends in purchased transport, 1954, 1958, 1963 in total and as per cent of net output; cost of own transport.

In [QRL 18] Edwards draws on the regional tabulations and gives payments for transport as a percentage of volume of sales and of net output. He explores regional variations in these percentages, in terms of rank scores, in terms of variation about national averages and in terms of rank correlation with road distance from Leicester as representing the population centroid of Great Britain.

3.14.3 Each of the subsequent censuses up to 1972 obtained data on payments for road transport, both outwards and inwards, to other companies or to separate transport organizations not covered on the same return: costs of OA transport by the same business, however, were excluded after 1968. Payments for other transport (rail, water, air, and Post Office combined) were obtained in 1971 and 1972. In the 1973 census, amounts paid to other organizations for transport were no longer separately distinguished—except for mining and quarrying.

3.14.4 The 1968 data for total and road transport expenditure are reproduced by Tulpule in [QRL 42] and analysed by SIC Industry Orders with a discussion on trends from 1963.

3.14.5 The data on payments for transport by road for 1970, 1971 and 1972 are published in the census series of *Business Monitors* [QRL 85].

3.14.6 The Board of Trade Inquiry into the Wholesale Trades carried out in 1965 also yielded data on expenditure on purchased transport, distinguishing between road haulage and other modes, and on OA fleets. The OA fleet costs omitted expenditure on wages and tyres. Results were published in the *Board of Trade Journal* for 26 July 1968 [QRL 72] and reproduced for individual trades with a marking-up to cover the missing wages and tyre costs, by Edwards in *Transport Costs in the Wholesale Trades* [QRL 21]. The discussion centres on inter-trade differences in the ratio of total transport costs to wholesalers' gross margin.

3.14.7 The Censuses of Distribution for 1966 and 1971, but not those for earlier years, asked for information on the use of road goods transport. The reports on the 1966 census [QRL 84] give data:

on numbers of goods vehicles owned by licence class and unladen weight, and by licence class by form of organization (co-operative, multiple, independent) and kind of business; on the numbers of personnel wholly or mainly engaged in operation and maintenance of B or C licence vehicles, and their wages; on transport costs in total, as average per vehicle and in relation to gross margin and turnover, analysed by form of organization and kind of business.

3.14.8 In the 1971 census, information was obtained on

costs, by headings, of operating own goods vehicles;
payments to other organizations for road or rail transport and for other modes including Post Office.

Results were due to be published in a summary report in the SD series of *Business Monitors* [QRL 84] but not in the individual area reports.

3.15 Survey of Transport from Manufacturing Establishments

3.15.1 This survey, carried out in 1966/7, was addressed to the users, rather than to suppliers, of transport services. Its primary purpose was to throw light on the factors determining choice of mode used. The modes covered were road haulage, road transport on own account, rail, Post Office, coastal shipping and others.

3.15.2 Two types of information were collected from some 720 establishments in manufacturing industry. Traders were asked by postal questionnaire for information on:

size of turnover and labour force;
ownership and use of rail sidings and canal berths;
frequency of A contract or C hiring arrangements;
annual traffic generated;
annual expenditure in operating own transport, and in payments to others for transport.

They were also asked to complete forms relating to each of a sample of consignments, some 64,000 in total, about weight, commodity, origin and destination, mode used, price (or cost if by own transport) and some other characteristics of the consignment; and to send postcards with consignments to obtain information on time taken and damage.

3.15.3 The survey was in two parts—a 'general survey' confined to firms within a catchment area around two corridors, London to Newcastle and Liverpool to Glasgow, being studied in connection with a transport cost model (later abandoned) then being developed in MOT; and a 'commodity survey' with no area constraint but confined to five particular commodities—foodstuffs, chemicals, iron and steel, electronic equipment and paper.

3.15.4 The sampling frame used was a listing of establishments made available under stringent conditions as to confidentiality by the then Ministry of Labour. Full details of methodology, with copies of the questionnaires, are given in the full report (*see* below).

3.15.5 The data were analysed by computer in two ways;

(a) by multiple regression analysis, on modal choice and on charges, and
(b) by analysis and cross-analysis in normal tabular form.

The results were published by MOT in a short summary report *Transport for Industry* [QRL 4] and subsequently at length in *Industrial Demand for Transport* [QRL 3].

3.15.6 Apart from detailed analysis on questions of choice between modes and on price structures as indicated by charges for consignments, the report includes a great deal of data on road goods transport, most of it of a type not available elsewhere. There are data on:

> the proportions of annual tonnage sent by FH and OA and by other modes, by size of establishment;
> consignments by weight group by length of haul by modes;
> consignments by commodity groups by modes;
> proportions of consignments delivered within various numbers of days by modes;
> proportions lost or damaged by consignment size by mode;
> expenditure on transport per ton by size of establishment by mode, and as a percentage of turnover for selected industries;
> average cost or charge per lb and per 100 lb/mile by consignment size, by road FH/rail, by length of haul, all for six commodities;
> size of own vehicle fleet by size of establishment.

3.16 Other Surveys of Industry's Use of Transport

3.16.1 Three sub-regional surveys examining, *inter alia*, industry's use of road and other modes of transport, by means including consignment surveys, should be mentioned.

1. A sample survey in the West Midlands in 1953 by Walters and Sharp.
2. The West Cumberland Transport Survey of 1966 by Edwards.
3. The Severnside Industrial Survey of 1967/8 also by Edwards.

3.16.2 The West Midland Survey, carried out when the nationalized British Road Services was in full operation, was based on interviews with representatives of a sample of firms and on an analysis of consignments. The results were first presented in Walters' and Sharp's unpublished *Report on Traffic Costs and Charges of Freight Transport in Great Britain 1953* [QRL 45]. Data from the survey are also set out in Walters' *Integration in Freight Transport* [QRL 44], an Institute of Economic Affairs (IEA) Monograph published in 1968. The data therein include estimates of total traffic carried out in the West Midlands in November 1953 by rail, BRS general haulage, BRS Parcels, private road hauliers and C licence operators, with analyses of

> proportions and average consignment weight by lengths of haul;
> consignment weight distribution by modes;
> firms' expenditure on transport by mode; and relative charges by consignment weight and mileage group.

3.16.3 The implications of the data on questions, e.g. of returns to scale, reasons for modal choice and rate structures, are argued in a discussion of issues of 'co-ordination' and 'integration', licensing and free competition arising out of proposals in the White Papers on *Transport Policy* [B 51] and *The Transport of Freight* [B 50] of 1966 and 1967.

3.16.4 The West Cumberland Transport Survey was supervised by Edwards for the Northern Economic Planning Board. The survey was designed to establish the current pattern of transport demand, to relate this demand to economic activity in the area and to possible changes in the activity, and so to provide a basis for forecasts of changes in transport demand which could be related to the capacity of existing facilities. Broad information was obtained from a sample of establishments (size not stated) about annual expenditure on transport and on transport generated. Also for a sample of about 7,400 consignments made in the course of a week (about one-third of the estimated total from the area) data were obtained on

consignment weight,
commodity,
origin/destination,
regularity,
mode of transport,
cost, and
route (for road transport).

Detailed analyses of the data, and maps of outward and inward flows are given in the report on the survey, the *West Cumberland Transport Survey* [QRL 22] with its separate *Statistical Appendix*.

3.16.5 The Severnside Industrial Survey was conducted as part of a larger planning study—the Severnside Feasibility Study. Data was collected by questionnaire on a voluntary basis from manufacturing industry and quarrying, accounting for two-thirds of the area's labour force in those industries, together with a survey on a week's consignments outwards and inwards. The enquiry was mainly concerned with industrial structure and location; the consignment survey was included for the purpose of analysing the economic linkages of Severnside industry within the area, and with the rest of the country's economy. For results and survey details see *Severnside Industrial Survey* [QRL 19].

MANPOWER AND EARNINGS

3.17 Department of Employment Publications

3.17.1 The range of Department of Employment publications including

British Labour Statistics Yearbook [QRL 54]
British Labour Statistics Historical Abstract 1886–1968 [QRL 53]
New Earnings Survey [QRL 80]
Department of Employment Gazette [QRL 62]

gives:
1. the standard range of figures for employees in employment and total of employees (including unemployed) for Road Haulage (1968 SIC MLH 703 and 704 separately) by GB standard regions and Northern Ireland (N.B. The 1969 Yearbook gave figures for Road Haulage Contracting (MLH 703) on both the 1958 and 1968 SIC definitions (*see* 1.1.2));
2. some figures of wage rates for Road Haulage Contracting, but others only for SIC Transport and Communication as a whole;
3. statistics of earnings in MLH 703, and
4. statistics of earnings, in occupational analyses, for lorry or van drivers, by vehicle size ranges.

3.17.2 There are no separate employment (or wage rate) figures for OA transport as a whole, since the great majority of the employees concerned are classified with the industries of main activity.

3.17.3 It is to be noted that the figures given of numbers of employees in road haulage do not even approximate to the manpower at work since, *inter alia*, they exclude employers and the self-employed working in the large numbers of single-vehicle and other small fleets (*see* 3.13.13 above). (Figures of the self-employed, with or without employees, are however given in *Census of Population* Industry tables [QRL 58] together with employees by categories.)

3.17.4 There are in fact no official figures or series for the total labour force in road goods transport. The 1965 *Operating Cost Survey* [QRL 23] (*see* 3.13 above) yielded estimates of full-time and part-time manpower. *Basic Road Statistics* [QRL 51] gives annual figures of total workers employed by 'road transport' which here includes passenger transport, motor manufacture, garage and motor sales, and road construction and maintenance. It includes the DE figures for insured workers employed in road haulage contracting and a by-and-large, and inadequate, figure for OA transport.

3.17.5 The concept of total labour force in road goods transport is in any case a very hazy one, because of the problem of how to treat the very large number of drivers of OA light vans used only incidentally or occasionally for carriage of goods.

3.17.6 *Census of Population* tables [QRL 58] give figures of the total numbers giving their occupations as 'driver of goods vehicles' and 'lorry drivers' mates or van guards'. As noted in 3.13.13 above there are reasons for concluding that most of the drivers of light OA vans regard and state their main occupation as something other than driving.

3.17.7 From 1975, *TS* [QRL 108] reproduces the DE June census figures of employees in employment for all transport MLH industries for the latest five years, with breakdowns for the latest year by sex, by full-time/part-time/all and by EC Pl regions.

3.18 Annual Reports of the Road Transport Industry Training Board (RTITB) [QRL 95]

3.18.1 The RTITB was established in 1966 for the organization of training in the transport industry through levy/grant arrangements. In the Board's context, the road transport industry covers, in addition to FH road haulage and passenger transport, motor vehicle distribution and repair, agricultural and horticultural machinery, vehicle-and body-building, warehousing, motoring-schools and motor factors. OA transport units are not covered. The Board conducted statutory censuses of manpower in the industry so defined in 1968 and 1971. A report on the latter, in an Appendix to the Board's Report for 1971/2, examined trends in manpower in relation to road haulage output and forecasts for the future. Apart from such occasional material, the annual reports normally include an analysis of numbers of employers and employees on the register analysed by size of firms. From the 1972/3 report, the analysis is for leviable employers (those with a pay-roll of more than £7,500 raised to £10,000 in 1974). In 1972, the non-leviable amounted to 6,500 employers with 16,000 employees out of the totals of 15,000 registered employers with 236,000 employees. There are also statistics on employees, leavers and recruits by occupational group and data on numbers and time spent in training.

NATIONAL ACCOUNTS AND INPUT–OUTPUT ANALYSES

3.19 The National Accounts

3.19.1 The principal industry analyses in the annual Blue Books on *National Income and Expenditure* [QRL 78]—Tables 1.11 and 3.1 in the 1965–75 issue—show the contributions to gross domestic product in terms of value added, for broad industry groups. 'Transport' appears as one group, covering SIC MLH 701 to 707 and 709, but of course excluding the great bulk of own-account road goods transport not within MLH 704, whose contribution to GDP is subsumed in that of the industries using it.

3.19.2 The industry contributions are built up by the CSO by the addition of estimates of income from employment (wages or salaries plus employers' contributions), gross profits of companies and income from self-employment and gross trading profits of public corporations and other public enterprises, based on DE data by industry on numbers employed and average earnings, public corporations accounts, and on Inland Revenue data (*see* Notes in Blue Books and [B 16] for more information). Separate estimates are not made for MLH 703 and 704 in building up the 'Transport' totals.

3.19.3 *Index Numbers of Output at constant factor cost*

In the set of industry index numbers of output at constant factor cost (Table 2.2 of the 1965–75 Blue Book), which are combined by weights proportional to net output in the base year (at present 1970) to provide the output-based estimates of movements in GDP at constant factor cost, Transport and Communication (SIC MLH 701 to 709) share a single output index with the total weight of 85 per 1,000. This is itself built up by weighting together indicators for the separate industries included. For road haulage the indicator is a measure of physical output, ton-mileage, which sidesteps the problem of deflating in the absence of an output price index, but which is not an ideal index of real, or net, output because of its great heterogeneity and changing 'mix' over time (*see* 2.2.5 above).

3.19.4 For years from 1958 until the re-basing on 1970, the indicator is total ton-mileage, including that on own account (in the absence of a reliable separate estimate of FH ton-mileage), though strictly most of the OA output is relevant to the other industries owning the vehicles involved.

3.19.5 For the 1958-based series, the weight for road haulage contracting—MLH 703 in the 1958 SIC—was 17 per 1,000. For the re-basing on 1963 for the industry now defined as MLH 703 and 704 in the 1968 SIC, the weight was increased by transfers from other industries employing C licence vehicles, to 20·3 per 1,000—*see* [B 30]. Later, with the availability of improved annual ton-mileage data from the continuing survey, the indicator for the 1970-based series was changed to exclude own-account transport after 1968 and given a weight of 13·58 per 1,000. This represents the estimated contribution of road haulage to GDP in 1970, and is very close to the estimates for 1965 of 1·4% (out of a total of 5·5% for FH and OA together) from the 1965 cost survey [QRL 23] —*see* 3.13.14.

3.19.6 More information about the rebasing to 1970 of the index numbers of real output is to be found in No. 25 in the *Studies in Official Statistics* series [B 30]. *See also* notes in the Blue Books.

3.19.7 For years before 1958 the indicator for goods transport by road was an index of the numbers of goods vehicles with carriers' licences, including all C licence vehicles, weighted to allow for changes in the mix by unladen-weight groups, but not for changes in vehicle-mileage from year to year. The weight for the sector was 21·53 per 1,000 in the 1948-based series, and 10·7 per 1,000 in the series based on 1958—*see* [B 32].

3.19.8 *Expenditure-based estimates of GDP*

In the expenditure-based approach to GDP— Tables 1.8 and 2.1 in the 1965–75 Blue Book—the component of main interest in the context of this review is gross domestic fixed capital formation (GDFCF). This is analysed by industry by type of asset (vehicles, ships and aircraft, plant and machinery, and new buildings and works) in Table 11.8

3.19.9 The estimates of GDFCF for the road haulage component are based on sample enquiries on capital expenditure conducted by the Business Statistics Office (BSO) under Statistics of Trade Act powers. Sample size over a period of years has been typically about 5,000 hauliers, stratified by fleet size. From 1974 the VAT register has been used as the sampling frame with a £200,000 turn-over cut-off. *National Accounts Statistics Sources and Methods* [B 16], p. 376, refers to various difficulties and shortcomings in the returns, which were then (1968) precluding publication in the Blue Books of separate estimates for road haulage. Estimates for MLH 703 and 704 together for the years 1966 to 1968 inclusive were however published in the *Board of Trade Journal* [QRL 52] for 12 August 1970 and for 1966 to 1969 in *Trade and Industry* [QRL 52] for 28 April 1971. Consideration is being given to publishing *Business Monitors* to continue the series.

3.19.10 In the Blue Book GDFCF analyses before 1973, road haulage was buried in a large residual item 'Other transport and services' including miscellaneous non-transport services. From 1973, however, 'Road haulage and storage' has been separately distinguished. This corresponds to SIC MLH 703, 704 and 709, the last including miscellaneous transport services, e.g. travel agents, brokers and motoring-schools as well as storage. Road haulage must account for the great bulk of the GDFCF for this group. No doubt it is difficult to obtain reliable estimates for MLH 709 which precludes a further split and publication of the road haulage component separately.

3.19.11 In using the Blue Book figures of capital expenditure it should be noted

(1) that in the 'vehicles, ships and aircraft' element, vehicles include business cars;
(2) that since 'Road haulage and storage' includes, *inter alia*, motoring-schools, a significant proportion of its capital expenditure on vehicles may be for cars as against goods vehicles;
(3) that capital expenditure by other industries for their own-account transport is included with these industries' other capital expenditure, mainly in the 'vehicles, etc.' element, but here too including all purchases of business cars.

3.19.12 The Blue Book figures for gross capital expenditure by the inland transport industries are reproduced with some rearrangement in *TS* [QRL 108] in a table on capital expenditure on transport in the UK (which in addition includes data for capital expenditure on roads).

3.19.13 The Blue Book tables on capital consumption and net domestic fixed capital formation by industry group (Tables 12.3, 12.4, 12.7 and 12.8 in the 1965–75 edition) treat transport and communication as a single group, but Table 12.12 on gross capital stock at 1970 replacement costs distinguishes 'Road haulage and storage'. For sources and methods for these tables *see* [B 16] and Notes in Blue Books, which give information on changes.

3.19.14 *Quarterly estimates of GDP*
For the purposes of the quarterly expenditure-based estimates of GDP published in *Economic Trends* [QRL 67], which have no industry breakdown, estimates for road haulage are obtained by Department of Industry from an enquiry on capital expenditure in the distributive industries, addressed to a panel of some 200 of the larger transport firms.

3.20 Input–Output Analyses

3.20.1 The Input–Output tables based on the 1954 and 1963 Censuses of Production were not disaggregated sufficiently to distinguish road transport as an industry or 'commodity'. The 1954 tables treated transport and communication together as one of forty-five industries; the 1963 tables with seventy industries treated road and rail together, though separating them from other transport—mainly air and water.

3.20.2 However, the 90×90 industry analyses in the CSO's *Input–Output Tables for UK for 1968* [QRL 71], and the updated 1970 and 1971 versions in *Business Monitors PA 1004* [QRL 71], making use, *inter alia*, of the data on industries' payments for transport by road obtained in the 1968, 1970 and 1971 Censuses of Production, break transport down into railways, road transport and other. Road goods and road passenger transport are still shown combined as a single industry or commodity. However, since virtually all road passenger transport is purchased as final output by consumers, and virtually all the road transport shown as purchased by industries and services producing intermediate output is goods transport, it is possible to derive from the tables good indications of the distribution among purchasers—the other industries and the classes of final buyers—of the sales output of road goods transport (but *see* 3.20.4) and of how these purchases of road goods transport figure in relation to all other inputs for the various industries and commodities produced.

3.20.3 On the other hand, the data yielded by the analysis of the various inputs into road transport are not readily divisible as between goods and passenger transport.

3.20.4 It should be noted that under the conventions of the analysis, road goods transport as an *industry* is restricted in effect to road haulage, i.e. what is covered by SIC MLH 703 and 704, though road goods transport as a commodity is shown as including also all own-account transport in production industries, the cost of which is included in delivered prices of products. (This is because sales of goods are valued at ex-works prices in the analysis.) On the other hand, the 'commodity' includes no own-account transport of the construction, distribution and other service industries —considerably the greater part of OA transport.

3.20.5 Much care is necessary in interpreting and using the data in the tables. The concepts and conventions of input–output analysis are specialized and pitfalls abound: the non-expert will be well advised to study carefully the general explanations, as well as those on the treatment of the transport industry and its services, in the admirable accompanying text in [QRL 71].

3.20.6 The best input analysis for road goods transport relates to 1965 operations and is found in *Operating Costs in Road Freight Transport* [QRL 23], Appendix 3. This analysis updated to 1968 was in fact used by CSO in estimating the joint input analysis for road goods and passenger transport for the 1968 Input–Output tables.

GOODS TRANSPORT AS TRAFFIC ON THE ROADS

3.21 Road Traffic Censuses and Counts

3.21.1 Data on road goods transport as a user of the road system are available in the results of road traffic censuses. These have a long history—*see* [B 17] for references to road censuses in the inter-war period.

3.21.2 This section is concerned with censuses on a national scale: those carried out *ad hoc* in local and regional contexts are treated in 3.22 below. The national censuses are of three kinds:

a continuing survey to measure trends and short-period variations in the general level of traffic,

occasional large bench-mark censuses to estimate the absolute level of traffic on the road system,

periodical censuses, covering major roads only, designed to obtain information on variations in the traffic flow from section to section of road for highway planning, assessment of priorities for improvement, maintenance, programming and other purposes.

3.21.3 *The continuing survey* started in 1956 and has been conducted at 50 points on the trunk and classified roads of Great Britain according to a scheme initiated by the then Road Research Laboratory (now Transport and Road Research Laboratory (TRRL)). The points were selected at random within each of eight categories—Trunk, Class I, Class II and Class III roads in urban and in rural areas. (For road classifications, *see* explanation in Notes to *Transport Statistics* [QRL 108].) Every point on the roads in each category had an equal chance of selection, so that the flow of traffic observed at the census points in any period of time is a random sample of the flows over the road category as a whole. The average observed flow at the census points, multiplied by the total lengths of road in each category, gives an estimate of the number of vehicle-miles travelled on those roads during the period.

3.21.4 At each of the 50 sites an automatic counter was established to provide a continuous record of motor vehicles (strictly, half the number of axles) passing the point. In addition, starting in 1958, at each site manual counts of each class of vehicle were carried out between 6 a.m. and 10 p.m. on a consecutive Friday, Saturday and Sunday each month. The results of the manual counts, when combined with those of the automatic counts, gave estimates of the monthly vehicle-mileage performed by each class of motor vehicle.

3.21.5 In January 1966 the system of manual counts was expanded to cover over 200 points, including 45 of the original 50 sites. These points include a number of motorway sites, and provision has been made for those to be added to as the motorway network is extended. Since May 1971, for reasons of economy, counting at non-motorway sites has been reduced to two months in every three. A rotating sample enables estimates to be made for the remaining one-third sub-sample on a month-to-month basis. At the beginning of 1974, twenty-three motorway census points were in operation as well as 192 sites on all-purpose trunk and classified roads. Unclassified roads are not represented in either the 50-point or the 200-point survey; although they form about half the total mileage of road in Great Britain, they convey less than one-fifth of the total motor traffic.

3.21.6 *Bench-mark estimates* of the absolute level of traffic in 1960, 1966 and 1973, including traffic on unclassified roads, were made by the TRRL on the basis of short-period censuses conducted at 1,100 sites in 1959/60, at 1,300 in 1966/7 and again in autumn 1973/spring 1974. The sites for these bench-mark censuses, like those for the continuing survey, were selected as a stratified random sample.

3.21.7 Large-scale censuses of the third type (which began in 1922) were conducted in 1961 and 1965. Another was spread over a four-year cycle from 1969 to 1973 to provide a more continuous flow of information and a steadier work-load. A further cycle started in August 1974. (A note in *Statistical News* 26.20 refers to both cycles.) In these censuses the sites—6,500 in the current cycle—are selected strategically to cover the motorways and class A roads section by section. The main counts are in August in order to measure maximum flows, with supplementary counts in the spring to give a measure of seasonal variation.

3.21.8 In all the manual counts, enumerators classify vehicles by appearance-currently into ten classes:

pedal cycles   light goods vehicles
mopeds   heavy goods vehicles with 2
scooters   axles
motorcycles   heavy goods vehicles with 3
cars and taxis   axles or more (rigid)
buses and coaches   heavy goods vehicles (articulated or with trailer)

For some but not all counts the penultimate class is subdivided into vehicles with 3 and 4 axles, and the last class into those with 3, 4 and 5 or more axles in total.

3.21.9 Because they are based on appearance, the class definitions for the road traffic statistics derived, including those for goods vehicles, necessarily differ in some respects from those used in the vehicle registration and licensing statistics—see 2.1.4 *et seq.* above.

3.21.10 Road traffic data from the first two types of counts are published in *HS* [QRL 70] from 1963 to 1973, and in *TS* [QRL 108] from 1974. Formerly, they were published in *Roads in England and Wales* [QRL 97] and the equivalent Scottish publications.

3.21.11 Fuller accounts of census design and methodology, and more detailed results are given —for the 50/200 point counts—in *Road Research Technical Paper No. 63* [QRL 37] and TRRL Reports No. 45 and LR 119, 371 etc. [QRL 16]; and for the 1100/1300 point census in Road Research Technical Paper No. 62 [QRL 38] and RRL Report No. LR 206 [QRL 39]. *See also* [QRL 34] for data on trends 1938–60 and [QRL 17] on traffic distribution through twenty-four hours of the day.

3.21.12 The data in *HS* and *TS* comprise:
Vehicle-miles by light vans/other goods vehicles
    annual—all roads in GB
    annual × urban/rural (index 1966 = 100)—all roads in GB
    monthly × motorways/urban/rural—all roads in GB
    monthly average × months—motorways, trunk and classified roads in GB (not separately)
    daily average × weekdays/Sats/Sundays × months (as previous item)
    average annual per vehicle (goods vehicles in total)
and, for *motorways*, based on counts at some points additional to those in the monthly census:
Vehicle-miles (annual) on the whole motorway system
average flows in vehicles per day at some 20 selected points
    both by
        light vans
        other goods vehicles, 2 axles rigid
        other goods vehicles, 3 or more axles rigid
        other goods vehicles, articulated or with trailer.
It should be noted that figures for goods vehicle traffic on unclassified roads cannot be obtained by taking the difference between the latter figures and 'all roads' figures because the residual would be distorted by sampling errors.

3.21.13 The detailed data tabulated in the TRRL Reports mentioned above include breakdowns for 'other goods vehicles' by axle configuration for most of the above data given in *HS* and *TS*; analyses by MOT Traffic Engineering Division (for definitions see *Roads in England and Wales* [QRL 97]) of vehicle-miles per day by road types, urban and rural and by light/heavy goods vehicles, and of average daily flow by urban/rural, light/heavy goods.

3.21.14 Data from the general traffic census in 1965 were published in *HS* [QRL 70] for 1967 in map form, showing for each site:

(1) the average number of motor vehicles per sixteen-hour August day (calculated from four-day counts as $1/7(\text{Fri} + \text{Sat} + \text{Sun} + 4 \times \text{Mon}))$;
(2) the average annual percentage growth since the previous census in August 1961;
(3) the percentage of heavy goods vehicles (those of $1\frac{1}{2}$ tons unladen weight or more) in the total flow.

3.21.15 Results from the 1969–73 cycle were not published, but may be seen or purchased (£6 per annual volume) at the offices of the DTp Directorate of Statistics—Traffic Census Unit, St Christopher House, Southwark St., London S.E.1, and at offices of the Scottish Development Department and Welsh Office at addresses given in the *SN* 26.20 note, where more information about these censuses and the cycle started in 1974 can be obtained.

3.21.16 Statistical information on roads in Northern Ireland may be found in the annual *Reports of the Ministry of Development*, Belfast [QRL 87] and in the *Ulster Year Book* [QRL 112] in its chapter on transportation and communications.

3.22 Traffic and Transportation Studies and Surveys

3.22.1 A very large number of studies and surveys varying from the simple to the highly complex and for study areas ranging from point locations and villages up to and including all the major conurbations, have been carried out over recent years, for a variety of planning purposes. Many of them contain data on goods vehicle movements and other aspects of road goods transport, generally as part of a comprehensive analysis of passenger travel and goods flows by different modes of transport for the purpose of estimating future demand and the implications for transport planning and investment.

3.22.2 The data may be derived by various techniques—roadside counts at cordons and screen-lines, interview and postal surveys, and analysis in conjunction with land/use, demographic and economic data. As a rule private car travel and other personal travel are treated much more fully than goods transport.

3.22.3 Most of the data relate to purely local movement, but some of the studies yield data on long-distance flows between the study area and other parts of the country and a number of the studies are of much interest from the point of view of methodology.

3.22.4 Because of the great number and variety of type of the studies and surveys, and of the vast number of localities and areas concerned, it is not possible to give here any sort of listing or summary of the data available. However, DTp (Statistics Transport, A Division) maintains an index of traffic and transportation surveys carried out in Great Britain as a reference source for people or organizations interested in various aspects of transport policy or research. By late 1975 details of over 1,000 surveys had been stored on microfilm, with a system for identifying surveys covering a particular area, or topic, or using a particular computer or analytical technique (see *SN* 31.38). The range of information on the microfilm entries corresponds to the questionnaire used in compiling the index—*see* copy in Appendix A of this review. A free summary listing of the surveys held in the index was published in the DOE Headquarters Library Information Series No. 21. Further information about the index can be obtained from DOE/DTp Headquarters Library Research Section, 2 Marsham Street, London SW1P 3EB (01-212-4328).

3.22.5 References are given in the QRL to two of the conurbation studies—for the West Midlands [QRL 109] and Glasgow [QRL 69], also to a publication by the British Road Federation—*Traffic in the Conurbations* [QRL 43] which brings together data from eight of these studies. For a summary of the techniques used in the studies, see *Urban Traffic Engineering Techniques* 1965 [B 52] and *Traffic and Transport Plans (Road Circular 1/68)* [B 44]. Regional plans may also include transportation studies.

3.23 Road Accidents

3.23.1 DTp's annual *Road Accidents in Great Britain* [QRL 88], much expanded as from the 1973 issue, gives some statistics relating to road accidents in which goods vehicles are involved. The data include statistics of numbers of goods vehicles involved in injury accidents, by severity of accident and by two/three/four unladen-weight groups, and in built-up and non-built-up areas by month, by daylight/darkness and by road surface conditions. Casualties and casualty rates per 100 million vehicle-miles to drivers and passengers of goods vehicles are given, but no regular data on casualties to occupants of other vehicles or to pedestrians involved in accidents with goods vehicles. *TS* [QRL 108] includes a selection of these data, with figures for other modes of transport.

3.23.2 The statistical tables in [QRL 88] are preceded by a review of the year's experience, highlighting different aspects from time to time, and drawing on special studies and additional data. The review in the 1972 issue included data on the overall involvement record of heavy goods vehicles, and on the associated casualties to pedestrians and users of other vehicles (*see* also the 1976 issue).

3.23.3 For a detailed discussion of the accident record of goods vehicles relative to those of other vehicles, *see* Chapter 6 of Sharp's *Living with the Lorry* [QRL 35] in which he draws on data from *Road Accidents in Great Britain* [QRL 88] and from a number of TRRL reports. Among the latter are LR 394 [QRL 29] with data on pedestrian casualties and vehicles involved, LR 481 [QRL 105], with data on accidents involving various combinations of vehicles as well as on vehicle/pedestrian accidents, and LR 316 [QRL 32], a study of fatal injuries in vehicle collisions, based on coroners' reports.

3.23.4 TRRL Report LR 283 [QRL 28] gives more detailed analyses of road accidents and casualty rates by class of road in rural and urban areas, with some data for goods vehicles for 1966, and has references to some earlier similar analyses. *See also* LR 348 [QRL 28] for 1968 data.

3.23.5 Data on road accidents in Northern Ireland are published in *Annual Reports on Road Accident Statistics in N. Ireland* [QRL 50]. Other data arising from special studies are obtainable from Ministry of Home Affairs, Belfast.

3.23.6 *Cost of road accidents*
Estimates of the cost of road accidents, including medical costs, the cost of lost output, damage to vehicles and property, as well as the cost of damage-only accidents (on which there are no regular data) have been made by Reynolds [QRL 30] and Dawson [QRL 11]. *See also Road Truck Costs*, Annex 12 [QRL 94] and *Transport Policy*, Vol 2, Paper 6, Appendix I [B 55], and [QRL 88], e.g. for 1976.

3.24 Studies of Environmental Effects of Road Goods Transport

3.24.1 In recent years growing concern with the adverse effects of road traffic and transport on the environment—human, natural and built—has prompted a large and increasing volume of studies and research of all kinds into e.g. danger, noise, vibration, emissions and visual intrusion, and how they can be measured, evaluated, limited or avoided. Some of the work is related to road goods transport, but most to road traffic and transport generally. Statistical data arising from the work are scattered through a large literature, and another volume in the series is to review in detail the sources of data on these and other kinds of pollution of the environment.

3.24.2 Here it is appropriate to draw attention to the many studies undertaken by the TRRL which can be picked out from the list of TRRL Reports, regularly updated and available to enquirers in libraries or from TRRL, Crowthorne, Berks.

3.24.3 Among TRRL studies of particular interest for the data presented and/or the methodology used are two on the effects of urban freight distribution in Putney High Street and in two less busy shopping streets in Newbury and Camberley, with the object of providing estimates of the total impact on people in the streets. (*See* LR 556 [QRL 9] and LR 603 [QRL 8].) Activities comprised

    collection of data on goods deliveries, etc. from shop managers,
    direct observation and time-lapse photography of traffic and freight operations,
    measurement of noise,
    surveys of attitudes of pedestrians and residents.

Results given in the reports include

data on the distribution of goods visits by type of business, floor-space area and time,
delays and costs to other traffic by parking, etc.,
relation of classified vehicle flows, speed pattern and loading on noise levels and peaks,
opinions of pedestrians and residents, e.g. percentages ascribing various degrees of 'bother' to noise, smells, vibration, delay, etc. analysed by age, location, etc.

3.24.4 A pioneering TRRL survey covering a whole town has been carried out at Swindon with the objects of obtaining (1) detailed data on flows of commodities and goods vehicles in the town, and (2) a computer model to predict how some possible measures to control goods vehicle movements are likely to affect e.g. flows of vehicles, distribution costs, traffic congestion and quality of the environment. Two preliminary reports have been issued—TRRL SR 126 UC [QRL 27] and SR 158 UC [B 1].

3.24.5 Data collection in 1973 involved interviews with operators and detailed vehicle movement surveys by log-books for internally based vehicles and roadside interviews at ten cordon sites for externally based vehicles. Preliminary results given in [QRL 27] include data on

distribution by weight of goods vehicles entering the town,
proportions of through and stopping traffic,
goods vehicles stopping in town centre,
commodities delivered by land use.

[B 1] describes the data collection and the construction of the computer model.

3.24.6 Further studies of the same type are being undertaken in Hull and in a sector of S.E. London.

3.24.7 An article, 'Road Traffic and the Environment', in *Social Trends*, No. 5 [QRL 33] gives data from a survey sponsored by DOE in 1970 to investigate attitudes of the general public as to how they are affected by road traffic in their homes and immediate locality. The survey involved some 5,700 interviews in a number of localities of different types. Results are presented in terms of percentages of people bothered by the effects of noise, vibration, fumes, dust and dirt, parking, danger to pedestrians and visual intrusion, related to level of exposure to traffic, with analysis by age, socio-economic group and by type of locality—on bus routes, in cul-de-sac, in conurbations and by three ranges of population density outside conurbations.

3.24.8 The subject of wear and tear on the roads by heavy vehicles and the implications for road construction and maintenance costs has been widely studied. Data sources should be covered in the review in this series dealing with the road system. *Road Track Costs* [QRL 94] is relevant: Paper 6 in *Transport Policy*, Vol 2 [B55] is more up-to-date. See also *Commercial Traffic Studies* [QRL 10] for data on axle loading characteristics of goods vehicles and traffic count/axle weight studies.

3.24.9 For a wide-ranging study of goods vehicles in the environment and the social and economic issues involved, see *Living with the Lorry* [QRL 35] by C. Sharp, sponsored by the FTA and RHA. This draws on a great deal of data from chapters in other listed studies on demand for freight transport and goods vehicles, noise, pollution of the atmosphere, vehicle weights and road wear, accidents, other effects with social costs including vibration, delays, visual intrusion and direct damage, 'the rail solution' and 'the road solution'. Studies listed at [B 6, B 11, B 14, B 24, B 25 and B 34] are also of potential interest.

3.25 Digest of Energy Statistics

3.25.1 The annual publication of the Department of Energy [QRL 63] includes data on inland deliveries in the UK of petroleum products by end use, in tonnage terms and distinguishing figures for motor spirit and for derv fuel, for goods vehicles. These figures are reproduced in *TS* [QRL 108], which also includes data on expenditure on fuel excise duty allocable to road goods operators—both in eleven-year series form—from *Annual Reports of HM Customs and Excise* [QRL 86].

3.26 Prices and Charges

3.26.1 There is no organized collection or publication of information on prices.

3.26.2 Some concerns issue tariffs or pricing guides as a basis for negotiation: a twice-yearly publication *Rates* [QRL 82] lists some of these as quoted by various named or unnamed carriers and forwarding agents.

3.26.3 Three reports [QRL 59, QRL 90, QRL 91] followed references to the National Board for Prices and Incomes (NBPI) in 1965 on increases in rates recommended by the Road Haulage Association, and in 1967 on charges, costs and wages and the scope for productivity. They contain some scanty generalized statistics, based on relatively small sample surveys addressed by the Board to operators, on the make-up and trend of costs and rates, and in greater detail on averages and distributions of hours worked and weekly earnings.

3.26.4 The Select Committee Report [QRL 99] includes some comparisons of parcel tariffs quoted by National Carriers Ltd. and British Road Services Parcels Ltd., and the minutes of evidence contain much on the pricing policies of the National Freight Corporation and these subsidiaries.

3.26.5 A good deal of light has been thrown on charges by means of data obtained in surveys on a consignment basis described in 3.15 and 3.16 above. Thus Bayliss and Edwards [QRL 23] analyse the charges paid on consignments by manufacturing firms by various modes of transport in relation to consignment weight, distance and other factors, and evaluate the relative importance of price among other factors as an influence on the choice of mode. *See also* Edwards [QRL 22], Walters [QRL 44], Chisholm [QRL 6] and Chisholm and O'Sullivan [QRL 7], the last two with particular reference to transport cost as a function of distance.

3.26.6 In [QRL 15], a study of productivity trends in a number of transport industries, Deakin and Seward give details of a sample survey carried out in 1967, addressed to a random sample of FH operators drawn from the MOT Index. The object was to obtain, from individual consignment data, average charges per ton-mile for thirty-one commodities in order to produce an aggregate index of ton-mileage output weighted by price relatives, so as to improve on aggregate unweighted ton-mileage as an indicator of real output for use in productivity calculations.

INTERNATIONAL TRAFFIC AND EEC STATISTICS

3.27 Goods Vehicle Roll-on/Roll-off Traffic at Ports

3.27.1 The number of goods vehicles entering and leaving Great Britain as roll-on/roll-off traffic on shipping services has been growing rapidly. Statistics on this traffic have been published annually by the National Ports Council (NPC) since 1965 in *Container and Roll-on Port Statistics* [QRL 79]. These statistics provide measures not only of the use of port facilities for traffic of this type, but also some indication of the volume of international road goods traffic on the roads of Great Britain—not in vehicle-mile terms, but perhaps better than nothing.

3.27.2 The publication contains data on the numbers of road goods vehicles/trailers and the tonnage they carry, entering or leaving ports in GB on roll-on shipping services. There are analyses by inwards/outwards, loaded/empty, by overseas country in foreign trade and by Northern Ireland/other in coastwise trade; and some data for individual ports for 'wheeled units' which at some ports include rail wagons. The data are also reproduced in summary form in *TS* [QRL 108].

3.28 DTp Roll-on/Roll-off Goods Survey

3.28.1 The survey was begun in 1971 to monitor the movements of road goods vehicles on roll-on ferry services between GB and the Continent. The stimulus was the need to begin collection of data to satisfy the requirements of EEC Directive 69/467 on Regional/International movements of goods by road, or its successor (*see* 3.29 below).

3.28.2 Ferry operators complete a questionnaire for each quarter of the year for each service operated, giving the number of powered vehicles and the number of unaccompanied trailers and semi-trailers carried. Figures for powered vehicles are required by country of registration, but this is not required for unaccompanied trailers because the nationality of a trailer can be difficult to determine simply by inspection. Every effort is made to ensure that all ferry services are covered. This has not always been achieved, particularly in 1971 and 1972, but comparisons with the statistics published by the NPC (3.27 refers) show only a small shortfall, possibly due partly to inaccuracy of figures provided by operators.

3.28.3 Data are published in *TS* [QRL 108]. The 1975 issue gives:

numbers of vehicle movements in 1975 between GB and Europe and v.v., by country of registration,
total vehicle movements between GB and Europe by powered vehicles/trailers and semi-trailers shipped without a tractive unit, by in/out, annually 1971 to 1975.

The analysis by country of registration is less reliable than would be desired, due to inaccurate returns and, in several cases, the lack of any information on nationality. The survey is, however, at present the only source of such information.

3.28.4 The survey was extended in 1975 to include traffic on ferry services to Ireland.

3.29 EEC Statistical Requirements

3.29.1 Three EEC statutes requiring annual returns to the Commission are relevant. One includes references to road traffic, the other two, still in draft form and subject to final agreement, relate to domestic and international road goods transport respectively.

3.29.2 EEC Regulation 1108/70 introduced an accounting system for expenditure on infrastructure in respect of transport by rail, road and inland waterway, and provides for collection of detailed statistics of the traffic using the respective infrastructures. For road traffic, the data required annually in respect of goods vehicles are total vehicle-kilometres on roads outside built-up areas, by road classes, for:

vans with maximum gross weight not over 3 tons,
goods vehicles by number of axles,
goods vehicles with trailers by combinations of axle numbers of vehicle and trailer,
tractors with semi-trailers by combinations of axle numbers of tractor and trailer,
agricultural vehicles.

Every five years, including 1975, a vastly more detailed analysis is specified, also for roads outside built-up areas by classes. This is an analysis of distance run by commercial vehicles, cross-classified by maximum gross weight, by axle arrangement, by *actual* loads on front and rear axles in class intervals of 1 tonne of actual axle load.

DOE have used weighbridges at a number of sites in 1975 to determine actual axle loadings for a sample of vehicles as a basis for this return. The fine classification of axle load reflects the findings that wear on road surfaces is proportional to a high power of axle loading—generally taken to be the fourth power—see TRRL Report LR 628 [QRL 10] for results of some traffic count/axle weight studies.

3.29.3 The information called for by Regulation 1108/70 was intended primarily as an aid to developing future policies on charging for the use of infrastructure, and it is not certain how far it will be formally published by EEC. Further information can be obtained from: European Economic Commission Division C1: Infrastructure charging, D. G. VII, Rue de la Loi 200, 1049 Bruxelles.

3.29.4 On domestic road goods transport, the proposals under consideration are for annual returns based on sample surveys, in respect of operations by all goods vehicles with payload capacity of 3 tonnes or more. The data required comprise

total tonnes/tonne-kilometres, for FH/OA/total, analysed by type of service (ordinary/collection and delivery/shuttle) by distance groups (0–49, 50–149, 150 km +) and by commodity groups, and type of service (total collection and delivery only)

tonnes by FH/OA/total by commodity groups by distance groups (as above)

tonnes by EEC region of loading by EEC region of destination

tonnes by EEC regions by received/despatched/intra-regional by commodity groups.

3.29.5 Shuttle service is defined as carriage of a repeated and identical nature as concerns goods, distance and places of loading and unloading. A list of twenty-three commodity groups is proposed (possibly one or two more)—a condensation of the fifty-two groups of headings in the NST, the EEC's commodity classification for transport statistics—see [B 33]. The list of EEC regions for UK are the Standard Regions, Scotland and Northern Ireland: the full list for the purpose is still to be agreed.

3.29.6 The proposals for statistics on international carriage of goods by road (which includes carriage involving sea crossings) are intended to supersede those of an existing directive which involves frontier formalities and has caused problems for most of the member states. The current draft proposal provides for annual returns, in respect of national vehicles only, with a carrying capacity of 3 tonnes or more, to cover the following data:

tonnes/tonne-kilometres for FH/OA by commodity groups,

tonnes by commodity groups by distance ranges (0–49, 50–149, 150–499, 500–999, 1,000 km +),

tonnes loaded/unloaded by commodity groups analysed by member states and by third countries.

Commodity groups are as for domestic goods transport.

3.29.7 The data requirements in the three sets of returns to EEC, actual or proposed, are in each case considerably more detailed than data so far (early 1977) collected and published by DTp. Presumably, the data submitted to EEC will be published by DTp.

REGULAR STATISTICAL PUBLICATIONS

3.30 Highway Statistics [QRL 70]
3.30.1 From 1963 to 1973 the main official publication for regular statistics on road transport other than passenger transport (published in

Passenger Transport in GB (PTGB)) and road accidents (published in *Road Accidents in GB* [QRL 88]), was *Highway Statistics* [QRL 70]. This annual publication brought together statistics on

> motor vehicles currently licensed
> new registrations
> road traffic
> road goods transport
> taxation receipts from road users
> consumers' expenditure in UK on road transport
> household car ownership
> driving licences
> driving tests.

The data under the first four headings relevant to this review have been described earlier in discussing the primary sources. The data on taxation receipts did not distinguish goods transport from public passenger transport and motoring.

3.31 Transport Statistics, Great Britain [QRL 108]

3.31.1 From 1974 (i.e. with 1974 data initially, but with many tables for 1964 to 1974 in annual series form) this new and much more comprehensive annual publication by DTp replaced *HS* and *PTGB*. *TS* incorporates, in some respects more fully, the data coverage of these two publications, and also has extensive coverage of rail, air, inland waterways, sea transport and pipelines. There are tables bringing together data for all modes, e.g. on users' expenditure, on public expenditure on transport, on capital expenditure, on goods transport output and on accidents; and there is a section with comparative data for other European countries, the USA and USSR. There are also data, not distinguishing modes, on motor insurance and on offences.

3.31.2 In addition to the data described earlier in Section 3 on vehicle stock and new registrations (3.2.5–3.2.8), operators' fleets (3.3.6 and 3.5.4), testing and smoke emission checks for heavy goods vehicles (3.3.7), road transport output (3.4.50), users' expenditure (3.12.2), employment in road haulage (3.17.7) capital expenditure (3.19.12), road traffic (3.21.10), road accidents (3.23.1), fuel consumption (3.25.1) and roll-on/roll-off international traffic (3.27 and 3.28), *TS* also includes data on expenditure on fuel duties, vehicle licences and other taxes, in which figures for road goods transport are separately distinguished. There is a section with forecasts *inter alia* on vehicle numbers, vehicle-kilometres and inland freight tonnes and tonne-kilometres.

3.31.3 *TS* uses metric units except for unladen and gross weight classifications of vehicles and for length of journey or haul distance ranges which are still in imperial units.

3.32 CSO Monthly Digest [QRL 73]
Annual Abstract of Statistics [QRL 47]

3.32.1 The principal series on road transport output, vehicle-miles, current licences and new registrations, and road traffic, are reproduced in these publications. [QRL 73] gives

> annual ton-mile output and a quarterly index of ton-miles (*see* 3.4.48);
> annual current licence data for goods vehicles with a quarterly index based on licence issues and refunds, and monthly data on new registrations;
> index numbers for road traffic by light vans, others and total goods vehicles and for articulated vehicles also.

3.32.2 [QRL 47] gives
> the annual tonnage and ton-mileage series—total, FH and OA;
> current licence and new registration data, for GB and Northern Ireland, on goods vehicles by unladen-weight groups;

annual vehicle-miles for light vans, other and total goods vehicle traffic on the roads.

3.33 Basic Road Statistics

3.33.1 The British Road Federation publishes a useful unofficial annual, *Basic Road Statistics* [QRL 51]. This compilation reproduces various official series on motor vehicles, road traffic, road accidents, road transport, road mileage, road finance and expenditure, road administration and motor taxation, with a section on data for Northern Ireland. It also includes a useful compact outline in historical sequence of road transport legislation.

3.34 Publications by International Organizations

3.34.1 Reflecting the more usual size-categorization of vehicles by carrying capacity used abroad, the *UN Annual Bulletin of Transport Statistics for Europe* [QRL 48] gives figures of new registrations and stock of goods vehicles by carrying-capacity ranges. The UK figures are based on conversion of figures for ranges of unladen weight using factors derived from a sample of details of gross weight and payload given by vehicle manufacturers.

3.34.2 The figures for other countries include numbers of semi-trailers and trailers (by capacity) which cannot be provided by UK since they are not subject to licensing and registration here.

3.34.3 This source also has a table on international road traffic and transport including data on entries of road goods vehicles, in total and for foreign vehicles separately, and of those which are empty; also of tonnage carried on vehicles entering, leaving and in transit. In addition there are figures of total (including international) traffic on the roads in terms of vehicle-kilometres, and of total road goods transport in tonnage and tonne-kilometres with separate figures for FH transport. Country by country, there are more gaps than entries in the latter table. There are some figures for GB.

3.34.4 International road traffic and transport naturally loom larger in relation to domestic traffic on the Continent with its land frontiers, than in this island. But they are of increasing importance here, both in policy contexts and in connection with EEC statistical requirements.

3.34.5 *The Annual Reports of the European Conference of Ministers of Transport* [QRL 68] also contain some data relating to goods vehicles by capacity ranges and to traffic in international transport. But the latter are not shown for many countries.

3.34.6 *World Road Statistics* [QRL 110], an unofficial publication by the International Road Federation also publishes some vehicle and road traffic data available elsewhere, but in addition some data on imports of goods vehicles, and some examples of comparative average annual taxation of road goods vehicles of different sizes—of unknown reliability.

3.34.7 A snag with these international publications is that there is often a time-lag of a year, sometimes more, between publication of figures in domestic sources and their appearance in the international publication. By the latter time the figures may be out of date because of amendments, which may not consistently or promptly be passed on to the international organization concerned. There can also be muddles over conversions to metric units. It is desirable, wherever practicable, to check with domestic publications before taking data as correct.

3.34.8 *EEC Yearbook of Transport Statistics* [QRL 111]. This year book covers all modes of transport. Tables on road transport cover infrastructure (length of roads), vehicle stock and new registrations and numbers of road haulage enterprises and their fleets. There are also tables on domestic and international road goods transport. The latter include country of origin and destination data distinguishing ten NST commodity chapters—so far only for the six original members. Future coverage will presumably include detailed data submitted in implementation of the provisions described in 3.29 above.

4 Regional Statistics

4.1 The Regional Abstracts and Digests

4.1.1 As is apparent from the detailed account of sources in Part 3, the amount of data relevant to road goods transport analysed by Economic Planning or Standard Regions is relatively limited.

4.1.2 *Regional Statistics*, formerly *The Abstract of Regional Statistics* [QRL 46], includes only figures of goods vehicles (in total) with current licences, and new registrations, and these in less detail than in *HS* and *TS*.

4.1.3 *The Digest of Scottish Statistics* [QRL 64] up to 1971 gave new registration and current licence figures for goods vehicles (in total) by type of fuel, figures of vehicles on carriers' licences, of insured employees in Road Haulage Contracting (employers, and employees in employment from October 1967) and of average weekly earnings in Road Haulage Contracting (excluding British Road Services). The Digest's successor, *The Scottish Abstract of Statistics* [QRL 98], maintains the series except for the data on vehicles with carriers' licences.

4.1.4. *The Digest of Welsh Statistics* [QRL 66] has figures of goods vehicles (total) currently licensed in three unladen-weight groups; goods vehicle driver and passenger casualties in road accidents; numbers of employees and average weekly earnings in road haulage contracting.

4.1.5 *The Digest of Statistics—Northern Ireland* [QRL 65] has figures of current licences and new registrations of motor vehicles for goods vehicles in total, and statistics of vehicles involved in road accidents, with vans and lorries shown together.

4.2 Other Sources

4.2.1 Statistics on a standard region or administrative area basis are available from a number of the sources reviewed in Section 3 above, in particular

current licence and new registration data, by registration and licensing authority within Ec Pl Regions—from *HS* and *TS* (*see* 3.2.5 *et seq.*); and for Northern Ireland—from [QRL 83] (*see* SN 23.24).

Data on Carriers' and Operators' Licences and fleet structure, and enforcement and other administrative data, by Licensing Authority Area—from [QRL 49], *see* 3.3.3 *et seq*—and on licensed operators in N. Ireland from *The Ulster Year Book* [QRL 112].

Goods traffic origin/destination analyses by standard regions—from [QRL 103, QRL 104], *see* 3.4.30, 3.4.37.

Industries' expenditure on transport—from [QRL 18], *see* 3.14.2.

Employment and earnings data by Standard Regions—from DE publications and from [QRL 108], *see* 3.17.1 and 3.17.7.

Detailed road accident statistics for Northern Ireland from [QRL 50] and Ministry of Home Affairs, Belfast, *see* 3.23.5 and for Scotland from Scottish Development Department, Edinburgh. Statistics on road traffic for Northern Ireland from [QRL 87] and for Scotland from Scottish Development Department, Edinburgh.

Some other data, e.g. roll-on traffic data at ports can be assembled for regions.

4.2.2 In addition, data from a variety of major sub-regional surveys may have added regional relevance.

5 Modelling and Forecasts

5.1 It may be useful to give some references to examples of secondary analysis of available data for the purposes of modelling and forecasting and to papers on relevant theory, methodology and statistical data requirements.

5.2 The TRRL have published several studies forecasting vehicle population and traffic on the roads by process of analysing past trends to derive simple regression models for total ton-mileage as a function of GDP, making assumptions about other modes of traffic, and extrapolating trends in vehicle capacity, to obtain forecasts of vehicle numbers and vehicle-mile traffic. *See* Tanner [QRL 36] and Tulpule [QRL 40, QRL 42] and for a study of world trends and projections, Tulpule [QRL 41].

5.3 Figures of past trends and forecasts for some of the more important indicators in the transport field are given in Paper 1 in Volume 2 of *Transport Policy* [B 55]. DTp's official departmental forecasts are based on the TRRL work—the most recent ones on [QRL 36] but with slightly modified assumptions—*see* DOE Technical Memorandum H3/75, *Standard Forecasts of Vehicles and Traffic* [QRL 101]. Paper 7 in [B55], Vol 2 describes the forecasting methods and assumptions and discusses some criticisms.

5.4 Brown and Maultby [B 5] discuss the unreliability of simple GDP/total ton-mileage relationships and the advantages and possibilities of alternative methods of forecasting based on input–output analyses, and on the combination of separate forecasts for the industries which are the main generators of transport demand. Bayliss [B 2] also discusses instability and other inadequacies of 'total ton-mile' models and reviews other approaches with emphasis on modal-split models.

5.5 Chisholm [QRL 5] discusses an MOT forecast study of 1963 [B 49] and some other forecasts, and various simple regression model approaches; and also considers the possibility of forecasting transport demand in regional disaggregation.

5.6 Other work uses data on inter-regional and zone-to-zone flows such as that obtained from the MOT/DOE road goods survey in 1962 (*see* 3.4.28 *et seq.*) in attempts to develop models for transport demand in terms of inter-regional flows of goods and vehicle flows on the trunk road network. Chisholm and O'Sullivan's major study at [QRL 7] and some DOE work at [B 8] have already been mentioned in 3.4.32. *See also* O'Sullivan [B 20] and Edwards and Gordon's discussion [B 7] of the potential use of freight flow data for developing inter-regional input–output models for regional forecasting.

5.7 Schneider [B 22] examines in depth the concept of transport demand and possible methods by which it can be described and analysed for forecasting and other purposes. *See also* Noortman [B 19] on transport demand.

6 Comments and Suggestions

6.1 In his contribution on Road and Rail Statistics to the RSS series of reviews of sources in the late 1940s [B 17], F. A. A. Menzler reported the almost complete absence of statistical information on the volume, nature and cost of work done by road goods transport, with nothing more tangible available than numbers of carriers' licences and rough estimates based on traffic census figures. There had been no material advance since A. E. Kirkus of the then Ministry of Transport had addressed the Institute of Transport in 1936 on road transport statistics [B 13].

6.2 In the 1950s, MOT's sample surveys of 1952 and 1958 (3.4) threw much-needed light on the structure and characteristics of the vehicle fleet and on the nature and volume in physical terms of the work done; and the RRL's 50-point road traffic census provided continuous information from 1956 on vehicle-mile trends by vehicle types. Munby, writing in 1960 [B 18], could thus report a useful advance in available data, but had to point to large remaining gaps, particularly in financial information.

6.3 The 1960s saw much progress. The MOT's 1962 survey (3.4) expanded the information on commodities carried and added the first extensive information on the geographical element in terms of zone-to-zone flows; the 1966 survey of operating costs and expenditure (3.13) yielded the first actual data (as distinct from broad estimates and cost formulae) on vehicle- and fleet-operating costs on FH and OA transport, on FH receipts, on total users' expenditure and on net output; and the major 1966/7 survey on the use of transport by manufacturers (3.15), analysing data on consignments sent by FH and OA road transport, rail and other modes, threw light both on the factors determining choice of mode, and indirectly on transport prices—the latter through a detailed analysis of the structure of charges actually made and how they varied with consignment size, length of haul, commodity, etc. The Board of Trade's Censuses of Production and Distribution (3.14) began to provide estimates of each industry's expenditure on road transport and the National Ports Council began to assemble data on roll-on/roll-off traffic at the ports (3.27). The expansion of the 50-point road traffic census to 200 points and larger-scale bench-mark traffic censuses by the RRL (3.21) increased the precision of relevant road traffic data. In the 1960s also, in addition to various other studies in regional and sub-regional contexts—partly making use of the growing stock of data—land use/transportation studies mounted in all the large conurbations and in many other major towns obtained comprehensive data on traffic generation, attraction, flows and modal distribution (though with more attention to passenger than freight traffic) to provide bases for transportation planning in the areas concerned.

6.4 In the 1970s to date, the main developments have been the start of the continuing road goods transport survey (3.4.39), taking the place of the roughly quinquennial surveys of operations and physical output; a variety of studies mainly by the TRRL on the effects of transport on the environment (3.24); a continuous survey of roll-on/roll-off international goods vehicle traffic (3.28); and on the publications side, the début of DTp's comprehensive annual *Transport Statistics*, [QRL 108], with a considerable increase in content of data on road goods transport and copious data on other modes.

6.5 In the last ten years or so, therefore, a great deal of new data has been published on road goods transport, throwing light on a number of previously dark areas. Much, however, has been in physical rather than financial terms and much or most has been from one-off or occasional surveys. The mid-1960s surveys on operating costs and on industry's use of transport have not been repeated, and the data, though highly revealing and useful at the time, are now years out of date. The Business Statistics Offices (BSO) production enquiries are tending to reduce or omit coverage of purchases of transport services. There has still been no census-type enquiry concerned with financial structure and assets, inputs, turnover or sales and manpower, though the 1966 survey of operating costs went a good way in this direction. There are no data on current sales by public hauliers or expenditure in OA transport: the resumed publication by DTp, in *Transport Statistics* [QRL 108], of estimates of total users' expenditure by the Rudd/Dawson method (*see* 3.12) is welcome, for the broad indications they provide, and would be more so if they were more accurate and detailed.

6.6 With the passing of ten years since the previous operating cost survey and given the recent enormous increases in fuel costs and large increases in wage costs, there appears to be a strong case for DTp to draw up a programme for filling the gaps in financial data on road goods transport. Among possibilities which might be considered are:

(1) a census-type economic enquiry in comprehensive but simple terms for bench-mark purposes, with a subsample providing detailed information on fleet and other assets, operating costs for individual vehicles and the whole fleet, in adequate input detail with, *inter alia*, input–output analysis in mind, and turnover;

(2) the addition of questions on current turnover, or total expenditure for OA operators, either to the continuing survey (at present only yielding data in physical terms), and/or to the annual BSO enquiry on capital expenditure (as was done in 1974 for purposes of proving the VAT register used for the first time as the sampling frame).

6.7 It is to be hoped that BSO's production enquiries to industries will carry questions on expenditure on both purchased and own road transport at close intervals if not annually.

6.8 As regards capital expenditure, DTp might explore with the BSO the possibility of making the latter's enquiries more informative in the road goods transport context by separating expenditure on goods vehicles from that on cars, both in the enquiries addressed to road haulage firms, and in those addressed to other industries (so as to show capital expenditure on goods vehicles for own-account fleets). If practicable, also, the capital investment data for road haulage should be published separately from those for 'storage, etc.', if not in the National Income Blue Books, at least in Business Monitors.

6.9 The more detailed data published in *Transport Statistics* [QRL 108] from the Goods Vehicle List are a big improvement, but they could still be extended with advantage, by giving analyses by vehicle capacity ranges: these are more relevant for some purposes than either unladen weight or gross weight analyses, and are normal in Europe. It would be useful to build up trends of total tonnage capacity of the fleet with breakdown by ranges of capacity. The GVL might also be exploited to yield data on acquisition, disposals and net changes.

6.10 As regards data on physical output, the data from the continuing survey published in *Highway Statistics* [QRL 70] for years up to 1973 were meagre. *Transport Statistics* publishes much more detail but only in terms of traffic tonnage and tonne-kilometres. These give only part of the output picture. Lacking are any data on the deployment and operation of the fleet, e.g. in vehicle-kilometre and other terms, in carrying the traffic, as also are data on annual tonnage, tonne-kilometres and vehicle kilometres per vehicle. Many of the analyses and cross-analyses used in publishing the 1962 and 1967/8 survey data (see 3.4.23 and 3.4.37) are useful and should be provided annually, including analyses by vehicle-carrying capacity as well as origin/destination data —the raw data are on the questionnaires. Detailed analyses on fuel consumption could also be provided. As data builds up, as much detail as is feasible should be given in series form to preclude the need to refer to previous issues. A full review in DTp of the potential of the continuing survey data for analysis and publication could be rewarding.

6.11 Further study of the possibility of devising a better indicator of real output for national income purposes than total FH ton-miles, possibly by disaggregating output into components and re-assembling with weights approximately proportional to value added per unit of physical output, could be worth while. Disaggregated vehicle-mile output (or vehicle-hour output if data from tachographs become available), might be as good a basis or better than the present aggregate ton-miles indicator.

6.12 The absence of a price index, or any pressure for one, probably reflects *inter alia*, the fact that very little road goods transport is purchased by consumers or other final buyers, as well as the availability of output data in physical terms, which lessens the need for a price index as a deflator of output data at current prices. Nevertheless, some data to indicate price trends in different sectors of road goods transport, short distance, long distance, international, own account in various industries and so on, in which price trends may be different, would appear desirable. The difficulties of compiling such indicators are considerable. Consignment surveys, addressed to transport users, which could incidentally yield price or charges data for other transport modes as well, might be considered for this purpose and indeed for others where the greater scope for analysis of data for individual consignments, as compared with data for total vehicle loads, would be valuable.

6.13 The vehicle-mile data for goods vehicles derived from road censuses have been of limited usefulness because of the lumping together, in much of the published data, of all goods vehicles other than 'light vans' as 'heavy goods vehicles'. The more detailed breakdown by axle configuration now available should be carried as fully as possible into published data.

6.14 Studies of the actual flows of traffic on the main arteries of the road system, including those serving ports and those avoiding towns, are likely to become of increasing importance in investment planning and for lorry routeing purposes. Local Authorities' obligations under the Heavy Commercial Vehicles Act of 1973 (the Dykes Act) [B 27] to specify through routes and/or forbidden zones or roads may involve studies and subsequent monitoring of traffic. Data resulting from these studies will be of wide interest and should be liberally published.

6.15 A last point on publication: in addition to annual publication in the new *Transport Statistics* [QRL 108], which will necessarily be subject to time-lags, there would appear to be a case for publishing more data than at present on a quarterly basis to provide up-to-date trends, possibly with some use of moving twelve-month series.

Quick Reference List—Table of Contents

Vehicles   61
   (1) *with current excise licences*   61
   (2) *new registrations*   61
   (3) *with Operators' or Carriers' Licences*   61
   (4) *deployed in operation*   61

Operators   62

Licensing Administration   62

Output   62
   (1) *tons/ ton-miles (or metric)*   62
   (2) *vehicle-miles (or metric)*   63
   (3) *journeys*   63
   (4) *net output*   63

Operating Costs   63
   (1) *total costs*   63
   (2) *vehicle costs*   63

Receipts   63

Capital Investment   64

Fuel Consumption and Duty   64

Manpower   64

Wage Rates, Earnings   64

Users' Expenditure   65

Consignments   65

Charges Paid   65

Road Traffic (Goods Vehicles)   65

Road Accidents 65

International Roll-on/Roll-off Traffic 66

Notes:
1. The full breakdowns shown may not apply throughout the period, nor, in full, to each source where two or more are grouped for convenience.
2. For details of cross-analyses, see text.
3. Three-digit text references may be either to the beginning of discussion of the source, or to a relevant paragraph within the discussion.
4. In addition to the specific text references given, Section 1 (Introduction) and Section 2 on matters of usage, definition, coverage and measurement are usually relevant.
5. The list is not exhaustive of data and sources reviewed in the text. Other references may be found in the Subject Index.

Quick Reference List

Subject	Breakdown	Area (if not GB)	Frequency	Publication (see QRL key)	Text reference
Vehicles					
(1) Vehicles currently licensed	Excise category: unladen wt; yrs of first registration; Ec Pl Regions; Licg. Authorities	GB, UK	Annual	[QRL 108], [QRL 70], [QRL 92], [QRL 51]	3.2.1
(2) New registrations	As above and fuel used	GB, UK	Annual	[QRL 74]	3.2.9
	Excise category: unladen wt; fuel used		Monthly	[QRL 76], [QRL 92]	3.2.7
			Annual	[QRL 70], [QRL 108], [QRL 51]	3.2.7
	As above and newly subject to HP agreements		Monthly	[QRL 100]	3.33.1
	New vehicles, by make British/foreign: vans/other		Annual	[QRL 74]	3.2.9
(3) With Operators' or Carriers' Licences	Rigid/articulated; gross weight; body type; year of first registration; fleet size; Areas		Annual	[QRL 108], [QRL 49], [QRL 51]	3.3, 1.3
	Licence categories; unladen weight; Areas		Annual	[QRL 70], [QRL 49], [QRL 51]	3.3, 1.3
	Fleet size; FH/OA or licence category; Areas		1963, 1964 1966, 1969	[QRL 81], [QRL 70] [QRL 23], [QRL 70]	3.5.1, 3.13.7 3.5.2
(4) Deployed in operation	FH/OA or lic. cat., unladen wt; type of fuel; carrying capacity; year of first registration; body type; nature of business (C vehicles); main type of work (C vehicles); deployment		1962, 1967/8	[QRL 103], [QRL 104]	3.4.19, 3.4.33
	Licence categories; mean carrying capacity; age; propn. diesel; mean idle days; propn. wholly or mainly carrying specified commodities; propn. running different numbers of journeys per week		1952, 1958	[QRL 25], [QRL 106]	3.4.2, 3.4.9
	Fleet size, unladen weight; vehicle type; nature of business; return load factor; whether operated beyond 75 miles radius (C vehicles)		1958	[QRL 102]	3.6.1

Subject	Breakdown	Area (if not GB)	Frequency	Publication (see QRL key)	Text reference
Operators					
Holders of Operators' or Carriers' licences	Areas; (with vehicle numbers) licence categories (when applicable)		Annual	[QRL 49], [QRL 108]	3.3, 1.3
	Fleet size; main work categories; others (FH)		1971	[QRL 1]	3.8
	Fleet size		1969	[QRL 70]	3.5
	Fleet size (FH)		1963, 1966	[QRL 81], [QRL 70], [QRL 23]	3.5
	Fleet size (C vehicles)		1964, 1966	[QRL 70], [QRL 23]	3.5
	Fleet size; various others (FH)	South-east Area	1932, 1936 1953, 1965	[QRL 2]	3.7
Licensing Administration					
Applications, objections, hearings, suspensions, etc., prosecutions, convictions	Areas		Annual	[QRL 49]	3.3, 1.3
HGV drivers' licences—applications, issues suspensions, etc.	Areas		Annual	[QRL 49]	3.3, 1.3
Vehicle examination, testing, prohibitions, noise and smoke checks	Areas		Annual	[QRL 49], [QRL 108]	3.3, 1.3
Output					
(1) Tons, tonnes and/or ton-miles, tonne-km	Total (and other modes)		Annual Annual 1964–	[QRL 47] [QRL 108]	3.32.2, 1.5, 2.2 3.4.39, 3.31.1, 1.5, 2.2
	Total; FH/OA or licence category		Annual 1963–	[QRL 70], [QRL 108]	3.30, 3.31, 3.4, 1.5, 2.2
	FH/OA; Rigid/artic. vehicle; gross weight; unladen weight; length of haul; commodities		Annual 1974–	[QRL 108]	3.31, 3.4, 1.5, 2.2
	FH/OA or licence category; length of haul; unladen weight; carrying capacity; commodities; within/to/from regions; region to region; type of work (C vehicles); nature of business (C vehicles)		1962, 1967/68	[QRL 103] [QRL 104]	3.4.19, 3.4.33, 2.2
	Total		1952, 1958	[QRL 25], [QRL 106], [QRL 24]	3.4.2, 3.4.9, 3.4.14, 2.2

Quick Reference List 63

Index of ton-miles	Current base 1970 = 100	Quarterly	[QRL 73]	3.4.48, 3.32.1, 2.2
Average tons, ton-miles per vehicle per annum or per week	FH/OA or licence category; unladen weight	1952, 1958 1962, 1967/8	[QRL 25], [QRL 106] [QRL 103], [QRL 104]	3.4.2, 3.4.9, 2.2 3.4.19, 3.4.33, 2.2.
(2) Vehicle-miles	Loaded/empty; journey type; length of haul; FH/OA or licence category; unladen weight; carrying capacity; type of work (C vehicles)	1962, 1967/8	[QRL 103], [QRL 104]	3.4.19, 3.4.33, 2.2
Average vehicle-miles per vehicle per annum or per week	Loaded/empty; FH/OA or licence category; unladen weight	1952, 1958 1962, 1967/8	[QRL 25], [QRL 106] [QRL 103], [QRL 104]	3.4.2, 3.4.9, 2.2 3.4.19, 3.4.33, 2.2
(3) Journeys	Journey type; length of haul licence category; unladen weight within/to/from regions; region to region	1962	[QRL 103]	3.4.9, 2.2
(4) Net output	Salaries and wages/depreciation/profits	1965	[QRL 23]	3.13.14, 3.19
Operating Costs				
(1) *Total costs*				
Annual costs; Cost per ton of fleet unladen weight; Cost per vehicle-mile	Cost headings; FH/OA; fleet size (all GB operators)	1965	[QRL 23]	3.13
Cost per ton carried; Cost as per cent of receipts (FH)	Cost headings; fleet size; principal work category (sample of FH operators)	1971	[QRL 1]	3.8
(2) *Vehicle costs* per annum; per hour; per mile; per ton carried;	Cost headings; FH/OA; unladen weight; carrying capacity; rigid/artic.	1965	[QRL 23]	3.13
per week; per mile; per mile	Cost headings; miles per week or per annum; vehicle types; carrying capacity (including value of vehicle occupants' time) vans other goods; vehicle speed	Annual Occasional Most years	[QRL 66], [QRL 75], [QRL 26], [QRL 96] [QRL 10]	3.10 3.11 3.10
Receipts				
Receipts per mile	Fleet size	1965	[QRL 23]	3.13
Receipts per mile, per ton of fleet unladen wt, per ton carried	Fleet size; category of main work (sample of FH operators)	1971	[QRL 1]	3.8
Annual, FH		1965	[QRL 23]	3.13

64 Road Goods Transport

Subject	Breakdown	Area (if not GB)	Frequency	Publication (see QRL key)	Text reference
Annual, NFC	Subsidiary companies		Annual	[QRL 77]	3.9.4
Annual, BTC (BRS)	Collection and delivery/other		Annual (until 1962)	[QRL 55]	3.9.2
			4-weekly (until 1962)	[QRL 56]	3.9.3
Capital Investment					
Road Haulage (MLH 703 and 704)	New buildings/vehicles/plant and machinery		Annual 1966–9	[QRL 52]	3.19.8
Road Haulage and Storage (MLH 703, 704, 709)	New buildings/vehicles/plant and machinery		Annual 1973–	[QRL 78]	3.19.8
For sample of FH operators at constant 1967 prices	New buildings/vehicles/plant and machinery		Annual 1969 to 1970	[QRL 1]	3.18
Fuel Consumption and Duty					
(1) Tons delivered to transport undertakings	Goods vehicles/other; derv/petrol		Annual	[QRL 63], [QRL 108]	3.25
(2) Fuel excise duty allocable to road goods transport			Annual	[QRL 86], [QRL 108]	3.25
Manpower					
Employees	Road haulage contracting/other road haulage; regions; sex	UK	Annual	[QRL 54], [QRL 62]	3.17
	Occupied as van/lorry drivers by industries	UK	Annual	[QRL 54], [QRL 62]	3.17
Total, including employers and self-employed	Self-employed/managers/foremen, etc.		1951, 1961 1966, 1971	[QRL 58]	3.17
Occupied	FH/OA	GB	1965	[QRL 23]	3.13
	Drivers, mates, etc; age; marital condition		1951, 1961 1966, 1971	[QRL 58]	3.17
Employers, employees registered/leviable by RTITB	Size of firm; leavers/recruits		Annual	[QRL 95]	3.18
Wholly engaged in OA transport in distributive trades	Total		1966	[QRL 84]	3.14.5
Wage Rates, Earnings					
Wage rates, road haulage contracting	Categories of workers; areas		Annual and as changed	[QRL 54]	3.17
Earnings	Sex; adults/youths; part-time	UK	Biennial	[QRL 54], [QRL 62]	3.17
Earnings—distributions	Various categories		Annual	[QRL 80]	3.17

Quick Reference List 65

Users' Expenditure

		GB, UK		
Total annual	By road transport modes		1949, 1950 1960, annual from 1963 1965	[QRL 31], [QRL 12] [QRL 70], [QRL 108] [QRL 23]	3.12 3.12 3.13
Annual spent on transport by production and distributive industries	FH/OA Purchased/own account by expenditure headings; industries; areas; regions and secondary analysis in		1963, 1966 1968, 1970 1971, 1972	[QRL 85], [QRL 84] [QRL 72]	3.14 3.14
Average cost per ton despatched	Transport modes; size of establishment (5 industries)		1966/7	[QRL 20], [QRL 21] [QRL 42], [QRL 18] [QRL 3], [QRL 4]	3.14 3.15
Average cost per lb and per 100 lb/mile for consignments	Haulier/rail; commodities Consignment size; length of haul		1966/7 1967/8	[QRL 3], [QRL 4] [QRL 44], [QRL 15]	3.15 3.16, 3.26.6

Consignments

Annual tonnage	FH/OA/other modes; size of establishment		1966/7	[QRL 3], [QRL 4]	3.15
Consignments (number)	Weight; length of haul; modes; commodities; days to delivery; propns. lost or damaged; origin/destination		1953, 1966 1967 1966/7	[QRL 44], [QRL 19] [QRL 22] [QRL 3]	3.16 3.13

Charges Paid

Average per/lb	Haulier/rail; commodities;		1966/7	[QRL 3], [QRL 4]	3.15
Average per 100 lb/mile	consignment size; length of haul		1967, 1968	[QRL 44], [QRL 15]	3.16, 3.26.5, 1.2.6.

Road Traffic (Goods Vehicles)

Vehicle-miles	Light vans/HGV by axles; all roads, urban/rural/motorways; months; weekdays/Saturdays/Sundays		1938 and 1949–	[QRL 70], [QRL 108] [QRL 16], [QRL 38], [QRL 34]	3.21, 2.1, 2.2
Vehicles per day, per hour, flows	Light vans/HGV by axles; type of road; area; hours of the day; urban/rural/motorways		1960, 1966 1968, 1970	[QRL 37], [QRL 39] [QRL 17]	3.21
Vehicles per day	Sites on trunk roads; proportion of heavy goods vehicles		1965, 1969–73	[QRL 70]	3.21, 2.1

Road Accidents

Goods vehicles involved (numbers)	Severity; unladen weight; built-up/non-built-up areas; months; daylight/darkness; road surface condition as above and by class of road		Annual 1966, 1968	[QRL 88] [QRL 27]	3.23, 2.1 3.23, 2.1

Subject	Breakdown	Area (if not GB)	Frequency	Publication (see QRL key)	Text reference
Casualties to occupants of goods vehicles	Drivers/others; severity; unladen weight; built-up/non-built-up areas; months		Annual	[QRL 88]	3.23, 2.1
Casualty rates per 100 million vehicle-miles	as above and by class of road		1966, 1968	[QRL 27]	3.23, 2.1
Casualties to pedestrians and occupants of other vehicles			1970, 1972	[QRL 32], [QRL 61]	3.23, 2.1
Goods vehicles involved, casualties	Northern Ireland	NI	Annual	[QRL 50]	3.23, 2.1
Cost of road accidents	Damage; medical costs; lost output, etc.		1971, 1956	[QRL 11], [QRL 30]	3.23, 2.1
International Roll-on/Roll-off Traffic					
Vehicle movements	Country of registration; rigid vehicles/trailers; in/out		Annual	[QRL 108]	3.28
	Loaded/empty; countries to/from; rigid vehicles/trailers; in/out accompanied/unaccompanied		Annual	[QRL 79], [QRL 108]	3.28
Tonnage carried	Loaded/empty; countries to/from; rigid vehicles/trailers; in/out accompanied/unaccompanied		Annual	[QRL 79], [QRL 108]	3.28

Quick Reference List: Key to Publications

With few exceptions, the publications listed are to be found in the Department of the Environment/Department of Transport Library at 2 Marsham Street, London SW1P 3EB, and most also at the library of the Chartered Institute of Transport, 80 Portland Place, London W1. The DOE/DTp Library produces an annual list of DOE and DTp publications, available from DOE/DTp Library Services, Room P3/178 at the above address, with details of exactly where they may be obtained, as well as a monthly Bulletin of accessions, with brief abstracts.

The Transport and Road Research Laboratory, Crowthorne, Berkshire, maintains a list of its publications, available on request.

In the case of continuous publications where titles, or names of organizations responsible or of the publishers have changed over time, the most recent designation is, in general, used.

Quick Reference List Key to Publications

Reference Number	Author and/or Organization Responsible	Title	Publisher	Frequency or date of Publication
[QRL 1]	Bayliss, B. T. Dept. of the Environment	The Road Haulage Industry since 1968	HMSO, London	1973
[QRL 2]	Bayliss, B. T. Committee of Inquiry on Small Firms	The Small Firm in the Road Haulage Industry	HMSO, London	1971
[QRL 3]	Bayliss, B. T. and Edwards, S. L. Ministry of Transport	Industrial Demand for Transport	HMSO, London	1968
[QRL 4]	Bayliss, B. T. and Edwards, S. L. Ministry of Transport	Transport for Industry: Summary Report on 1966 Survey	HMSO, London	1968
[QRL 5]	Chisholm, M.	'Forecasting the Generation of Freight Traffic in GB', in Chisholm, M., Frey, A. E. and Haggett, P. (eds.), *Regional Forecasting*	Butterworth, London	1970
[QRL 6]	Chisholm, M.	'Freight Transport Costs, Industrial Location and Regional Development' in Chisholm, M. and Manners, G., (eds.), *Spatial Policy Problems of the British Economy*	Cambridge University Press	1971
[QRL 7]	Chisholm, M. and O'Sullivan, P.	Freight Flows and Spatial Aspects of the British Economy	Cambridge University Press	1973
[QRL 8]	Christie, A. W., Blackett, D. S., Cundill, M. A. and Prudhoe, J. Dept. of the Environment	Urban Freight Distribution: studies of operations in shopping streets at Newbury and Camberley (TRRL Report LR 603)	TRRL, Crowthorne	1973
[QRL 9]	Christie, A. W., Prudhoe, J. and Cundill, M. A. Dept. of the Environment	Urban Freight Distribution: a study of operations in High Street, Putney (TRRL Report LR 556)	TRRL, Crowthorne	1973
[QRL 10]	Currer, E. W. H. Dept. of the Environment	Commercial traffic studies (TRRL Report 628)	TRRL, Crowthorne	1973
[QRL 11]	Dawson, R. F. F. Dept. of the Environment	The Cost of Road Accidents in GB and Current Costs of Road Accidents in GB (TRRL Reports LR 79, 396)	TRRL, Crowthorne	1967, 1971

Quick Reference List: Key to Publications

Ref	Author	Title	Publisher	Date
[QRL 12]	Dawson, R. F. F.	'Estimated Expenditure on Road Transport in GB 1960' in *Journal of the Royal Statistical Society*, series A (General), Vol. 125, Part 3	Royal Statistical Society	1962
[QRL 13]	Dawson, R. F. F. Ministry of Transport	*Estimated Expenditure on Road Transport in GB 1965 and 1966* (TRRL Report LR 134)	TRRL, Crowthorne	1967
[QRL 14]	Dawson, R. F. F.	*Vehicle Operating Costs in 1970, 1973* (1973 with P. Vass) (TRRL Reports LR 439, 661)	TRRL, Crowthorne	1972, 1974
[QRL 15]	Deakin, B. M. and Seward, T. Dept. of the Environment	*Productivity in Transport* (Univ. of Cambridge, Dept. of Applied Economics, Occasional Paper No. 17)	Cambridge University Press	1969
[QRL 16]	Dunn, J. B.	*Traffic Census Results for 1965–1972* (TRRL Reports No. 45 and LR 119, 222, 302, 371, 428, 548, 618)	TRRL, Crowthorne	Annual
[QRL 17]	Dunn, J. B. and Hutchings, I. J. Ministry of Transport Dept. of the Environment	*The Distribution of Traffic in GB through the 24 Hours of the Day in 1968* (TRRL Report LR 295)	TRRL, Crowthorne	1969
[QRL 18]	Edwards, S. L.	'Regional Variations in Freight Cost' in *Journal of Transport Economics and Policy*, Vol. IX, No. 2.		May 1975
[QRL 19]	Edwards, S. L. Dept. of the Environment	*Severnside Industrial Survey* (Part of Severnside Feasibility Study)	Dept. of the Environment	1971
[QRL 20]	Edwards, S. L.	'Transport Cost in British Industry' in *Journal of Transport Economics and Policy*, Vol. IV, No. 3		1970
[QRL 21]	Edwards, S. L.	'Transport Costs in the Wholesale Trades' in *Journal of Transport Economics and Policy*, Vol. III, No. 3		1969
[QRL 22]	Edwards, S. L. Northern Economic Planning Board	*The West Cumberland Transport Survey and Statistical Appendix*	Northern Economic Planning Board	1967
[QRL 23]	Edwards, S. L. and Bayliss, B. T. Dept. of the Environment	*Operating Costs in Road Freight Transport*	Dept. of the Environment	1968
[QRL 24]	Glover, K. F. Ministry of Transport	'Statistics of the Transport of Goods by Road' (Report of 1958 Survey) in *Journal of RSS*, Series A, Vol. 123, Pt. 2	Royal Statistical Society	1960
[QRL 25]	Glover, K. F. and Miller, D. N. Ministry of Transport	'The outlines of the Road Goods Transport Industry' (Report of 1952 Survey) in *Journal of RSS*, Series A, Vol. 117, Pt. 3	Royal Statistical Society	1954
[QRL 26]	Harrison, A. J.	'Some Notes on Road Transport Costs' in *Bulletin of Oxford University Institute of Statistics*, Vol. 27, No. 2	Oxford Institute of Statistics	1965
[QRL 27]	Hitchcock, A. J. M., Christie, A. W. and Cundill, M. A. Dept. of the Environment	*Urban freight: Preliminary results from the Swindon freight survey* (TRRL Report SR 126 UC)	TRRL, Crowthorne	1974
[QRL 28]	Johnson, H. D. Dept. of the Environment	*Road Accident and Casualty rates based on the 1300 pt Census, and . . . in 1968* (RRL Reports 283, 348)	TRRL, Crowthorne	1969, 1970

Reference Number	Author and/or Organization Responsible	Title	Publisher	Frequency or date of Publication
[QRL 29]	Johnson, H. D. and Garwood, F. Dept. of the Environment	*Notes on Road Accident Statistics* (TRRL Report LR 394)	TRRL, Crowthorne	1971
[QRL 30]	Reynolds, D. J.	'The Cost of Accidents in GB' in *Journal of RSS, Series A*, Vol. 119, Pt. IV	Royal Statistical Society	1956
[QRL 31]	Rudd, E.	'Estimates of Expenditure on Road Transport in GB' in *Journal of RSS, Series A*, Vol. 125, Pt. 3	Royal Statistical Society	1962
[QRL 32]	Ruffell-Smith, H. P. Dept. of the Environment	*A study of fatal injuries in vehicle collisions based on coroners' reports* (TRRL Report LR 376)	TRRL, Crowthorne	1970
[QRL 33]	Sando, F. D. and Batty, Miss V. Dept. of the Environment	'Road Traffic and the Environment' in *Social Trends*, No 5	HMSO, London	1974
[QRL 34]	Scott, J. R. and Tanner, J. C.	'Traffic trends and vehicle-miles in GB 1938-60' in *The Surveyor*, 12.5.62		1962
[QRL 35]	Sharp, C. Freight Transport Association	*Living with the Lorry*	Freight Transport Association	1973
[QRL 36]	Tanner, J. C. Dept. of the Environment	*Forecasts of vehicles and traffic in GB: 1974 revision* (TRRL Report LR 650)	TRRL, Crowthorne	1974
[QRL 37]	Tanner, J. C. and Scott, J. R. Dept. of Scientific and Industrial Research	*Fifty-point Traffic Census: the First 5 years* (Road Research Technical Paper, No. 63)	HMSO, London	1962
[QRL 38]	Tanner, J. C., Johnson, H. D. and Scott, J. R. Dept. of Scientific and Industrial Research	*Sample Survey of the Roads and Traffic of GB* (Road Research Technical Paper No. 62)	HMSO, London	1962
[QRL 39]	Timbers, Janice A. Dept. of the Environment	*Traffic Survey at 1300 sites* (TRRL Report LR 206)	TRRL, Crowthorne	1968
[QRL 40]	Tulpule, A. H. Dept. of the Environment	*Forecasts of Vehicles and Traffic in GB 1969* (TRRL Report LR 288, 543)	TRRL, Crowthorne	1969
[QRL 41]	Tulpule, A. H. Dept. of the Environment	*An analysis of some world transport statistics* (TRRL Report LR 622)	TRRL, Crowthorne	1974
[QRL 42]	Tulpule, A. H. Dept. of the Environment	*Trends in transport of freight in GB* (TRRL Report LR 429)	TRRL, Crowthorne	1972
[QRL 43]	Voorhees, A. M. and Associates	*Traffic in the Conurbations*	British Road Federation	1970

Quick Reference List: Key to Publications 71

[QRL 44]	Walters, A. A.	Integration in Freight Transport (IEA Research Monograph)	Institute of Economic Affairs	1968	
[QRL 45]	Walters, A. A. and Sharp, C.	Report on Traffic Costs and Charges of Freight Transport in Great Britain 1953	Unpublished, but copies available to interested research workers on written application to the Chief librarian, DOE DTp Library		
[QRL 46]	Central Statistical Office	Abstract of Regional Statistics, later Regional Statistics	HMSO, London	Annual	
[QRL 47]	Central Statistical Office	Annual Abstract of Statistics	HMSO, London	Annual	
[QRL 48]	United Nations, Economic Commission for Europe	Annual Bulletin of Transport Statistics for Europe	United Nations, New York	Annual	
[QRL 49]	Dept. of Transport	Annual Reports of the Licensing Authorities to the Minister for Transport	Dept. of Transport, London	Annual	
[QRL 50]	Royal Ulster Constabulary	Annual Reports on Road Accident Statistics in Northern Ireland	Royal Ulster Constabulary, Traffic Division Headquarters, Alexander Road, Belfast	Annual	
[QRL 51]	British Road Federation	Basic Road Statistics	British Road Federation	Annual	
[QRL 52]	Board of Trade, Dept. of Industry	Board of Trade Journal, later Trade and Industry	HMSO, London	Weekly	
[QRL 53]	Dept. of Employment	British Labour Statistics Historical Abstract 1886–1968	HMSO, London	1971	
[QRL 54]	Dept. of Employment	British Labour Statistics Yearbook	HMSO, London	Annual	
[QRL 55]	British Transport Commission	British Transport Commission: Annual Report and Accounts 1948–1962	HMSO, London	Annual	
[QRL 56]	British Transport Commission	British Transport Commission: Transport Statistics 1948–1962	BTC	4-weekly	
[QRL 57]	Ministry of Transport	Carriers' Licensing. (Report of the 'Geddes' Committee on Carriers' Licensing)	HMSO, London	1965	
[QRL 58]	Office of Population Censuses and Surveys, and General Register Office, Scotland	Census 1961, (a) England and Wales—Industry Tables, (b) England and Wales—Occupation Tables, (c) Scotland, Vol. 6, Occupation Industry and Workplace (Sample) Census 1966. Great Britain. Economic Activity Tables	HMSO, London HMSO, London HMSO, Edinburgh HMSO, Edinburgh and London	1966 1966 1966 1968	
		Census 1971, Great Britain, Economic Activity Tables	HMSO, London	1967	
[QRL 59]	National Board for Prices and Incomes	Charges, Costs and Wages in the Road Haulage Industry Report No. 48 and Statistical Supplement, Cmnd. 3482, 3482-1	HMSO, London	1968	
[QRL 60]	Commercial Motor	Commercial Motor Tables of Operating Costs for Goods and Passenger Vehicles	IPC Transport Press Ltd	Annual	
[QRL 61]	Dept. of the Environment	Contributions to the Accident Situation by all types of Road Vehicles. TRRL Leaflet LF 320 and in LR 481 (see QRL 105)	TRRL, Crowthorne	1972	

Reference Number	Author and/or Organization Responsible	Title	Publisher	Frequency or date of Publication
[QRL 62]	Dept. of Employment	Department of Employment Gazette	HMSO, London	Monthly
[QRL 63]	Dept. of Energy	Digest of Energy Statistics	HMSO, London	Annual
[QRL 64]	Scottish Development Dept.	Digest of Scottish Statistics (April 1953–April 1971)	HMSO, Edinburgh	April, October
[QRL 65]	Ministry of Finance, Northern Ireland	Digest of Statistics N. Ireland	HMSO, Belfast	Twice Yearly
[QRL 66]	Welsh Office	Digest of Welsh Statistics (1954–)	HMSO, Cardiff	Annual
[QRL 67]	Central Statistical Office	Economic Trends	HMSO, Cardiff	Annual
[QRL 68]		European Conference of Ministers of Transport, Annual Report of Council of Ministers	OECD, Paris	Annual
[QRL 69]	Glasgow Corporation	Greater Glasgow Transportation Study, Vols 1, 2, 3, 4	Glasgow Corporation	1967, 1968, 1971
[QRL 70]	Dept. of the Environment	Highway Statistics (1963–73)	HMSO, London	Annual
[QRL 71]	Central Statistical Office	Input-Output Tables for the UK for 1968. (Studies in Official Statistics No. 22) for 1970 and for 1971 (Business Monitor PA 1004)	HMSO, London	1973, 1974, 1975
[QRL 72]	Board of Trade	'Inquiry into the Wholesale Trades 1965' in Board of Trade Journal for 26 July 1968	Board of Trade	1968
[QRL 73]	Central Statistical Office	Monthly Digest of Statistics	HMSO, London	Monthly
[QRL 74]	Society of Motor Manufacturers and Traders	The Motor Industry of Gt. Britain	SMMT, London	Annual
[QRL 75]	Motor Transport	Motor Transport: Cost Tables	IPC Transport Press Ltd	Annual
[QRL 76]	Dept. of Transport	Motor Vehicle New Registrations (Business Monitor M1)	HMSO, London	Monthly
[QRL 77]	National Freight Corporation	National Freight Corporation Annual Report and Accounts	HMSO, London	Annual
[QRL 78]	Central Statistical Office	National Income and Expenditure (Blue Book)	HMSO, London	Annual
[QRL 79]	National Ports Council	National Ports Council: Container and Roll-on port statistics	National Ports Council, 1–19 New Oxford St., London WC1A 1DZ	Annual
[QRL 80]	Department of Employment	New Earnings Survey	HMSO, London	Annual
[QRL 81]	Ministry of Transport	Public Haulage Operators Analysis by Size of Fleet 1963	Ministry of Transport	1964
[QRL 82]		Rates (formerly Road Rates)	Freight Information Services, Formby, Lancs.	Twice yearly
[QRL 83]	Home Office, N. Ireland	Report on Administration of Home Office Services, Belfast	HMSO, Belfast	Annual
[QRL 84]	Dept. of Trade and Industry	Report on the Census of Distribution and Other Services 1966 (GB), Vol. 1 Main Details, Vol. 2 Tables of Transport Costs, Floorspace etc.	HMSO, London	1970, 1971
		For 1971: Summary Report in Business Monitor SD Series	HMSO, London	1975–

Quick Reference List: Key to Publications

[QRL 85]	Dept. of Trade and Industry	Report on the Census of Production 1963, Introductory Notes, Industry volumes, Summary Tables 1968, as 1963 1970, Business Monitor, C series 1971, 1972, Business Monitor, P series	HMSO, London	1968 1971– 1973– 1974–, 1975–
[QRL 86]	HM Customs and Excise	Reports of Commissioners of H.M. Customs and Excise	HMSO, London	Annual
[QRL 87]	Ministry of Development, Northern Ireland	Report of the Ministry of Development, Northern Ireland	HMSO, Belfast	Annual
[QRL 88]	Dept. of Transport Scottish Development Dept., Welsh Office	Road Accidents in Gt. Britain	HMSO, London	Annual
[QRL 89]	Ministry of Transport	The Road Goods Survey 1962: The Magnetic Tapes from the Geographical Analysis . . . (Mathematical Advisory Unit, Note 101)	Ministry of Transport	
[QRL 90]	National Board for Prices and Incomes	Road Haulage Charges, Cmnd. 2968	HMSO, London	1966
[QRL 91]	National Board for Prices and Incomes	Road Haulage Rates	HMSO, London	1965
[QRL 92]	Ministry of Transport	Road Motor Vehicles (to 1962)	HMSO, London	Five returns per year, 1946–56 Annual, 1957–62
[QRL 93]	Ministry of Transport	Road Research 1958	HMSO, London	1959
[QRL 94]	Ministry of Transport	Road Track Costs	HMSO, London	1968
[QRL 95]	Department of Employment	Road Transport Industry Training Board: Report and Statement of Accounts	Road Transport Industry Training Board, Wembley (from 1972/73)	Annual
[QRL 96]	Road Haulage Association	Road Way (Journal of the Road Haulage Association)	Road Haulage Association	Monthly
[QRL 97]	Ministry of Transport	Roads in England and Wales	HMSO, London	Annual
[QRL 98]	Scottish Office	Scottish Abstract of Statistics, 1971–	HMSO, Edinburgh	Annual
[QRL 99]		Second Report from the Select Committee on Nationalised Industries Session 1972–73: National Freight Corporation	HMSO, London	1973
[QRL 100]	Society of Motor Manufacturers and Traders	S.M.M.T. Monthly Statistical Review	SMMT, London	Monthly
[QRL 101]	Dept. of the Environment	Standard Forecasts of Vehicles and Traffic (DOE Technical Memorandum H3/75)	DOE, London	1975
[QRL 102]	Traders Road Transport Association	Survey of C Licensed Vehicles (1958)	Traders Road Transport Assocn.	1959
[QRL 103]	Ministry of Transport	Survey of Road Goods Transport 1962, Final Results, Part I, Final Results Geographical Analysis, Final Results Commodity Analysis, Methodological Report	HMSO, London	1964, 1966, 1964, 1966

Reference Number	Author and/or Organization Responsible	Title	Publisher	Frequency or date of Publication
[QRL 104]	Dept. of the Environment	Survey of the Transport of Goods by Road 1967–1968	Dept. of the Environment	1971
[QRL 105]	Dept. of the Environment	Towards Safer Road Vehicles (TRRL Report LR 481)	TRRL Crowthorne	
[QRL 106]	Ministry of Transport	The Transport of Goods by Road (Report of the 1958 Survey)	HMSO, London	1959
[QRL 107]	Dept. of the Environment	The Transport of Goods by Road 1970–1972, 1975	Dept. of Transport, Dept. of the Environment	June 1973 Oct. 1976
[QRL 108]	Dept. of Transport	Transport Statistics Great Britain 1964–1974, 1965–1975 . . .	HMSO, London	Annual
[QRL 109]	West Midlands Transport Study Technical Committee	West Midlands Transport Study, Vol. 1	Freeman Fox Miller Smith and Associates	1968
[QRL 110]	International Road Federation	World Road Statistics,	IRF, Geneva 63 Rue de Lausanne	Annual
[QRL 111]	Statistical Office of the European Economic Community	Yearbook of Transport Statistics	EEC, Luxembourg, Brussels	Annual
[QRL 112]		The Ulster Year Book	HMSO, Belfast	Annual

Select Bibliography

[B 1] Atkins Planning, *Swindon Freight Study, Collection of Data and Construction of Computer Model*, TRRL Report SR 158 UC, 1975.

[B 2] Bayliss, B. T., 'Demand for Freight Transport, Practical Results of Studies on Market Operation', in *Report of 20th Round Table on Transport Economics*, ECMT (from OECD, 2 rue André-Pascal 75775, Paris), 1973.

[B 3] Bayliss, B. T., *European Transport*, Kenneth Mason Publications Ltd., London, 1965.

[B 4] Bayliss, B. T. and Hebden, Julia, 'Theory and Application of Index Numbers to the Transport Sector', *UN Economic Commission for Europe W/TRANS/WP6/262 (22.5.70)*.

[B 5] Brown, A. H. and Maultby, A. S., 'Methods of Forecasting the Quantities of Freight in Great Britain', *Statistical News*, 25.14, May 1974.

[B 6] Burt, M. E., *Roads and the Environment*, TRRL Report LR 441, 1972.

[B 7] Edwards, S. L. and Gordon, I. R., 'The Application of Input–Output Methods to Regional Forecasting: the British Experience', in Chisholm, Frey and Haggett (eds.), *Regional Forecasting*, Butterworth, London, 1970.

[B 8] Heyman, Ruth, 'Initial Attempts at Modelling Freight Flows', *Mathematical Advisory Unit Note 211*, Dept. of the Environment, March 1971.

[B 9] Hobson, T. F. J., 'Survey of Road Goods Transport 1967/8 (Methodology)', *Statistical News*, 9.6, May 1970.

[B 10] Hobson, T. F. J. and Taylor, R. M., 'A National Heavy Goods Vehicle Register', *Statistical News*, 20.20, February 1973.

[B 11] Jennings, A., Sharp, C. and Whibley, D., *Delivering the Goods, a Study of the Watford Service-only Precinct*, Freight Transport Association Research Report No. 2, 1972.

[B 12] Kent-Smith, D. B. and Prichard, A., 'Development of Statistical Regions in UK', *Statistical News*, 27.1, November 1974.

[B 13] Kirkus, A. E., 'Road Transport Statistics', *Journal of the Institute of Transport*, 1936, Vol. 18, p. 62.

[B 14] Lassiére, A. and Bowers, P., 'Studies on the social costs of Urban Road Transport (noise and pollution)', in *Report of 18th Round Table on Transport Economics, EMCT 1972* (from OECD, see [B 2]).

[B 15] Lockyer, M. J. G., 'Commodity Classifications and Codings', *Statistical News*, 24.5, February 1974.

[B 16] Maurice, Rita, *National Accounts Statistics Sources and Methods*, HMSO, London, 1968.

[B 17] Menzler, F. A. A., 'Rail and Road Statistics', in *Sources and Nature of the Statistics of the U.K.*, Royal Statistical Society, Oliver and Boyd, London, 1972.

[B 18] Munby, D. L., 'Road Transport. A Gap in National Statistics', in *Bulletin of the Oxford University Institute of Statistics*, Vol. 22, No. 4, November 1960.

[B 19] Noortman, H. J., 'Economic Criteria for Determining the Capacity of Goods Transport by Road with a View to Obtaining an Optimum Balance between Supply and Demand', in *Report of 11th Round Table on Transport Economics*, EMCT, 1971 (from OECD, see [B 2]).

[B 20] O'Sullivan, P., 'Forecasting Inter-regional Freight Flows', in Chisholm, Frey and Haggett (eds.), *Regional Forecasting*, Butterworth, London, 1970.

[B 21] Rubra, N., *Transport and Communication* (unit 13 in a Second Level Course in Statistical Sources), Open University Press, 1975.

[B 22] Schneider, W. L., 'Studies (notably from the Econometric Approach) of Factors Determining the Demand for Freight Transport', in *Report of the 16th Round Table on Transport Economics*, ECMT, 1972 (from OECD, see [B 2]).

[B 23] Walker, G., *Road and Rail*, Allen and Unwin, London, 1947.

[B 24] Watkins, L. H., *Urban Transport and Environmental Pollution*, TRRL Report LR 455, 1972.

[B 25] Whiffin, A. C. and Leonard, D. R., *A Survey of Traffic Induced Vibrations*, TRRL Report LR 418, 1972.

[B 26] UN Economic Commission for Europe, *Commodity Classification for Transport Statistics in Europe (CSTE)* (with SITC, BTN, NCM, NST classifications in parallel), W/TRANS/WP/6/194/Rev 1, July.

[B 27] Department of the Environment, *A Guide to Operators' Licensing*, 1973.

[B 28] *Heavy Commercial Vehicles (Control and Regulation) Act* (the 'Dykes' Act), 1973.

[B 29] Civic Trust Report *Heavy Lorries*, Civic Trust, London, October 1970.

[B 30] Central Statistical Office, *The Index of Industrial Production and Other Output Measures*, CSO. Studies in Official Statistics, No. 17, HMSO, 1970. *The Measurement of Changes in Production*, CSO Studies in Official Statistics, no. 25, HMSO, 1976.

[B 31] *The Motor Vehicles (Construction and Use) Regulations*, HMSO, London, 1973.

[B 32] *National Income Statistics Sources and Methods*, HMSO, London, 1956.

[B 33] Statistical Office of the EEC, *Nomenclature Uniforme Marchandise pour les Statistiques des Transports* (NST). Luxembourg, 1968.

[B 34] Department of the Environment, *A Review of Road Traffic Noise*, TRRL Report LR 357, 1970.

[B 35] *Road and Rail Traffic Act 1933*, HMSO, London.

[B 36] *Road Safety Act 1967*, HMSO, London.

[B 37] *Road Traffic Act 1960*, HMSO, London.

[B 38] *Standard Industrial Classification 1958*, HMSO, London.

[B 39] *Standard Industrial Classification 1968*, HMSO, London.

[B 40] Statistics of Inland Goods Transport, *Economic Trends*, February 1960, reprinted in *CSO New Contributions to Economic Statistics, Second Series*, 1962.

[B 41] *Statistics of Trade Act 1947*, HMSO, London.

[B 42] Central Statistical Office, *Statistical News*, HMSO, London (Quarterly).

[B 43] Department of Transport *Stats 20—Instructions for the Completion of Road Accident Reports* Dept. of Transport, Statistics Transport A Division, 2 Marsham St., London SW 1 (1974 revision).

[B 44] Ministry of Transport, *Traffic and Transport Plans*, (Ministry of Transport, Roads Circular No. 1/68), HMSO, London, 1968.

[B 45] *Transport Act 1953*, HMSO, London.

[B 46] *Transport Act 1962*, HMSO, London.

[B 47] *Transport Act 1968*, HMSO, London.

[B 48] Department of the Environment, *Transport and Road Research*, Transport and Road Research Laboratory, HMSO, London (Annual).

[B 49] Ministry of Transport, *The Transport Needs of Great Britain in the Next Twenty Years*, HMSO, London 1963.

[B 50] *The Transport of Freight* (White Paper), Cmnd. 3740, HMSO, London, 1967.

[B 51] *Transport Policy* (White Paper), HMSO, London, 1966.

[B 52] Ministry of Transport Scottish Development Department, *Urban Traffic Engineering Techniques* HMSO, London, 1965.

[B 53] *Vehicles Excise Act 1962*, HMSO, London.

[B 54] *Vehicles Excise Act 1971*, HMSO, London.

[B 55] Department of the Environment, *Transport Policy*, (Consultation Document), (2 vols), HMSO, London, 1976.

Appendices

Appendix A *DTp Index of Traffic and Transportation Surveys*
  (a) Extract from *Statistical News* No. 31
  (b) Questionnaire used for compiling entries   78
Appendix B *Copies of Forms*
  (a) Questionnaires used for:
    DOE Continuing survey of Road Goods Transport (form R for *rigid*   93
    vehicles reproduced in full, only p. 2 of form A for *articulated* vehicles is
    given, as pp. 1, 3–4 are identical with form R)
    MOT Sample Survey of Road Goods Transport 1967/8   98
    Business Statistics Office Enquiry into the Distributive and Service Trades
      for 1974—Road Passenger Transport and Road Haulage   108
  (b) Local Taxation Office Return to DOE for Census of Road Motor Vehicles   116

Appendix A

TRANSPORT
Index of Traffic and Transportation Surveys

An index of traffic and transportation surveys carried out in Great Britain has been compiled by the Department of the Environment as a reference source for people or organizations interested in various aspects of transportation policy or research.

The index was started several years ago when organizations sponsoring surveys were asked to complete a detailed questionnaire covering the subject-matter of research for each survey. The index was updated in 1973 and details of over 1,000 surveys are currently held on microfilm.

Full details of the surveys are available upon application to the Department. If the identification of surveys covering particular topics or using particular techniques in sampling or analysis is of interest then it is possible to isolate such surveys by using an 'optical feature card' system which scans the file of records for surveys having the relevant features. A list of the main feature headings is given below.

SECTION A. GENERAL INFORMATION

Type of survey
Area covered
Dates of fieldwork
Size of sample
Size of population
Sampling technique
Geographical zone codes
Zoning system
Number of businesses
Type of businesses
Method of analysis
Tabulations
Form of storage for basic data
Programming language used
Availability of reports
Further studies

SECTION B. SURVEYS OF VEHICLE MOVEMENTS

Traffic volumes
Transportation inventories
Speed of flow
Public passenger transport
Freight transport fleets

Vehicle classifications
Vehicle movements

SECTION C. SURVEYS OF PERSON MOVEMENTS

Where and how information was obtained
Mode of transport
Journey purpose
Times of journeys
Cost of journeys
Origin and destinations
Additional data

SECTION D. SURVEYS OF FREIGHT MOVEMENTS

Commodity classification
Individual freight consignments
Other details of journey
Pipelines
Air
Inland waterways
Coastal shipping
Non-coastal shipping
Road
Rail

SECTION E. PARKING SURVEYS

Facilities
Type of parking
Characteristics (duration, usage, etc.)
Operation (public/private)
Survey method

A summary listing of the surveys held in the index is to be published in the Department of the Environment Headquarters Library Information Series No. 21 and will be free of charge.

Further details concerning the index can be obtained from

Headquarters Library Research Section,
2 Marsham Street,
London,
SW1P 3EB
(01-212 4328).

INDEX OF TRAFFIC AND TRANSPORTATION SURVEYS

NOTES FOR GUIDANCE IN COMPLETING THE QUESTIONNAIRE

1. Please make entries in BLACK INK. This produces a clearer microfilm.

2. In sections being completed please ensure that in all cases where there is a 'YES' or 'NO' box against a question that one of the boxes contains a tick. If asked to specify details to a 'YES' answer—do NOT leave blank—if the answer is not known please say so.

3. QUESTION A7 'A COMPREHENSIVE TRAVEL SURVEY' is one that includes SEVERAL aspects of traffic and transportation study such as those specified in the first four boxes of Question A7, may also include other types of survey which have not been specified here.

4. QUESTION A10 'SIZE OF SAMPLE'. Please quote the ACHIEVED sample (not the DRAWN sample). State if not available.

    QUESTION A10 'SIZE OF POPULATION'. This is the number of persons/households/vehicles etc. from which the sample is drawn, and to which the survey results would normally be grossed up (e.g. population of Manchester).

Appendix A 81

INDEX OF TRAFFIC AND TRANSPORTATION SURVEYS

Mrs J S Andrews Room 4/08
DIRECTORATE OF STATISTICS
DEPARTMENT OF THE ENVIRONMENT
ST CHRISTOPHER HOUSE
SOUTHWARK STREET
LONDON SE1

TELEPHONE 01- 928 7999 Ext 2610

FOR OFFICE USE ONLY	Survey No
	Page No. A/1

Our ref: S3/49/014 (_ _ _ _ _ _ _ _ _ _ _)

Your ref:

Section A

GENERAL INFORMATION: TO BE COMPLETED FOR ALL SURVEYS

The information on this document will be stored on microfilm.
Please type or write clearly in BLACK INK
Answers should be indicated by a tick [✓] *or written in the spaces provided*

A1. Title of Survey	
A2. Short summary of scope, objectives and survey method	
A3. NAME and ADDRESS of sponsoring organisation(s) or department(s)	
A4. NAME, ADDRESS and TELEPHONE NUMBER of person to whom application for further details should be made	Position in organisation._ _
A5. NAME and ADDRESS of organisations actually carrying out the survey if different from A3 above	
A6. TITLES OF PUBLICATIONS RELATING TO THE SURVEY NAME OF PUBLISHER AND DATES	
A7. TYPE OF SURVEY	Origin and Destination [ ] Parking [ ] Land use [ ] Traffic Generation [ ] Comprehensive Travel Survey [ ] Special Survey [ ] Other [ ] _ please specify
A8. Please describe the extent of the AREA COVERED BY THE STUDY with the location of any roadside survey points	
A9. DATES OF FIELDWORK	Starting date (Actual or expected) _ _ _ _ _ _ _ _ _ _ _ _ _ _ Completion date (Actual or expected) _ _ _ _ _ _ _ _ _ _ _ _ _ _

A

(SPECIMEN)

82 Road Goods Transport

Section A
GENERAL INFORMATION

FOR OFFICE USE ONLY

Survey No

Page No. A/2

A10. SIZE AND TYPE OF SAMPLE
SAMPLING TECHNIQUE
(eg simple random, stratified, multi-stage etc.
- please describe briefly)

Size of sample ....
Size of population ....

A11.
a) Was a system of GEOGRAPHICAL ZONE CODES used?   YES ☐   NO ☐

b) Was the zoning system used for any of the following?
- Household Interview ☐
- Cordon Road Survey ☐
- Cordon Bus Survey ☐
- Cordon Rail Survey ☐
- Commercial vehicle operators interview ☐

c) Were planning data (eg type of dwelling, car ownership) obtained at zonal level?   YES ☐   NO ☐

d) Were data specially collected on any of the following topics?
- Population ☐
- Employment ☐
- Shopping ☐
- Land Use ☐
- Environmental topics - please specify ☐

A12. Did the sampling frame include businesses?   YES ☐   NO ☐

Approximately how many firms were involved? _____

Please describe briefly the type of business (eg manufacturing, distribution _____

A13. Please indicate METHOD OF ANALYSIS used

GENERATION	i) Growth factor ☐	ii) Regression analysis ☐	iii) Category analysis ☐
DISTRIBUTION	i) Analogue ☐	ii) Gravity model ☐	iii) Opportunity model ☐
ASSIGNMENT	i) Minimum path without capacity restraint ☐	ii) Speed/flow (Linear programming) ☐	iii) Multiroute ☐
MODAL SPLIT	i) Pre-distribution ☐	ii) Post-distribution ☐	
EVALUATION	i) Engineering ☐	ii) Cost/benefit ☐	iii) Environment ☐
SEPARATION PARAMETER USED IN DISTRIBUTION	i) Time ☐	ii) Distance ☐	iii) Generalised cost ☐

Other methods - please specify ☐

A14. TABULATIONS

Please indicate nature of tabulations produced, eg number and type of tabulations

Attach list of tabulations if available.

A

Appendix A 83

Section A
GENERAL INFORMATION

FOR OFFICE USE ONLY

Survey No. _ _ _ _ _

Page No. A/3

A15. FORM IN WHICH BASIC DATA ARE STORED   Quantity (no. of questionnaires/cards/reels of tape)

- On questionnaires/schedules only ☐   - - - - -
- On punched cards ☐   - - - - -
- On punched tape ☐   - - - - -
- On magnetic tape ☐   - - - - -
- Other - please specify ☐   - - - - -
- Programming language used _____   - - - - -

A16. Is a report available?   YES ☐   NO ☐

If 'NO', do you intend to produce one within the next 12 months?   YES ☐   NO ☐

A17. Do you intend to repeat this study or carry out a similar one within the next 12 months   YES ☐   NO ☐

A18. Please include where possible specimen survey documents (eg questionnaire)

Please include other documents if it is not possible to accommodate important items of information on this questionnaire.

DOCUMENTS ENCLOSED: NUMBER OF DOCUMENTS

	FOR OFFICE USE ONLY
Questionnaire specimen _ _	- - - - -
List of tabulations _ _	- - - - -
Details of survey points _ _	- - - - -
Report _ _	- - - - -
Other (please specify) _ _	- - - - -

SPECIMEN

DATE _ _ _ _ _   SIGNED _ _ _ _ _ _ _ _ _ _

POSITION IN ORGANISATION _ _ _ _ _ _ _ _ _ _ _ _ _ _ _ _

To facilitate completion of the remainder of the questionnaire a section has been alloted to each major type of transportation survey.
Please complete all sections appropriate to your survey and place ticks in the corresponding boxes below. The sections are as follows:

SECTION COMPLETED

- A. GENERAL INFORMATION ☐
- B. SURVEYS OF VEHICLE MOVEMENTS ☐
- C. SURVEYS OF PERSON MOVEMENTS (BY ANY MODE) ☐
- D. SURVEYS OF FREIGHT MOVEMENT ☐
- E. PARKING SURVEYS ☐

A

84 *Road Goods Transport*

Section B

VEHICLE MOVEMENTS

FOR OFFICE USE ONLY

Survey No.

Page No. B/1

B1. TRAFFIC VOLUMES

WAS INFORMATION COLLECTED ON TRAFFIC VOLUMES?

NO ☐

YES, by:-

Postal questionnaire ☐	Number plate count ☐	
Manual volume count ☐	Automatic volume count ☐	Other - please specify ☐
Roadside interview ☐	Attachment to vehicles ☐	

IF by 'ROADSIDE INTERVIEW' were the surveys:-

Inbound cordon ☐	Outbound cordon ☐	Screenline ☐

Other - please specify ☐

B2. TRANSPORTATION INVENTORIES

WAS INFORMATION COLLECTED ON ANY OF THE FOLLOWING?

1. ROAD LENGTHS, WIDTHS, LAYOUTS .... YES ☐   NO ☐

   If 'YES' was the highway network CODED TO A SYSTEM?

   NO ☐

   YES ☐ TO __ 'TFA' (SIA) ☐   'TRAP' (CRD) ☐   'MULTIFLOW' (CRD) ☐

   'CAPRE' (IBM/TRAVERS MORGAN) ☐   'BPR': Current suite (PTRC) ☐

   'TRIPS' (AM VORHEES) ☐   OTHER - please specify ☐

2. SPEED OF FLOW

   — By vehicle in traffic   YES ☐   NO ☐

   — By number plate check   YES ☐   NO ☐

   — By other means - please specify

3. PUBLIC PASSENGER TRANSPORT

   — routes, frequencies, capacities etc .... YES ☐   NO ☐

   Was the public transport system coded?

   NO ☐

   YES ☐ TO _ 'PUBLIC' (SCOTT WILSON KIRKPATRICK) ☐   'TRANSITNET' (CRD) ☐

   'NAPRO' (IBM/TRAVERS MORGAN) ☐   'HUD' (SIA) ☐   'OMNIBUS' (SIA) ☐

   'TRIPS' (AM VORHEES) ☐   OTHER - please specify ☐

B

Appendix A 85

Section B

VEHICLE MOVEMENTS

FOR OFFICE USE ONLY

Survey No.
Page No. B/2

B2. TRANSPORTATION INVENTORIES (Continued)
   4. FREIGHT TRANSPORT FLEETS
      - vehicle utilisation, economics of operation etc.

   YES ☐   NO ☐

B3. VEHICLE CLASSIFICATION

   WERE ANY VEHICLE CLASSIFICATIONS USED?

   NO ☐

   YES –

Heavy goods ☐	Light goods van ☐	Car ☐
Bus/Coach ☐	Motorcycle/moped/scooter ☐	Taxi ☐
Pedal Cycle ☐	Other classifications – please specify ☐	

B4. ADDITIONAL DATA ON VEHICLE MOVEMENTS

	YES	NO
1(a) Was JOURNEY PURPOSE established?	☐	☐
(b) If 'YES' was DIRECTION of journey recorded? (eg. 'TO work' or 'FROM work')	☐	☐
2(a) Was information on ORIGINS and DESTINATIONS collected?	☐	☐
(b) If 'NO', was directional information collected in any other way? (eg. 'NORTH-bound' or 'SOUTH-bound', 'INTO study zone' or 'OUT OF study zone')	☐	☐
3. Were journeys 'TO HOME' AND 'FROM HOME' separately identified?	☐	☐
4(a) Was LAND USE of the ORIGIN identified?	☐	☐
(b) Was LAND USE of the DESTINATION identified?	☐	☐
5. Were commercial vehicles classified according to INDUSTRIAL CLASSIFICATION of operator?	☐	☐
6(a) Was information obtained on CAR OCCUPANCY?	☐	☐
(b) Was information obtained on PUBLIC TRANSPORT OCCUPANCY?	☐	☐
(c) Was information obtained on COMMERCIAL VEHICLE OCCUPANCY?	☐	☐

Please indicate at the bottom of page A/3 that you have completed this section.

B

86 Road Goods Transport

Section C

PERSON MOVEMENTS

FOR OFFICE USE ONLY

Survey No _____

Page No. C/1

C1. DATA COLLECTION

Was Information on PERSON MOVEMENTS collected?

NO ☐

YES –

PLEASE INDICATE HOW THE DATA WERE COLLECTED	by Interview	by Questionnaire left and collected	by Postal Questionnaire	by Count
at the household	☐	☐	☐	☐
at workplace	☐	☐	☐	☐
at travel termini	☐	☐	☐	☐
in course of travel	☐	☐	☐	☐
other sources - please specify	☐	☐	☐	☐

If collected 'IN COURSE OF TRAVEL' were any of the following operated?

Inbound Cordon ☐   Outbound Cordon ☐
Screen line ☐   Other - please specify ☐

C2. JOURNEY MODE

Was information collected on MODE OF TRANSPORT?

NO ☐

YES –

Air ☐	Pedal cycle ☐	Car/Van/Taxi ☐
Train ☐	Bus/Coach ☐	Motorcycle/Scooter/Moped ☐
Walking ☐	Other - please specify ☐	

C3. JOURNEY PURPOSE

Was Information on TRAVEL MOTIVATION collected?   YES ☐   NO ☐

If 'YES' –

Were any PERSONAL JOURNEY PURPOSE classifications used?

NO ☐

YES:-

To/from work ☐	To/from school or college ☐	Employer's Business ☐
Shopping ☐	Personal Business ☐	Leisure activities ☐
Holidays ☐	Other - please specify ☐	

Was DIRECTION OF JOURNEY recorded?   YES ☐   NO ☐
(eg 'TO work' or 'FROM work')

C

Appendix A 87

Section C

PERSON MOVEMENTS

FOR OFFICE USE ONLY	Survey No
	Page No. C/2

C4. ADDITIONAL JOURNEY INFORMATION

Was information collected on

(a) the times of journeys YES [ ] NO [ ]

(b) the cost of journeys (if public transport used) YES [ ] NO [ ]

(c) public transport accessibility YES [ ] NO [ ]

C5. ADDITIONAL DATA ON PERSON MOVEMENTS

YES NO

1(a) Was information on ORIGINS AND DESTINATIONS collected? [ ] [ ]

(b) If 'NO' was directional information collected in any other way? (eg 'NORTH-bound' or 'SOUTH-bound'; 'INTO study zone' or 'OUT OF study zone') [ ] [ ]

2(a) Was LAND USE of the ORIGIN identified? [ ] [ ]

(b) Was LAND USE of the DESTINATION identified? [ ] [ ]

3. Where applicable, was distinction made between driver and passenger? [ ] [ ]

4. WAS INFORMATION ON ANY OF THE FOLLOWING COLLECTED?

Sex [ ]

Age [ ] Social class [ ]

Marital Status [ ] Family composition [ ]

Occupation [ ] Income [ ]

Car/Van Ownership [ ] Possession of driving licence [ ]

Ownership of dwelling [ ] Type of dwelling [ ]

Other - please specify [ ]

Please indicate at the bottom of page A/3 that you have completed this section

C

Road Goods Transport

Section D

FREIGHT MOVEMENTS

FOR OFFICE USE ONLY

Survey No. _____

Page No. D/1

D1. GENERAL INFORMATION

1. Was information collected on FREIGHT MOVEMENTS?   YES ☐   NO ☐

    If 'YES', please indicate whether the survey identified separately freight movements by:

Road	☐	Inland Waterways	☐
Rail	☐	Coastal Shipping	☐
Pipeline	☐	Non-coastal Shipping	☐
Air	☐		

2. Was information collected on FREIGHT COMMODITIES?   YES ☐   NO ☐

    If 'YES' was a COMMODITY CLASSIFICATION used?

    NO ☐

    YES –

		Standard Form	Modified* Form
C.S.T.E.	– Commodity Classification for Transport Statistics in Europe (Economic Commission for Europe Inland Transport Committee 1968)	☐	☐
S.I.T.C.	– Revised Standard International Trade Classification (United Nations 1961)	☐	☐
B.T.N.	– Brussels Tariff Nomenclature (Customs Cooperation Council 1955)	☐	☐
N.S.T.	– Uniform Goods Nomenclature for Transport Statistics. (The Statistical Office of the European Communities 1968)	☐	☐

    OTHER ☐ please specify

    *eg. With additional detail or at more than one level.

3. Was information collected on INDIVIDUAL FREIGHT CONSIGNMENTS?   YES ☐   NO ☐

4. Was information collected on OTHER DETAILS OF FREIGHT JOURNEY? (eg journey purpose, origin and destination)   YES ☐   NO ☐

    If 'YES', please specify

D

Appendix A 89

Section D

FREIGHT MOVEMENTS

FOR OFFICE USE ONLY

Survey No

Page No D/2

D2. DATA COLLECTION

If information was obtained on freight movement by any of the following modes please indicate the source of the information and the type of survey below

	By interview	By delivery and collection of questionnaire	By postal questionnaire
ROAD			
1. From firms despatching and receiving goods	☐	☐	☐
2. From haulage and transport operators.	☐	☐	☐
3. From other sources – please specify	☐	☐	☐
RAIL (including freightliners)			
1. From firms despatching and receiving goods	☐	☐	☐
2. From haulage and transport operators	☐	☐	☐
3. From other sources – please specify	☐	☐	☐
PIPELINE			
1. From firms despatching and receiving goods	☐	☐	☐
2. From haulage and transport operators	☐	☐	☐
3. From other sources – please specify	☐	☐	☐
AIR TRANSPORT			
1. From firms despatching and receiving goods	☐	☐	☐
2. From haulage and transport operators	☐	☐	☐
3. From other sources – please specify	☐	☐	☐

SPECIMEN

/D

Section D	FOR OFFICE USE ONLY	Survey No
FREIGHT MOVEMENTS		Page No D/3

D2. DATA COLLECTION (Continued)

	By Interview	By delivery and collection of questionnaire	By postal questionnaire
INLAND WATERWAYS			
1. From firms despatching and receiving goods	☐	☐	☐
2. From haulage and transport operators	☐	☐	☐
3. From other sources – please specify	☐	☐	☐
COASTAL SHIPPING			
1. From firms despatching and receiving goods	☐	☐	☐
2. From haulage and transport operators	☐	☐	☐
3. From other sources – please specify	☐	☐	☐
NON-COASTAL SHIPPING			
1. From firms despatching and receiving goods	☐	☐	☐
2. From haulage and transport operators	☐	☐	☐
3. From other sources – please specify	☐	☐	☐

Please indicate at the bottom of page A/3 that you have completed this section

D

Appendix A 91

Section E

PARKING SURVEYS

FOR OFFICE USE ONLY

Survey No

Page No. E/1

E1. FACILITIES

Was information collected on parking facilities YES ☐ NO ☐

DID THE SURVEY COVER

(1) PUBLICLY AVAILABLE ON-STREET PARKING?

NO ☐

YES -

- Parking free of charge ☐
- Parking restricted by regulation ☐
- Metered parking ☐

(2) PUBLICLY AVAILABLE OFF-STREET PARKING?

NO ☐

YES, parking with -

- No charge, period unrestricted ☐
- No charge, period restricted ☐
- Charge made ☐

(3) PRIVATELY AVAILABLE OFF-STREET PARKING?

NO ☐

YES, parking with -

- No charge, period unrestricted ☐
- No charge, period restricted ☐
- Charge made ☐

E2. TYPE OF PARKING

Please indicate whether any of the following TYPES OF PARKING were included

- Surface ☐
- Underground ☐
- Multi-Storey ☐

Did the survey cover parking within the precints of individual properties?

NO ☐ YES, properties were -
- Office ☐
- Shop ☐
- Industrial ☐
- Residential ☐

/E

Section E
PARKING SURVEYS

FOR OFFICE USE ONLY

Survey No _____

Page No E/2

E3. CHARACTERISTICS

Please indicate which of the following characteristics were established:-

- Parking duration ☐
- Charge Structure ☐
- Provision of visitor parking ☐
- Extent of car park usage ☐
- Vehicle classification ☐

Were trip generation characteristics examined YES ☐   NO ☐

E4. OPERATION

Did the survey identify any of the following categories of ownership of car parks?

NO ☐

YES, -
- Publicly owned ☐
- Publicly owned but privately operated ☐
- Privately owned ☐

E5. SURVEY METHOD

Was the survey carried out by:-

- Direct observation ☐
- Interview ☐
- Self completion questionnaire ☐
- Other means - please specify ☐

Please indicate at the bottom of page A/3 that you have completed this section

E

Appendix B   93

COMMERCIAL IN CONFIDENCE   Ref: _____ /R

DEPARTMENT OF TRANSPORT
Continuing Survey of Road Goods Transport

DTp
(Directorate of Statistics)
1 Selden Hill
Hemel Hempstead
Herts HP2 4SZ

Hemel Hempstead
(STD 0442) 2561
Ext 262
or 309
or 306
or 308

	1	2
	1	0

Vehicle Reg Mark

3	4	5	6	7	8	9

Operator licence No

10	11	12	13	14	15

Survey Week .... to ....

Dear Sirs

1. The Department of Transport is conducting a continuing survey of the transport of goods by road, by obtaining information about a sample of goods vehicles. The vehicle specified above has been selected for inclusion in the sample and you are required, under Section 1 of the Statistics of Trade Act, 1947 to provide the information requested in this form for the survey week shown above, and to return the completed form to the Department of Transport at the above address within SEVEN days of the end of the survey week.

2. This notice is given under section 1 of the Act for the purpose of obtaining the information necessary for the discharge by the Department of its functions, for emergency and defence planning purposes and for the provision of a statistical service for industry, in particular to enable the trends relating to the use of vehicles in the road goods transport industry, including the quantities and kinds of goods carried thereby, to be satisfactorily estimated.

3. THE INFORMATION PROVIDED BY YOU WILL BE USED SOLELY FOR STATISTICAL PURPOSES. THE DATA WILL BE TREATED AS STRICTLY CONFIDENTIAL, in accordance with the Statistics of Trade Act, and statistics which are published or made publicly available will be prepared in such a way that particulars relating to any individual undertaking will not be disclosed.

4. If you have any difficulties or queries regarding the completion of this questionnaire, we will be pleased to help you, and will accept a reverse charge telephone call, (after 1 pm if possible, please).

Yours faithfully

G. Penrice

G PENRICE
Principal Director of Statistics

SPECIMEN

1   If the vehicle is not in your possession:

If vehicle was sold before the survey week please give date sold, delete your name and address and insert that of new owner.   Date sold _____

If vehicle has been scrapped give date scrapped.   Date scrapped _____

In either case please return form immediately in the envelope supplied.

2   If you still have the vehicle

Please complete the questionnaire.

16	17	18	19	20	21	22	23
T	A	R	Y	BT	T	S	W

Road Goods Transport

PLEASE COMPLETE THIS PAGE EVEN IF THE VEHICLE WAS NOT USED DURING THE SURVEY WEEK.

Name of the person in your organisation who should be consulted if questions arise about this Return. _____

Name of business or organisation _____

Address of business _____

_____

Nature of business _____ Tel. _____

Official Use: 24 25 26 27 28 29 30 31 32 33 34 35 36 37 38 39 40 41 42 43 44
REG SIC

Please give the following information relating to the vehicle with registration mark shown on Page 1.

1

Unladen weight ☐☐☐☐☐ Kilogrammes

Carrying capacity ☐☐☐☐☐ Kilogrammes

Plated weight or GVW if not plated ☐☐☐☐☐ Kilogrammes

4

How many miles has the vehicle travelled in the last 12 months .... miles

If the vehicle has not been in your possession for 12 months give:

(a) Date vehicle acquired ....

(b) Miles travelled since vehicle acquired .... miles

49 50 51 52 53 54

2

Number of axles

SPECIMEN

5

Please give the average fuel consumption for the vehicle in miles per gallon. If not known exactly give an estimate.

Fuel consumption .... miles per gallon.

55 56 57 58 59

3

During the seven day period of the survey was the vehicle operated:

Wholly for hire or reward? ☐ 1.

Wholly on contract work for a single customer? ☐ 2.

Wholly on own account? ☐ 3.

Partly for hire and partly on own account? ☐ 4.

Please tick the appropriate box. If no work was carried out in the survey week tick the box which would normally apply had there been work.

46 47 48

6

If the vehicle was not used at all on the public roads during the seven day period of the survey was this because of:

Please tick the appropriate box.

Repair ☐ 1.

Holiday ☐ 2.

No driver ☐ 3.

No work ☐ 4.

Site work ☐ 5.

Prohibition ☐ 6.

Not taxed ☐ 7.

Other reason ☐ 8.

If you have ticked (8) please state here what the other reason is ....

Official Use   NJC   60 61 ☐☐

Appendix B

Please enter on this page details of journeys with four or less stops for collection and/or delivery.

If there is an overnight stop without change of load, enter the whole journey under the first day of the journey. If the vehicle is not in use any day write in the reason. Please account for all seven days. Continue on a separate sheet if necessary. Show all empty journeys. Include details of international journeys where the vehicle travels overseas.

SINGLE STOP JOURNEYS: Enter each journey on a separate line. Empty return journeys can be entered on the same line as the outward journey. If however the return journey is loaded, start a new line. Show all empty journeys.

MULTI–STOP JOURNEYS with FOUR or less stops for collection and/or delivery: Enter each part of the journey on a separate line. Bracket the parts of the journey together, or mark them "Increasing" or "Reducing load". Show return journeys separately.

MULTI-STOP JOURNEYS with FIVE or more stops: Enter details on page 4.

DAY OF WEEK	JOURNEYS		TYPE OF GOODS	NUMBER OF MILES	NUMBER OF MILES	WEIGHT OF GOODS CARRIED
	ORIGIN (If "London" or other major city please give district)	DESTINATION	Give full details (see notes below)	LOADED	EMPTY	(If empty put zero; if unknown give estimate) Kilogrammes

SPECIMEN

IF FOOD, PLEASE GIVE DETAILS eg TINNED CARROTS, FROZEN BEEF etc.

IF MIXED GOODS PLEASE GIVE DOMINANT COMMODITY.

IF GENERAL GOODS WITH NO DOMINANT COMMODITY WRITE SUNDRIES.

IF EMPTIES OR PALLETTES WERE CARRIED WRITE EMPTIES.

On this page enter details of journeys on which there were FIVE or more intermediate collection and delivery points.

Enter each base to base journey on a separate line. Start a new line for each day even if the vehicle is not garaged overnight at normal base. If fewer than FIVE stops for collection and/or delivery, do not shew below but enter details on page 3.

Continue on a separate sheet if necessary.

DAY OF WEEK	JOURNEY		TYPE OF GOODS (give full details) See notes below	NUMBER OF MILES LOADED	NUMBER OF MILES EMPTY	TOTAL WEIGHT OF GOODS DELIVERED Kilogrammes	NUMBER OF STOPS FOR DELIVERY	TOTAL WEIGHT OF GOODS COLLECTED Kilogrammes	NUMBER OF STOPS FOR COLLECTION
	ORIGIN (If "London" or other major city please give district)	FINAL DESTINATION							

SPECIMEN

IF FOOD, PLEASE GIVE DETAILS eg TINNED CARROTS, FROZEN BEEF etc.

IF MIXED GOODS GIVE DOMINANT COMMODITY.

IF GENERAL GOODS WITH NO DOMINANT COMMODITY WRITE SUNDRIES.

IF EMPTIES WERE CARRIED WRITE EMPTIES.

Scrutiny
Coding

SB 25600 (Rev Jan 1977)

Appendix B   97

PLEASE COMPLETE THIS PAGE EVEN IF THE VEHICLE WAS NOT USED DURING THE SURVEY WEEK

Name of the person in your organisation who should be consulted if questions arise about this Return._____

Name of business or organisation_____

Address of business _____

Nature of business _____   Tel._____

Official Use: 24 25 | 26 27 | 28 29 30 31 32 | 33 34 35 36 | 37 38 39 | 40 41 42 43 44
           REG   SIC

Please give the following information relating to the tractive unit with registration mark shown on Page 1 and its trailer. If more than one trailer is used during the seven days of the survey please give details on this page for the trailer with the greatest unladen weight.

1
- Unladen weight (tractive unit) ☐☐☐☐☐ Kilogrammes
- Unladen weight (trailer) ☐☐☐☐☐ Kilogrammes
- Carrying capacity (unit plus trailer) ☐☐☐☐☐ Kilogrammes
- Plated weight or gross train weight ☐☐☐☐☐ Kilogrammes

2 Number of axles:
- Tractive unit ☐ 45
- Trailer ☐ 46

3 Please tick the body type which best describes the trailer.
- Flat or sided, including skeletals ☐ 1.
- Insulated or refrigerated ☐ 2.
- Box body or van ☐ 3.
- Liquid food tanker ☐ 4.
- Other liquid tanker ☐ 5.
- Tanker or bulk carrier for solids ☐ 6.
- Livestock carrier ☐ 7.
- Any other type not listed above, please describe
.... 47

4 During the seven day period of the survey was the tractive unit operated:
- Wholly for hire or reward? ☐ 1.
- Wholly on contract work for a single customer? ☐ 2.
- Wholly on own account? ☐ 3.
- Partly for hire and partly on own account? ☐ 4.

Please tick the appropriate box. If no work was carried out in the survey week tick the box which would normally apply had there been work. 48

5 How many miles has the tractive unit travelled in the last 12 months.....................miles

If the unit has not been in your possession for 12 months give:
(a) Date vehicle acquired.....................
(b) Miles travelled since vehicle acquired ....miles

49 50 51 52 53 54
☐☐☐☐☐☐

6 Please give the average fuel consumption for the vehicle in miles per gallon. If not known exactly give an estimate.

Fuel consumption .... miles per gallon

55 56 57 58 59
☐☐☐☐☐

7 If the tractive unit was not used at all on the public roads during the seven day period of the survey was this because of:

Please tick the appropriate box.
- Repair ☐ 1.
- Holiday ☐ 2.
- No driver ☐ 3.
- No work ☐ 4.
- Site work ☐ 5.
- Prohibition ☐ 6.
- Not taxed ☐ 7.
- Other reason ☐ 8.

If you have ticked (8) please state here what the other reason is ....

SPECIMEN

Official Use   NJC   60 61 ☐☐

Road Goods Transport

CONFIDENTIAL

MINISTRY OF TRANSPORT

SAMPLE SURVEY OF GOODS VEHICLES

3

Ministry of Transport
(Statistics Division)
Albion Court
Marlowes
Hemel Hempstead
Herts.

Hemel Hempstead 2561/7
Ext. 262
or 306
or 308
or 309

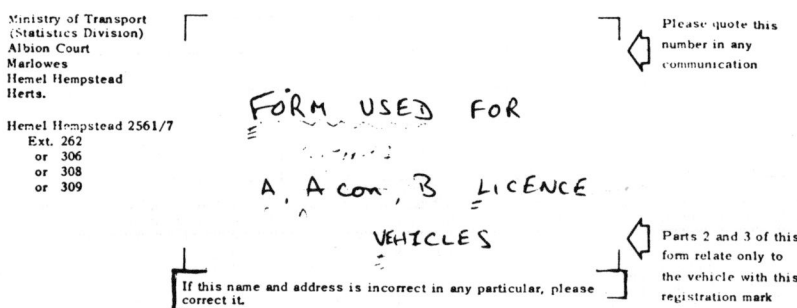

FORM USED FOR
A, A con, B LICENCE VEHICLES

Please quote this number in any communication

If this name and address is incorrect in any particular, please correct it.

Parts 2 and 3 of this form relate only to the vehicle with this registration mark

Dear Sir(s),

As you may already have seen in the Press or heard from your Association, the Ministry of Transport is conducting a survey on the transport of goods by road by means of a sample survey of goods vehicles. The vehicle specified above has been selected for inclusion in the sample and you are required, under Section 1 of the Statistics of Trade Act, 1947, to provide the information requested on pages 2 and 3 of this form, and to return the completed form to the Ministry of Transport at the address above.

The purpose of this inquiry is to bring up to date and extend the information obtained in previous inquiries about the transport of goods by road in this country. The information obtained from the last survey of this type, conducted in 1962, has been of importance and value both to the Government and industry for a variety of purposes but is now dated. There have been substantial developments in the country's goods transport system and it is now essential to have more up-to-date information.

Although this inquiry is on a rather larger scale than its predecessor in 1962, only a sample of operators is being approached, and only a small number of vehicles is selected. In order that the results of the inquiry may reflect the experience of all kinds of operators and all types of vehicles, it is therefore necessary for every operator included in the sample to complete and return the form in respect of the vehicle actually selected. IF THE VEHICLE HAS BEEN SCRAPPED OR IS NO LONGER IN YOUR POSSESSION, PLEASE INDICATE THIS AND RETURN THIS FORM AT ONCE.

The week covered by the questionnaire begins on Monday morning August 7th, 1967 and ends at midnight on Sunday August 13th, 1967. The form should be completed accurately in all particulars and returned to this office not later than August 23rd, 1967; a franked addressed envelope is enclosed for this purpose.

The questionnaire has been divided into three sections: part 1 asks for particulars of the business of the owner of the vehicle, part 2 asks for details of the vehicle specified above, and part 3 is intended to serve as a record of that vehicle's work during the week of the inquiry.

If the vehicle is not used at all during the week of the inquiry, or is engaged wholly on work off the public highway (e.g. on site work), parts 1 and 2 and the first column only of part 3 should be completed.

Before completing the form would you please read the notes on pages 2 and 4? If you have any queries we shall be glad to answer them; our address and telephone number are given at the top of this page.

The information provided by you will be treated as strictly confidential, as provided in the Act, and will be used solely in the compilation of statistics which will be prepared and published in a way which will not reveal the particulars relating to any individual undertaking except with the written consent of the undertaking concerned.

On the completion of the inquiry a report will be published similar to the report in the 1962 inquiry ("Survey of Road Goods Transport 1962" published by HMSO in four Parts: Ministry of Transport Statistical Paper Nos. 2, 4, 5 and 6). In addition to the published report, and in so far as resources permit, the Ministry will in due course be prepared to entertain requests for the provision of special tabulations or analyses at a charge which would cover any additional work entailed.

On behalf of the Minister, I should like to ask for your co-operation in this inquiry by completing your return promptly and with care.

Yours faithfully,

A. H. Watson
Director of Statistics

Appendix B   99

PART 1: DETAILS OF BUSINESS

1. Do you undertake any other business as well as haulage? (describe) _____
_____

PART 2: DETAILS OF THE VEHICLE SPECIFIED ON PAGE 1
Answer questions 1, 2, 5, 6, 7 by placing a tick in the appropriate box or boxes.

1. Carrier's licence for this vehicle:
   1 ☐ A
   2 ☐ Contract A
   3 ☐ B

   If 'B' licence, state whether the vehicle was used during the week of this enquiry mainly for the carriage of goods on:-
   4 ☐ own account
   5 ☐ hire or reward

2. Type of fuel:
   1 ☐ petrol
   2 ☐ diesel
   3 ☐ other

3. Unladen weight: _____ tons _____ cwt.

4. Year of first registration: _____

5. Is the vehicle an articulated vehicle?
   1 ☐ Yes   2 ☐ No
   If "yes", does the tractive unit weigh more than 2 tons?
   3 ☐ Yes   4 ☐ No

6. Type of body (you may need to tick more than one box)
   1 ☐ tipper (not tanker)
   2 ☐ platform or sided
   3 ☐ insulated or refrigerated van
   4 ☐ box body (includes vans, Lutons, etc.)
   5 ☐ demountable container or tank
   6 ☐ tanker, liquids
   7 ☐ tanker or other bulk carrier, solids
   8 ☐ inflatable container or tank
   9 ☐ livestock carrier
   10 ☐ other: describe _____

7. Does the vehicle normally carry a demountable container or tank?
   1 ☐ Yes   2 ☐ No

8. Carrying capacity: _____ tons _____ cwt.

9. Plated weights if allocated: _____ tons _____ cwt.

10. Number of axles: _____

SPECIMEN

To the best of my knowledge and belief the information given in this return is complete and correct.

Date: _____   Signature: _____

Telephone No.: _____   Status in organisation: _____
(e.g. proprietor, manager, director)

Address where vehicle specified is normally garaged: _____
_____

PART 3: RECORD OF WEEK'S WORK OF VEHICLE SPECIFIED ON PAGE 1

Each row is to be used as the record of one journey (but see column (2)).

Before completing the form, please read the notes at the foot of the page.

this enquiry is August 7th, 1967 to 1967.

licence number: _____

Vehicle registration mark: _____

(1)	(2)	(3) Journey (see notes)					(4) Nature of journey (see notes) Select X or Y, whichever best describes the particular journey. X. Straight run with no collecting or delivery points along the route. Y. Journey with a number of collecting or delivery points on the route.							(5) Was this an overnight driving trip? Answer "yes" or "no"	(6) If a large freight container (see notes) was used on this trip:		(7) Was there any intermediate change-over of drivers on this trip? Answer "yes" or "no"	(8) Were short drivers used at the start or end of this trip? Answer "yes" or "no"	(9) Goods carried – state main types. Empties should be shown as such when they are carried.
		From			To		If loaded		If empty	If loaded			Part of journey run empty (miles)	Number of stops for loading and unloading		Was it of I.S.O. standard cross-section (8'×8')? Answer "yes" or "no"	What length was it? (feet)		at start / at end	
Day of week on which journey was started, or vehicle not used. If vehicle not used, give reason (see notes). Each day of the week must be accounted for.	If number of identical journeys made, state number below and give details for one journey only.	Address (town & county)	terminal type (see notes). Tick either box if applicable		Address (town & county)	terminal type (see notes). Tick either box if applicable	Miles run loaded	Estimated tons carried	Miles run empty	Part of journey run loaded (miles)	Estimated total tons carried									
			rail	dock		rail	dock													
			rail	dock		rail	dock													
			rail	dock		rail	dock													
			rail	dock		rail	dock													
			rail	dock		rail	dock													
			rail	dock		rail	dock													
			rail	dock		rail	dock													
			rail	dock		rail	dock													
			rail	dock		rail	dock													
			rail	dock		rail	dock													
			rail	dock		rail	dock													
			rail	dock		rail	dock													
			rail	dock		rail	dock													
			rail	dock		rail	dock													

Continued overleaf

SPECIMEN

Appendix B   101

NOTES ON COMPLETING PART 3 OF THE FORM

General notes

Please start by entering the carrier's licence number and the registration number of the specified vehicle at the head of the page. List each journey made during the week, except in those cases where a number of identical journeys are made. Enter the day of the week in column (1) followed by particulars of the journey in columns (3) and (4). If a "container" was used (see definition below) the size of the container should be shown in column (5). The goods carried should be described in column (9).

For identical journeys you should state the number of journeys made on each day in column (2) and give details of one journey only in the other columns. Each day's journeys should be recorded separately.

A journey which takes more than one day should be counted as one journey, even if a change-over of drivers was made. Record such a change-over in column (7).

Containers

For the purposes of this enquiry a "container" means a rigid or collapsible piece of transport equipment in which goods in bulk or package form are carried. It can be used many times and can be transferred to other forms of transport, for example, railway "Freightliner" wagons, or ships. Large containers are usually as wide as the vehicle platform on which they are put, about 8 feet high and at least 10 feet long. The I.S.O. standard container is 8 ft. by 8 ft. in cross-section and of 3 different lengths, 10 ft., 20 ft. and 30 ft., but non-standard containers are also in use.

In answering the questions in column (6), only include containers that are at least 500 cu.ft. in capacity.

Column (1): day of week

You should make some entry for each day of the week. If the vehicle was not in use on a particular day, give the reason, e.g. holiday, no work, repairs, etc. If the vehicle was engaged on site work, state this beside the appropriate day in column (1).

Column (3): journey

Give the starting point (town and county) and destination for each journey in the "address" column. In the "terminal type" column, if the goods were picked up or set down at a rail depot or at a dock, tick the appropriate box – this applies to type X journeys only (see note below). For type Y journeys, ignore the "terminal type" column. For type X journeys, if collecting and delivery stops are few (as for example, on a journey London – Croydon – Guildford – London) these stops should be shown in column (3). If, however, the journey is a circular trip with many collecting or delivery points, as, for example, in local delivery work, this should be stated in column (3); intermediate points need not then be given.

Column (4): nature of journey

For each journey, decide whether it is of type X or type Y and enter the details of the journey (miles run and tons carried) in the appropriate column. You should not complete both X and Y columns for the same journey.

Type X journeys involve a straight run with no collecting or delivery points along the route. Show as separate journeys (a) each trip which involves carrying a load from a single pick-up point to single destination where the whole load is dropped; (b) each empty run from
  (i) base to pick-up point,
  (ii) one dropping-off point to another collecting point, and
  (iii) a dropping-off point back to base.

If the journey consists mainly of a long-distance straight run but there are several stops for picking up done at the beginning of the trip, or for unloading at the end of the trip (for example, a haul from London to Birmingham, but two or more stops in Birmingham to unload) this should be counted as a single journey of type X.

Type Y journeys involve setting down or picking up goods at several points during the journey, and are often circular trips. Count as single journeys each mainly circular trip, and each trip which, though not circular, involves many short hauls (under 100 miles) and a frequently changing load. In the appropriate column, give the number of stops made on such a trip for picking up and setting down loads.

Column (4): tons carried

For loaded journeys you are asked to state the tonnage carried. If not known please estimate; if the load is less than 1 ton, estimate to the nearest ¼, ½ or ¾ ton.
Exclude tare weight of "containers" or "lift vans" where these are used, but include weight of contents. Record carriage of empties as a loaded journey, giving an estimate for the weight of the empties, and writing "empties" in column (9) (goods carried).

For type Y journeys include the weight of the load, if any, at the start of the journey, plus any additional loads picked up along the route.

- 3 -

PART 3 (Continued)

(1)	(2)	(3) Journey				(4) Nature of journey								(5) Was this an overnight driving trip? Answer "yes" or "no"	(6) If a rail freight container was used				(7) Weather only	(8) Were you driving within hours (yes/no)		(9)
Day	Number of identical journeys	From		To		terminal type (type X journeys only)	X. Straight run with no collecting or delivery points along the route.				Y. Journey with a number of collecting or delivery points on the route.												Particulars which can be seen when they are carried
		address	terminal type (type X journeys only)	address			if loaded		if empty		part of journey run loaded (miles)	estimated total tons carried	part of journey run empty (miles)	number of stops for loading and unloading		Was truck used?	"Type" or "size"			at start	at end	
							miles run loaded	estimated tons carried	miles run empty								(feet)					
TOTALS BROUGHT FORWARD:-																						
			rail		rail																	
			dock		dock																	
			rail		rail																	
			dock		dock																	
			rail		rail																	
			dock		dock																	
			rail		rail																	
			dock		dock																	
			rail		rail																	
			dock		dock																	
			rail		rail																	
			dock		dock																	
			rail		rail																	
			dock		dock																	
			rail		rail																	
			dock		dock																	
			rail		rail																	
			dock		dock																	

SPECIMEN

Appendix B   103

CONFIDENTIAL   MINISTRY OF TRANSPORT

SAMPLE SURVEY OF GOODS VEHICLES   **12**

Ministry of Transport
(Statistics Division)
Albion Court
Marlowes
Hemel Hempstead
Herts.

Hemel Hempstead 2561/7
  Ext. 262
    or 306
    or 308
    or 309

Please quote this number in any communication

If this name and address is incorrect in any particular, please correct it.

Parts 2 and 3 of this form relate only to the vehicle with this registration mark

Dear Sir(s),

As you may already have seen in the Press or heard from your Association, the Ministry of Transport is conducting a survey on the transport of goods by road by means of a sample survey of goods vehicles. The vehicle specified above has been selected for inclusion in the sample and you are required, under Section 1 of the Statistics of Trade Act, 1947, to provide the information requested on pages 2 and 3 of this form, and to return the completed form to the Ministry of Transport at the address given above.

The purpose of this inquiry is to bring up to date and extend the information obtained in previous inquiries about the transport of goods by road in this country. The information obtained from the last survey of this type, conducted in 1962, has been of importance and value both to the Government and industry for a variety of purposes but is now dated. There have been substantial developments in the country's goods transport system and it is now essential to have more up-to-date information.

Although this inquiry is on a rather larger scale than its predecessor in 1962, only a sample of operators is being approached, and only a small number of vehicles is selected. In order that the results of the inquiry may reflect the experience of all kinds of operators and all types of vehicles, it is therefore necessary for every operator included in the sample to complete and return the form in respect of the vehicle actually selected. IF THE VEHICLE HAS BEEN SCRAPPED OR IS NO LONGER IN YOUR POSSESSION, PLEASE INDICATE THIS AND RETURN THIS FORM AT ONCE.

The week covered by the questionnaire begins on Monday May 6th, 1968, and ends at midnight on Sunday May 12th, 1968. The form should be completed accurately in all particulars and returned to this office not later than May 22nd, 1968; a franked addressed envelope is enclosed for this purpose.

The questionnaire has been divided into three sections: part 1 asks for particulars of the business of the owner of the vehicle, part 2 asks for details of the vehicle specified above, and part 3 is intended to serve as a record of that vehicle's work during the week of the inquiry.

If the vehicle is not used at all during the week of the inquiry, or is engaged wholly on work off the public highway (e.g. on site work), parts 1 and 2 and the first column only of part 3 should be completed.

Before completing the form would you please read the notes on pages 2 and 4? If you have any queries we shall be glad to answer them; our address and telephone number are given at the top of this page.

The information provided by you will be treated as strictly confidential, as provided in the Act, and will be used solely in the compilation of statistics which will be prepared and published in a way which will not reveal the particulars relating to any individual undertaking except with the written consent of the undertaking concerned.

On the completion of the inquiry a report will be published similar to the report in the 1962 inquiry ("Survey of Road Goods Transport 1962" published by HMSO in four Parts: Ministry of Transport Statistical Paper Nos. 2, 4, 5 and 6). In addition to the published report, and in so far as resources permit, the Ministry will in due course be prepared to entertain requests for the provision of special tabulations or analyses at a charge which would cover any additional work entailed.

On behalf of the Minister, I should like to ask for your co-operation in this inquiry by completing your return promptly and with care.

Yours faithfully,

A. H. Watson
Director of Statistics

PART 1: DETAILS OF BUSINESS

NOTES:

Question 1: Where the vehicle is owned by a transport subsidiary of a parent company, give the nature of business of the parent company.

Question 2: Answer by placing a tick in the appropriate box.

---

1. Nature of business of owner of vehicle (describe): _____

2. Is business mainly a manufacturing activity ☐

    or building and construction ☐

    or wholesale distribution ☐

    or retail distribution ☐

    or other activity ☐

SPECIMEN

PART 2: DETAILS OF THE VEHICLE SPECIFIED ON PAGE 1

Answer questions 1, 2, 5, 6, 7 by placing a tick in the appropriate box or boxes.

1. Indicate type of work vehicle mainly engaged on during the week of this enquiry

    1 ☐ retail delivery in urban areas

    2 ☐ retail delivery in mainly rural areas

    3 ☐ wholesale delivery (including finished goods from docks):

        from docks ☐

        other ☐

    4 ☐ maintenance and repair work

    5 ☐ carriage of materials to or from building sites

    6 ☐ delivery of materials (raw or semi-finished) or fuel to factories:

        from docks ☐

        other ☐

    7 ☐ delivery of export goods to docks

    8 ☐ other: describe _____

    9 ☐ not working

2. Type of fuel:

    1 ☐ petrol

    2 ☐ diesel

    3 ☐ other

3. Unladen weight: _____ tons _____ cwt.

4. Year of first registration: _____

5. Is the vehicle an articulated vehicle?

    1 ☐ Yes   2 ☐ No

    If "yes", does the tractive unit weigh more than 2 tons?

    3 ☐ Yes   4 ☐ No

6. Type of body (you may need to tick more than one box)

    1 ☐ tipper (not tanker)

    2 ☐ platform or sided

    3 ☐ insulated or refrigerated van

    4 ☐ box body (includes vans, Lutons, etc.)

    5 ☐ demountable container or tank

    6 ☐ tanker, liquids

    7 ☐ tanker or other bulk carrier, solids

    8 ☐ inflatable container or tank

    9 ☐ livestock carrier

    10 ☐ other: describe _____

7. Does the vehicle normally carry a demountable container or tank?

    1 ☐ Yes   2 ☐ No

8. Carrying capacity: _____ tons _____ cwt.

9. Plated weight, if allocated: _____ tons _____ cwt.

10. Number of axles: _____

To the best of my knowledge and belief the information given in this return is complete and correct.

Date: _____ Signature: _____

Telephone No.: _____ Status in organisation: _____

(e.g. proprietor, director, manager)

Address where vehicle specified is normally garaged: _____

_____

Appendix B   105

The week of this enquiry is May 6th, 1968 to May 12th, 1968.

PART 3: RECORD OF WEEK'S WORK OF VEHICLE SPECIFIED ON PAGE 1
Each row is to be used as the record of one journey (but see column (2)).
Before completing the form, please read the notes at the foot of the page.

Carrier's licence number: _____

Vehicle registration mark: _____

[SPECIMEN form — blank tabular record with columns (1) through (9):
(1) Day of week on which journey made or started, or vehicle not used. If vehicle not used, give reason (see notes). Each day on which the work must be accounted for.
(2) If number of identical journeys made, state number below and give details for one journey only.
(3) Journey (see notes) — From / To, each with Address (town & county) and terminal type (see notes, Tick either box if applicable): rail / dock.
(4) Nature of journey (see notes). Select X or Y, whichever best describes the particular journey. X. Straight run with no collecting or delivery points along the route. Y. Journey with a number of collecting or delivery points on the route. Sub-columns: If loaded — Miles run loaded, Estimated tons carried; If empty — Miles run empty; Part of journey run loaded (miles); Estimated total tons carried; Part of journey run empty (miles); Number of stops for loading and unloading.
(5) Was there an overnight driving trip? Answer "yes" or "no".
(6) If a large freight container (see notes) was used on this trip — Was it of I.S.O. standard cross-section (8' x 8')? Answer "yes" or "no". What length was it? (feet).
(7) Was there any intermediate change-over of drivers on this trip? Answer "yes" or "no".
(8) Was sheet drivers used at the start or end of this trip? Answer "yes" or "no". at start / at end.
(9) Goods carried — state main types. Empties should be shown as such when they are carried.]

Continued overleaf

Continued overleaf

106 Road Goods Transport

NOTES ON COMPLETING PART 3 OF THE FORM

General notes

Please start by entering the carrier's licence number and the registration number of the specified vehicle at the head of the page. List each journey made during the week, except in those cases where a number of identical journeys are made. Enter the day of the week in column (1) followed by particulars of the journey in columns (3) and (4). If a "container" was used (see definition below) the size of the container should be shown in column (6). The goods carried should be described in column (9).

For identical journeys you should state the number of journeys made on each day in column (2) and give details of one journey only in the other columns. Each day's journeys should be recorded separately.

A journey which takes more than one day should be counted as one journey, even if a change-over of drivers was made. Record such a change-over in column (7).

Containers

For the purposes of this enquiry a "container" means a rigid or collapsible piece of transport equipment in which goods in bulk or package form are carried. It can be used many times and can be transferred to other forms of transport, for example, railway "Freightliner" wagons, or ships. Large containers are usually as wide as the vehicle platform on which they are put, about 8 feet high and at least 10 feet long. The I.S.O. standard container is 8 ft. by 8 ft. in cross-section and of 3 different lengths, 10 ft., 20 ft. and 30 ft., but non-standard-containers are also in use.

In answering the questions in column (6), only include containers that are at least 500 cu.ft. in capacity.

Column (1): day of week

You should make some entry for each day of the week. If the vehicle was not in use on a particular day, state the reason, e.g. holiday, no work, repairs, etc. If the vehicle was engaged on site work, state this beside the appropriate day in column (1).

Column (3): journey

Give the starting point (town and county) and destination for each journey in the "address" column, and the terminal type in the "terminal type" column. For type X journeys, if the goods were picked up or set down at a rail depot or at a dock, tick the appropriate box — this applies to type X journeys only (see note below). For type Y journeys enter the address in the "terminal type" column. For type Y journeys, if collecting and delivery stops are few (as for example, on a journey London – Croydon – Guildford – London) these stops should be stated in column (3). If, however, the journey is a circular trip with many collecting or delivery points, as, for example, in local delivery work, this should be stated in column (3); intermediate stops need not then be given.

Column (4): nature of journey

For each journey, decide whether it is of type X or type Y and enter the details of the journey (miles run and tons carried) in the appropriate column. You should not complete both X and Y columns for the same journey.

Type X journeys involve a straight run with no collecting or delivery stops along the route. Show as separate journeys (a) each trip which involves carrying a load from a single pick-up point to single destination where the whole load is dropped; (b) each empty run from
  (i) base to pick-up point,
  (ii) one dropping-off point to another collecting point, and
  (iii) a dropping-off point back to base.

If the journey consists mainly of a long-distance straight run but there are several stops for picking up done at the beginning of the trip, or for unloading at the end of the trip (for example, a haul from London to Birmingham, but two or more stops in Birmingham to unload) this should be counted as a single journey of type X.

Type Y journeys involve setting down or picking up goods at several points during the journey, and are often circular trips. Count as single journeys each mainly circular trip, and each trip which, though not circular, involves many short hauls (under 100 miles) and a frequently changing load. In the appropriate column, give the number of stops made on such a trip for picking up and setting down loads.

Column (4): tons carried

For loaded journeys you are asked to state the tonnage carried. If not known please estimate; if the load is less than 1 ton, estimate to the nearest ¼, ½ or ¾ ton. "Exclude tare weight of "containers" or "lift vans" where these are used, but include weight of contents. Record carriage of empties as a loaded journey, giving an estimate for the weight of the empties, and writing "empties" in column (9) (goods carried).

For type Y journeys include the weight of the load, if any, at the start of the journey, plus any additional loads picked up along the route.

PART 3 (Continued)

(2)	(3) Journey				(4) Nature of journey							(5)	(6) If a large freight container was used:—		(7)	(8) Were shunt drivers used? Answer "yes" or "no"		(9)
	From		To		X. Straight run with no collecting or delivery points along the route.				Y. Journey with a number of collecting or delivery points on the route.			Was this an overnight driving trip? Answer "yes" or "no"	Was it of I.S.O. standard cross-section? (8' x 8') "yes" or "no"	What length was it? (feet)	Was there any intermediate change-over of drivers on this trip? Answer "yes" or "no"			
Number of identical journeys	address	terminal type (type X journeys only)	address	terminal type (type X journeys only)	if loaded		if empty		part of journey run loaded (miles)	estimated total tons carried	part of journey run empty (miles)	number of stops for loading and unloading					at start	at end	Goods carried — state main types. Empties should be shown as such when they are carried.
					miles run loaded	estimated tons carried	miles run empty												

BROUGHT FORWARD:—

[Blank specimen form with repeating rows labeled "rail" and "dock" in columns (3) and (4)]

- 4 -

Road Goods Transport

BUSINESS STATISTICS OFFICE Newport Gwent NPT 1XG
Telephone: Newport (0633) 56111 ext. 2610 Telex: 497121/2   FV   GA 521

← Please quote in any enquiry

Department of Industry

If the name or address shown above is incorrect in any respect, please correct it, and insert postal code if appropriate.

IN CONFIDENCE

INQUIRY INTO THE DISTRIBUTIVE AND SERVICE TRADES FOR 1974

ROAD PASSENGER TRANSPORT AND ROAD HAULAGE

Dear Sir(s)

The purpose of this inquiry is to obtain up-to-date information about the distributive and service trades in this country. The information is needed for the appreciation of economic trends and the compiling and publishing of statistical information.

If possible your return should be for the calendar year 1974, but if no figures are available for this period the return may be made for a business year ending on any date from 6 April 1974 to 5 April 1975 inclusive. Please forward your completed return to this office within two months of the date of receipt, or within two months of the end of your business year.

This inquiry is conducted under the terms of Section 1 of the Statistics of Trade Act, 1947, which requires that you complete and return this form. The information that you provide will be treated as confidential in strict accordance with the terms of the Act.

If you have any queries about the form, or wish to obtain further information about the inquiry please write to, or telephone the Business Statistics Office at the address above.

Yours faithfully

M C Fessey

M C FESSEY
Director

GENERAL NOTES

1. This inquiry covers firms who operate in Great Britain and are engaged in road passenger transport (including operators of bus and coach services, taxi-cabs and private hire cars) and road haulage contracting (including furniture removals and hire of commercial vehicles).

2. Your return should cover only the activities of the business whose name and address is given on the front of this form.

3. Separate businesses, or subsidiary companies, which operate mainly outside Great Britain should be excluded.

4. If you cannot give precise figures you should give the best estimates that you can. All values should be stated to the nearest £. Do not leave blanks; where none state NONE.

FOR OFFICIAL USE ONLY

SECTION A - PARTICULARS OF BUSINESS

1. If this return covers the business of a member of a group of companies please give below the name and address of the parent company of the group.

　　　　Name of parent company ....

　　　　Head office
　　　　Address　　　　　..
　　　　(including
　　　　postal code)　　　..

　　　　　　　　　　　　　..

2. Your value added tax registration number is shown on the label on the front of the form. If this number is incorrect please state the correct number in the box below:

　　　　　　Value added tax registration number　[_ _ _ | _ _ _ | _ _ _]

SPECIMEN

SECTION B - PERIOD COVERED BY THE RETURN

If possible your return should be made for the calendar year 1974 but if no figures are available for this period the return may be made for a business year ending on any date from 6 April 1974 to 5 April 1975 inclusive.

		Day	Month	Year
Period covered by the return　From	11	/	/	
To	12	/	/	

Appendix B III

SECTION C - ANALYSIS OF TOTAL TURNOVER

The total turnover required in this section should cover all the activities of the business to which this form is addressed. Turnover is defined as the gross takings or total sales and commissions of the business before any deductions.

INCLUDE any amounts received or expected in grants and/or allowances from the Government or any Statutory Body or Local Authority.

EXCLUDE a Sales of fixed assets and exceptional receipts e.g. sales of capital goods, insurance claims etc.

b Value added tax, agents' commissions, trade discounts etc.

C1 Turnover derived from the transport activities covered in note 1 of the General Notes should be entered against this heading.

C2 Any other turnover of the business to which this form relates should be entered against the appropriate heading.

Please give an estimated breakdown of the total amount where precise records are available.

SPECIMEN

SECTION C – ANALYSIS OF TOTAL TURNOVER

State your total turnover for the year of the return . . . . | 20 | £ |

State against the appropriate headings below the breakdown of this total turnover

1. Transport . . . . | 21 | £ |

2. Other activities £

   a. Agriculture, forestry and fishing . . . . | 22 |
   b. Mining and quarrying . . . . | 23 |
   c. Manufacturing . . . . | 24 |
   d. Construction . . . . | 25 |
   e. Retailing . . . . | 26 |
   f. Wholesaling . . . . | 27 |
   g. Catering . . . . | 28 |
   h. Motor trades . . . . | 29 |
   i. Other non-transport activities . . . . | 30 |
      (please specify) ....
      ....

SPECIMEN

Appendix B   113

SECTION D - CAPITAL EXPENDITURE

The amounts entered should be exclusive of value added tax, except that the value added and special taxes paid on <u>passenger cars</u> only should be included.

INCLUDE:

    a.   All expenditure charged to capital asset accounts together with any amounts charged to revenue but ranking as capital items for tax purposes.

    b.   The total cost (excluding interest payments) of capital items bought on hire purchase.

    c.   Any expenditure in the year on additions to capital assets which is temporarily being carried forward under other headings, e.g. work in progress on capital assets in course of construction, or deposits or other payments on account of capital assets in process of acquisition.

    d.   Expenditure on replacing assets destroyed in circumstances (e.g. fire) which have given rise to an insurance claim.

    e.   Expenditure on vehicles, plant and machinery, etc., let out on hire, except when these are charged to current account.

    f.   Capital expenditure at any location belonging to the company where operations have not yet begun.

EXCLUDE:

    a.   The value of any assets acquired in taking over an existing business or disposed of in selling part of your business as a going concern.

    b.   Expenditure on intangible assets such as goodwill, patents and trade marks.

    c.   Transfers to capital asset accounts during the year brought forward under other headings from previous years.

    d.   Expenditure on any items which are to be used mainly outside Great Britain.

    e.   Expenditure on vehicles, plant, machinery, etc., obtained on hire.

DO NOT deduct any amounts received or expected in grants and/or allowances from the Government or any Statutory Body or Local Authority.

DO NOT deduct any amounts for depreciation, amortization or obsolescence.

D1 AND D2 LAND AND BUILDINGS

INCLUDE:

    a.   Against heading 1 expenditure on the construction of new buildings; the extension or improvement of old buildings (including fixtures, e.g. lifts, heating and ventilating systems), and on site preparation and other civil engineering work. Include the cost of any newly constructed buildings bought.

    b.   Against heading 2 the capital cost of freeholds bought and the capital cost or premium payable for leaseholds acquired and against heading 3 amounts receivable.

    c.   Against headings 1 and 2 architects' and surveyors' fees and any legal charges, stamp duties, agents' commissions, etc.

    d.   Against heading 3 proceeds of disposals.

D4 AND D5 VEHICLES

INCLUDE:

Against headings 4 and 5 road goods vehicles (including delivery vans), passenger cars and bicycles.

EXCLUDE:

Mechanical handling equipment such as fork lift trucks, used within warehouse, stock rooms, etc., and any other mobile powered equipment.

D6 AND D7 PLANT, MACHINERY AND OTHER CAPITAL EQUIPMENT

INCLUDE:

Against headings 6 and 7 plant, machinery and other capital equipment, e.g. office machinery, furniture, mechanical handling equipment and mobile powered equipment.

SECTION D - CAPITAL EXPENDITURE

LAND AND BUILDINGS (exclusive of VAT)

		£
1. Cost of new building work or other constructional work of a capital nature	40	
2. Cost in the year of land and existing buildings purchased	41	
3. Proceeds of land and buildings disposed of	42	

VEHICLES

(passenger cars inclusive of VAT and special taxes, other vehicles exclusive of VAT)

		£
4. Cost of new and second-hand vehicles purchased	43	
5. Proceeds of vehicles disposed of	44	

PLANT AND MACHINERY AND OTHER CAPITAL EQUIPMENT (exclusive of VAT)

		£
6. Cost of new and second-hand items purchased	45	
7. Proceeds of items disposed of	46	

PLEASE COMPLETE DECLARATION ON PAGE 8

Appendix B 115

SECTION E - DECLARATION

I hereby declare that the information contained in this return is complete and correct to the best of my knowledge and belief.

STATUS IN THE BUSINESS (PROPRIETOR, DIRECTOR, SECRETARY, ETC.) ....

Signature .... **Telephone No/Ext** ....

Date ....

Name and address of person who should be consulted if questions arise about this return (BLOCK CAPITALS PLEASE)

....

....

....

....

.... **Telephone No** ....

SPECIMEN

Department of the Environment

Census of Road Motor Vehicles

Quarter ending 30th September 19........

....County (Borough or Burgh) Council

CARS Etc.
VEHICLES (EXCISE) ACT 1971 FIFTH SCHEDULE

	CODE	Totals from STATS. 1
CLASSIFIED BY CYLINDER CAPACITY		
Up to 700 c.c.	1	
701 to 1000 c.c.	2	
1001 to 1200 c.c.	3	
1201 to 1500 c.c.	4	
1501 to 1800 c.c.	5	
1801 to 2000 c.c.	6	
2001 to 2500 c.c.	7	
2501 to 3000 c.c.	8	
Over 3000 c.c.	9	
TOTAL: CARS CLASSIFIED BY c.c.		
ALL CARS CLASSIFIED BY HORSE POWER	10	
ELECTRICALLY PROPELLED CARS	11	
TOTAL: ALL CARS ETC.		

TOTAL OF UNLICENSED CARS ☐

TOTAL OF TRANSFERRED VEHICLES (CARS) ☐

SUMMARY

TOTAL (STATS 5)—Cars, etc.	
TOTAL FROM ,, 6—Cycles, P.C.V.s and tractors	
,, ,, ,, 7—Goods	
,, ,, ,, 8—Hackneys and Exempt Vehicles	
GRAND TOTAL	

Vehicles exempt from payment of Licence Duty during the year ended 30th September 19   under Sect.7(1) and by virtue of the definition of "public road" in Sect. 38(1) of the Vehicles (Excise) Act, 1971

Stats 5
(*Revised 1975*) Final Sheet and Grand Total

Appendix B 117

Department of the Environment   L.T.A. No................

Census of Road Motor Vehicles

Quarter ended 30th September 19........

....County (Borough or Burgh) Council

MOTOR BICYCLES, AGRICULTURAL TRACTORS Etc. (£5 Class)
VEHICLES (EXCISE) ACT 1971 FIRST AND THIRD SCHEDULES

MOTOR BICYCLES Etc.	CODE	Totals from STATS. 2
Mopeds	1	
MOTOR CYCLES AND SCOOTERS:— Up to 50 c.c.	2	
51 c.c. to 125 c.c.	3	
126 c.c. to 150 c.c.	4	
151 c.c. to 200 c.c.	5	
201 c.c. to 250 c.c.	6	
251 c.c. to 350 c.c.	7	
351 c.c. to 500 c.c.	8	
501 c.c. and over	9	
Electric bicycles	10	
Total bicycles		
Tricycles (£10 licence duty)	11	
Total bicycles and tricycles		
PEDESTRIAN CONTROLLED VEHICLES	12	

AGRICULTURAL TRACTORS, ETC. (£5 Class)		Totals from STATS. 2
Agricultural tractors	13	
Combine Harvesters and other Agric. Machines	14	
Digging Machines	15	
Mobile Cranes	16	
Works Trucks	17	
Mowing Machines	18	
Others (£5 Class)	19	
TOTAL: AGRICULTURAL TRACTORS ETC. (£5 CLASS)		
General Haulage and Showmen's Tractors	20	

TOTAL FOR THIS SHEET

BICYCLES AND TRICYCLES	
P.C.V.s	
AGRICULTURAL TRACTORS Etc. (£5 Class)	
GENERAL HAULAGE AND SHOWMEN'S TRACTORS	
TOTAL	
TOTAL OF UNLICENSED BICYCLES ETC.	
TOTAL OF UNLICENSED TRACTORS ETC.	
TOTAL OF TRANSFERRED VEHICLES (BICYCLES ETC.)	
TOTAL OF TRANSFERRED VEHICLES (TRACTORS ETC.)	

Stats 6
(Revised 1975) Final Sheet

Department of the Environment   L.T.A. No. ....

Census of Road Motor Vehicles

Quarter ended 30th September 19........

....County (Borough or Burgh) Council

GOODS VEHICLES
VEHICLES (EXCISE) ACT 1971 FOURTH SCHEDULE

FARMERS' GOODS UNLADEN WEIGHT	CODE	Totals from STATS. 3A
Not over 16 cwt	1	
Over 16 cwts not over 1 ton	2	
„ 1 ton „ „ 1½ „	3	
„ 1½ „ „ 2 „	4	
„ 2 „ „ 3 „	5	
„ 3 „ „ 5 „	6	
„ 5 „ „ 8 „	7	
„ 8 „ „ 10 „	8	
Over 10 „	9	
TOTAL: FARMERS' GOODS VEHICLES		

INCLUDED ABOVE

Vehicles licensed to draw trailers

ALL OTHER GOODS UNLADEN WEIGHT		Totals from STATS. 3
Not over 16 cwt	10	
Over 16 cwts not over 1 ton	11	
„ 1 ton „ „ 1½ „	12	
„ 1½ „ „ 2 „	13	
„ 2 „ „ 3 „	14	
„ 3 „ „ 4 „	15	
„ 4 „ „ 5 „	16	
„ 5 „ „ 6 „	17	
„ 6 „ „ 7 „	18	
„ 7 „ „ 8 „	19	
„ 8 „ „ 9 „	20	
„ 9 „ „ 10 „	21	
Over 10 „	22	
TOTALS: GENERAL GOODS VEHICLES		

INCLUDED ABOVE

Tower Wagons (not used for street lighting) ..

Showmen's Goods Vehicles .. .. ..

Vehicles licensed to draw trailers .. .. ..

TOTAL FOR THIS SHEET

FARMERS' .. ..

ALL OTHER GOODS .. ..

                             TOTAL ..

TOTAL OF ALL UNLICENSED GOODS VEHICLES .. .. ..

TOTAL OF ALL TRANSFERRED GOODS VEHICLES .. ..

Stats 7

(Revised 1975) Final Sheet

Appendix B 119

Department of the Environment   L.T.A. No................

Census of Road Motor Vehicles

Quarter ended 30th September 19........

....County (Borough or Burgh) Council

HACKNEY VEHICLES AND EXEMPT VEHICLES
VEHICLES (EXCISE) ACT 1971 SECOND SCHEDULE

HACKNEY VEHICLES (Other than tramcars) SEATING CAPACITY	CODE	Totals from STATS. 4
Not more than 4	1	
5 to 8	2	
9 „ 15	3	
16 „ 32	4	
33 „ 40	5	
41 „ 48	6	
49 „ 56	7	
57 „ 64	8	
65 „ 72	9	
73 and over	10	
Total Hackney Vehicles		

TOTAL OF UNLICENSED HACKNEYS

TOTAL OF TRANSFERRED HACKNEYS

SPECIMEN

EXEMPT VEHICLES (bearing "Nil" Licences)	CODE	Totals from STATS. 4A
CARS	11	
CARS—PERSONAL EXPORT	12	
CARS—DIRECT EXPORT	13	
CARS MODIFIED FOR DISABLED PERSONS	14	
INVALID VEHICLES	15	
AMBULANCES	16	
MOTOR CYCLES	17	
MOTOR CYCLES—PERSONAL EXPORT	18	
MOTOR CYCLES—DIRECT EXPORT	19	
AGRICULTURAL TRACTORS	20	
OTHER TRACTORS	21	
GOODS VEHICLES	22	
BUSES and COACHES	23	
FIRE APPLIANCES	24	
ROAD ROLLERS	25	
ROAD CONSTRUCTION VEHICLES	26	
LOCAL AUTHORITY STREET CLEANSING	27	
LOCAL AUTHORITY STREET LIGHTING	28	
MOBILE CRANES and WORKS TRUCKS	29	
SNOW PLOUGHS	30	
OTHER VEHICLES	31	
TOTAL EXEMPT VEHICLES		

TOTAL NON-RENEWED LICENCES IN "EXEMPT" CLASS

TOTAL TRANSFERRED VEHICLES IN "EXEMPT" CLASS

Stats 8
(Revised 1975) Final Sheet

Subject Index

A-, B- and C-licensed vehicle figures, 3.3.2, 3.3.3, 3.3.5
A-licensed vehicles, 1.3.1, 1.3.2, 1.3.3, 1.3.4
Accident reporting, goods vehicle in, 2.1.8
Accidents, cost of road, 3.23.6
Accidents in Northern Ireland, road, 3.23.5
Accidents, road, 3.23
Accounting system for expenditure on infrastructure, EEC, 3.29.2
Accounts, national, 3.19
Agricultural goods vehicle, 2.1.6, 2.1.12
Annual Abstract of Statistics, 3.32.2
Applications for Operators' Licences, 3.3.4
Area licensing authority reports, 3.3
Attitudes of the public to road goods transport, 3.24.7
Attitudes to effects of road traffic, surveys of, 3.24.3, 3.24.7
Axle loadings, 2.1.10, 3.24.8, 3.29.3
Axle weight, maximum, 2.1.10

B- and C-licensed vehicle figures, A, 3.3.2, 3.3.3, 3.3.5
B-licensed vehicles, 1.3.1, 1.3.2, 1.3.3, 1.3.4
Basic Road Statistics, 3.33.1
Bench-mark estimates, road traffic, 3.21.6
Blue books, national income and expenditure, 3.19
Board of trade inquiry into the wholesale trades, 3.14.6
Breakdown of road goods transport industry, 1.2
BRF, *see* British Road Federation
British Labour Statistics Historical Abstract, 3.17.1
British Labour Statistics Yearbook, 3.17.1
British Road Federation, 1.4.1, 3.33.1
British Road Services, 1.2.5, 3.9.2
British Transport Commission, 3.4.2, 3.9
BRS parcels, 1.2.5, 3.26.4
BRS, *see* British Road Services
BTC, *see* British Transport Commission

C-licensed vehicle figures, A, B and 3.3.2, 3.3.3, 3.3.5
C-licensed vehicles, 1.3.1, 1.3.2, 1.3.3, 1.3.4
C-licensed vehicles, TRTA survey of, 3.6
Capital equipment, investment in, 3.8.3
Capital expenditure, 3.19
Capital expenditure in road haulage and storage, 3.19.10
CAPS, *see* Cost and Productivity Scheme
Carriers Licensing, Geddes Committee on, 1.3.5, 1.3.7
Carriers' licensing, working of, 1.3.7
Carriers' licensing system, 1.3, 3.3
Carrying capacity, definition of maximum, 2.1.10
Census counts, goods vehicle in roadside, 2.1.7
Census of distribution, 3.14
Census of production, 3.14, 3.20.1, 3.20.2
Censuses, large-scale road traffic, 3.21.7

Censuses, methodology in road traffic, 3.21.11
Censuses, national road traffic, 3.21
Censuses, population, 3.13.13, 3.17.6
Census, results of road traffic, 3.21.10, 3.21.11, 3.21.12, 3.21.13, 3.21.14, 3.21.15
Centre for Interfirm Comparisons, 3.11.1
Channel Islands, 3.2.9
Charges for coastal shipping, 3.15.1
Charges for Post Office transport, 3.15.1
Charges for rail transport, 3.15.1
Charges for road transport, 3.15.1
Charges in road haulage industry, 1.2.6, 3.26
Charges, multiple regression analysis on, 3.15.10
Charges related to weight and distance by mode, 3.15
Chemicals, transport of, 3.15.3
CIC, *see* Centre for Interfirm Comparisons
Circular journeys, 2.2.7
Classification of vehicles, 2.1.4, 2.1.5, 2.1.6, 2.1.7, 2.1.8, 2.21.8
Classification, road, 3.21.3
Coastal shipping, 1.5, 3.4.8
Coastal shipping, charges for, 3.15.1
Commercial Motor Tables of Operating Costs, 3.10, 3.12.1
Commercial Vehicles Act 1973, Heavy, 6.14
Committee of Inquiry on Small firms, 3.7.1
Commodity analysis in 1962 survey, 3.4.26, 3.4.27
Commodity classification, EEC, 3.29.5
Commodity Classification for Transport Statistics in Europe, ECE, 3.4.26
Commodity classifications, review of, 3.4.26
Commodity survey, 3.15.3
Comparative data on European countries, 3.31.1
Comparative data on USA, 3.31.1
Comparative data on USSR, 3.31.1
Comparisons, Centre for Interfirm, 3.11.1
Comparisons of expenditure, inter-industry, 3.14.2
Consignment surveys, 3.16, 6.12
Consignment weight distribution, 3.16.2
Consignments delivery time by modes, 3.15.6
Consignments proportion lost or damaged by modes, 3.15.6
Construction industry expenditure on transport, 3.14.1
Continuing road traffic survey, 3.4.11, 3.4.15, 3.21.3, 3.21.4, 3.21.5
Continuing survey, DOE, 3.4.39, 3.4.40, 3.4.41, 3.4.42, 3.4.43, 3.4.44, 3.4.45, 3.4.46, 3.4.47, 3.4.48, 3.4.49, 3.4.50
Continuing survey, methodology in, 3.4.40, 3.4.45
Continuing survey, sample size in, 3.4.41
Contract A-licensed vehicles, 1.3.1, 1.3.2, 1.3.3, 1.3.4
Contribution to gross domestic product, 1.5.2, 3.13.14, 3.19.1, 3.19.2, 3.19.5, 3.19.14

Conurbation studies, 3.22.5
Conurbation study, Glasgow, 3.22.5
Conurbation study, West Midlands, 3.22.5
Cost and Productivity Scheme, 3.11.1
Cost of road accidents, 3.23.6
Costs, Commercial Motor Tables of Operating, 3.10, 3.12.1
Costs, fleet operating, 3.13.8
Costs, fuel, 3.10, 3.11, 3.13
Costs in distributive industries, transport, 3.14.7, 3.14.8
Costs in road freight transport, survey of operating, 3.13
Costs, joint, 3.13.6
Costs, Motor Transport Tables of Operating, 3.10, 3.13.11
Costs, operating, 3.10, 3.11, 3.13
Costs reports, Road Haulage Association, 3.11
Costs, vehicle operating, 3.13.9
Coverage of road goods transport, 2.1.12
Coverage of road haulage and storage, 3.19.10
Crown vehicles, 2.1.5, 2.1.7, 2.1.8, 2.1.12
CSO index of industrial production, 3.4.17
CSTE, *see* Commodity Classification for Transport Statistics in Europe
Cumberland transport survey, West, 3.16.4
Current vehicle licence figures, 3.2.2, 3.2.3, 3.2.5, 3.2.6, 3.2.9
Customs and Excise, Reports of HM, 3.25

Data from vehicle licensing and registration, 3.2
Dawson expenditure estimates, Rudd, 3.12
Definition of a shuttle service, 3.29.5
Definition of for hire transport, 2.1.2
Definition of goods vehicle, 2.1.4, 2.1.5, 2.1.6, 2.1.7, 2.1.8
Definition of gross weight, 2.1.10
Definition of heavy goods vehicle, 2.1.11
Definition of maximum carrying capacity, 2.1.10
Definition of own-account transport, 2.1.1
Definition of plated weight, 2.1.10
Definition of professional haulage, 2.1.1
Definition of public haulage, 2.1.1, 2.1.2
Definition of road haulage, 2.1.1, 2.1.2
Definition of train weight, 2.1.10
Definition of unladen weight, 2.1.9
Definitions, usage and, 2.1
Delivery time by modes, consignments, 3.15.6
Demand for transport, 5.7
Demand for transport, industrial, 3.15
Demand, forecasting transport, 5
Department of Employment Data, 3.17
Department of Employment Gazette, 3.17.1
Department of the Environment Library, 3.22.4
Development of road goods transport statistics, 6
Digest of Energy Statistics, 3.25
Dimensions of transport output, 2.2.5
Distribution, Census of, 3.14
Distribution through 24 hours, traffic, 3.21.11
Distributive industries, transport costs in, 3.14.7, 3.14.8
DOE continuing survey, 3.4.39, 3.4.40, 3.4.41, 3.4.42, 3.4.43, 3.4.44, 3.4.45, 3.4.46, 3.4.47, 3.4.48, 3.4.49, 3.4.50
DOE roll-on-roll-off goods vehicle survey, 3.28
DOE sample surveys, MOT and 3.4
DOE, *see also* Department of the Environment

Domestic product, contribution to gross, 1.5.2, 3.13.14, 3.19.1, 3.19.2, 3.19.5, 3.19.14
Domestic road goods transport, 2.1.13, 2.1.14
Driver and Vehicle Licensing Centre, 3.2.1
Drivers' licences, heavy goods vehicle, 1.3.8, 3.3.4
DTp data, *see* DOE
Dykes Act, 6.14

Earnings, manpower and, 3.17, 3.18
Earnings, weekly, 3.26.3
Earnings Survey, New, 3.17.1
ECE Commodity Classification for Transport Statistics in Europe, 3.4.26
Economy, importance of road goods transport in the, 1.5.2
EEC accounting system for expenditure on infrastructure, 3.29.2
EEC commodity classification, 3.29.5
EEC regulations, 1.3.9, 3.29
EEC statistical requirements, 3.29
EEC *Yearbook of Transport Statistics*, 3.34.8
Effect of goods transport in Putney High Street, 3.24.3
Effect of road goods transport in Camberley, 3.24.3
Effect of road goods transport in Newbury, 3.24.3
Effect of road goods transport in Swindon, 3.24.4
Effects of road goods transport, environmental, 3.24
Effects of urban freight distribution, 3.24.3
Electricity industry expenditure on transport, 3.14.1
Electronic equipment, transport of, 3.15.3
Employment, 3.13.12, 3.17
Employment data, Department of, 3.17
Employment Gazette, Department of, 3.17.1
End-to-end journeys, 2.2.7
Energy Statistics, Digest of, 3.25
Environmental effects of road goods transport, 3.24
Equipment, investment in capital, 3.8.3
Equipment, transport of electronic, 3.15.3
Establishments, industrial classification of transport, 1.1.2
Establishments repairing vehicles, 1.1.5
Europe, ECE Commodity Classification for Transport Statistics in, 3.4.26
European Conference of Ministers of Transport, Reports of, 3.34.5
European countries, comparative data on, 3.31.1
Examinations, vehicle, 3.3.4
Excise licensing and registration, 2.1.5, 3.2
Excise, Reports of HM Customs and, 3.25
Exempt vehicles, 2.1.5, 2.1.7, 2.1.8, 2.1.12
Expenditure, 3.12, 3.13.4, 3.13.5, 3.13.6
Expenditure-based estimates of GDP, 3.19.8, 3.19.9, 3.19.10, 3.19.11, 3.19.12, 3.19.13, 3.19.14
Expenditure Blue Books, National Income and, 3.19
Expenditure, capital, 3.19
Expenditure estimates, Rudd/Dawson, 3.12
Expenditure in road haulage and storage, capital, 3.19.10
Expenditure, inter-industry comparisons of, 3.14.2
Expenditure on coastal shipping, 3.15.1
Expenditure on infrastructure, EEC accounting system for, 3.29.2
Expenditure on Post Office transport, 3.15.1
Expenditure on rail transport, 3.15.1
Expenditure on road goods transport, industries', 3.14

Subject Index

Expenditure on transport, construction industry, 3.14.1
Expenditure on transport, electricity industry, 3.14.1
Expenditure on transport, gas industry, 3.14.1
Expenditure on transport, manufacturing industry, 3.14.1
Expenditure on transport, mining industry, 3.14.1
Expenditure on transport, water supply industry, 3.14.1

Factors determining modal choice, 3.15.1, 3.16.3
Farmers' goods vehicle, 2.1.6, 2.1.12
FH, *see* for hire
Fleet operating costs, 3.13.8
Fleet size structure, 3.5, 3.6, 3.7, 3.8, 3.13.7
Flows in 1962 survey, inter-regional, 3.4.29, 3.4.30, 3.4.31
Flows in 1962 survey, inter-zonal, 3.4.31, 3.4.32
Flows in 1967/68 survey, inter-zonal, 3.4.36
Flows, regional origin-destination, 3.4.29, 3.4.44, 5.6, 6.10
Foodstuffs, transport of, 3.15.3
For hire transport, definition of, 2.1.2
Forces vehicles, 2.1.5, 2.1.7, 2.1.8, 2.1.12
Forecasting, modelling and, 5
Forecasting output, 3.4.17, 5
Forecasting road traffic, 5.2, 5.3
Forecasting transport demand, 5
Forecasting vehicle population, 5.2, 5.3
Foreign-registered vehicles, 2.1.14, 2.1.15
Freight transport association, 1.4.1
Freightliners Ltd, 1.2.5, 3.9.4
FTA, *see* Freight Transport Association
Fuel costs, 3.10, 3.11, 3.13
Fuel duties, 3.31.2
Fuel used by goods vehicles, 3.25

Gaps in road goods transport statistics, 6.6
Gas industry expenditure on transport, 3.14.1
GDFCF, *see* gross domestic fixed capital formation
GDP, expenditure-based estimates of, 3.19.8, 3.19.9, 3.19.10, 3.19.11, 3.19.12, 3.19.13, 3.19.14
GDP, *see* gross domestic product
Geddes Committee on Carriers' Licensing, 1.3.5, 1.3.7
General goods vehicle, 2.1.6, 2.1.12
Geographical analysis in 1962 survey, 3.4.28, 3.4.29, 3.4.30, 3.4.31, 3.4.32
Glasgow conurbation study, 3.22.5
Goods vehicle, agricultural, 2.1.6, 2.1.12
Goods vehicle, definition of, 2.1.4, 2.1.5, 2.1.6, 2.1.7, 2.1.8
Goods vehicle, definition of heavy, 2.1.11
Goods vehicle, farmers', 2.1.6, 2.1.12
Goods vehicle, general, 2.1.6, 2.1.12
Goods vehicle in accident reporting, 2.1.8
Goods vehicle in licensing and registration, 2.1.5
Goods vehicle in roadside census counts, 2.1.7
Goods Vehicle Index, 3.4.20, 3.5.1
Goods Vehicle List, 3.4.42, 3.5.3
Gross domestic fixed capital formation, 3.19.8, 3.19.9, 3.19.10
Gross domestic product, contribution to, 1.5.2, 3.13.14, 3.19.1, 3.19.2, 3.19.5, 3.19.14
Gross domestic product, quarterly estimates of, 3.19.14
Gross weight, definition of, 2.1.10
Growth of firms, multiple regression analysis on, 3.7.2

GVI, *see* Goods Vehicle Index
GVL, *see* Goods Vehicle List

Haulage and storage, capital expenditure in road, 3.19.10
Haulage and storage, coverage of road, 3.19.10
Haulage, definition of professional, 2.1.1
Haulage, definition of public, 2.1.1, 2.1.2
Haulage, definition of road, 2.1.1, 2.1.2
Haulage, industrial classification of road, 1.1.2, 1.1.4
Heavy Commercial Vehicles Act 1973, 6.14
Heavy goods vehicle, definition of, 2.1.11
Heavy goods vehicle drivers' licences, 1.3.8, 3.3.4
Heavy goods vehicle testing scheme, 3.3.7
HGV, *see* heavy goods vehicle
Highway Statistics, 3.30.1
History of road administration and legislation, 3.33.1
Hours, maximum working, 1.3.8
Hours worked, 3.26.3

Importance of road goods transport in the economy, 1.5.2
Importance of road goods transport relative to other transport, 1.5, 3.4.8, 3.4.12
Income and Expenditure Blue Books, National, 3.19
Incomes, National Board for Prices and, 3.26.3
Index, Goods Vehicle, 3.4.20, 3.5.1
Index numbers of output at constant factor cost, 3.19.3
Index of Industrial Production, CSO, 3.4.17
Index of Inland Goods Transport-Monthly, 3.4.18
Index of traffic and transportation surveys, 3.22.4
Industrial classification of own-account transport, 1.1.2
Industrial classification of road haulage, 1.1.2, 1.1.4
Industrial classification of transport establishments, 1.1.2
Industrial demand for transport, 3.15
Industries' expenditure on road goods transport, 3.14
Industries' payments for transport as per cent of net output, 3.14.2
Industries' use of road goods transport, 3.14, 3.15, 3.16
Infrastructure, EEC accounting system for expenditure on, 3.29.2
Input–output analyses, 3.20
Inter-industry comparisons of expenditure, 3.14.2
Inter-regional flows in 1962 survey, 3.4.29, 3.4.30, 3.4.31
Inter-zonal flows in 1962 survey, 3.4.31, 3.4.32
Inter-zonal flows in 1967/68 survey, 3.4.36
Interfirm Comparisons, Centre for, 3.11.1
International publications, 3.34
International road goods transport, 2.1.13, 2.1.14, 3.27, 3.28, 3.29, 3.34
Investment in capital equipment, 3.8.3
Iron and steel, transport of, 3.15.3
Isle of Man, 3.2.9

Joint costs, 3.13.6
Journeys, end-to-end, 2.2.7
Journeys, multiple-stop, 2.2.7
Journeys with intermediate stops, 2.2.7

Labour force, 3.17
Land use transportation surveys, 3.22

Large-scale road traffic censuses, 3.21.7
Licence figures, current vehicle, 3.2.2, 3.2.3, 3.2.5, 3.2.6, 3.2.9
Licence figures, Operators', 3.3.2, 3.3.3, 3.3.6
Licence, Operators', 1.3.5, 3.8
Licence, place of vehicle, 3.2.4
Licensed vehicles, TRTA survey of C, 3.6
Licences, applications for Operators', 3.3.4
Licences, heavy goods vehicle drivers', 1.3.8, 3.3.4
Licensing and registration, data from vehicle, 3.2
Licensing and registration, excise, 2.1.5, 3.2
Licensing and registration, goods vehicle in, 2.1.5
Licensing Authority reports, Area, 3.3
Licensing Centre, Driver and Vehicle, 3.2.1
Licensing offences, 3.3.4
Licensing, quality, 1.3.5
Licensing, quantity, 1.3.2, 1.3.6
Licensing system, carriers', 1.3, 3.3
Licensing system, present operators', 1.3.5, 3.3, 3.8
Licensing, working of carriers', 1.3.7
List, Goods Vehicle, 3.4.42, 3.5.3
Loading, maximum permitted, 1.3.8
Local Taxation Office, 3.2.2, 3.2.3
LTO, see Local Taxation Office

Mail services, Post Office, 2.1.12
Manpower and earnings, 3.17, 3.18
Manufacturing establishments, survey of transport from, 3.15
Manufacturing industry expenditure on transport, 3.14.1
Maximum axle weight, 2.1.10
Maximum carrying capacity, definition of, 2.1.10
Maximum permitted loading, 1.3.8
Maximum tractor plus trailer weight, 2.1.10
Maximum working hours, 1.3.8
Measures of physical output, 2.2
Methodology in continuing survey, 3.4.40, 3.4.45
Methodology in road traffic censuses, 3.21.11
Methodology in 1952 survey, 3.4.2, 3.4.2, 3.4.5
Methodology in 1958 survey, 3.4.10, 3.4.11
Methodology in 1962 survey, 3.4.20
Methodology in 1967/68 survey, 3.4.34
Midlands conurbation study, West, 3.22.5
Midlands, sample survey in the West, 3.16.2, 3.16.3
Minimum List Headings, relevant, 1.1.2, 1.1.4, 2.1.1
Mining industry expenditure on transport, 3.14.1
Ministry of transport, see MOT
MLH, see Minimum List Heading
Modal choice, factors determining, 3.15.1, 3.16.3
Modal choice, multiple regression analysis on, 3.15.10
Modal split models, 5.4
Modelling and forecasting, 5
Monthly Digest of Statistics, 3.32.1
MOT and DOE sample surveys, 3.4
MOT survey 1952, 3.4.2, 3.4.3, 3.4.4, 3.4.5, 3.4.6, 3.4.7, 3.4.8
MOT survey 1958, 3.4.9, 3.4.10, 3.4.11, 3.4.12, 3.4.13, 3.4.14, 3.4.15, 3.4.16, 3.4.18
MOT survey 1962, 3.4.19, 3.4.20, 3.4.21, 3.4.22, 3.4.23, 3.4.24, 3.4.25, 3.4.26, 3.4.27, 3.4.28, 3.4.29, 3.4.30, 3.4.31, 3.4.32
MOT survey 1967/68, 3.4.33, 3.4.34, 3.4.35, 3.4.36, 3.4.37, 3.4.38

Motor taxation, 3.33.1
Motor Transport Tables of Operating Costs, 3.10, 3.13.11
Movements to and from GB of foreign-registered vehicles, 3.28
Multiple regression analysis on charges, 3.15.10
Multiple regression analysis on growth of firms, 3.7.2
Multiple regression analysis on modal choice, 3.15.10
Multiple regression analysis on operating costs, 3.13.10
Multiple-stop journeys, 2.2.7

National accounts, 3.19
National Board for Prices and Incomes, 3.26.3
National Carriers Ltd, 1.2.5, 3.9.4, 3.26.4
National Freight Corporation, 1.2.5, 3.9, 3.26.4
National Income and Expenditure Blue Books, 3.19
National Ports Council, 3.27.1
National road traffic censuses, 3.21
Nationalized element in road goods transport, 1.2.5, 3.9
NBPI, see National Board for Prices and Incomes
Net output, industries payments for transport as per cent of, 3.14.2
Net output-road goods transport, 1.5.2, 3.13.14, 3.14.2
New Earnings Survey, 3.17.1
New registrations, 3.2.7, 3.2.8, 3.2.9
NFC, see National Freight Corporation
Nomenclature for Statistics of Transport-EEC Classification, 3.29.5
Northern Ireland, road accidents in, 3.23.5
Northern Ireland, roads in, 3.21.16
Northern Irish data, 4.1.5
NPC, see National Ports Council
NST, see Nomenclature for Statistics of Transport

OA, see own-account
Offences, licensing, 3.3.4
Operating costs, 3.10, 3.11, 3.13
Operating Costs, Commercial Motor Tables of, 3.10, 3.12.1
Operating costs, fleet, 3.13.8
Operating Costs in Road Freight Transport, Survey of, 3.13
Operating Costs, Motor Transport Tables of, 3.10, 3.13.11
Operating costs, multiple regression analysis on, 3.13.10
Operating costs, vehicle, 3.13.9
Operators' licence, 1.3.5, 3.8
Operators' licence figures, 3.3.2, 3.3.3, 3.3.6
Operators' licences, applications for, 3.3.4
Operators' licensing system, present, 1.3.5, 3.3, 3.8
Operators' output, 3.4
Operators, regulations for, 1.3.8
Organization of road goods' transport industry, 1.2
Other transport, importance of road goods transport relative to, 1.5, 3.4.8, 3.4.12
Output at constant factor cost, index numbers of, 3.19.3
Output, dimensions of transport, 2.2.5
Output, forecasting, 3.4.17, 5
Output, industries' payments for transport as per cent of net, 3.14.2
Output, measures of physical, 2.2
Output, operators, 3.4
Output-road goods transport, net, 1.5.2, 3.13.14, 3.14.2

Subject Index

Own-account transport, definition of, 2.1.1
Own-account transport, industrial classification of, 1.1.2

Paper, transport of, 3.15.3
Passenger Transport in Great Britain, 3.30.1, 3.31.1
Passenger transport, road, 1.5
Payments for transport as per cent of net output, industries', 3.14.2
Physical output, measures of, 2.2
Place of vehicle licence, 3.2.4
Plated weight, definition of, 2.1.10
Pollution due to road goods transport, 3.24
Population censuses, 3.13.13, 3.17.6
Ports, roll-on/roll-off traffic at, 3.27
Post Office mail services, 2.1.12
Post Office transport, charges for, 3.15.1
Post Office transport, expenditure on, 3.15.1
Present operators' licensing system, 1.3.5, 3.3, 3.8
Prices, 3.26
Prices and Incomes, National Board for, 3.26.3
Principal publications, 3.30, 3.31, 3.32, 3.34
Production, Census of, 3.14, 3.20.1, 3.20.2
Production, CSO Index of Industrial, 3.4.17
Productivity calculations, 3.26.6
Productivity Scheme, Cost and, 3.11.1
Professional haulage, definition of, 2.1.1
Public haulage, definition of, 2.1.1, 2.1.2
Publications, international, on road transport, 3.34
Publications, principal, on road transport, 3.30, 3.31, 3.32, 3.34
Purpose of traffic and transportation surveys, 3.22.1
Putney High Street, effect of goods transport in, 3.24.3

Quality licensing, 1.3.5
Quantity licensing, 1.3.2, 1.3.6
Quarterly estimates of gross domestic product, 3.19.14

Rail transport, 1.5, 3.4.8
Rail transport, charges for, 3.15.1
Rail transport, expenditure on, 3.15.1
Regional origin-destination flows, 3.4.29, 3.4.44, 5.6, 6.10
Regional statistics, 3.4.28, 4
Registration, data from vehicle licensing and, 3.2
Registration, excise licensing and, 2.1.5, 3.2
Registration, goods vehicle in licensing and, 2.1.5
Registrations, new, 3.2.7, 3.2.8, 3.2.9
Regression analyses, 3.4.32
Regression analysis on charges, multiple, 3.15.10
Regression analysis on growth of firms, multiple, 3.7.2
Regression analysis on modal choice, multiple, 3.15.10
Regression analysis on operating costs, multiple, 3.13.10
Regression analysis on traffic, 3.4.32
Regression models, 5.2, 5.5
Regulations, EEC, 1.3.9, 3.29
Regulations for operators, 1.3.8
Relative to other transport, importance of road goods transport, 1.5, 3.4.8, 3.4.12
Relevant Minimum List Headings, 1.1.2, 1.1.4, 2.1.1
Repairing vehicles, establishments for, 1.15

Reports of European Conference of Ministers of Transport, 3.34.5
Reports of HM Customs and Excise, 3.25
Reports of undertakings, 3.9
Results of continuing survey, 3.4.46, 3.4.47, 3.4.48, 3.4.49, 3.4.50
Results of road traffic censuses, 3.21.10, 3.21.11, 3.21.12, 3.21.13, 3.21.14, 3.21.15
Results of TRTA survey, 3.6.5
Results of 1952 survey, 3.4.5, 3.4.6, 3.4.7, 3.4.8
Results of 1958 survey, 3.4.12, 3.4.14
Results of 1962 survey, 3.4.22, 3.4.23, 3.4.24, 3.4.25, 3.4.26, 3.4.27, 3.4.28, 3.4.29, 3.4.30, 3.4.31, 3.4.32
Results of 1967/8 survey, 3.4.36, 3.4.37, 3.4.38
Review of commodity classifications, 3.4.26
RHA, *see* Road Haulage Association
Road accidents, 3.23
Road accidents, cost of, 3.23.6
Road accidents in Northern Ireland, 3.23.5
Road and Rail Traffic Act 1933, 1.3.1, 1.6.1, 3.3.1
Road classification, 3.21.3
Road goods transport, coverage of, 2.1.12
Road goods transport, domestic, 2.1.13, 2.1.14
Road goods transport, environmental effects of, 3.24
Road goods transport, industries' expenditure on, 3.14
Road goods transport, industries' use of, 3.14, 3.15, 3.16
Road goods transport industry, breakdown of, 1.2
Road goods transport industry, organization of, 1.2
Road goods transport, international, 2.1.13, 2.1.14, 3.27, 3.28, 3.29, 3.34
Road goods transport statistics, development of, 6
Road haulage and storage, capital expenditure in, 3.19.10
Road haulage and storage, coverage of, 3.19.10
Road Haulage Association, 1.2.6, 1.4.1, 3.11, 3.26.3
Road Haulage Association costs reports, 3.11
Road haulage, definition of, 2.1.1, 2.1.2
Road haulage, industrial classification of, 1.1.2, 1.1.4
Road Haulage Industry since 1968, Study on the, 3.8
Road Haulage Industry, Small Firm in the, 3.7
Road passenger transport, 1.5
Road Research Laboratory, Transport and, 3.10.3, 3.12.1, 3.21, 3.23, 3.24, 5.2
Road Safety Act 1967, 1.3.8, 2.1.10
Road Traffic Act 1960, 1.6.1
Road traffic bench-mark estimates, 3.21.6
Road traffic censuses, large-scale, 3.21.7
Road traffic censuses, national, 3.21
Road traffic, forecasting, 5.2
Road traffic survey, continuing, 3.4.11, 3.4.15, 3.21.3, 3.21.4, 3.21.5
Road Transport Industry Training Board Reports, 3.18
Roads in Northern Ireland, 3.21.16
Roads, unclassified, 3.21., 3.21.12
Roads, wear and tear on the, 3.24.8
Roadside census counts, goods vehicle in, 2.1.7
Roll-on/roll-off goods vehicle survey, DOE, 3.28
Roll-on/roll-off services, trailers and semi-trailers on, 3.28.1, 3.28.2
Roll-on/roll-off traffic at ports, 3.27
RTITB, *see* Road Transport Industry Training Board

RTITB definition of road transport industry, 3.18.1
Rudd/Dawson expenditure estimates, 3.12

Sample size in continuing survey, 3.4.41
Sample size in TRTA survey, 3.6.2
Sample size in 1952 survey, 3.4.2, 3.4.5
Sample size in 1958 survey, 3.4.10
Sample size in 1962 survey, 3.4.19, 3.4.20
Sample size in 1967/68 survey, 3.4.33, 3.4.34
Sample survey in the West Midlands, 3.16.2, 3.16.3
Sample surveys, MOT and DOE, 3.4
Scope of review, 1.1
Scottish data, 4.1.3
Screenline surveys, 3.22.3
Select Committee on Nationalized Industries, 1.2.5, 3.9.5, 3.26.4
Self-employed persons, 3.17.3
Severnside Industrial Survey, 3.16.5
Shipping, coastal, 1.5, 3.4.8
Shuttle service, definition of a, 3.29.5
SIC, see Standard Industrial Classification
Small Firm in the Road Haulage Industry, 3.7
Small Firms, Committee of Inquiry on, 3.7.1
SMMT, see Society of Motor Manufacturers and Traders
Society of Motor Manufacturers and Traders, 3.2.5, 3.2.9
Standard Industrial Classification, 1.1.2, 1.1.4, 2.1.1
Statistics of Trade Act 1947, 1.6.2, 3.4.4, 3.19.9
Statistics, regional, 3.4.28
Steel, transport of iron and, 3.15.3
Stock of vehicles, 3.2.5, 3.2.6
Storage, capital expenditure in Road haulage and, 3.19.10
Storage, coverage of Road haulage and, 3.19.10
Study on the Road Haulage Industry since 1968, 3.8
Suggestions for the future, 6
Survey, continuing road traffic, 3.4.11, 3.4.15, 3.21.3, 3.21.4, 3.21.5
Survey, DOE continuing, 3.4.39, 3.4.40, 3.4.41, 3.4.42, 3.4.43, 3.4.44, 3.4.45, 3.4.46, 3.4.47, 3.4.48, 3.4.49, 3.4.50
Survey, DOE roll-on/roll-off goods vehicle, 3.28
Survey, New Earnings, 3.17.1
Survey of C-licensed vehicles, TRTA, 3.6
Survey of Operating Costs in Road Freight Transport, 3.13
Survey of transport from manufacturing establishments, 3.15
Survey, Severnside Industrial, 3.16.5
Survey, West Cumberland Transport, 3.16.4
Survey 1952, MOT, 3.4.2, 3.4.3, 3.4.4, 3.4.5, 3.4.6, 3.4.7, 3.4.8
Survey 1958, MOT, 3.4.9, 3.4.10, 3.4.11, 3.4.12, 3.4.13, 3.4.14, 3.4.15, 3.4.16, 3.4.17, 3.4.18
Survey 1962, MOT, 3.4.19, 3.4.20, 3.4.21, 3.4.22, 3.4.23, 3.4.24, 3.4.25, 3.4.26, 3.4.27, 3.4.28, 3.4.29, 3.4.30, 3.4.31, 3.4.32
Survey 1967/68, MOT, 3.4.33, 3.4.34, 3.4.35, 3.4.36, 3.4.37, 3.4.38
Surveys, MOT and DOE sample, 3.4
Surveys of attitudes to effects of road traffic, 3.24.3, 3.24.7
Surveys, Traffic and transportation, 3.22

Tachographs, 1.3.8, 1.3.9, 6.11
Taxation, motor, 3.33.1
Taxation Offices, Local, 3.2.2, 3.2.3
Testing scheme, heavy goods vehicle, 3.3.7

Ton-mileage, 2.2.3, 2.2.7
Tonnage, 2.2.2
Tractor plus trailer weight, maximum, 2.1.10
Trade associations, 1.4.1
Traders Road Transport Association, 1.4.1, 3.6
Traffic and transportation surveys, 3.22
Traffic and transportation surveys, index of, 3.22.4
Traffic and transportation surveys, purpose of, 3.22.1
Traffic Areas, 3.3.1
Traffic attraction, 3.4.32
Traffic censuses, methodology in road, 3.21.11
Traffic censuses, national road, 3.21
Traffic censuses, results of road, 3.21.10, 3.21.11, 3.21.12, 3.21.13, 3.21.14, 3.21.15
Traffic data, 3.21, 3.22, 3.23
Traffic distribution through 24 hours, 3.21.11
Traffic generation, 3.4.32, 5.4
Trailer weight, maximum tractor plus, 2.1.10
Trailers and semi-trailers in UK registration, 3.34.2
Trailers and semi-trailers on roll-on/roll-off services, 3.28.1, 3.28.2
Train weight, definition of, 2.1.10
Training Board Reports, Road Transport Industry, 3.18
Transport Act 1953, 1.3.3
Transport Act 1968, 1.2.5, 1.3.5, 1.3.6, 1.6.1, 3.8.1
Transport and Road Research Laboratory, 3.10.3, 3.12.1, 3.21, 3.23, 3.24, 5.2
Transport costs in distributive industries, 3.14.7, 3.14.8
Transport establishments, industrial classification of, 1.1.2
Transport of chemicals, 3.15.3
Transport of electronic equipment, 3.15.3
Transport of foodstuffs, 3.15.3
Transport of iron and steel, 3.15.3
Transport of paper, 3.15.3
Transport output, dimensions of, 2.2.5
Transport Statistics, 3.31
Transportation surveys, index of traffic and, 3.22.4
Transportation surveys, land use, 3.22
Transportation surveys, purpose of traffic and, 3.22.1
Transportation surveys, traffic and, 3.22
TRRL, see Transport and Road Research Laboratory
TRTA survey of C-licensed vehicles, 3.6
TRTA survey, results of, 3.6.5
TRTA survey, sample size in, 3.6.2

UN *Annual Bulletin of Transport Statistics*, 3.34.1
Unclassified roads, 3.21.5, 3.21.12
Undertakings, reports of, 3.9
Unladen weight, definition of, 2.1.9
USA, comparative data on, 3.31.1
Usage and definitions, 2.1
USSR, comparative data on, 3.31.1

Vehicle examinations, 3.3.4
Vehicle licence, place of, 3.2.4
Vehicle licence figures, current, 3.2.2, 3.2.3, 3.2.5, 3.2.6, 3.2.9
Vehicle licensing and registration, data from, 3.2
Vehicle Licensing Centre, Driver and, 3.2.1
Vehicle operating costs, 3.13.9

Subject Index 127

Vehicle population, forecasting, 5.2
Vehicle weights, 2.1.9, 2.1.10, 2.1.11
Vehicle-mileage, 2.2.4
Vehicles, classification of, 2.1.4, 2.1.5, 2.1.6, 2.1.7, 2.1.8, 2.21.8
Vehicles, stock of, 3.2.5, 3.2.6

Wage rates, 3.2.6, 3.17
Water supply industry expenditure on transport, 3.14.1
Wear and tear on the roads, 3.24.8
Weekly earnings, 3.26.3
Weight, definition of gross, 2.1.10
Weight, definition of plated, 2.1.10
Weight, definition of train, 2.1.10
Weight, definition of unladen, 2.1.9

Weight distribution, consignment, 3.16.2
Weight, maximum axle, 2.1.10
Weight, maximum tractor plus trailer, 2.1.10
Weights, vehicle, 2.1.9, 2.1.10, 2.1.11
Welsh data, 4.1.4
West Cumberland Transport Survey, 3.16.4
West Midlands conurbation study, 3.22.5
West Midlands, sample survey in the, 3.16.2, 3.16.3
Wholesale Trades, Board of Trade Inquiry into the, 3.14.6
Working hours, maximum, 1.3.8
Working of carriers' licensing, 1.3.7
World Road Statistics, 3.34.6

Zones in 1962 survey, 3.4.28